Bloody Brilliant Women

Bloody Brilliant Women

The Pioneers, Revolutionaries and
Geniuses Your History Teacher Forgot
to Mention

CATHY NEWMAN

WILLIAM
COLLINS

William Collins
An imprint of HarperCollins*Publishers*
1 London Bridge Street
London SE1 9GF

WilliamCollinsBooks.com

First published in Great Britain in 2018 by William Collins

4

Copyright © Cathy Newman 2018

Cathy Newman asserts the moral right to
be identified as the author of this work

A catalogue record for this book is
available from the British Library

ISBN 978-0-00-824171-1 (hardback)
ISBN 978-0-00-824170-4 (trade paperback)

Printed and bound in Great Britain by
CPI Group (UK) Ltd, Croydon, CR0 4YY

MIX
Paper from
responsible sources
FSC C007454

This book is produced from independently certified FSC paper
to ensure responsible forest management.

For more information visit: www.harpercollins.co.uk/green

To John and our two bloody brilliant little women

Contents

1

Introduction

Education, Education, Education

This is definitely one to file under *You Wouldn't Get Away with It Nowadays*, but when I was at school studying for my History A Level, our teacher used to take select groups of pupils to visit the bomb shelter from the Second World War at the bottom of his garden. I think he'd just watched *Dead Poets Society*, which had recently come out, and decided to portray himself as an inspirational eccentric.

I was never invited; but I like to imagine the group sitting on the damp earth beneath the corrugated tin roof as Mr Dead Poet read to them in faltering torchlight, breaking off every so often to quote Churchill. Perhaps even my favourite Churchillism: 'My education was interrupted only by my schooling.'

That's how I feel about school too. The vagaries of the curriculum in the late 1980s meant I studied the Anglo-Saxons about three times. For years I knew all about the Venerable Bede but almost nothing about anything that happened after 1066.

To this day, I remain embarrassed by the holes in my knowledge. Throughout my adult life I've bought – though admittedly not read – every history book I can lay my hands on. 'History of Britain'-type books promising a broad overview are my particular pleasure.

Recently, when I was fifty or so pages into one of these great tomes, I had a bit of a eureka moment. I noticed that, apart from Mrs Thatcher and Queen Elizabeth II, who are in a category of their own, not a single woman had so far been mentioned.* I read on, increasingly incredulous, until finally one appeared: Agatha Christie, in the context of something about her influence on the 'national imagination'.

Perhaps I'm being unfair. A book like the one I was reading, whose opening chapters dealt with war and its management by male politicians, was always going to be light on women. Still, many accounts of modern British history are patchy when it comes to gender, celebrating the achievements of, say, the suffragettes in a burst of fluorescent righteousness, only to pack women away again in a cupboard marked 'Lowly, Ancillary Roles; Housewives, etc.' until the 1960s. At which point they are allowed out to be totems of the sexual revolution, burn their bras and go on strike at Dagenham's Ford plant.

The truth had to be more nuanced. And the deeper I delved into the history of twentieth-century Britain, the more it appeared that the shape and extent of female influence was far greater than generally acknowledged. I'm not just talking about the arts or education, where talented women have long been celebrated, but in traditionally 'male' fields like medicine, politics, law, engineering and the military. Were it not for women, those significant features of modern Britain such as council housing, hospices and the humane laws relating to property ownership, child custody and divorce might not exist in the same form.

The more I read about these women pioneers, the more frustrated I became that so many are so little known outside academic literature. Not only did these women achieve remarkable things,

---

* I am also discounting a glancing reference to Clement Attlee's self-effacing wife Violet.

but they usually had to battle hostility and discrimination as they did so. This book is my attempt to bring these women and their accomplishments to a wider audience; to tell *their* story – and ours.

One of its working titles was *The Class of 1918*, because that is how I thought of these women while I was writing: 1918 being, if not exactly a feminist Year Zero, then the year when the ball started rolling in the direction of equality. It was the year when the Representation of the People Act allowed women to vote if they were over the age of 30 and met a 'property qualification'. At the same time, the Parliament (Qualification of Women) Act in 1918 gave women over twenty-one the right to stand for election as MPs. Which was momentous, although it did mean that between 1918 and 1928 some women were in the odd position of being able to stand for Parliament but unable to vote: Jennie Lee was twenty-three when she stood as the North Lanark Labour candidate in the 1929 by-election, just before the rules were changed.

The Class of 1918 are those women who either prepared the ground for or immediately benefited from the burst of empowerment which followed getting the vote. For Western women, 1918 is the start of the modern era. Just as historians use the term 'the long twelfth century' as shorthand for the period between 1050 and 1250 – a way of rationalising the massive changes that occurred in those two hundred years – so you can argue that, for women, the twentieth century started later than it did for everyone else and hasn't yet ended. Not until 1928 was the voting franchise in Great Britain and Northern Ireland extended to all women over the age of twenty-one, finally giving them the vote on the same terms as men.

To make sense of the modern era, you need to understand the years which immediately preceded it. So my history includes women who predate even first-wave feminism – the activist Ada Nield Chew, for example, and Octavia Hill, whose National Trust for Places of Historic Interest or Natural Beauty arose out of her campaigning for better quality housing for the poor.

————————

That women have the same rights and opportunities as men is practically a given for my two young daughters. They watch *Channel 4 News*, see me interviewing what must seem like an endless procession of female politicians, bankers, lobbyists, CEOs, etc. The fact that a little over a hundred years ago most British women couldn't even vote is scarcely credible to them. They have only the vaguest notion of what today's modern, successful women have inherited from their forebears; of what they need to be thankful for; of how painfully slow the process of being taken seriously has been and, indeed, continues to be.

This is where the idea of 'women's history' comes in. Do we still need such a thing? We certainly *did* – the first 1885 edition of the prestigious *Dictionary of National Biography* found room for only 3 per cent of women in its sixty-two volumes – and I would argue we still do.

Of course, the danger of gathering together the experiences of so many different women (black, white and Asian; straight or LGBTQ+) is that the specificity of those experiences to those particular women gets overlooked. They may have trodden similar paths and faced similar pitfalls. But oppression comes in many shapes and sizes.

Even primary-school children now learn that the kind of discrimination Florence Nightingale had to overcome as a wealthy, upper-middle-class, well-connected English woman was very different to that experienced by her fellow nurse Mary Seacole as a mixed-race woman (a 'mulatto', in the language of the day) who identified as both Scottish and Jamaican. I have done my best in what follows to bear this in mind.

This is not a textbook. I have tried to write about these remarkable women in an accessible and entertaining way. At its heart, though, are two basic questions: what were the sources of female power in the twentieth century? And what have women used this power to achieve?

The answers are complex because female power is complex. Even if we accept that, for much of human history, women have conducted their lives in a patriarchal bubble – subordinate in law, custom and religion to the men around them; not even *wanting* equality with men, so ridiculous did the idea seem – it doesn't mean they lacked purpose and agency. And it doesn't mean we shouldn't celebrate their achievements.

As modern women, we are instinctively drawn to a certain species of trailblazer – the women it's easy and satisfying to claim as proto-feminists. But not all of them would be pleased to wear the T-shirt.

Take the eighteenth-century writer and philanthropist Hannah More for starters. It was fine, she thought, to teach poor women to read so that they could understand the Bible; but she was shocked by women she had heard about in France who 'run to study philosophy, and neglect their families to be present at lectures in anatomy', and she loathed the sort of education reforms proposed by Mary Wollstonecraft: 'How many ways there are of being ridiculous!'

When the explorer Mary Kingsley returned from the second of her expeditions to West Africa in October 1895, she distanced herself from the New Women then being discussed in news-papers, arguing that women's suffrage was 'a minor question; while there was a most vital section of men disenfranchised women could wait.' The polymathic explorer Gertrude Bell – one of the cleverest, most remarkable British women of the early twentieth century – couldn't understand why women wanted the vote. Believing the whole business to be a silly distraction from the grand imperial project to which she was committed, she became first secretary of the Women's National Anti-Suffrage League.

Another modern feminist reflex – and I must plead guilty here – is to scoff at traditional 'homemaker' roles. It's one thing to believe, as I do, that too many women remained trapped in them for too long, their intellectual freedom of movement curbed; but it's quite another to claim that they have no value. The opposite is the case: it was domestic power that many of the women featured in this book harnessed.

High-born historical heroines wouldn't have been doing the dishes, yet frequently their lot was to be also-rans: nearly-queens such as Matilda, daughter of Henry I, who just missed out on the throne in 1153; or queens who stood in for absent monarchs such as Eleanor of Aquitaine, who governed England while her son Richard the Lionheart was off fighting the crusades. In her brilliant book about these pre-Tudor queens, *She-Wolves* (2010), the historian Helen Castor notes that their power was perceived as 'a perversion of "good" womanhood, a distillation of all that was most to be feared in the unstable depths of female nature'.[1] It was a view promoted most famously by the Scottish reformer John Knox in his polemic of 1558, *The First Blast of the Trumpet Against the Monstrous Regiment of Women*: 'For nature hath in all beasts printed a certain mark of domination in the male and a certain subjection in the female which they keep inviolate.'

Gems like this kept me entertained as I was writing. But how, I wondered in my ignorance, did Knox feel justified in writing this stuff in the sixteenth century when in many ways women had been bossing it for hundreds of years before that?

'The history of England,' wrote the historian and politician Macaulay, 'is emphatically the history of progress.' Not for women, it isn't. In key respects, they were better off in 800 than they were in 1800. I didn't notice this sufficiently when I was eighteen and studying history. (I barely noticed *anything* when I was eighteen. I was too busy bemoaning my curly hair and bottle-top glasses.) Now, in my forties, I found myself wondering what had gone wrong since Anglo-Saxon times, when women were accorded considerable respect.

Surviving evidence, some of which I'll outline below, led the historian Doris Stenton to conclude that Anglo-Saxon women were 'more nearly the equals of their husbands and brothers than at any other period before the modern age'.[2] At this point the fake-news klaxon sounds in the back of my head. Some historians[3] dispute Stenton's 'Golden Age' thesis, so I should note that we have little concrete information about how women *actually* lived. Anglo-Saxon culture was mostly oral, so what we know comes from clerical and legal records and, least reliably of all, heroic poems.

Still, language tells its own story, and it's significant that the Old English word *mann* can also be used of women. A charter from 969 that relates to a grant of land near Worcester concludes: 'Aelfweard was the first man, and now it is in the hands of his daughter and she is the second man.' As we in the twenty-first century tussle over gender-neutral toilets, our Anglo-Saxon ancestors might have wondered what on earth all the fuss was about.

Anglo-Saxon marriage, too, sounds almost progressive, especially compared to the bond of misery endured by many Victorian women. A husband had to pay his prospective wife a *morgengifu* or 'morning-gift', often a considerable amount of money or land, over which she had total control. Finances were the joint responsibility of husband and wife. According to the laws of Aethelbert, a woman could walk out on a marriage if she was unhappy, and if she took her children with her then she was entitled to half the marital home. How very equitable.

'Cunning women' had considerable power in Anglo-Saxon communities, practising folk magic, using their powers to heal, hex and hunt down stolen goods. Pendants, crystal balls, shells and other amulets thought to have magical properties have been found in the graves of female Anglo-Saxons. And although we might bridle when we read, in the tenth-century anthology of Anglo-Saxon poems and other literature known as the Exeter Book, that 'the place of a woman is at her embroidery', cloth-making and embroidery were in fact high-prestige occupations. In the households of large-estate owners, many of whom were women, the mistress of the house and her daughters would have worked making adorned gifts or, after the arrival of Christianity, church vestments. More mundane soft furnishings such as wall-hangings, table linen and bed clothes were handed down as heirlooms, and more commonly mentioned in the wills of women than men, suggesting they were thought of as female property.

The needle was by no means the only tool in women's armoury. Female warriors wielded more traditionally masculine weapons to great effect. We know that a strong tradition of female warriors existed in pre-Anglo-Saxon Britain from Tacitus' account of the Iceni queen Boudica's rebellion against the Romans. He puts into her mouth a rousing speech in which she assures her troops that it is 'customary … with Britons to fight under female captaincy'. Boudica rides in a chariot with her daughters in front of her and fights not as a queen but as a 'woman of the people' to avenge 'her liberty lost, her body tortured by the lash, the tarnished honour of her daughters'.

High-born Anglo-Saxon women, too, could be every bit as blood-thirsty as the men. Queen Cynethryth, wife of Offa of Mercia, is a Lady Macbeth figure who not only had coins struck in her name, but is supposed to have encouraged Offa to kill Aethelberht II of East Anglia. Aethelflaed, daughter of King Alfred (of cakes infamy) assumed power after her husband Aethelred, Lord of the Mercians, died in 911. A formidable warrior who 'protected her own men and terrified aliens' (according to William of Malmesbury), she ruled for the next seven years, implementing an ambitious programme of fortification and fending off attacks from marauding Vikings and Danes.

The arrival of Christianity in the British Isles is usually dated to 597, the year Augustine became the first Archbishop of Canterbury and baptised the first Christian Anglo-Saxon king, Aethelberht of Kent. Many of the monasteries that subsequently dotted the landscape were 'double monasteries' where an abbess ruled over both monks and nuns, who lived in separate buildings.

Thanks to good old Eve, notions of female inferiority are hard-wired into Christianity. Nevertheless, women emerge in this period as effective religious leaders, not least because of their apparent gifts for diplomacy and realpolitik. Medieval historian Henrietta Leyser thinks women adapted to Christianity more easily than men because they were better at reconciling new demands with old codes: '[Women] take up its challenges with alacrity and with evident success. They become saints apace, exercising power in life and in death: in life in positions of influence as abbesses, in death through miracles worked at their shrines.'[4]

Most of what we know about these abbesses comes to us via my old friend from the history class, the Northumbrian monk Bede, aka 'the godfather of history'. His favourite seems to have been Hilda of Whitby, who founded Whitby Abbey and was famously wise: according to Bede, 'not only ordinary people but also kings and princes sometimes sought and received her counsel when in difficulties.' One of her most celebrated feats was her discovery and encouragement of the cowherd-poet Caedmon, composer of one of the earliest known vernacular poems, 'Caedmon's Hymn'.

These 'brides of Christ' could be flamboyant, glamorous figures, their celebrity an important source of local pride. St Edith, abbess of Wilton Abbey in Wiltshire, was famous for dressing in ornate, golden clothes (albeit with a hair shirt worn underneath). William of Malmesbury tells how, when she was ticked off for this by Aethelwold of Winchester, she retorted that this opulence didn't matter because God could see through superficial trappings to the soul beneath: 'For pride may exist under the garb of wretchedness; and a mind may be as pure under these vestments as under your tattered furs.'

After 1066, many (though not all) historians agree, a lot of that girl power withered on the vine, in the church and beyond. Freedoms taken for granted in Anglo-Saxon society were undermined by new canon (religious) law and the Normans' insistence on making land ownership a condition of military service to a lord. From 1066, the number of female land-owners drops. Women can no longer make wills. Husbands are permitted to beat their wives. Primogeniture transforms inheritance law so that first-born sons are valued over daughters. If a woman kills her husband, it's classed as treason and punished accordingly by burning at the stake.

The idea that women are second-class citizens, physically and mentally inferior to men, becomes a commonplace as medieval Catholic theology sets up new and troubling archetypes that remain with us – on the one hand, Eve; on the other, the Virgin Mary.

Consider the Bayeux Tapestry, the 230-foot long piece of embroidered cloth thought to have been commissioned by William the Conqueror's brother. As all schoolchildren know, it tells the story of the Norman conquest, culminating in the Battle of Hastings. Although it was *made* by English women – women whose needlework skills were so famous throughout Europe that their work had a special name, *Opus Anglicanum* ('English work') – it *depicts* only three women: Queen Edith of Wessex, wife of Edward the Confessor and sister of the slain Harold; a mysterious figure called Aelfgyva, whose presence seems to be a reference to some unknowable contemporary sex scandal; and finally, an anonymous war refugee fleeing with her child from a burning building. Notice the way these women fall neatly into three categories: inheritors of and revellers in wealth and status; sources of gossip and intrigue; and helpless victims. Is the Bayeux Tapestry a precursor of the *Daily Mail Online*'s notorious 'sidebar of shame'?

Still, our medieval sisters struggled on. They oversaw births and deaths as midwives and layers-out of bodies. Some ran businesses from their houses. If they were married they could and often did declare themselves unmarried in order to escape the common-law disadvantages of being wives. (Their husbands were happy to be complicit in this as it absolved them of liability for any debts.) This was known as trading *feme sole* and gave women a bit of economic independence, especially in areas like the silk trade; in trades less female-dominated they probably fared worse.

Alice Chester carried on her husband's business after his death in 1473. She used her own ships to trade in cloth, wine and other commodities with Ireland, Spain, Portugal and Flanders and made enough money to afford a town house in Bristol and to lavish expensive gifts on her local church, which included elaborate carved figures and a new rood loft. Margaret Paston ran her lawyer husband John's malt and wool business when he was away, as well as defending the family estates in Norfolk from armed bandits. When they were separated, Margaret kept in contact with John by letter, many of which have survived to provide us with arresting insights into life in England during the War of the Roses. In 1449 she wrote to John demanding crossbows, grappling irons and shooting bolts for use in defending the Paston castle at Gresham against an attack by Lord Molynes. Margaret and her twelve comrades-in-arms never stood a chance against Molynes' thousand-strong army, and she was duly evicted and the castle sacked. But she didn't lack courage or resourcefulness.

We learn a fair bit about the lifestyle of a bourgeois woman in a thriving provincial town from Margery Kempe, the Christian mystic whose dictated autobiography, dating from the 1420s and surviving in a single manuscript discovered in the 1930s, is one of the earliest known memoirs by a woman. Much of it relates to her spiritual journey, undertaken in the grip of what sounds like post-partum psychosis.

Among the religious revelations is the more fascinating one that Kempe ran a microbrewery in her home town of Norwich. *The Book of Margery Kempe* is pleasingly graphic about what ensued on the day a batch of ale became contaminated: 'When the ale had as fine a froth on it as anyone might see, suddenly the froth would go flat, and all the ale was lost in one brewing after another, so that her servants were ashamed and would not stay with her.'[5] Having only taken up brewing in the first place 'out of pure covetousness', Kempe interpreted this stalled fermentation as a punishment from God.

Less heavenly patriarchs intervened over the next century. A woman's work was reduced to child-rearing and caring. Acquiring education, power, money? Not so much. There were exceptions such as the entrepreneur Katherine Fenkyll who, like Alice Chester, took over her husband's business (he had been a draper) with huge success after his death in 1499. But apprentices to trades were usually male: only seventy-three women are known to have been enrolled as apprentices in sixteenth-century London, compared with thousands of men.[6]

Women weren't thought to be worth properly educating, so they couldn't acquire skills the blokes took for granted. In the early modern period, female education was generally a religious affair, designed to get round the fact that women were 'born in sin' as daughters of Eve, the 'weaker vessel'; gossipy and obstinate, prone to idleness, volatility, hysteria – or any other vice which could be hurled at them.

Exceptions to this rule tended to be royal, or as good as. Sir Thomas More treated Margaret Roper and his other daughters to the same education as he had. Margaret could read Aesop's *Fables* by the age of three and went on to study languages, history, philosophy, rhetoric and – her particular passion – astronomy. She married, as she was expected to do, but when More discovered that she and her husband William Roper were both studying astronomy, he wrote a bold, inspiring letter to her that sounds –

sounds – as if it is legitimising her intellectualism: 'I am ever wont to persuade you to yield in everything to your husband; now, on the contrary, I give you full leave to strive to surpass him in the knowledge of the celestial system.'

Yet there remained a sense that a woman's mind was 'naturally bad'; that Margaret was remarkable not in herself but because her education represented a triumph over women's inherent defects – defects which, More conceded, 'may be redressed by industry'.[7]

So it was that the future Queen Elizabeth I was tutored industriously by Roger Ascham between 1548 and 1550. Ascham was impressed by Elizabeth's intellect: 'Yea, I believe, that beside her perfect readiness in Latin, Italian, French, and Spanish, she readeth here now at Windsor more Greek every day than some prebendary of this church doth read Latin in a whole week.' Aged eleven, she presented her stepmother with a translation from the French of Navarre's *Mirror of the Sinful Soul* protected by a needlepoint canvas cover she had made herself. Truly, she possessed all the virtues!

But the adult Elizabeth justified her success by declaring that she was *different* from other women, possessing the (male) heart and stomach of a king. Pictures show her armoured, manly. But she was the exception which proved the rule. Edmund Spenser's female knight Britomart in Book III of his epic Gloriana poem *The Faerie Queene* is supposed to represent Elizabeth. But as the poet makes clear: 'virtuous women wisely understand/That they were born to base humility/Unless the heavens them lift to lawful sovereignty.'

Elizabeth Joscelin's *The Mothers Legacie* (1624), a conduct manual written in the form of a letter to an unborn child, is revealing about prevailing attitudes towards female education. While it was vital that women be taught 'good housewifery', writes Joscelin, 'other learning a woman needs not.' She goes on: 'Though I admire it in those whom God hath blest with discretion, yet I desired not much in my owne, having seene that sometimes women have greater portions of learning than wisdome.'

One female Restoration writer who bucked the trend for feminine modesty was Margaret Cavendish, Duchess of Newcastle. She craved reputation, recognition, visibility – all the markers of success men believed were their due, for, as she wrote in the preface to *Poems, and Fancies*, 'they hold books as their crown, and the sword as their sceptre, by which they rule and govern.' Not only was Cavendish prolific, but she refused to be restricted to a single genre, turning her hand to biography, poetry, science fiction, philosophical and scientific treatises – anything she felt like. Thanks to her talent for self-promotion – she designed her own extravagant, daringly masculine costumes and travelled with a full complement of carriages and servants – she became one of fashionable society's must-see attractions.

When Cavendish visited London in 1667, Samuel Pepys became obsessed with obtaining a sighting of her. After several failed attempts, he finally caught up with her when she addressed the Royal Society on 23 May – the first woman ever to do so. Unfortunately, Cavendish was overcome with nerves, possibly because of the presence in the room of so many scientists she had been rude about in print, and she gave a poor account of herself. Pepys was scathing: 'The Duchess hath been a good comely woman; but her dress so antic and her deportment so unordinary, that I do not like her at all, nor did I hear her say anything that was worth hearing.'

This was pretty unfair, especially as Cavendish had received 'no formal education in even the most basic writing skills'.[8] In fact, as an aristocratic woman, she had arguably received a *worse* education than her immediate social inferiors, who'd been trained up as governesses, ladies' companions and teachers. Yet her instinct, as with so many latter-day women, was to blame her failings on herself, rather than an unjust society. 'It cannot be expected I should write so wisely or wittily as men, being of the effeminate sex, whose brains Nature hath mixed with the coldest and softest elements.'

The sense that education for women might be genuinely important – because the lack of it isolates them from spheres of legal and political influence – doesn't gain momentum until the end of the eighteenth century when radical ripples from revolutionary France cause turbulence in Britain.

'Talents put a man above the World, & in a condition to be feared and worshipped, a Woman that possesses them must be always courting the World, and asking pardon, as it were, for uncommon excellence,' wrote the aristocratic social-reformer Elizabeth Montagu to a friend in 1763. To help level the playing field, Montagu and like-minded ladies such as Mary Monckton turned their houses into salons where women and men could meet and mix as intellectual equals. The salon was a French import and the point was conversation, not debauchery – no drink was allowed, or card playing. Montagu's function as hostess was to encourage and bestow patronage on writers she liked.

Salonieres became known as 'bluestockings' – not, at this stage, a pejorative term for a studious woman – after a male guest, Benjamin Stillingfleet, turned up to one wearing blue worsted stockings because he hadn't been able to afford black silk ones. Exactly how the term came, by the late eighteenth century, to apply only to women isn't clear – possibly because it was two women, Monckton and Elizabeth Vesey, who decided to 'own' it by calling their salon the Blue Stockings Society. James Boswell, biographer of Samuel Johnson (he of the Dictionary) went along to one of Monckton's salons and noted that 'her vivacity enchanted the Sage [i.e. Johnson], and they used to talk together with all imaginable ease.' The novelist Fanny Burney was sceptical, describing Monckton in 1782 as 'between thirty and forty, very short, very fat ... [and] palpably desirous of gaining notice and admiration', and Montagu as having 'the air and manner of a woman accustomed to being distinguished, and of great parts'. So much for the sisterhood.

If Johnson was happy to drink tea and chat with educated women, he still thought of them as essentially decorative; still believed, like most of his kind, that 'a man is in general better pleased when he has a good dinner upon his table than when his wife speaks Greek. My old friend Mrs Carter [a celebrated female linguist, who tutored her brother so that he, unlike her, could have the privilege of going to Cambridge] could make a pudding as well as translate Epictetus from the Greek and work a handkerchief as well as compose a poem.'

Some feminist historians go so far as to argue that the Enlightenment – the period from the late seventeenth to the late eighteenth centuries when intellectual discourse was dominated by thinking about human reason, science and our relationship to the natural world – didn't benefit women at all: 'Just as there was no Renaissance or Scientific Revolution for women, in the sense that the goals and ideas of those movements were perceived as applicable only to men, so there was no Enlightenment for women.'[9]

Certainly, its defining philosopher Jean-Jacques Rousseau, in his people-power bible *The Social Contract* (1762), declared that educated women were 'unpleasing and unnecessary'. His influential novel *Emile* (1762) promoted his belief in biologically determined difference between the sexes, even recasting wit, the salonieres' stock-in-trade, as a harmful vice: 'A female wit is a scourge to her husband, her children, her friends, her servants, to everybody.' Even if timidity, chastity and modesty were not innate female attributes, he argued in *Letter to D'Alembert* (1758) that 'it is in society's interest that women acquire these qualities; they must be cultivated in women, and any woman who disdains them offends good morals.'

Passages such as this infuriated the English feminist pioneer Mary Wollstonecraft – that 'hyena in petticoats', as the politician

Horace Walpole called her. In just six weeks she bashed out the scrappy but momentous manifesto *Vindication of the Rights of Women* (1792), its key goal the demolition of Rousseau's arguments. 'The first object of laudable ambition,' she wrote, 'is to obtain a character as a human being, regardless of the distinction of sex.' Once women were given the same education as men, they could go on to be doctors and lawyers or run complex businesses, just as men did. Why, she thought, liberating women in this way would even make them nicer to be around! As she put it: 'Would men but generously snap our chains, and be content with rational fellowship instead of slavish obedience, they would find us more observant daughters, more affectionate sisters, more faithful wives, more reasonable mothers – in a word, better citizens.'

The process of intellectual stunting began in childhood, Wollstonecraft argued. Gender stereotyping had the effect of returning grown, mature women 'back to childhood when they ought to leave the go-cart for ever':

> Every thing that they see or hear serves to fix impressions, call
> forth emotions, and associate ideas, that give a sexual character
> to the mind. False notions of beauty and delicacy stop the
> growth of their limbs and produce a sickly soreness, rather than
> delicacy of organs; and thus weakened by being employed in
> unfolding instead of examining the first associations, forced on
> them by every surrounding object, how can they attain the
> vigour necessary to enable them to throw off their factitious
> character?

By the 1790s, when Wollstonecraft was writing this, 'bluestocking' had become an insult and the fledgling women's movement fatally associated with the 'Jacobin' values of revolutionary France. On 10 September 1797, at the age of just thirty-seven, Wollstonecraft's chaotic, itinerant life ended after she gave birth to her daughter Mary, future author of *Frankenstein*, and developed septicaemia.

The light of progress flickered only dimly. Some dedicated girls' schools had been founded in the early eighteenth century, endowed by merchants and livery companies, but as a rule they focused on 'accomplishments' such as needlework rather than the kind of learning laid on for boys. Between 1785 and 1786 (when the money ran out), Jane Austen and her sister Cassandra studied at the Abbey School in Reading, a boarding school run by a Mrs La Tournelle who had a cork leg and a passion for theatre.

It was probably similar to Mrs Goddard's school as described in Austen's 1815 novel *Emma* – 'a real, honest, old-fashioned Boarding-school, where a reasonable quantity of accomplishments were sold at a reasonable price, and where girls might be sent to be out of the way and scramble themselves into a little education without any danger of coming back prodigies.'

The loss of ground in the mid to late eighteenth century was a real blow for women. Even if she had acquired a smattering of education, the most an intelligent, independent-minded woman could hope for was to be a governess or a teacher or a ladies' companion. As their husbands ventured out into the world and were rewarded for their thrusting virility, they would stay at home being chaste and docile, reading the sort of novels Jane Austen would later parody in her mock-gothic *Northanger Abbey*. This so-called 'cult of sensibility' seems to have been a very British phenomenon. As the critic and historian Janet Todd remarks: 'Foreigners marvelled at the idleness thrust on English women, whose business was little more than coquetry in youth and motherhood or fashion in later years.'[10]

For feminist academics Bonnie Anderson and Judith Zinsser, the early nineteenth century 'marked the nadir of European women's options and possibilities'[11]. Paradoxically, though, by embracing the most traditional female virtues, women acquired a moral authority as the 'consciences of society' that they later put to radical use.

The tradition of female radicalism and dissent ushered in by Mary Wollstonecraft would bear fruit in the new century – eventually. First, though, the relationship between men and women would have to become more equal as part of a broader process of social reform. Women would have to stop being virtuous and passive simply because it was expected of them. They would have to be able to divorce their husbands and seek legal redress in cases of abuse and rape.

This started to happen as early as 1837 when a woman called Caroline Norton fought for the right to have access to (though not custody of – that would be a crazy idea!) her three young sons after walking out on her drunken, abusive husband, the MP and failed barrister George Chapple Norton. Her fastidiously detailed list of the obstacles married women encountered in existing law makes for grim reading:

> An English wife may not leave her husband's house. Not only can he sue her for restitution of 'conjugal rights', but he has a right to enter the house of any friend or relation with whom she may take refuge … and carry her away by force …
>
> If her husband take proceedings for a divorce, she is not, in the first instance, allowed to defend herself … She is not represented by attorney, nor permitted to be considered a party to the suit between him and her supposed lover, for 'damages'.
>
> If an English wife be guilty of infidelity, her husband can divorce her so as to marry again; but she cannot divorce the husband … however profligate he may be.

Sadly, Norton failed in her bid to secure formal access to her children. She was only allowed supervised visits after her youngest son, William, died after falling from a horse in 1842. But her campaigning blasted a path for transformative legislation like the Custody of Infants Act 1839, the Matrimonial Causes Act 1857 and the Married Women's Property Act 1870.

Before long, a new generation of bluestockings was exploiting the zest for reform. They understood only too well that far-reaching change was required and that it was as important to improve the lot of working-class women as it was to lift restrictions on middle-class women looking for work.

Education was vital because of the insight it gave women into the way men controlled the world. At the end of the day, irrespective of whatever other rights they secured, it was education that would give women the keys to the kingdom and enable them to insert themselves into history in the way they deserved.

———

On the morning of 7 April 1853 Dr John Snow, renowned at the time as Britain's most skilful anaesthetist, took a cab from his home in Sackville Street in central London to Buckingham Palace. He made contact with Sir James Clark, Queen Victoria's Physician in Ordinary, and Dr Charles Locock, Queen Victoria's first Physician Accoucheur – from the French, meaning 'one who is present at the bedside' – and the three men waited in an anteroom next to the Queen's bedroom to be summoned. In the early stages of labour, Victoria preferred to be attended only by her beloved Prince Albert and 'monthly nurse' (nanny-cum-midwife) Mrs Lilly.

At around midday, the Queen asked Snow to come to her bedside. He measured out 15 minims (0.9ml) of chloroform onto a handkerchief which he folded into a cone before placing it over the royal mouth and nose. It had taken six years to persuade the Palace that chloroform was safe, but finally, on the occasion of her eighth pregnancy, the Queen had decided to give it a go. Leopold's proved to be her easiest birth so far. As Snow noted: 'Her Majesty expressed great relief from the application, the pains being very trifling during the uterine contractions, whilst between the periods of contractions there was complete ease.'

Victoria had always hated pregnancy and childbirth, which she nicknamed the *Schattenseite* or 'shadow side' of marriage. She called her own pregnancies 'wretched' and when her eldest daughter Vicky fell pregnant for the first time and wrote to her mother in anticipation of sage advice, Victoria replied: 'What you say of the pride of giving life to an immortal soul is very fine, dear, but I own I cannot enter into that; I think much more of our being like a cow or a dog at such moments; when our poor nature becomes so very animal and unecstatic.'

'In the Christian tradition,' the historian of anaesthesia Stephanie Snow points out, 'suffering during labour provided a permanent reminder of Eve's original sin in the Garden of Eden and opponents of anaesthesia were swift to draw on the Biblical admonition that "in sorrow shalt thou bring forth children".[12] By agreeing to use chloroform during Leopold's birth, Victoria had done something modern, dangerous and radical, horrifying one notable contemporary obstetrician, who admonished her for 'a too-bold step'.[13] She'd taken a huge medical risk, in the process scotching the centuries-old notion that pain during labour was natural and virtuous.

If *Anaesthesia a la Reine* was at first an option only for wealthy, fashionable ladies, it didn't stay that way for long, becoming part of a portfolio of new medical techniques – for example, sterilisation with phenol; wearing gloves to perform internal examinations – which made childbirth not just less onerous for women but not as frequently fatal.

The Victoria who wrote so candidly to Vicky sounds nothing like the Victoria we think we know. Ditto the Victoria who, in 1860, is considering suitors for Princess Alice when she suddenly confesses: 'All marriage is such a lottery – the happiness is always an exchange – though it may be a very happy one – still the poor woman is bodily and morally the husband's slave. That always sticks in my throat.'

Does this mean Queen Victoria was a feminist? It's possible, as Simon Schama has pointed out, that Victoria was familiar with early feminist writing, particularly Barbara Leigh Smith's exposé of the harsh realities of marriage, *Brief Summary in Plain Language of the Most Important Laws Concerning Women* (1854). In 1862, in an act which could be interpreted as sisterly, she appointed the women's-rights activist Emily Faithfull as her Printer and Publisher in Ordinary – 'not a position she would have given to someone who had incurred her disapproval'.[14]

But Victoria had her limits. The idea that women might want to work; might want rights; might want, through suffrage, *actual involvement* in the running of the country – this enraged her. 'It is', she wrote, 'a subject which makes the Queen so furious she cannot contain herself.' The whole idea was a 'mad, wicked folly … with all its attendant horrors on which her poor feeble sex is bent, forgetting every sense of womanly feeling and propriety.'

Two steps forward, three steps back.

The unnoticed contradictions here suggest a Queen and a society stumbling, blindfolded, through new territory. By the end of her reign, as we shall see, the way ahead would be rather clearer.

———————

One of the joys of writing this book was the numerous lively conversations with friends, family, colleagues and contacts I had along the way. So many people made inspired suggestions of women who deserved to be included. I thank them all at the back, but here at the front I want to pay tribute to two women, both dead now, who were incredibly important and inspirational to me when I was growing up. This book is their legacy.

In 1968, shortly after graduating from Oxford – the first person in her family to go to university – my mum joined the staff of the west London girls' school Godolphin and Latymer as a chemistry teacher. Helping to run the department was a woman called Frances Eastwood. Frances was much older than my mum and only two years away from retiring, but she was helpful and welcoming and before long the pair had become firm friends. She lived with another Godolphin teacher, Dorothy Newman (no relation), who had been Head of Classics before retiring in 1961.

While I was growing up my parents' relationship with their parents was always slightly tense and strained. As a result, Frances and Dodo (as we called Dorothy) became de facto grandparents to my sister Sarah and me; we regularly stayed at their house in Hythe where they would feed us hunks of bread they baked, topped with a thick layer of home-made cherry jam. But their gentle kindness and generosity never blinded us to the fact that they were fiercely clever, independent-minded women who had known hardship as well as opportunity.

Frances had read chemistry at Lady Margaret Hall, Oxford (and lived just long enough to see me win a place at the same college). Dorothy, meanwhile, had read Classics at Newnham College, Cambridge in the 1920s and remembered with fury how until 1948 – 1948! – women were not allowed to be full members of the university. Like many clever women of the period they never married or had children, blaming a lack of suitable men left alive after the First World War. It feels intrusive to speculate whether this was the whole story. Intrusive, but necessary, as the social historian Virginia Nicholson makes clear in *Singled Out*, her brilliant book about Frances and Dodo's generation of what used to be called 'spinsters'. They were known collectively as the Surplus Women after the 1921 Census revealed that there were 1.7 million more women than men in the population.

Remembering women like Frances and Dodo she encountered in her childhood, Nicholson recalls the questions that went unanswered because they were too rude to ask:

Why didn't they ever marry? Did they mind? Did they harbour secret sadness? What did they do about the lack of love in their lives, and the lack of sex? Did they care that they had never had children? Did their spectacles and tweed jackets protect them from terrible vulnerabilities?[15]

As it happens, I don't think Frances and Dodo were sad or loveless or vulnerable. The point for me is that they existed in an atmosphere of quirky female self-sufficiency and, while obviously bluestockings, were practical as well as cerebral. When Godolphin and Latymer was evacuated from Hammersmith to Newbury during the war – it shared a building with Newbury Grammar School – Dorothy as Senior Mistress helped to ensure its smooth operation and, with Frances' help, ran one of the hostels for evacuated pupils.

I often wonder what Frances and Dodo would make of the way the modern world treats women. I think they would be horrified by the volume of abuse women are expected to soak up on Twitter – actually, they would be horrified by Twitter, full stop – but thrilled by such developments as the celebrity of historian Dame Mary Beard, Jane Austen's appearance on a bank note and Laura Bates' Everyday Sexism campaign.

I hope they would be proud of my journalism, especially my work on *Channel 4 News* – and of this book, which I humbly offer up to them in tribute.

2

Old Battles, New Women

1880–1914

By the 1880s, when our tale roughly begins, a time-traveller from Britain at the start of the nineteenth century would have found much of the country unrecognisable. Its urban centres, linked by a sophisticated rail network, boasted street lighting, paved roads and – if you were lucky – state-of-the-art sewers. In the industrial north and Midlands, especially, these towns and cities were thrumming symbols of imperial pomp and civic pride. Just beyond them, in soon-to-be suburbia, the sort of houses many of us still inhabit were being thrown up at breakneck speed.

But one thing remained resolutely unchanged. Politics was still a game played almost entirely by men – and old men at that. Benjamin Disraeli was sixty-nine when he became Prime Minister in 1874. William Gladstone, who succeeded him in 1880, was seventy at that point – and eighty-two by the time he was elected for the fourth time in 1892. Queen Victoria was dismayed at the prospect of her precious empire being at the mercy of the 'shaking hand of an old, wild and incomprehensible man'. But then she had always disliked Gladstone, once complaining of the esteemed orator: 'He always addresses me as if I were a public meeting.'

Queen Victoria had to get along with ten British prime ministers during her reign, which gives you a sense of just how much change she witnessed.

The nineteenth century was a time of massive expansion, especially for London. The capital's population rose from 960,000 in 1801, when the first national census was taken, to nearly 6.6 million by 1901 – roughly the same as the combined populations of Paris, Berlin, Vienna and St Petersburg.[1] Cities swelled because of migration from rural areas: the aftershocks of 1873's agricultural depression, triggered by a collapse in grain prices, didn't ease until the 1890s.

Immigration was also a factor in this urban drift. Jews fled the pogroms in Eastern Europe and Irish Catholics escaped from poverty and famine. In 1765, the *Morning Gazette* estimated there were 30,000 black servants in the country.[2] After slavery's abolition the numbers fell dramatically, though there would still have been a significant black presence in ports like Cardiff, Liverpool and Grimsby, as well as London, where, according to Peter Ackroyd, most former slaves and their offspring were absorbed into society's underclass as beggars and crossings-sweepers and became 'almost invisible'.[3]

This might be overstating it. You don't have to look far to find examples of visible black Victorian Britons,[4] but history books tend to have less to say about the women than the men. Or perhaps there were just fewer of them. Nurse-cum-hotelier Mary Seacole is now as well known among primary school children as her supposed rival Florence Nightingale (in fact, the two were on friendly terms), and was in many respects as effective a nurse on the killing fields of the Crimea. The African-American actor and playwright Ira Aldridge moved to London and had two daughters, Luranah and Amanda, who both became opera singers.[5] Laura Bowman, the African-American star of the musical *In Dahomey* – so popular it was performed at Buckingham Palace on 27 June 1903 – settled in Wimbledon with her common-law husband and performing partner Pete Hampton. Jane Roberts, a former slave who also moved to London from America and lived in a quiet street off Battersea Park, died in 1914, aged ninety-five.

She's buried in Streatham cemetery: plot 252, class H, block F.[6] Caroline Barbour-James and her five children moved from Guyana to west London in 1905. Upright Christians, they were always so smart and clean that local working-class youths thought they were millionaires.[7]

There was a fuss when the most recent BBC adaptation of E. M. Forster's *Howards End* gave the Schlegel siblings a black maid. It was anachronistic, some said. Political correctness gone mad. But as Jeffrey Green's fascinating *Black Edwardians: Black People in Britain 1901–1914* shows, there were plenty of women of African descent in domestic service in Britain at this time, for example Ann Styles, a freed slave from Jamaica who moved to London in around 1840 with the white family she worked for. She continued in their service all her working life. Green's own grandmother, Martha Louisa Vass, worked as a maid for a suffragette. Vass worked every day, often late into the night when the woman gave dinner parties. Every other Sunday she was allowed the afternoon off.

And then there's Sara Forbes Bonetta, who deserves to be far better known. In 1850, at the age of around eight, Bonetta was delivered by a Captain Frederick E. Forbes to Queen Victoria as a 'gift' from King Ghezo of Dahomey, in what is now Benin in West Africa. Forbes named her after his ship, the HMS Bonetta, which had been patrolling the area with orders to intercept and destroy any slaving vessels.

Forbes worried about the 'burden' of bringing a child back on the ship but concluded he had no choice as Sara was now the property of the crown. He saw for the girl a future as a missionary and wrote her a glowing character reference:

> For her age, supposed to be eight years, she is a perfect genius;
> she now speaks English well, and has a great talent for music.
> She has won the affections with but few exceptions, of all who
> have known her; by her docile and amiable conduct, which

nothing can exceed. She is far in advance of any white child of her age, in aptness of learning, and strength of mind and affection ... Her mind has received a moral and religious impression and she was baptised according to the rites of the Protestant Church.[8]

When Sara finally met Queen Victoria at Windsor Castle the queen was delighted with her, agreeing with Forbes that she was 'sharp and intelligent'. 'Sally', as Victoria called her, became the queen's goddaughter and for the next year was raised by the Forbes family like any other upper-middle-class English child. She visited the royal household several times and struck up a friendship with Princess Alice, Victoria and Albert's second daughter, who was a similar age.

In 1851, however, Sara developed a persistent cough. Victoria's doctors concluded that Britain's wet climate was bad for Sara's health and she was sent back to Africa to be educated at mission-ary school. But she was unhappy there and a few years later, when Sara was twelve, Victoria gave her permission to return to Britain.

She attended the wedding of Victoria, the Princess Royal, and in August 1862 was herself married at St Nicholas' Church in Brighton to a Yoruba businessman, Captain James Pinson Labulo Davies. The couple returned to West Africa, where Sara gave birth to a daughter, named – you guessed it – Victoria. The queen became *her* godmother too, and when Sara brought the baby to meet her namesake, Victoria observed: 'Saw Sally, now Mrs Davies, & her dear little child, far blacker than herself ... a lively intelligent child with big melancholy eyes.' Sara went on to have two more children. But she developed tuberculosis and died in 1880, the year our imaginary time-traveller arrives in Britain.

Sara Forbes Bonetta is fascinating because, simply by existing and behaving as she did, she debunked contemporary theories about race which held that anyone who wasn't Anglo-Saxon was an example of a lower evolutionary form. John Beddoe, author of

The Races of Britain (1862) and President of the Anthropological Institute 1889–1891, believed 'Africanoids' were related to Cromagnon man. But remember Captain Forbes' extraordinary assessment: 'She is far in advance of any white child of her age …'

It's a shame neither Bonetta nor Seacole, who died in 1881, lived to see the new age that was dawning. Everywhere there was evidence of a rupture with the past, with everything known and familiar. The telegraph network made it possible to communicate quickly and reliably over huge distances. The first petrol-driven internal combustion engine was constructed in 1884 by Edward Butler. By the 1880s most new houses would have come with gas pipes and lamps as standard. Not surprisingly, the pace of development left many struggling to keep up.

Foremost among those left behind were the poor. The Poor Law Amendment Act of 1834 meant that if you wanted help, you had to go to the workhouse to get it, with all the hardship that entailed. Disease, starvation and overcrowding were still widespread, though by the 1880s the middle classes had acquired a greater capacity to be shocked and/or titillated by them: books and pamphlets such as Andrew Mearns' *The Bitter Cry of Outcast London* (1883) and George R. Sims' *How The Poor Live* (1883) found a ready readership.

To a significant degree, the job of sorting this mess out fell into the laps of women, as if women alone had the necessary resources to make a difference. In most cases these sorter-out women were upper middle class. The respectable helped the 'lowly' – until the battle for suffrage turned serious, at which point factory workers and MPs' wives suddenly found themselves members of the same team.

The virtuous militancy that had powered protest groups like the Chartists – who wanted greater political representation for the working classes – was still in the air in the 1870s and 1880s. But increasingly it was being harnessed by women like the social reformers Clementina Black; Rachel and Margaret McMillan;

Beatrice Webb; and Lydia Becker, who founded the first national suffrage campaign group, the National Society for Women's Suffrage (NSWS), in 1867. It was hearing Lydia speak at a NSWS meeting in 1872 which radicalised a young Emmeline Pankhurst.

What these women had in common was, mostly, determination; though sometimes hardship too.

Clementina Black certainly knew how tough life was for many women. Her mother had died from a rupture while attempting to lift her invalid father, leaving twenty-one-year-old Clementina to look after him and her seven younger siblings. That she managed to write her first novel, *A Sussex Idyll*, while doing this speaks volumes; though it's for her work with the Women's Industrial Council (WIC), which she founded in 1894, and the Women's Trade Union League (WTUL) rather than her fiction that Black is remembered.

Rachel and Margaret McMillan had to overcome tragedy too. Born in New York in 1859 and 1860 respectively, they returned to their parents' native Inverness with their mother after scarlet fever had killed their father and infant sister and left Margaret deaf. (Her hearing returned when she was fourteen.) Their conversion to Christian socialism in the late 1880s ignited an obsession with educational reform. They paid particular attention to working-class children, and their campaigning led to a change in the law to provide free school meals for children and the proper training of nursery teachers. They would go on to open school-cum-clinics like the Deptford Clinic, which acted as a medical centre for local children, and 'night camps' where children from deprived areas could camp outside as well as wash and obtain clean clothes.

Before activism dominated her life, home-schooled Lydia Becker had been an amateur scientist – specialist subjects: botany and astronomy – who published a book, *Botany for Novices* (1864), and corresponded regularly with Charles Darwin. Becker would send Darwin specimens of plants indigenous to Manchester and contributed to his work on plant dimorphism. In return, Darwin acted as her unofficial tutor and mentor and, when Becker asked if he had a spare paper she might read out at the inaugural meeting of her quietly radical Manchester Ladies' Literary Society – 'Of course we are not so unreasonable as to desire that you should write anything specially for us' – he generously sent over three.[9]

Beatrice Webb is better-known. With her husband Sidney, she would go on to be a founding member of what is now Britain's oldest political think tank, the Fabian Society and, in 1895, the London School of Economics. Her approach to social reform was to drip-feed socialist ideas into the minds of Britain's ruling elite. As young, unmarried Beatrice Potter, however, she worked with the sociologist Charles Booth on his monumental study of the Victorian slums *Life and Labour of the People in London*, published between 1889 and 1903.

Webb didn't call herself a socialist until February 1890, when she declared her conversion in her diary, but she wrote several years earlier of the 'growing uneasiness, amounting to conviction' she felt that 'the industrial organisation, which had yielded rent, interest and profits on a stupendous scale, had failed to provide a decent livelihood and tolerable conditions for a majority of the inhabitants of Great Britain'.[10]

More and more women like these five were feeling that they had a role to play in improving society. They knew they could answer the question of what constituted a 'decent livelihood' or 'tolerable conditions' as capably as the men. But the late-Victorian expectation was that women would suppress their intellects, the better to boost men's sense of their own superior brainpower.

All four parts of Coventry Patmore's best-known poem, the sickly paean to marriage 'The Angel in the House', were first published together in 1863. By the 1880s this piece of sludge epitomised the Victorian ideal where women were concerned. 'Man must be pleased,' wrote Patmore, 'but him to please is woman's pleasure.'

For Patmore, women – being both altruistic and obedient by nature – were best employed in the home, making their husbands happy and looking after any children. Even if their husbands stopped loving them, they must continue to love these men out of loyalty: 'Through passionate duty love springs higher, as grass grows taller round a stone.'

What became known as the doctrine of separate spheres – that women belonged at home while only men could cope with the demands of the workplace – found its most famous expression in an essay by the writer and art critic John Ruskin called 'Sesame and Lilies', published in 1865. The job of a woman, Ruskin argues, is to patrol the domestic front: her intellect, such as it is, is 'not for invention or creation, but for sweet ordering, arrangement, and decision':

> By her office, and place, she is protected from all danger and temptation. The man, in his rough work in open world, must encounter all peril and trial; – to him, therefore, must be the failure, the offence, the inevitable error: often he must be wounded, or subdued; often misled; and always hardened. But he guards the woman from all this …[11]

Pity Ruskin's poor wife! Indeed, his own marriage to Euphemia 'Effie' Gray was annulled after six years on the grounds of non-consummation. Supposedly the sight of her pubic hair and menstrual blood on their wedding night disgusted him.

If the 'separate spheres' doctrine sounds a bit barmy to us today, plenty of women at the time couldn't get their heads round it either. The suffragist and campaigner for female education Emily Davies declared that 'men have no monopoly of working, nor women of weeping'.[12] She railed against a 'double moral code, with its masculine and feminine virtues, and its separate law of duty and honour for either sex'.[13]

Nowhere was this moral code more obviously unfair than in the bedroom. If a man committed adultery, it was a regrettable but understandable lapse. (It was in men's nature to have sex whenever they felt like it, so what could you do to stop them?) For a woman, however, it was catastrophic, unforgivable, life changing. The Matrimonial Causes Act of 1857 ruled that a woman could be divorced on the grounds of their adultery alone, whereas a man needed to be found guilty of other additional offences. He'd have to have committed incest, or not only been unfaithful but also deserted his wife.

The Act had led to an explosion in the divorce rate because middle-class couples could afford to split. Before the Act and its creation of a dedicated Court of Divorce and Matrimonial Causes, a marriage could be dissolved only by an Act of Parliament, at massive expense. In 1858, its first year in operation, there were three hundred divorce petitions compared to three the previous year.

One of these three hundred was brought by the industrialist Henry Robinson and became notorious. Despite having several mistresses and two illegitimate children, Robinson sought to divorce his wife Isabella on grounds of *her* infidelity, even though the only proof was a diary in which Isabella had been unwise enough to confide her erotic fantasies; a diary which shocked the nation when it was read out in court and extracts from it printed in newspapers.

Letters sent to Isabella by the object of her lust, a married homeopath called Edward Lane, proved nothing; nor did the diary prove anything save the lively sexual imagination of its author. But it was used against Isabella in court to protect Edward's reputation. Broken and humiliated, she was obliged to defend herself by claiming that the diary was a dream-vision, a hallucination, and that a uterine disorder she suffered from had induced 'erotomania'.[14]

By 1880 the idea of a woman being imprisoned by an unhappy marriage was grimly commonplace. Though of course, it was hardly a new one. The heroine of Mary Wollstonecraft's 1797 novel *The Wrongs of Woman: or, Maria: A Fragment* is locked up by her husband, first in their home and later in a mental institution. In the asylum Maria writes a memoir for her infant daughter who has been taken away from her: 'But a wife being as much a man's property as his horse, or his ass, she has nothing she can call her own!' she protests. 'He may use any means to get at what the law considers as his, the moment his wife is in possession of it, even to the forcing of a lock.'[15]

Under nineteenth-century marriage law a woman's legal identity was absorbed into her husband's – a principle known as 'coverture'. Without her husband's consent a wife was unable to make a will, sue or be sued. All her property became her husband's, including anything she had owned before and brought to the marriage. And her husband had custody of their children.

A change came in 1870 with the Married Women's Property Act, which permitted women to be the legal owners of any money they earned and to inherit property. And in 1884 the Matrimonial Causes Act denied a husband the right to lock up his wife if she refused to have sex with him – although it wasn't ratified until 1891 after an incident which became known as the 'Jackson Abduction'.

On 5 November 1887, Emily Hall, a respectable solicitor's daughter, married Edmund Jackson, the feckless son of an army officer. The couple never lived together and on their wedding night, before they had the chance to consummate their marriage, Edmund left for New Zealand, telling Emily he would send for her once he and his friend Dixon had established themselves there as farmers.

But Emily decided she didn't want to go to New Zealand after all, feeling that 'it would be impossible for me to hope to endure the rough life of a colonial settler'.[16] So she wrote to Edmund telling him this, adding that she no longer wanted any contact with him. The begging tone of his letters to her from New

Zealand worried her and she suspected he had married her for her money rather than out of love. Edmund's angry reply asserted his husbandly rights in no uncertain terms:

> Do not make any mistake. There shall be a perfect understanding between us, but I will make it, not you. It is most ridiculous for you to say you will have this or that; it depends on whether I approve or no.[17]

Four years passed. Then, without telling Emily, Edmund returned to Britain. Having obtained a decree for restitution of conjugal rights, he tracked Emily down to the Lancashire village of Clitheroe, where she had been brought up and her family still lived, and he kidnapped her as she was leaving church one Sunday. He bundled her into a waiting carriage with such haste that he knocked the bonnet off her head, drove her to a house he had rented in Blackburn and locked her in. Outside the house, to stop her trying to escape, he planted a team of hired heavies. Emily's friends tracked her down and demanded entry. When this was refused they called the police, but to no avail.

A crowd gathered outside the house and watched as supplies were delivered. On the morning after the abduction, reported *The Times*, 'milk and the papers were taken in by means of a string let down from one of the bedroom windows, and, later on, all kinds of provisions were obtained in the same way. At noon a box of cigars was hoisted up to the garrison.' On 11 March 1891, Edmund was forced to leave the house after Emily's sister filed a charge of assault against him for injuries she'd sustained trying to defend Emily during the abduction. Even as he left, though, his heavies swarmed around the house waving sticks.

Emily was fortunate to come from a legally literate family. They filed a writ of habeas corpus, which, if granted, meant Emily could be brought before a court which ought to declare her detention unlawful. But on 16 March, the High Court rejected the

application on the basis that, while generally the forcible detention of a subject by another was 'prima facie illegal', where the
relation was that of husband and wife, different rules applied.

Infuriated, Emily's family took the case to the Court of Appeal
– and, amazingly, got a sympathetic hearing. The Court agreed
that Edmund had no right to force his wife to live with him: the
very idea was uncivilised and derived from what Lord Halsbury,
delivering the first judgement, called 'quaint and absurd dicta'. The
judges suspected that Edmund had married Emily for her money,
displaying the sort of predatory behaviour to which men were
prone and from which women needed protecting.

Lord Halsbury's judgement was a landmark because, notwithstanding its reflexive sexism, it rejects the idea of the 'absolute
dominion of the husband over the wife', calling Edmund's counsel's defence of wife-beating 'outrageous to common feelings of
humanity' and 'inconsistent with the rights of free human creatures'. This echoed the language of contemporary women's-rights
campaigners, though Lord Halsbury went on to specify instances
in which husbands might be entitled to use limited, temporary
powers of restraint, if, for example, a woman 'were on the staircase
about to join some person with whom she intended to elope'.[18]

But while the educated middle classes had the freedom and
resources to use the courts in this way, for working-class women
in 1880 it was a different story. Their lives, based around laundry
and childcare – six or more children was the norm – were exhausting and terrifyingly unpredictable. Money trickled in uncertainly
and there was no safety net if it ran out. Everything (clothes,
furniture, cooking and cleaning utensils) was in short supply. Any
meat was fed to the man of the house as the breadwinner. As a
result, girls growing up in working-class households were under-
nourished, prone to tuberculosis and other diseases, and less able
to withstand the ravages of pregnancy and childbirth.

Many working-class women went into service. By 1901, 91.5
per cent of all English servants were women.[19] Some started

young: as late as 1911, more than 39,000 13- and 14-year-olds were working as servants. The 1870 Education Act had theoretically opened up avenues for women by making education a matter of state provision rather than the whimsical, unregulated gift of charities, churches and other voluntary associations. But many girls were unable to take advantage of school places because their families were poor. A child in service, rather than in school, meant financial security, a situation that is portrayed in Flora Thompson's semi-autobiographical *Lark Rise to Candleford* sequence of novels:

> As soon as a mother had even one daughter in service, the strain upon herself slacked a little. Not only was there one mouth less to feed, one less pair of feet to be shod, and a tiny space left free in the cramped sleeping quarters; but every month, when the girl received her wages, a shilling or more would be sent to 'our Mum'.[20]

Most middle-class families had at least one servant. As the feminist historians Bonnie Anderson and Judith Zinsser pithily observe: 'For men, the dividing line between middle and working class was usually measured in income; for women, it lay in the difference between being a servant and being able to afford one.'[21]

Charles Booth estimated that 30 per cent of London families could not live on a man's wages alone. In order to supplement their husbands' earnings, working-class wives took on piecework – usually sewing or knitting – either at home or in attics or cellars supervised by a 'sweater'. Abuse and malpractice in the 'sweated work' industry was rife, both at home and in factories. The extent of it was exposed by one of the late-Victorian period's great whistleblowers and one of the most impressive activists of the era: Ada Nield Chew.

The second child in a family of thirteen, Chew was born on 28 January 1870 to William Nield, a brickmaker, and his wife Jane, in Audley, Staffordshire. At the age of eleven she left school to help look after her family, which included an epileptic younger sister; she fitted in paid work where she could.

After the family moved to Crewe in 1887, Chew found work in the Compton Brothers clothing factory. But it was miserable and exploitative, so in 1894 she sent the *Crewe Chronicle* a series of anonymous letters savagely criticising the pay and conditions of the women who worked at the factory, especially as compared to those of their male colleagues doing the same work.

This was a risky undertaking, but for Chew the alternative was unthinkable: 'As long as we are silent ourselves and apparently content with our lot, so long shall we be left in enjoyment of that lot.'[22] Bear in mind, when reading this extract from her second letter to the *Chronicle*, published on 19 May 1894, that Chew had no formal secondary education and taught herself to write by reading novels and magazines:

And now to take an average of a year's wage of the 'average ordinary hand', which was the class I mentioned in my first letter, and being that which is in a majority may be taken as fairly representative. The wages of such a 'hand', sir, will barely average – but by exercise of the imagination – 8 shillings [approximately £42 in today's money] a week. I ought to say, too, that there is a minority, which is also considerable, whose wages will not average above 5 shillings [approximately £26] a week. I would impress upon you that this is making the very best of the case, and is over rather than understating. What do you think of it, Mr Editor, for a 'living' wage?

I wish some of those, whoever they may be who mete it out to us, would try to 'live' on it for a few weeks, as the factory girl has to do 52 weeks in a year. To pay board and lodging, to provide herself decent boots and clothes to stand all weathers, to pay an occasional doctor's bill, literature, and a holiday away from the scope of her daily drudging, for which even the factory girl has the audacity to long sometimes – but has quite as often to do without. Not to speak of provision for old age, when eyes have grown too dim to thread the everlasting needle, and to guide the worn fingers over the accustomed task.[23]

As well as paying for their own materials, women workers had to shell out for hot water to make the tea they drank. Their managers were so inefficient at apportioning labour that the only way the women could earn a living wage was by taking work home with them, which added another four or five hours to the working day – and this had to be fitted in, remember, around household chores like cooking, cleaning and looking after small children.

Once her identity as the author of the letters was exposed, Chew lost her job. But she had been talent-spotted by the Independent Labour Party – a precursor of today's Labour party – and the burgeoning suffragist movement.

Plenty of other women shared Chew's passion and panache. By the time Annie Besant helped to organise a strike of the female workers at Bryant & May's match factory in east London in 1888, Besant was already well known for her part in a notorious obscenity trial. Besant and Charles Bradlaugh, head of the Secular Society she had joined in 1875, used the *National Reformer* magazine to promote a progressive agenda that included education, suffrage and, especially, birth control. The pair were arrested after they published a cheap book intended to educate poor women about contraception.

Although Besant and Bradlaugh were found guilty of obscenity, the verdict was overturned on a technicality. Bradlaugh went on to become an MP. Besant was, predictably, hit harder: the scandal of the trial cost her custody of her daughter. But the trauma of this loss seems only to have catalysed her activism.

She was moved to righteous fury when she learned at a Fabian Society meeting of the conditions endured by Bryant & May's mostly female workers. As if the litany of industrial injustices (fourteen-hour working days, poor pay made poorer still by an unfair system of fines) wasn't long enough, the 'matchgirls' had to endure a uniquely horrible side-effect of handling the white phosphorous used in match-making: 'phossy jaw'.

Vapour from the phosphorous caused the lower jaws of workers to become distended and deformed – and even glow in the dark. Abscesses would form and over time the jaw bone would simply rot away. On 23 June 1888, Besant published an article in *The Link*, the newspaper she co-edited with the campaigning journalist W. T. Stead, exposing practices at the factory. A follow-up piece took the form of a letter to Bryant & May's middle- and upper-class shareholders. It's a masterpiece of campaigning rhetoric:

> Do you know that girls are used to carry boxes on their heads
> till the hair is rubbed off, and the young heads are bald at fifteen
> years of age? Country clergymen with shares in Bryant &
> May's, draw down on your knee your fifteen-year-old daughter;
> pass your hand tenderly over the silky, clustering curls, rejoicing
> in the dainty beauty of the thick shining tresses …[24]

Bryant & May's response was swift and brutal: they tried to force their workers to sign a statement saying they were content with their lot. When one group refused and were sacked, 1,400 other workers went on strike in solidarity. With the help of trade-union pioneer Clementina Black, and Catherine Booth, who with her husband William co-founded the Salvation Army, Besant helped the women to organise and fight back. She became head of the Matchgirls' Union and secured a significant climbdown. On 21 July 1888, stung by the bad publicity, Bryant & May agreed to end the fines system and re-hire the women it had sacked.

It was the first time a union of unskilled workers had got what they wanted from a strike. But it was in some ways a Pyrrhic victory as Bryant & May continued to use white phosphorous until 1901, despite knowing full well it was toxic. After Catherine

Booth died in 1890, William honoured her memory by opening the Salvation Army's own match factory where only the harmless but more expensive red phosphorous was used. 'Remember the poor matchgirls!' cried their adverts.

Not until the new century were other trades regulated in the same way. Part of the problem was that, while unions existed for men, they were reluctant to allow women to join them. Women were regarded as cheap rival labour, threatening men's livelihoods. Frustrated by this, bookbinder Emma Paterson founded the Women's Protective and Provident League (WPPL) in 1874. It soon represented women in a mass of industries, including making jam, tights and cigars.

The nail- and chain-making industry, based in the Black Country, was one of the most dangerous. In 1910 it became one of the first trades to be regulated when the Scottish trade unionist Mary MacArthur, who had become secretary of the WPPL after it turned into the Women's Trade Union League (WTUL) in 1891, organised a strike of female chain workers at Cradley Heath. In a landmark ruling she secured for them a minimum wage, famously observing that 'women are unorganised because they are badly paid, and poorly paid because they are unorganised.'[25]

In 1893 the WTUL's treasurer May Abraham became one of the first two female factory inspectors. The other was Mary Paterson, who was based in Glasgow. Abraham's *Royal Commission on the Employment of Labour*, focusing on the weaving industry, stresses the massive regional variation in women's pay – 24 shillings a week in Lancashire compared with 18 in Yorkshire – and describes in horrifying detail the damp but boiling-hot conditions where the weavers worked. Adelaide Anderson's 1922 study *Women in the Factory* is even worse. She describes how the dust inhaled by women spinning silk caused them to cough up silkworms.

Abraham and Paterson were paid salaries of £200 a year, much less than their male counterparts, but they achieved impressive results, including the early identification of asbestos as a health risk. Inspector Lucy Deane warned in a 1898 report of the 'sharp glass-like jagged nature of the particles', and pointed out that 'where [the particles] are allowed to rise and to remain suspended in the air of the room in any quantity, the effects have been found to be injurious as might have been expected.'[26] Her report was ignored until 1911 when clinical evidence linking asbestos to lung disease was finally gathered.

Thanks to these women's efforts the Factory Act of 1895, which extended and amended previous Factory Acts, would place a much greater emphasis on workers' 'health and safety' – a phrase coined, by the way, by a woman: Audrey Pittom, Deputy Chief Inspector of Factories in the mid 1970s.

The WTUL also claimed credit for later legislation such as the Workmen's Compensation Act 1897, which established the principle that those injured in the workplace should be compensated, and was ultimately responsible for the Shops Act 1911. One of the great welfare reforms of Lloyd George's Liberal government, this set a maximum working week of sixty hours and gave shop assistants a weekly half-day holiday. Happy days!

Being a shop assistant in one of the newfangled department stores springing up in towns and cities across the country or waitressing was now an option for working- and lower-middle-class women, who had previously had something of a Hobson's choice of factory work or service.

At first, shop owners exploited the abundance of cheap, deferential labour with predictable cynicism. When assistants 'lived in' a store – a common practice at the time – their lodgings were often squalid. What's more Thomas Sutherst, president of the Shop Hours Labour League in the 1880s, wrote: 'the shop assistant in these days is obliged to submit to the intolerable fatigue of standing for periods, varying according to the locality, from thirteen to seventeen hours a day.' We might bemoan twenty-first-century interning, but it was nothing to what women then experienced. They were often 'apprenticed' for several years during which they were paid pocket-money wages.

A young woman called Margaret Bondfield took a leaf out of Ada Nield Chew's book when she wrote a series of pseudonymous articles for *The Shop Assistant* exposing shoddy, exploitative practices in department stores in Brighton and London. Living in, she experienced overcrowded, insanitary conditions and awful food as well as what she called 'an undertone of danger'. Bondfield was expected to work between 80 and 100 hours a week for 51 weeks per year. Little wonder she had already become an active trade unionist by 1896, when the Women's Industrial Council suggested she work as an undercover agent, reporting back to them – and the wider world, through a column in the *Daily Chronicle* – on the abuses she found.

Despite her limited education, Bondfield went on to enjoy a long, illustrious political career, founding the Women's Labour League (WLL) in 1906 and becoming both the first woman to chair the general council of the Trades Union Congress (TUC) and the first female cabinet minister, as Minister of Labour in Ramsay MacDonald's Labour government of 1929–31.

Decades before Bondfield made history in this role, the choice of work available to women was expanding. As early as the 1860s, Jessie Boucherett and Maria Rye had managed, through their Society for Promoting the Employment of Women, to secure jobs for women in banks and insurance companies. The booming communications sector offered other opportunities. In 1869, the year the Telegraph Act of 1869 handed the Post Office a monopoly on telegraph services, most of the 6.8 million telegrams sent in Britain would have been dictated to women. By 1914, 7,000 women were employed by the Post Office and 3,000 in other government services. But there were massive barriers remaining, not least that women had to give up their jobs once they married. And, of course, they were paid significantly less than men.

Actually, the gender pay gap was an issue in all white-collar clerical jobs. At the Prudential insurance company, male clerks earned up to £350 a year while few women made more than £60. Women had to shoulder the burden of dressing smartly on low wages or risk losing their jobs for being scruffy.

While equal opportunity at work was still a distant dream for late-Victorian feminists, there were plenty of battles to be fought at home. The nature of the middle class was changing. The difference between lower-middle and upper-middle was becoming more defined in terms of manners and outlook, and the number of servants a family could afford to hire: just a cook and a maid-of-all-work? Or an array of different kinds of help? At the top of the scale, what mattered was that the house was beautiful – and by extension the woman beautiful, for she occupied the centre of this world, holding its elements in genteel suspension.

Rooms in late-Victorian upper-middle-class homes grew cluttered as hoarding fine things became a moral prerogative – conveniently for those who wanted to be both genteel *and* righteous; to reconcile, as George Eliot put it in *Middlemarch*, 'piety and worldliness, the nothingness of this life and the desirability of cut glass'.[27] As the design historian Deborah Cohen notes: 'Women's sense of themselves seems from the 1890s onward to have been tied up increasingly in their décor.'[28]

The continuing popularity of Mrs Beeton's *Book of Household Management* is revealing. It's fair to assume most families read it aspirationally. Mrs Beeton, who died in 1865, four years after it came out, directs her advice to the manager of a large household whom she compares to the commander of an army, the assumption being that this woman has a team of servants at her beck and call to engineer show-offy dinner-party *coups de théâtre*, such as *Service à la Russe*, in which as many as fourteen courses are presented one after the other.

While husbands went off to work, middle-class 'womenfolk' remained at home as pampered dependents. Katharine Chorley grew up in the well-to-do Manchester suburb of Alderley Edge where 'pheasants whirred out of copses, the crack of guns sounded through the winter, [and] cattle churned to a muddy porridge the good Cheshire soil at the entrance gates of fields.'[29] Happily, this bucolic idyll existed a mere fifteen minutes' train journey from the centre of Manchester. Chorley recalled in her memoir *Manchester Made Them* that once the 8.25, 8.50 and 9.18 trains had left in the morning the Edge became 'exclusively female':

> You never saw a man on the hill roads unless it were the doctor or the plumber, and you never saw a man in anyone's home except the gardener or the coachman. And yet it was a man-made and a man-lorded society.[30]

Businessmen using the trains travelled First Class. But if a wife or daughter needed to go into Manchester she would always travel Third Class because 'to share a compartment with the gentlemen (we were taught never to call them just plainly "men") would have been unthinkable'. In this situation 'business trains' were avoided if possible: 'It was highly embarrassing, a sort of indelicacy, to stand on the platform surrounded by a crowd of males who had to be polite but were obviously not in the mood for feminine society.'[31] Chorley's less-deceived gaze is unsparing: women in such a society, she recognises, 'existed for their husbands' and fathers' sakes and their lives were shaped to please masculine vanity.'[32]

Life for upper-middle-class women was, if anything, even stranger and more isolated. Privilege infantilised them: Gwen Raverat, granddaughter of Charles Darwin, wrote in *Period Piece*, her very funny memoir of her 1890s childhood, that at the end of the century there were thousands of British women like her Aunt Etty who had 'never made a pot of tea ... been out in the dark alone ... travelled by train without a maid ... or sewn on a button.'[33]

'There were always people to do these things for her. In fact, in some ways, she was very like a royal person. Once she wrote when her maid, the patient and faithful Janet, was away for a day or two: "*I am very busy answering my own bell.*"[34]

How had this situation arisen? Because the behaviour of 'respectable' women was governed by strict social rules. By the 1880s public transport was making it easier for women to get around, but there were still places where they needed to be accompanied. Women who walked the streets themselves were seen as 'either endangered or dangerous', as one historian puts it,[35] and as a rule 'a lady was simply not supposed to be seen aimlessly wandering the streets or eating alone.'[36]

Virginia Woolf's *The Pargiters*, an early version of the 'essay-novel' that would become *The Years*, her last work to be published in her lifetime, is partly set in the 1880s, at which point the middle-class Pargiter sisters 'could not possibly go for a walk alone':

> For any of them to walk in the West End by day was out of the
> question. Bond Street was as impassable, save with their
> mother, as any swamp alive with crocodiles … To be seen alone
> in Piccadilly was equivalent to walking up Abercorn Terrace in
> a dressing gown carrying a bath sponge.[37]

One middle-class woman who made it her moral business to walk the streets – admittedly with a companion for safety – was the social reformer Mary Higgs. The difference was that Higgs disguised herself as a homeless woman. In 1906, twenty-seven years before George Orwell went 'on the tramp' to write *Down and Out in Paris and London*, Higgs published *Glimpses Into the Abyss*, an extraordinary account of life on the streets, in lodging houses and the wards of workhouses.

Born in Wiltshire in 1854, Higgs (née Kingsland) was the daughter of a Congregational minister and in 1873 became the first woman to study for the Natural Science Tripos at Cambridge. She drifted into teaching, but after marrying Thomas Kilpin Higgs, a minister like her father, devoted much of her time to philanthropic works: helping to manage a home for destitute women in Oldham; and engaging in utopian brainstorming with Ebenezer Howard, founder of the 'garden city' movement.

Higgs considered poverty to be a sort of disease, more or less infectious – she talks about the 'microbes of social disorder' – which the right sort of 'remedial treatment' could eradicate. In her introduction to *Glimpses into the Abyss*, Higgs describes the Oldham cottage she converted into a lodging house as a 'social microscope, every case being personally investigated as to past life, history and present need'.[38] What had been done to these women? What had they done to themselves? Higgs admitted ignorance. But she was determined to learn. The only way to do this, she decided, was to explore 'Darkest England' herself in a spirit of rational, scientific enquiry.

And so Higgs wandered through West Yorkshire, Lancashire and, briefly, London. She studied the Poor Law in Britain and its equivalent in Denmark. She also undertook a 'literary investigation into deterioration of human personality' – a 'necessary corollary to the acquisition of a wide collection of facts'. Her inquiries took on a eugenicist gloss, shocking to us now, though it would have shocked few people at the time:

> In any given individual the whole path climbed by the foremost classes or races may not be retraced. Therefore numbers of individuals are permanently stranded on lower levels of evolution. Society can quicken evolution by right social arrangements, scientific in principle.[39]

Higgs' sense that improving social conditions for the poor could transform them and set them back on the road to prosperity (or at least 'evolution' rather than 'devolution') sounds progressive. But for her, people could only retrace the path appropriate to their class or race; could only hope to reach a certain, pre-ordained level of attainment. Even with all the wind in the world behind her, a working-class woman could never hope to be as clever and accomplished as an upper-class woman.

Higgs brought along her own secret supply of provisions – sugar, tea, plasmon (a form of dried milk) – and tolerated the filthy bedding, fleas and lack of washing facilities. But the behaviour of the people she encountered baffled her:

> A conversation sprang up about the treatment of wives, and it was stated that a woman loved a man best *if he ill-treated her* … All the conversation was unspeakably foul, and was delivered with a kind of cross-shouting, each struggling to make his or her observations heard.[40]

In a workhouse tramp ward, naivety blinded Higgs to the ever-present sexual threat. A male 'pauper', charged with the responsibility for admitting women, 'talked to me in what I suppose he thought a very agreeable manner, telling me he wished I had come alone earlier, and he would have given me a cup of tea. I thanked him, wondering if this was usual, and then he took my age, and finding I was a married woman (I must use his exact words), he said, "Just the right age for a bit of funning; come down to me later in the evening." I was too horror-struck to reply.'[41]

Learning that 'single women frequently get shaken out of a home by bereavements or other causes, and drift, unable to recover a stable position once their clothing becomes dirty or shabby',[42] Higgs comes to understand the catch-22 of poverty. This led her, once she had returned to her own world of middle-class comfort, to campaign for such things as pensions for widowed mothers and family allowances – some sort of safety net that might break the cycle of destitution.

At Windsor Castle on the night of 14 December 1861, Prince Albert died of typhoid at the age of forty-two. Victoria was inconsolable: his loss was, she said, 'like tearing the flesh from my bones'. As she withdrew from the world, all that interested her was memorialising her husband and the miracle of their marriage through the likes of the Royal Albert Hall (opened in 1871) and the Albert Memorial (unveiled in 1872).

But however marvellous Victoria and Albert's often stormy relationship had been, as an institution marriage was becoming less and less popular. By 1871 there were 3.4 million unmarried women over the age of twenty, an increase from 2.8 million in 1851 – a mixture of spinsters and widows. Whatever their circumstances, these were 'surplus women', considered a significant social problem in late-Victorian Britain, unless they lived lives of sainted purity.

Among this number we can count the single, celibate Florence Nightingale, who referred to herself as a nun, her only 'sons' the soldiers she cared for. Other less fortunate surplus women lived in special lodgings on small annuities, devoting themselves to good works because to work for money was socially unacceptable. Nightingale was scornful of these 'lady philanthropists who do the odds and ends of charity': 'It is a kind of conscience-quieter,' she wrote, 'a soothing syrup.'[43]

For middle-class women who chose not to marry, options were limited. They could become governesses, educating the children of their social superiors but kept at arm's length by the host families so that they felt no more valued or involved than servants. Writing was also acceptable, but to make a success of it you needed private means. Back in the early nineteenth century, the prolific social theorist Harriet Martineu had been able to make a living entirely by the pen. But she was considered a brazen oddity, which may be why the novelist Margaret Oliphant wrote that Martineu was 'less distinctively affected by her sex than perhaps any other, male or female, of her generation'.[44]

In journalism, women's inability to forge the necessary old-school-tie connections made the job doubly hard. As Charlotte O'Connor Eccles wrote in 1893, in an anonymous article for *Blackwood's Edinburgh Magazine*:

> One is horribly handicapped in being a woman. A man meets other men at his club; he can be out and about at all hours; he can insist without being thought bold and forward; he is not presumed to be capable of undertaking only a limited class of subjects, but is set to anything … Where a man finds one obstacle, we find a dozen.[45]

When women *were* employed at a senior level, it was often as a gimmick. In November 1903, the newspaper proprietor Alfred Harmsworth – later Lord Northcliffe – decided to launch a paper 'for gentlewomen by gentlewomen'. Called the *Daily Mirror*, it would, Harmsworth announced in its inaugural editorial, arrange its stories so that 'the transition from the shaping of a flounce to the forthcoming changes in imperial defence, from the arrangement of flowers on the dinner-table to the disposition of forces in the Far East, shall be made without mental paroxysm or dislocation of interest.'[46] So far, so enlightened: in fact, it sounds rather like the UK edition of *Marie Claire* in its 1990s pomp.

To edit the *Daily Mirror* Harmsworth chose Mary Howarth, who had previously edited the women's pages of his incredibly successful *Daily Mail*, launched in 1896 and a classic example of the so-called 'ha'penny press' which catered to the newly literate beneficiaries of the 1870 Education Act. All Howarth's staff were women, and for a short time it looked as if Harmsworth's gamble had paid off: the first issue sold a healthy 276,000 copies. Within weeks, however, circulation had plummeted to 25,000. Howarth and her team were sacked and the *Mirror* transformed into a picture-driven (and male-edited) paper which went on to be almost as successful as the *Mail*.

Harmsworth called the first incarnation of the *Daily Mirror* 'the only journalistic failure with which I have been associated': 'Some people say that a woman never really knows what she wants. It is certain she knew what she didn't want. She didn't want the *Daily Mirror*.'[47] Bafflingly, the conclusion Harmsworth drew from this catastrophe was not that he had misjudged women's interests and catered to them poorly, but that 'women can't write and don't want to read.'[48] Oh dear.

Female journalists were consistently sidelined and belittled – a hazard of the job familiar to some in Fleet Street today. Emilie Peacocke, born in 1882, was the daughter of the editor of the *Northern Echo*, but even having journalism in the blood was of little help when she became the first full-time woman reporter on the *Daily Express*: she still wasn't allowed to use the paper's staff room.

Rachel Beer's installation as editor of both the *Sunday Times* and the *Observer* in the 1890s owed more than a little to the fact that her family owned them: her husband Frederick Beer had inherited the *Observer* from his father. She was a socialite, the great-granddaughter of the Sassoon family patriarch Sheikh Sason ben Saleh, an Iraqi Jew born in Baghdad in 1750 – the poet Siegfried Sassoon was her nephew – and arguably the papers were her playthings. Beer worked from home, a telephone line connecting her west London villa to the *Sunday Times'* office in Fleet Street.

Beer wrote copiously and was surprisingly hands-on as an editor. She had a weakness for puffery – she once altered George Bernard Shaw's copy to insert some society gossip, to his noisy displeasure – and was denied the confidence even of politicians she counted as friends, such as Gladstone. But on the whole she used her powers thoughtfully and responsibly, supporting women's causes whenever she could, although she thought equal pay and respect in the workplace more pressing issues for women than the vote.

Under her editorship the *Observer* achieved one of its biggest scoops: the admission by Count Esterhazy that he forged letters that had resulted in the false conviction of the Jewish artillery officer Captain Alfred Dreyfus for feeding military secrets to the German Embassy in Paris. But Beer's final years were not happy ones. She had contracted syphilis from Frederick and, after he died from the disease in 1903, her grief escalated into a full-scale mental breakdown. She was declared insane by the controversial psychiatrist George Savage, who counted Virginia Woolf among his patients, and the papers were sold off.

Instead of being forced into an asylum, Rachel was installed in a mansion in Tunbridge Wells and looked after by three nurses. Her nephew Siegfried visited her and wrote, in a passage he later cut from the final version of his memoir *The Weald of Youth*, that Rachel was reduced to staring at him, 'apathetic and unrecognising … a brooding sallow stranger, cut off from the rest of the world.'[49] She died on 29 April 1927.

A similar fate befell another talented woman journalist of the period, Lady Colin Campbell, aka Gertrude Elizabeth Blood, the youngest daughter of Anglo-Irish landowners from County Clare, Ireland. She contracted an unspecified venereal disease – probably gonorrhea – from her philandering Liberal MP husband. After a humiliating show trial in 1886 that left her a pariah, Gertrude was not allowed to divorce him. The illness robbed her of her vitality and striking looks and led eventually to her death in 1911, by which time she was more famous for having once worn a live snake around her neck than for her books and witty contributions to the *Pall Mall Gazette*.

Gertrude Elizabeth Blood's treatment showed that the sexual double-standard was alive and well relatively late in the century. It showed how little things had changed; how far, despite everything, women still had to go in their quest for representation and equality. For like it or not, the public sphere was still overwhelmingly male. Women who wished to make inroads into it were obliged to emphasise their homely, caring virtues, as the campaigner Josephine Butler did explicitly in 1869 when she wrote:

> I believe that nothing whatever will avail but the large infusion of Home elements into workhouses, hospitals, schools, orphanages, lunatic asylums, reformatories, and even prisons, and in order to attain this there must be a setting free of feminine powers and influence from the constraint of a bad education, and narrow aims, and listless homes where they are at present a superfluity.[50]

Butler had grown up in a staunchly liberal, abolitionist family where women were treated as intellectual equals. Like Mary Higgs, she married a clergyman and became interested in philanthropy, befriending an unmarried mother who had been imprisoned in Newgate after committing infanticide and finding the woman work as a servant in the Butler family home in Oxford – an early example of her 'rescue work'.

As with Annie Besant, personal tragedy turbo-charged her reforming zeal. In 1864 her five-year-old daughter Eva died after falling forty feet while trying to slide down a bannister. She had been rushing to greet her parents as they returned from a holiday in the Lake District. Josephine, who witnessed the event, wrote later that 'for twenty-five years I never woke from sleep without the vision of her falling figure, and the sound of the crash on the stone floor.'[51]

The Butlers moved to Liverpool in 1866 to begin a new life. Josephine remained depressed, but knew the only solution was to 'go forth and find some pain keener than my own ... I only knew that my heart ached night and day and that the only solace possible would seem to be to find other hearts which ached night and day, and with more reason than mine.'[52]

At the suggestion of a local Baptist minister, she visited Liverpool's docks where homeless women would gather to collect oakum, the untwisted fibres of old rope used to caulk ships – 'hard and degrading work, thought fit only for paupers or convicts'.[53] To their baffled amusement, Butler joined the women in their work and slowly won their trust and friendship. Many of them, she realised, were also prostitutes. They had to be, if they were to have enough money to live.

As before, Butler opened up her house, this time to the prostitutes she felt were especially deserving. One in particular became like a surrogate daughter: twenty-four-year-old consumptive Mary Lomax, a former under-maid in a grand house who had been raped by her employer and left pregnant, then drifted onto the streets after she was dismissed from service and then rejected by her own family.

Nothing summed up the sexual double standard quite like the Contagious Diseases Act 1864, which gave the police the power to arrest prostitutes and subject them to brutal, degrading internal examinations for venereal disease, on the grounds that they – not the men who used and abused them – were to blame for spreading it. Through her Ladies' National Association, Butler mobilised opposition to the Act and finally achieved success in 1885 when it was abolished and the age of consent for women raised from twelve to sixteen.

What took her so long? Partly it was the inability of the political patriarchy to come to terms with any sort of female agenda. In 1896 Butler would remember a 'fully sympathetic' MP admitting to a female friend, "Your manifesto has shaken us very badly in the House of Commons … We know how to manage any other opposition in the House or in the country, but this is very awkward for us – this revolt of the women. It is quite a new thing; what are we to do with such an opposition as this?"[54]

It was a more uncertain opposition than the MP perhaps supposed. Some middle-class women struggled to cast off their shackles and adjust to their new public prominence. Conditioned to be servile and law-abiding, they showed perverse respect for the rules that kept women in second place: educational reformer Mary Carpenter, for example, refused to chair meetings as she thought it wasn't respectable. Women who stood up at meetings were routinely praised for their 'heroism' – or treated as circus freaks. Suffrage campaigner Lilias Ashworth went on a speaking tour of the West Country in 1872 and noticed that audiences 'came expecting to see curious masculine objects walking on the platform, and when we appeared, with our quiet black dresses, the whole expression of the faces of the audience would instantly change'.[55]

Many men were also uncomfortable seeing women as Poor Law guardians – a sort of early social work. The work was considered unsuitable because of the unsavoury things they would witness in workhouses and hospitals. The first female English Poor Law guardian, Martha Merrington, was elected in 1875.

The historian Steven King recently discovered the diary of a female Poor Law guardian from Bolton in Lancashire called Mary Haslam. This entry for 27 February 1894 gives some idea of the day-to-day routine:

> Visited the Lying-in Ward again having tried to find out particulars of two of the women; one had left and the other had proved untruthful. Visited feeble-minded room. Saw lunatics in bed. Talked with Nurse Henry. Our Committee suggested to the guardians the possibility of brightening the lunatics' surroundings by reversing a day and night room; we had some conversation as to whether occasional nurses could be provided.[56]

Many women took advantage of the 1894 Local Government Act, which granted them the right to stand for election to local councils. Henrietta 'Nettie' Adler, daughter of the Chief Rabbi, was a school board manager until 1910 when she became a Progressive councillor for Hackney Central. Susan Lawrence – tall, haughty and monocled, with a cut-glass accent to match – began her career in 1910 as a Conservative councillor for West Marylebone but underwent an improbable conversion to socialism in 1913, eventually becoming one of the first three female Labour MPs alongside Margaret Bondfield and Dorothy Jewson.

What unites many of the women of the era is a willingness to play the long game. The female-dominated Fabian Society, founded in 1884, wanted to effect change on a grand scale by proceeding slowly and carefully. (Hence 'Fabian', honouring the Roman general Fabius Maximus who favoured attrition as a strategy rather than direct conflict.) When we think of nineteenth-century sanitary reform we think of someone like Bazalgette and his sewers – large-scale infrastructure designed and built by men. But other big, though perhaps less ostentatious, projects in this field – like the provision of public baths and wash-houses, found in nearly every British town by the 1920s – were the work of women.

Derbyshire-born Hannah Mitchell, a seamstress who went on to become a leading suffrage activist and Labour councillor, was elected as a Poor Law guardian in the market town of Ashton-under-Lyne in May 1904. Years later she became a member of the Manchester Baths Committee and wrote with pride of the 'really up-to-date little wash house' she had helped to get built, where 'a family wash could be done in a couple of hours, and the home kept free of wet clothes and steam'.[57]

From the 1850s onwards, a pressing social concern had been the woeful state of housing for the poor. One of Fabian-stalwart Beatrice Webb's sisters worked as a rent collector for the housing scheme run by Octavia Hill – the woman Webb said taught her 'the meaning of the poverty of the poor'. Webb first met Hill in 1886 at the home of their mutual friend Henrietta Barnett, the co-founder of Hampstead Garden Suburb and Toynbee Hall, the 'settlement' centre for the poor in London's Tower Hamlets. 'She is a small woman, with large head finely set on her shoulders,' Webb wrote in her diary:

> The form of her head and features, and the expression of the eyes and mouth, show the attractiveness of mental power. We talked on Artisans' Dwellings. I asked her whether she thought it necessary to keep accurate descriptions of the tenants. No, she did not see the use of it … She objected that there was already too much windy talk. What you wanted was action … I felt penitent for my presumption, but not convinced.[58]

The regal hauteur is immediately evident. Still, more than any other woman of her era, Hill could see that grand schemes only worked if you combined clarity of ambition with an infinite supply of patience.

Octavia Hill was born in 1838 in Wisbech, Cambridgeshire. Her father, James Hill, was a corn merchant who had fathered six children and been widowed twice by the time he married Octavia's mother, Caroline Southwood Smith – the family governess, hired after James was impressed by her writings on education.

In 1840 James Hill's business collapsed and he fell into a depression. The family moved to London where Caroline found work as manager and bookkeeper of the Ladies' Cooperative Guild. As soon as she was old enough, Octavia worked alongside her as her assistant and at fourteen began supervising the local ragged school children as they manufactured toys. But she was no callous 'sweater'– on the contrary, she took the children on regular trips to wide open green spaces like Hampstead Heath and noticed how much they valued and enjoyed them.

This sowed the seeds of a scheme for improving the working classes' quality of life by improving their environment – principally their homes, which were cramped and run-down even when 'well kept'. She wasn't the only one to come up with the idea. A mass of so-called 'model dwelling' companies emerged in London in the middle of the nineteenth century. There were thirty or more operating by the 1870s, of which the oldest, the Metropolitan Association for Improving the Dwellings of the Industrious Classes, had been around since 1841. Their goal – and Hill's – was solidly paternalistic, and at least one of their aims was the maintenance of the status quo, by nipping discontent in the bud. As Lord Shaftesbury put it: 'If the working man has his own house, I have no fear of revolution.'[59]

In other respects, though, Hill was different. For one thing there was the unusual matter of her key investor. John Ruskin had taken an interest in her as a fifteen-year-old after seeing her sketches – she was a talented artist – and had offered his services as an art tutor. He invested money he had inherited from his father in Hill's Charity Organisation Society for a 5 per cent dividend.

On the whole, as we know, Ruskin preferred his women to stay home by the hearth. But exceptions were permitted: if they were carrying out 'public work or duty which is also the expansion of that [i.e. their domestic role]' then they had his blessing, as such work was consistent with what Sheila Rowbotham calls Ruskin's 'organic vision of society as an interconnected household'.[60]

In 1865, Hill bought her first properties, close to Marylebone High Street in central London, but a million miles from the area as we now know it. She described her purchase a little later as 'a row of cottages facing a bit of desolate ground, occupied with wretched, dilapidated cow-sheds, manure heaps, old timber, and rubbish of every description':

> The houses were in a most deplorable condition – the plaster was dropping from the walls; on one staircase a pail was placed to catch the rain that fell through the roof. All the staircases were perfectly dark; the banisters were gone, having been burnt as firewood by tenants. The grates, with large holes in them, were falling forward into the rooms.[61]

Most 'model dwelling' companies had rules and regulations designed to exclude tenants of 'bad character' and attract the respectable working classes. Octavia went one step further. She believed that if you enabled people to develop self-respect and self-reliance then they wouldn't need charity. Any form of philanthropy which cultivated dependency was pointless and un-Christian. Reading one of her letters from 1890, I'm reminded of some of the twenty-first-century political rows over welfare reform:

> We have made many mistakes with our alms: eaten out the heart of the independent, bolstered up the drunkard in his indulgence, subsidised wages, discouraged thrift, assumed that many of the most ordinary wants of a working man's family must be met by our wretched and intermittent doles.[62]

Hill's tenants were closely monitored by teams of lady volunteers who distributed forms in which they were expected to review their weekly conduct. Hill favoured cottages rather than the barrack-like blocks popular with other housing associations – 'little houses' where lower-class people could 'get the individual feeling and notice which trains them in humanity'; though by the end of the century she was experimenting with maisonette-like 'compound houses', 'two distinct cottages one on the top of the other':

> People become brutal in large numbers who are gentle when they are in smaller groups and know one another, and the life in a block only becomes possible when there is a deliberate isolation of the family, and a sense of duty with respect to all that is in common.[63]

Any profits from the scheme were spent on what Hill considered to be improvements – like playgrounds and gardens. By 1874 she ran fifteen housing schemes and had around three thousand tenants. Ten years later she began to manage properties for the Ecclesiastical Commissioners.

But housing wasn't Hill's only focus. She wanted her tenants to be immersed in culture, education and nature. So she campaigned for the opening up of closed-off public spaces and the preservation of areas such as Hampstead Heath. In 1876, she and her sister Miranda founded the Society for the Diffusion of Beauty, later rechristened the Kyrle Society. This mutated over time into a 'holding trust' in which the ownership of threatened land or buildings could be vested. Hill suggested it be called 'The Commons and Gardens Trust'. But a colleague thought it should have a snappier title. What about 'National Trust'? She agreed and the society was registered in 1895.

Hill accomplished a good deal, but it didn't come easily to her. A workaholic perfectionist who hated delegating, she had several breakdowns triggered by a combination of overwork and a turbulent emotional life. But while she gave the world a blueprint for philanthropic property management, she worked on a small scale, smaller than her reputation perhaps suggests, and the housing crisis of the early twentieth century needed more far-reaching reform than she was able to provide.

Her influence on the debate about housing policy remains palpable. The historian and former MP Tristram Hunt writes that, as ministers 'grapple with re-engineering the welfare state, it is not Keynes, Marx or Giddens who provide the inspiration, but Hill, the most versatile of late Victorian social entrepreneurs.'[64]

Hill died of cancer in 1912, the year a woman cut from similar cloth, Maud Pember Reeves, published *Round About a Pound a Week*, compiled from tracts she had produced for the Fabian Society, distilling four years' worth of research into working-class housing. Reeves had established the Fabian Women's Group, working alongside Beatrice Webb, who was involved in the Royal Commission considering Poor Law reform. Through this she became interested in studying the lives of working-class families in Lambeth, focusing particularly on the women who held those families together.

Despite living in well-to-do Kensington and being the wife of the New Zealand government's Agent General, Reeves lacked Hill's air of genteel condescension and compulsion to moralise. But her indignation was just as fierce. As she watched children playing on the streets, she was infuriated by the way the poorer ones had had their futures stolen from them. You can tell them apart, she wrote, by the way they are 'comfortably dirty' and have 'the look of being small for their age': 'Had they been well housed, well fed, well clothed, and well tended, from birth, what kind of raw material would they have shown themselves to be?'[65]

What's astonishing about *Round About a Pound a Week* is how many of its suggested solutions came to pass: free school dinners, free health clinics, child benefit. Not since Rowntree's *Poverty* in 1901 had a book punched through so effectively, showing the middle classes and policy makers how the other half lived. It came at a time of general panic about the physical state of British men after the Boer War – concerns that would be raised again in 1914. Many were weakened by rickets and other diseases caused by poor nutrition.

Reeves and her helpers – including the anarchist Charlotte Wilson, who ran a Marxist debating society out of the Hampstead farmhouse she shared with her stockbroker husband – visited families trying to survive on a pound a week. She asked them to keep note of their outgoings and diaries detailing daily problems such as the struggle to heat their houses and keep vermin from disturbing children while they slept. Reeves was shocked by the way the families spent money they couldn't afford on burial insurance to avoid the embarrassment of a pauper's funeral for their children, few of whom lived to adulthood. The middle-class theory that the poor were 'bad managers' who squandered their money on drink was mostly not true. On the contrary, they did their best, living on bread with a scraping of dripping and sometimes potatoes. Once weaned, none of the children ever tasted milk again.

It is shocking that the families featured were by no means the worst off. A pound a week was a low wage, but not disastrously so.

Keeping body and soul together was only half the battle. There was also the life of the mind to consider.

Thanks to the 1870 Education Act, 92 per cent of the population of England and Wales were literate by 1910. But women were still not thought worth properly educating. The assumption was that they would – and would want to – stay at home raising children rather than go out to work.

Helena Swanwick, an early feminist and suffrage campaigner, wrote of her childhood in the 1880s that she 'could not help contrasting my condition with that of my three elder brothers, all at school and able to walk about freely in the daytime, while I was not allowed out alone and had to be content with some very poor piano lessons and a few desultory German lessons with two other girls who were quite beginners.'[66]

Slowly, this changed. The Girls' Public Day School Trust was founded in 1850, inspired by North London Collegiate, the first independent school for girls. This had been opened the previous year by Frances Mary Buss with the goal of enabling girls to study subjects usually thought of as 'male', such as science and mathematics.

Buss and her friend and associate Dorothea Beale, redoubtable members of the so-called Langham Place feminists, were the target of classic Victorian everyday sexism: 'Miss Buss and Miss Beale/Cupid's darts do not feel./How different from us,/Miss

Beale and Miss Buss', went one rhyme. Undeterred, they pressed on, and as schools opened, so did women's colleges like Girton, founded in Hitchin in 1869 but relocated to Cambridge in 1873. By 1879 Oxford also had three women's colleges: Lady Margaret Hall, Somerville and St Anne's.

Helena Swanwick was in raptures remembering her time at Girton: 'I had a study as well as a bedroom to myself ... my own fire, my own desk, my own easy-chair and reading lamp ... even my own kettle – I was speechless with delight ... To have a study of my own and to be told that if I chose to put "Engaged" on the door, no one would so much as knock was itself so great a privilege as to render me from sleep.'[67]

But Girton was expensive, costing £35 per term for board and tuition, and, even once they'd been accepted, women were at a disadvantage. Philippa Fawcett, daughter of the suffragist campaigner Millicent Garrett Fawcett (of whom more later), attended Newnham College in 1890 and came top in the Cambridge Maths Tripos exams. But she couldn't be named 'senior wrangler', the term for the university's top maths undergraduate, because women were not listed and would in any case not become full university members until 1948. Only then did they receive proper degrees rather than patronising 'certificates of achievement'.

Still, Fawcett had an easier time of it than her aunt Elizabeth Garrett Anderson, whose vocation to train as a doctor proved farcically hard to fulfil. Medical schools were rather conservative, and distinctly queasy about women attending classes in anatomy and physiology, as if the sight of a dead man's penis might be too much for the poor delicate creatures.

Elizabeth's father Newson Garrett, a successful but uneducated businessman, intended great things for his daughters – all that he had not had himself. After failing to get on with their governess, Elizabeth and her sister Louisa were packed off to the Academy for the Daughters of Gentlemen in Blackheath, where they were known as the 'bathing Garretts' because their father had instructed that they be given a hot bath once a week – an eccentric request in 1849. Elizabeth in particular hated its finishing-school atmosphere and the fact that she was not taught maths or science there.

At twenty-one, after a grand tour of the continent, Elizabeth found herself back at the family home in Aldeburgh, tutoring her numerous siblings; comfortable, but frustrated and intellectually restless. She became interested in the burgeoning women's movement and read about Elizabeth Blackwell, the first American (though British-born) female physician, in the *Englishwoman's Journal*. Anderson heard that Blackwell was visiting Britain and contacted Emily Davies, the educational reformer who co-founded Girton College, to arrange a meeting, after which she was more certain than ever that she wanted to train to be a doctor. With Davies' and Blackwell's encouragement, Anderson set about filling in the gaps in her education and talking her father round. Newson Garrett initially thought the idea 'disgusting' but changed his mind, writing to her:

> I have resolved in my own mind after deep and painful
> consideration not to oppose your wishes and as far as expense is
> concerned I will do all I can in justice to my other children to
> assist you in your study.

So Anderson enrolled as a nursing student at Middlesex Hospital, where she won round doubters with her competence, learned what she could from those doctors who were prepared to teach her and sneakily attended classes intended for male students only. To earn a medical degree, however, Anderson had to find a university that would allow her to matriculate. She applied to numerous English and Scottish medical schools, only to be refused entry on bizarre gender grounds. Her rejection letter from Aberdeen is priceless:

I must decline to give you instruction in Anatomy ... I have a strong conviction that the entrance of ladies into dissecting rooms and anatomical theatres is undesirable in every respect, and highly unbecoming. It is not necessary that fair ladies should be brought into contact with such foul scenes – nor would it be for their good, any more than for that of their patients.[68]

Frustrated, she spotted a loophole at the Society of Apothecaries, which didn't specifically forbid women sitting their exams. As it happened, the Society changed its rules to exclude women shortly afterwards, but the licence Anderson acquired allowed her to apply to a medical school in Paris where women *were* accepted. She obtained her degree in 1870, teaching herself French in order to do so, and returned to England to take up the post of chief medical officer at a children's hospital.

The following year, Elizabeth married James G. Skelton Anderson, the managing director of the Orient Steamship Company, in an unconventional ceremony in which she refused to say that she would 'obey' him. With his financial help she founded the New Hospital for Women in London, which had an all-female staff, and she worked there between 1886 and 1892, remaining the dean until 1902.

Several other Victorian female doctors went on to found hospitals after jumping through numerous hoops to qualify. Sophia Jex-Blake was one. A rival of Garrett Anderson's, she founded both a hospital and a school of medicine for women in Edinburgh. But she did so in the face of quite extraordinary discrimination.

Born in Hastings, Sophia had been working without pay at Queen's College, London as a maths tutor because her father, a proctor at a lawyers' society, wouldn't allow her to accept a salary. Deciding to train as a doctor, she went first to America, where she studied briefly with Elizabeth Blackwell in New York, before returning to England when her father died in 1869. But finding a British medical school to take her was harder than she expected. The University of London, 'of whose liberality one heard so much', rejected her, explaining that 'the charter had been purposely so worded as to exclude the possibility of examining women for medical degrees.' With the help of influential friends, she lobbied to be accepted by Edinburgh, which agreed to teach her only after she had personally advertised for more women entrants to make up numbers.

Sophia and four other women started their Edinburgh course in October 1869. Several curmudgeonly tutors refused to teach them, but they quickly proved themselves as capable as their male counterparts. One of them even won a prestigious Hope Scholarship, awarded to the top four students in the year, although Sophia later complained that it had been 'wrested from the successful candidate and given over her head to the fifth student on the list, who happened to be a man'.

The bullying Sophia and her colleagues endured in Edinburgh has passed into feminist legend. In her autobiography Sophia described how, after a meeting with the Royal Infirmary's management team, 'a certain proportion of the students with whom we worked became markedly offensive and insolent, and took every opportunity of practising the petty annoyances that occur to thoroughly ill-bred lads – such as shutting doors in our faces, ostentatiously crowding into seats we usually occupied, bursting into horse-laughs and howls when we approached – as if a conspiracy had been formed to make our position as uncomfortable as it might be'.[69]

Sophia's fellow Edinburgh medic Edith Pechey described the treatment she endured in a letter to the *Scotsman*:

If we happen to meet students on our way home in the evening … [they] find pleasure in following a woman through the streets, and take advantage of her being alone to shout after her

all the foulest epithets in their voluminous vocabulary of abuse
… I should be very sorry to see any poor girl under the care (!)
of such men as those, for instance, who the other night
followed me through the street, using medical terms to make
the disgusting import of their language more intelligible to
me.[70]

The more successful the women became in their studies, the more
the violence against them escalated. Mud was thrown at them and
fireworks attached to the doors of their lodgings. On 18 November
1870 the women arrived to sit an anatomy exam at Surgeon's Hall,
only to find a drunken mob blocking their entry and a live sheep
wandering around the room. The none-too-subtle message was
that a woman was as unwelcome there as a farmyard animal. 'The
unruffled lecturer advised his class to take no notice of the animal,
saying that it had more sense than those who sent it in.'

To add insult to injury, on 8 January 1872 Edinburgh's
University Court decided the university would not, after all, be
awarding the women a degree. But it was okay – they were still
free to study there, '*if we would altogether give up the question of
graduation*, and be content with certificates of proficiency'
(Sophia's italics). The students tried to sue Edinburgh University
for breach of implied contract. When this failed, they pursued the
matter through Parliament and after three years of squabbling,
during which Sophia founded the London School of Medicine
for Women, achieved victory in the form of the Russell Gurney
Enabling Act (1876), which obliged medical bodies to allow
women to sit exams – except in surgery – and gave women the
same rights as men to enter the profession.

Sophia Jex-Blake eventually sat her medical exams in 1877 at
the Irish College of Physicians in Dublin. She set up her own
practice in Edinburgh the following year and by the end of 1878
had treated 574 patients. From then on, women's progress through
the profession was unstoppable. In January 1882, 26 women in

England were registered as having medical qualifications, rising to 477 by 1911. How absurd that it had been such a struggle.

In a sense, these clever, educated women couldn't win. So-called New Women – with their bicycles, cheque books and eccentric desire to vote and hold down demanding jobs – were either shockingly erotic, in possession of a sex drive which was hard to control, or satirised as bluestockings: walking *Punch* cartoons, with their gaiters, loosely fitting skirts and, possibly, bloomers. They were in the curious position of knowing too much to be interesting to men, a position most of them enjoyed.

Elizabeth Blackwell had broken the news as early as 1881 that women had sex drives:

> The radical physiological error, which underlies ordinary thought and action in relation to the evils of sex, is the very grave error that men are much more powerfully swayed by this instinct of sex than are women. From this radical error are drawn the false deductions that men are less able to resist that instinct; that they are more injured by abstinence from its satisfaction; and that they require a licence in action which forbids the laying down of the same moral law for men and women.[71]

This was incendiary stuff. One of the scandals of Gertrude Blood's divorce trial in 1886 was her husband Lord Colin Campbell's allegation that she had had four adulterous relationships, one of them with the Duke of Marlborough. Of course, only men were allowed in the public gallery to hear the details as the evidence was considered not fit for female ears. Lord Colin Campbell's solicitor denounced her to the jury as 'grossly sensuous, guilty of yielding to the gratification of her passions, guilty of indecency of the grossest character as to time, place and circumstances'.[72]

Sexually liberated women were rather more sympathetically drawn in the popular novels of the day. One of the most widely read was *Anna Lombard* (1901) by 'Victoria Cross' – a *nom de plume* used by Annie Sophie Cory, the Indian-born daughter of a British army colonel.

It was the *Fifty Shades of Grey* of its day, selling an estimated six million copies, running through more than thirty editions and remaining in print until 1930, after which it mysteriously vanished from the nation's book shops and shelves. On publication it was denounced by critics as 'disgusting' (*Athenaeum*) and 'thoroughly impure' (*Academy*) because its eponymous New Woman heroine, while engaged to be married to an assistant commissioner in the Indian Civil Service called Gerald Ethridge, sleeps with and then marries her servant Gaida.

Gerald finds himself in a quandary. Should he abandon Anna or persist with the engagement in the hope that she will come to her senses and overcome the physical obsession for which, Gerald concedes with extraordinary post-feminist empathy, she is 'no more to be held responsible than she would have been for any physical malady'?

Adultery, interracial sex, infanticide ... Cory took every Victorian taboo she could think of and moulded a bestselling novel out of them, complete with prose which cleverly (or not so cleverly, depending on your viewpoint) displaces onto the natural world the sex it would have been illegal for her to describe: 'The purple sky above was throbbing, beating, palpitating ... What a night for the registration or the consummation of vows!'[73]

Just as intriguing was Cory's switching of gender roles – so that it is Anna who is the sexual adventurer and Gerald who nurtures and abstains. One contemporary reviewer who appreciated this was the journalist W. T. Stead, friend of Annie Besant, who wrote: 'Never before in English fiction can I remember so clearly cut a representation of an embodiment in a woman of what, alas!, is common enough in a man.'[74]

The cultural reign of the New Woman was long – from the early 1890s to 1911, though establishment newspapers tired of her early: 'Shall we never have done with the New Woman?' asked *The Times*, reviewing Ella Hepworth Dixon's only novel *The Story of a Modern Woman* in 1894. No one embodied her freewheeling sexual confidence like Amber Reeves – Maud Pember Reeves' daughter and the model for Ann Veronica Stanley in H. G. Wells' 1909 novel *Ann Veronica* – 'a girl of brilliant and precocious promise … [with] a sharp, bright, Levantine face under a shock of very fine abundant black hair, a slender nimble body very much alive, and a quick greedy mind'.[75] Educated at Newnham College, Cambridge, where she helped to found the Cambridge Fabian Society, Reeves read Moral Sciences and gained a double first in 1908.

Her affair with Wells was one of the great scandals of the day. When it was discovered, Wells was ostracised by many friends and obliged to resign from the Savile Club. But even though the relationship produced a child – a marriage of convenience to a lawyer called Rivers Blanco White followed hastily – there was never any suggestion that she was a victim. On the contrary, in the reckless, emancipated spirit of Anna Lombard, she had wanted sex with Wells as much as he had wanted it with her.

On 22 January 1901, Victoria died at the age of eighty-one. She had ruled over a fifth of the land area of the world, a population of four hundred million people. But imperial confidence was starting to crumble. The empire was expensive to maintain and, besides, other countries were catching up with Britain's technological invention, expansionist ambition and naval power.

As we saw earlier, Victoria had railed against the 'mad wicked folly' of women's rights. The next twenty years would show her to have been on the wrong side of history. But many women, particularly aristocratic ones, agreed with her. In 1889 a petition in the *Nineteenth Century* magazine signed by over a hundred mostly upper-class women rejected calls for equality because of 'disabilities of sex' (menstruation) and 'strong formations of custom and habit resting ultimately on physical difference, against which it is useless to contend'.[76]

Funnily enough, the first woman to vote did so accidentally. Lily Maxwell owned a crockery shop in Manchester and so met the property qualification that would have allowed her to vote had she been a man. Her name had been added to the electoral register in error. Encouraged by Lydia Becker, she voted in a by-election in 1867 (for her local Liberal MP, Jacob Bright), although her vote was subsequently declared illegal. 'We are told that Mrs Lily Maxwell is an intelligent person of respectable appearance,' the feminist *Englishwoman's Review* reassured its readers. 'It is sometimes said that women, especially those of the working class, have no political opinion at all, and would not care to vote. Yet this woman, who by chance was furnished with a vote, professed strong political opinions, and was delighted to have a chance of expressing them.'[77]

From the 1860s onwards there was constant fracturing and realignment of pro-suffrage groups; constant disputes over tactics and even goals. In 1897 another Women's Suffrage Bill passed its second reading with a seventy-one-vote majority, only to collapse when the government refused to allocate further time to it. Some saw this as evidence of progress, others as the exact opposite.

The most obvious split was between the 'suffragists' – whose most famous figurehead was Millicent Garrett Fawcett – and the 'suffragettes' – led by the Pankhursts. The suffragists, represented by the National Union of Women's Suffrage Societies (NUWSS), were committed to winning the vote by constitutional, non-violent means. Suffragettes, on the other hand, felt a defiant, militant path was the only appropriate one. They rallied to a different banner – that of the Women's Social and Political Union (WSPU), formed by Emmeline Pankhurst.

The Pankhursts occupy a curious place in our culture. They're synonymous with the fight for suffrage to the point where most people aren't aware that anyone else was involved. Like Florence Nightingale and the Brontës, they are better known as a heritage brand than as actual people. Remarkable though their idealism and crusading zeal undoubtedly was, Emmeline Pankhurst and her daughters could be, in their biographer Martin Pugh's words, 'ruthless, high-handed and self-righteous'; characters who on close inspection 'come as a shock'.

The Pankhursts' fame has overshadowed the contribution of Millicent Garrett Fawcett, who, in a quieter way, played a more effective role in acquiring the vote for women. She also found time to co-found Newnham College, Cambridge and, in 1901, travel to South Africa to investigate conditions in the concentration camps the British had set up there after the Boer War.

Pankhurst mania has also obscured fascinating figures like Sophia Duleep Singh, daughter of the last Maharaja of the Sikh Empire, Maharaja Duleep Singh. (He married a chambermaid, Ada Wetherill, after Sophia's mother died of typhoid, caught from ten-year-old Sophia who miraculously recovered.) Sophia was another of Queen Victoria's goddaughters, but turned against the Empire after visiting India in 1907. Once back in England, she campaigned for both the Women's Social and Political Union and Dora Montefiore's Women's Tax Resistance League (WTRL) – motto, 'No vote, no tax'. And despite her aristocratic credentials she was happy to stand on street corners selling *The Suffragette* newspaper.

So how did the Pankhursts come to own the suffrage story? The answer lies, rather prosaically, in the political scene of the 1880s and 1890s.

Gladstone's Third Parliamentary Reform Act of 1885 had massively expanded working-class suffrage for men, giving male agricultural labourers the vote but not women. As it happened, 1885 was also the year that a Manchester-based barrister and campaigner called Dr Richard Pankhurst stood for Parliament in Rotherhithe as a Liberal candidate, having tried his luck in

Manchester a couple of years before. This time he won 45.7 per cent of the vote. Close, but no cigar. Still, his campaign experience was, his wife Emmeline reflected, 'a valuable political lesson, one that years later I was destined to put into practice'.

Emmeline Goulden had been born in 1858 into a radical liberal Mancunian family. When Emmeline was still a child, the barrister and would-be politician Richard Pankhurst, already a key figure in the women's suffrage campaign, was something of a hero. In 1870 he had drafted the first Women's Suffrage Bill, a Private Members' Bill which had passed its first and second readings in the House of Commons before being thrown out by Gladstone.

After a spell studying in Paris, during which she nearly married a French man, Emmeline returned to Manchester. On 31 April 1878 her father took her to an anti-Disraeli rally at Manchester's Free Trade Hall, where she was charmed by the passion and erudition of Dr Pankhurst, who had a high-pitched voice, a red, pointy beard and a 'tendency to go over the top in his determination to set the world to rights' – a determination which would ultimately cost him a successful career.[78]

Richard and Emmeline married – he was forty-four, she twenty – and between 1880 and 1889 produced five children. Christabel was the eldest, followed by Sylvia, Frank, Adela and Harry. (Frank died aged four of diptheria.) In line with Richard's marital declaration to Emmeline that 'every struggling cause shall be ours', the children were brought up to be agents of 'social betterment' – drilled into moral shape by their ambitious, disciplinarian parents, who treated them as little adults.

The Pankhursts flitted between a new house in London's Russell Square and Manchester, Emmeline throwing herself into the role of political hostess while the children jostled for her attention which, when it was given at all, was usually lavished on confident, beautiful Christabel. Sylvia and Adela particularly suffered from this genteel neglect. Sylvia had poor eyesight, but since Emmeline disapproved of glasses she was never allowed a pair and so endured migraines for years.

In this charged environment, dysfunctionality reigned: the squabbles and more serious relationship breakdowns that blighted the Pankhursts' adult lives were, says Pugh, 'clearly foreshadowed in childhood'.[79] During this time Emmeline was always exquisitely dressed in the latest Paris fashions, and despised women who looked shabby. She would always take 'enormous trouble over her appearance in public', as if to reassure doubters that suffrage-seeking women were not the mannish caricatures of satirical cartoons. Sylvia, by contrast, was a notoriously shabby dresser – 'a proper scruff', in the words of one former trade union leader.[80]

Emmeline's involvement with the women's suffrage movement was, to begin with, politely constitutional, conforming to the widely held view that only single, unmarried women should get the vote. This was partly tactical, as it was thought that pressing for full female suffrage when 40 per cent of *men* still couldn't vote was pointless and unrealistic. Emmeline's subsequent change of tack had two catalysts. One was her election as a Poor Law guardian in Chorlton in 1894, which saw her campaign successfully for workhouse inmates to have private lockers for their possessions, warmer clothing and better food. The other was the death in 1898 of Richard – aged sixty-four – from a perforated ulcer.

Christabel, meanwhile, had been drifting aimlessly, and in 1901 wrote to her mother: 'Have you any ideas about me yet?' She befriended two powerful, highly politicised women, Eva Gore-Booth and Esther Roper, both members of the North of England Society for Women's Suffrage. They have sometimes been portrayed as a lesbian couple who drew Christabel into their relationship. The Pankhursts' biographer Martin Pugh thinks this unlikely, but they had a warming, softening influence on Christabel. At Gore-Booth and Roper's suggestion, she decided to study law. It would prove the perfect training for her quick, lively mind.

Emmeline seems to have been infuriated by Christabel's political awakening. In 1903, perhaps jealous of Christabel for picking up the suffrage baton, she founded the Women's Social and Political Union (WSPU), an extension of an earlier suffrage society she'd founded in 1889, the Women's Franchise League. The WSPU motto, 'deeds, not words', underwrote their manifesto of what Ray Strachey calls 'moral violence', which was born of impatience with Fawcett's slow attempt to obtain reform by constitutional means.

Emmeline sought a close relationship with the Independent Labour Party (ILP), but the ILP was ambivalent about female suffrage, fearing that if property-owning women got the vote as the WSPU demanded, they'd be more likely to vote Tory or Liberal. They also feared that allowing women to work would be bad for wages.

In 1905 the ILP leader Keir Hardie, to whom Sylvia had grown close, tried to introduce a bill proposing suffrage for female householders. His failure bolstered the Pankhursts' confidence and they vowed to turn the WSPU into an 'army in the field', recruiting key personnel such as Hannah Mitchell, Flora Drummond – a stout Scot nicknamed Precocious Piglet who liked dressing in military uniform – and Annie Kenney. Annie had met Christabel in Oldham in spring 1906 and pledged allegiance on the spot. The fifth child in a family of eleven, she had left school at thirteen and was needy and damaged – a naive dreamer looking for a good, brave cause. Sylvia Pankhurst would later write that 'her lack of perspective, her very intellectual limitations, lent her a certain directness of purpose when she became the instrument of a more powerful mind'.[81]

That powerful mind belonged to Christabel. For her, militancy was important because of the message it sent that women were capable of such behaviour. On 13 October 1905 she was arrested and imprisoned for deliberately spitting at a policeman outside Manchester's Free Trade Hall, an event which turned the suffragettes, as the *Daily Mail* called them, into martyr-heroes.

After the Liberals won the 1906 election, Christabel severed her links with the ILP, and the WSPU moved to London, its goal to attract fashionable, bourgeois women and acquire both a funding stream and (with Keir Hardie's help) a treasurer. A newspaper, *Votes for Women*, was launched and was selling 22,000 copies by May 1909. A car was bought for Emmeline and a chauffeur hired – former actress Vera Holme, who wore masculine attire and was always called Jack.

Artistic Sylvia, once a prize-winning student at Manchester School of Art and the Royal College of Art in London, oversaw the WSPU's visual branding – the flags, banners and a broad range of 'official' memorabilia – while Emmeline Pethick-Lawrence, a wealthy philanthropist who was co-editor of *Votes for Women*, came up with the iconic colour scheme: purple (for dignity), white (for purity) and green (for hope). Members were encouraged to wear the colours 'as a duty and a privilege'. Suffragette 'uniforms' were stocked by leading department stores like Selfridges and Liberty.

The WSPU fractured repeatedly over the next few years as new offshoots formed, such as the Women's Freedom League. On 21 June 1908, a staggering 250,000 people attended a WSPU rally in Hyde Park, only for Asquith to dismiss its significance. Christabel was roused to violence once more and the suffragettes stormed Parliament Square in October 1908, after which Emmeline, Christabel and Flora Drummond were put on trial charged with incitement to rush the House of Commons. Lawyer Christabel scored another PR victory when she called Lloyd George and Gladstone in evidence and ran rings round them, controlling the courtroom 'like a little singing bird' (as the caricaturist Max Beerbohm put it). Jailed again, Christabel became a huge celebrity, and Madame Tussaud's even commissioned her waxwork. But prison ground her down and the Liberal government, more distracted than ever by the effort of forcing through its radical programme under Lloyd George, continued to ignore female suffrage as an issue.

In the years leading up to the First World War, the WSPU continued to pursue its policy of seeking out violent conflict for propaganda purposes. When the suffragettes marched on Parliament again on 29 June 1909, Emmeline struck a policeman so that she would be arrested and tried for sedition. This ushered in a period of arson, chemical attacks and hunger strikes. The first imprisoned woman to refuse food was Marion Wallace Dunlop, who in July 1909 had been sentenced to a month in Holloway for vandalism. When she was denied political prisoner status, she refused food for ninety-one hours. Afraid that she would die and become a martyr, Gladstone released her early on medical grounds. This established a pattern other suffragettes would mimic – imprisonment followed by swift release. The government tried to break the pattern, first through barbaric methods of force-feeding (from September 1909), then later in April 1913 through the Prisoners (Temporary Discharge for Ill Health) Act, known as the Cat and Mouse Act. This enabled a hunger-striking prisoner to be released from prison when her health started to fail, then re-imprisoned when she had recovered so that her sentence could be served in full.

After 1910, Fawcett's NUWSS became the main players as support for militancy crumbled. The WSPU had announced a cessation of hostilities in January 1910, but it didn't last long. The eighteenth of November 1910 became known as Black Friday when Asquith's quashing of the Conciliation Bill, which would have extended the vote to property-owning women, caused wide-spread protests. Around two hundred women were assaulted by police and the event gave rise to one of the suffrage campaign's most famous photographic images: demonstrator Ada Wright lying on the ground, her hands covering her face while two men stoop over her.

By the end of 1911 there was *still* no real progress, despite Lloyd George being sympathetic to the cause. Asquith continued to voice his opinion that granting the vote to women would be a 'political mistake of a very disastrous kind'. He simply didn't understand why women would want to vote. After all, neither his wife nor his daughter did. He believed militancy – which he experienced personally when militants tried to tear off his clothes on the golf links at Lossiemouth in Scotland – was off-putting to the public and would kill popular support for the cause.

After the 1912 Reform Bill failed to give women the vote, Fawcett allied herself with the Labour Party, who agreed to vote against any future franchise bill that did not include women. The Pankhursts' response was to go into furious overdrive – more window-smashing, more imprisonment, more force-feeding. Tiring of the melée, Christabel bailed out and moved to Paris, leaving Annie Kenney in charge. 'Where is Christabel?' asked the headlines. In fact, she had booked herself into a hotel under the name 'Amy Richards' and for a while continued to exert control remotely, for example issuing the order for the MP Lewis Harcourt's house to be burned down. In practice, though, this was the beginning of her detachment from British politics. With Christabel out of the picture, Sylvia Pankhurst set up her own socialist-inclined suffrage campaign in the East End.

In January 1913 it looked as if women might win the vote at last, as the Franchise Bill was debated. But at the last minute the Speaker – Sir James Lowther, himself opposed to female suffrage – declared that any adoption of an amendment would so alter the bill that it would no longer be the same measure, so it would have to be cancelled and reintroduced in new form. The suffragettes took their anger out on Lloyd George, sending him sulphuric acid in the post and trying to burn down his country house.

The most notorious event in suffragette history was to follow: Emily Davison was trampled by the King's horse at the Derby on 4 June 1913 and died four days later. The thinking now is that she was trying to attach a scarf to its bridle, not throw herself under it. Then again, as a devoutly Christian radical, she had on previous occasions been willing to damage her body for the cause. Over the course of seven hunger strikes, she was force-fed forty-nine times. At one stage her cell was deliberately flooded with ice-cold water.

On YouTube you can watch flickering footage of her funeral procession: a solemn, stately affair, though judging by the number of caps and straw boaters – removed out of respect as the cortège goes past – the crowds lining the streets contained far more men than we might expect.

But of course, many men supported female suffrage, not just as theorists (John Stuart Mill) and proud domestic cheerleaders (Millicent Garrett Fawcett's blind husband, Henry) but as activists too. Frederick Pethick-Lawrence was imprisoned and force-fed alongside his wife, Emmeline, while George Lansbury MP, having resigned his seat to fight a by-election on the female suffrage issue, also found himself in a cell for defending the suffragettes' arson campaign in a speech at a WSPU rally.

It's somehow fitting that the best photos of the suffragettes were taken by a resourceful, enterprising woman. Christina Broom was a self-taught photographer who emerged as one of the key image-makers of the early twentieth century and is now celebrated as the first female press photographer. With her daughter Winnie helping, she would carry her heavy glass-plate camera onto the streets and photograph what she found – straightforward views of Tower Bridge or Oxford Street; royal events and sporting tournaments; Lyons tea boys brewing up at Victoria Station; the 1905 Earl's Court Exhibition, with its makeshift Red Indian village – turning the resulting images into postcards which she, her disabled husband and Winnie printed up at home in Fulham and sold in their thousands. She also submitted her photographs to agencies for publication in newspapers and magazines.

Broom's photos of the WSPU on parade take you beyond the Pankhurst family psychodrama, beyond the arid accounts of who did what to whom, and show you these extraordinary figures as they flit across the drab Edwardian landscape like exotic birds. Some of her finest 'suffragette' photos were taken on 23 July 1910 at a Hyde Park rally to celebrate the Conciliation Bill being debated, where over 150 campaigners were due to give speeches. Walking at the head of the 'Prisoners' Pageant' are three formerly imprisoned suffragettes: Emmeline Pethick-Lawrence, Sylvia Pankhurst and, wearing her academic robes and looking stern, Emily Davison.

Christina stopped photographing the women's suffrage movement in the summer of 1913. The following year, her health failing and increasingly confined to a wheelchair, she found a new subject: the military, especially soldiers before they left London for the Western Front.

Her photos of young men relaxing and on parade at their barracks are exceptionally moving – we know, as they do not, what fate has in store for them. But other more random pictures tell another parallel story. Among her First World War photos is a portrait taken in May 1916 that shows the direction of travel for women – a group of women police officers at a Women's War Work exhibition in Knightsbridge. In their long black skirts, barely mustering a smile, they look austere and forbidding. At the centre, holding her gloves, staring down the camera as if she is about to arrest it, is a former suffragette called Mary Allen, now a police inspector ...

An ambiguous, disturbing figure, Allen is the shape of things to come; a tidy emblem of the confusion many felt and would continue to feel as the twentieth century unwound; an example of what happens when a damaged personality grows convinced that the only meaningful solutions are extreme ones. But that is all in the future. For now, let us read the image as a celebration of female strength, solidarity and progress – a glorious summation of over thirty years of vigorous campaigning.

3

Of Soldiers and Suffrage

1914–18

The First World War might have been a 'total war' – a conflict in which opposing sides are ready to sacrifice anything and everyone to achieve victory – but in Britain this didn't extend to women being allowed to fight.

Not that this stopped them from trying.

In 1915, eighteen-year-old Dorothy Lawrence fulfilled her ambition to see action on the Western Front by selecting the only option open to her – pretending to be a man. Frustrated by the refusal of any Fleet Street editors to employ her as a war correspondent, Lawrence travelled to Paris where two English soldiers she met in a café helped her by smuggling out items of uniform with their washing.

'I'll see what an ordinary English girl, without credentials or money can accomplish,' she wrote several years later in a memoir, *Sapper Dorothy Lawrence*.[1] After darkening her skin with furniture polish, bulking out her shoulders with sacking and – a surreal touch, this – making tiny slashes in her cheeks with a razor to create the illusion of a shaving rash, Lawrence headed for the front with faked papers identifying her as Denis Smith, 1st Battalion Leicestershire Regiment.

The plan worked well, at first. Lawrence took a train to Amiens, then cycled to the small town of Albert, the Allies' centre of operations. There she befriended a soldier, a former coalminer called Tom Dunn, who risked court martial by smuggling her into the trenches.

'Now I see thoroughly the sort of girl yer are, I'll help yer,' Lawrence has Dunn say in her book. 'Yer no bad 'un. You're a lady.'[2] Lawrence would claim to have worked alongside Dunn laying mines in no-man's-land some four hundred yards from the German trenches, though the extent of her involvement has been disputed – it was, after all, highly skilled work for which she had not been trained. More probably she just kept a low profile during the day and, when night fell, slipped discreetly away to the derelict cottage in nearby Senlis Forest which Dunn had identified as a safe house, there to feast on the remnants of his rations and get a few hours' kip on a straw-bale bed.

Before long, however, problems arose. The tight swaddling around her chest grew painful – Lawrence had a 'robust figure' – and the stress of maintaining the subterfuge combined with the horrible conditions triggered a host of anxiety-related ailments. After just ten days she decided to give up, reasoning that it was better to be honest than to be discovered by accident.

When she made her announcement to the Sergeant in charge, his first reaction was to smile and pat her on the back. Lawrence was relieved: such heartiness surely meant he was going to allow her to stay at the front? In fact, he called the military police immediately and within minutes Lawrence was hauled out of her trench, screaming and shouting at her betrayer, 'You are the biggest blackguard I have ever met. If I *were* really a man I'd knock you down here and now.'[3]

Suspected of being a spy, Lawrence was interrogated by a panel of intelligence officers. 'So utterly ludicrous appeared this betrousered little female, marshalled solemnly by three soldiers and deposited before 20 embarrassed men,' she wrote. Rather than act manly and tough, however, Lawrence found herself '[lapsing] into feminine attitudes despite my little khaki uniform, concealment no longer being necessary'.[4] Her private letters were scrutinised for signs that she had been passing secrets to the enemy.

The discovery that Lawrence was neither a spy nor a 'camp-follower' (i.e. a prostitute) but a would-be journalist seemed to confuse military top brass, who had expected her to defend herself by professing patriotic loyalty. Still, her presence at the front was a serious security lapse, if nothing else. To avoid further embarrassment – and to stop Lawrence trying to file stories about the incident while preparations were underway for the imminent Battle of Loos – she was bundled off to a nearby convent while a decision was made about her future.

If Lawrence is to be believed, the nuns there loved her and were 'utterly enthralled at the adventures of a woman who had got out to the big world'.[5] So too the soldiers she had served alongside, a small crowd of whom queued up to shake her hand before her final expulsion from France.

On the ferry home, in a bizarre coincidence, Lawrence bumped into Emmeline Pankhurst, who was fascinated by Lawrence's story and tried to persuade her to speak at a WSPU event to encourage women to play an active part in the war effort. But the War Office had forbidden Lawrence from telling her story or discussing anything she had witnessed in the trenches until the end of the war. This was a professional blow to Lawrence, who pointed out: 'In making that promise I sacrificed the chance of earning by newspaper articles written on this escapade, as a girl compelled to earn her livelihood.'[6]

Not until 1919 did Lawrence's book see the light of day. It made little impact, possibly because it's brief and indifferently written; possibly because, even at the time, it felt a bit over-egged: not the sort of war story the British reading public wanted to hear. Its subtitle – 'the only English woman soldier' – has a whiff of fake news about it: Lawrence never served as a soldier and was only in the trenches for two weeks. What's more, other women found equally creative ways to see action.

The most famous of these other 'military maids' is Flora Sandes, a Yorkshire woman with close-cropped hair and a determined manner, whose career as a soldier seems partly to have been an expression of dissatisfaction with the limitations of her gender: 'When a very small child I used to pray every night that I might wake up in the morning and find myself a boy,' she admitted in her second volume of autobiography.[7]

Sandes' transformation from nurse at a military hospital in the then-Serbian city of Prilep, to soldier with the Serbian army was, she wrote, a result of her having 'naturally drifted' rather than any concerted effort to enlist. Female soldiers were not unusual in Serbia, where skill set was considered more important than sex, so given that the middle-class Sandes could shoot, ride and speak French and German as well as English, her appeal isn't hard to fathom. (Serbia was Britain's ally in the First World War, affiliated to the so-called Triple Entente linking Britain, France and Russia.)

Sandes' career ended in glory. Wounded by a grenade in 1916, she was promoted to the rank of Sergeant Major and awarded one of Serbia's highest military honours, the Order of Karađorđe's Star. At home, too, she was lionised. As Julie Wheelwright observes: 'In the English press she was catapulted from Red Cross nurse to the "Serbian Joan of Arc"'[8] – stopped in the street by taxi drivers; invited to dine with royals and generals. Her first autobiography, published in 1916 – presumably she wasn't bound as Dorothy Lawrence was by War Office demands for secrecy – received rave reviews and set her up for a successful career as a public speaker and unofficial ambassador for Serbia, whose post-war plight she was determined to alleviate.

Everywhere she went she relished her ambiguous, swaggering appearance (short hair, cane, full military regalia including sword) and the confusion it caused. In return, she was accorded the greatest respect. Introducing her to a capacity crowd at Sydney's King's Hall on 8 June 1920, the governor of New South Wales, Sir

Walter Davidson, declared: 'I have not heard of anything finer, or brighter, or more natural, or more modest, or braver or more skilful than the work of Lieutenant Flora Sandes.'[9]

Dorothy Lawrence, on the other hand, was unable to parlay her early daring into anything lasting or substantial. The career in journalism she craved eluded her and by 1925 her increasingly eccentric behaviour landed her in Colney Hatch Asylum in north London where she revealed to staff that she had been raped as a child by the church guardian who raised her after her parents died. She was locked up there until her death in 1964.

Lawrence's sense of herself as unique was clearly the point of her story. But this uniqueness would not have been much appreciated during the war when the prevailing sense among men (and many women too) was that women functioned best en masse as busy little worker bees. This is not to demean women's achievements at this time. After a century in which the First World War has been seen largely as a man's war – because it was the men who lost their lives and ran the show – the roles played by women have recently started to receive more attention.

Much of this wartime work, it's true, was traditional angel-in-the-house stuff. Thanks to Florence Nightingale's efforts during the Crimean War – trailblazing in some ways, constricting in others – the healing and caring professions were felt to be natural options for women. Not just by men, either: 'It was universally felt that there was work for women, even in war – the work of cleansing, setting in order, breaking down red tape, and soothing the vast sum of human suffering which every war is bound to cause,' wrote Millicent Garrett Fawcett, looking back on the 1850s from the pre-war, pre-suffrage vantage point of 1912.[10] And yet much of it was radically different from anything women had done before.

So let's begin at the beginning of the women's First World War.

Everyone knows that the First World War was triggered by the assassination of the Austrian Archduke Franz Ferdinand by nineteen-year-old Gavrilo Princip on 28 June 1914.

The American journalist Mabel Potter Daggett would write that on that day 'the door of *The Doll's House* [as in Henrik Ibsen's feminist play] opened – for the shot that was fired in Serbia summoned men to their most ancient occupation – and women to every other.'[11] In other words, the tragedy of the First World War ended up empowering women in a way no one could have predicted.

A global game of dominos began as countries resurrected long-dormant loyalties and alliances. Britain entered the war to support Belgium after Germany demanded free passage through it for its troops, according to its 'Schlieffen Plan' for a hypothetical European conflict. Although Britain was the only allied power to declare war on Germany rather than the other way round,[12] it didn't *want* a war. Nobody did. But European countries' huge armies, amassed to provide security and preserve the peace, 'carried the nations to war by their own weight', in A. J. P. Taylor's memorable phrase.[13]

The size of Britain's armed forces before 1914 was around 400,000 (compared to around 144,000 today), a figure the government initially thought satisfactory. It took the appointment of Lord Kitchener as Secretary of State for War to convince them that millions more men would be needed to defeat Germany. With the cabinet still opposed to conscription, Kitchener was placed in charge of voluntary recruitment and approved the use of his own image in propaganda posters, which played heavily on waverers' guilt and made it socially unacceptable not to sign up. The famous 'Lord Kitchener poster', designed by Alfred Leete and featuring a moustachioed Kitchener pointing at viewers, his eyes locking with theirs, appeared in September 1914.

Subsequent adverts deployed women as weapons. The 'Women of Britain say "Go!"' poster produced for the Imperial Maritime

League at around the same time as Kitchener's shows a mother clasping her two children to her as her husband marches away from their house. The woman stands not just for innocence, domesticity and morality, but for Britannia herself. As reports of rape and torture filtered through from Belgium and the other occupied territories, the necessity of defending Britannia at all costs seemed clear – and who better to do the defending than a husband?

Graphic atrocity propaganda depicted German soldiers spearing babies and raping nuns. In one poster a demon-eyed German soldier treads on a woman's corpse, blood dripping from his bayonet. Printed alongside it is an excerpt from what purports to be a British officer's letter to *The Times*:

> We have got three girls in the trenches with us, who came to us for protection. One had no clothes on, having been outraged by the Germans. I have given her my shirt and divided my rations among them. In consequence I feel rather hungry … Another poor girl has just come in, having had both her breasts cut off. Luckily I caught the Uhlan [cavalryman] officer in the act, and with a rifle at 300 yards killed him. And now she is with us, but, poor girl, I am afraid she will die. She is very pretty, and only about 19, and only has her skirt on …

A report by Viscount James Bryce's Committee on Alleged German Outrages detailed German atrocities against Belgian women. 'A witness gives a story, very circumstantial in its details, of how women were publicly raped in the market-place of the city, five young German officers assisting.'[14] The accuracy of Bryce's report was challenged after the Armistice, but there is no doubt that sexual violence against women in conflict zones is and was prevalent.

However, Millicent Garrett Fawcett – instinctively pacifist but a practical patriot who thought the war would ultimately advance the feminist cause – objected to these stories, arguing that 'it is surely no part of patriotism to stir up by speech or writing ungovernable rage and fury against the whole German people ... After nearly 2,000 years of Christianity we have but imperfectly learned one of its lessons if we think we can drive out cruelty by cruelty.'[15] She instructed her NUWSS to cease campaigning for suffrage and instead focus on sustaining the nation's vital energies: supporting Infant Welfare Centres, fundraising and keeping the food supply chain intact – for example, ensuring that ripe fruit did not rot on trees for want of workers to pick it.

While it suited the government to show women as passive, delicate creatures pining for their husbands, it was clear that with a third of the male labour force away fighting, they needed to roll up their sleeves and get to work doing 'men's jobs'. In March 1915, 80,000 women filled out a registration form declaring their willingness to do war work. Olive Schreiner, the South African writer and pacifist, observed cannily that 'the nation which is the first to employ its women may be placed at a vast advantage over its fellows in time of war'.[16] But ironically it was existing female workers – specifically working-class workers – who suffered most after the outbreak of war, as panicking wealthy households dismissed servants, and factories responded to drops in orders by laying off staff.

In September 1914, just over 44 per cent of all female employees were out of work. To address the problem, a system of relief work was created in the form of the Queen Mary's Work Fund, administered by the Central Committee for Women's Employment and run by labour-movement stalwarts such as Margaret Bondfield and Marion Phillips. The workrooms run by the fund paid notoriously badly – around 10 shillings a week; Sylvia Pankhurst called them 'Queen Mary's Sweatshops', though, as Gerry Holloway points out, 'unemployed women were probably grateful for any work they could get'.[17] There was also the Educated Woman's War Emergency Training Fund –

what a title! – which attempted to retrain women for clerical positions.

But as the war progressed and munitions and textiles factories went into overdrive, thousands of working-class women used their own initiative to find jobs, or rather new jobs, as most of them would have earned a wage before, doing piecework at home if not in a factory or in service. (In July 1914 there were already 200,000 women employed in the metal and chemical trades.)[18]

New soldiers needed new uniforms, and fast. Jane Cox from Mile End in London worked at Schneider's, which manufactured caps for the military. The poisonous khaki dye brought her out in boils: Cox developed a large, painful one on her spine but no treatment was offered. 'If you stopped to blow your nose you got the sack,' she remembered. 'You couldn't go to the toilet. You really worked in those days.'[19] At Ainsworth Mill in Cleator Moor in Cumbria, women produced khaki thread and were paid seven to nine shillings per week for sixty hours' work – little enough for the matter to be raised in the House of Commons by Labour MP William Anderson, husband of trade union leader Mary Macarthur.

During the cold winter of 1914 and 1915, women across Britain knitted gloves, scarves and balaclavas to send to troops. Special patterns could be bought for gloves that had a separate forefinger and thumb to make firing a gun easier, or garter-stitched eye patches supposed to hold dressings in place,[20] though the efforts of some of the new army of knitters were rather amateurish. Far more welcome, no doubt, was the decision by Mary Aitken, the wife of a Lancashire cotton merchant, to hand out ten thousand packets of cigarettes at the port of Le Havre to wounded soldiers after the Battle of the Marne.

One of the biggest employment opportunities for women arose because of a lack of munitions. Responsibility for munitions was taken away from Kitchener after the British Expeditionary Force (BEF) commander Sir John French blamed him for a shell shortage that he claimed had led to the failure of an attack at Aubers Ridge. Lloyd George took over, and set about negotiating with the unions over his pet policy of 'dilution', i.e. employing more women. The need became more pressing still after conscription was introduced in January 1916 to meet the Western Front's insatiable demand for troops.

For between £3 and £5 a week, women – inevitably dubbed the 'munitionettes' – filled shells with gas or the explosive compound trinitrotoluene (TNT). Woolwich Arsenal was employing 25,000 women by 1917. It was good money compared to what they might have earned in domestic service or from piecework, though much less than men would have been paid. Lloyd George thought pay equality 'a social revolution which … it is undesirable to attempt during war time'.

The inequity is all the more glaring because of the danger of the work, one belied by the jolly nickname given to the women: 'canaries', because of the way the TNT turned their skin yellow with jaundice. Aged just sixteen, Isabella Clark travelled all the way from Belfast to White Lund in Morecambe to get a job filling 9.2-inch gas shells. One day, as she and a friend were leaving the factory, they were stopped by a guard who noticed that the whites of their eyes were discoloured – a sign that they had ingested too much gas. Clark survived, but her friend died. Between May and October 1916, forty-one munitions workers died from TNT poisoning.

On 1 October 1917 an explosion at the White Lund factory killed ten people. The fire brigade was unable to contain the subsequent blaze. Workers were sent home with an extra fortnight's wages and the building decommissioned for the rest of the war. Among those dismissed was Clark, who found alternative work at an ordnance factory in Coventry, where conditions were better and workers had their own dedicated hostel with a maid to attend them, a piano in the hallway and bathrooms where the women could wash off the chemicals at the end of the day.

Factory explosions were more common than they ought to have been. When two hundred tonnes of TNT ignited at a plant in Faversham in 1916, 105 workers were killed. A blast at the TNT purifying plant at Silvertown in West Ham, Essex, on 19 January 1917 killed 73 and injured a further 400. The artist Winifred Knights witnessed it, and was so traumatised she had to abandon her studies at the Slade art college and leave London. Heard as far away as Sandringham in Norfolk, it was powerful enough to blow the glass out of windows in the Savoy Hotel in central London.

Britain's largest cordite factory was at Gretna on the border of Scotland and England. It had its own narrow-gauge railway and power station and was based around two purpose-built worker townships with their own police force, shops and laundries. Cordite was a highly explosive paste formed from nitroglycerine, nitrocellulose (or 'guncotton') and Vaseline. Mixed by hand in large vats, it became known as 'Devil's Porridge' after a remark made by Sir Arthur Conan Doyle when he visited the plant. Around 11,500 women were employed there – 45 per cent of them former domestic servants – compared with 5,900 men. They were put up in 'dormy houses' such as Barrow Women's Hostel, sometimes on a hot-bedding principle, so the same bed was used for workers on different shifts.

'There are good girls in the shell shops …, also there are some very bad ones,' noted a local newspaper. 'I have heard dreadful stories of girls who have maddened their landladies with their unclean habits when in lodgings. Yet, they keep coming; they are brought from all parts of the country, from north, south, east and west; from Scotland, Wales, Ireland and the Isle of Man.'[21]

Female workers at Gretna were renowned for their drunkenness and 'loose' morality to the point where the government, worried about its impact on the war effort, invoked the Defence of the Realm Act (DORA) to close or reform pubs in nearby Carlisle. It was a social experiment known as the State

Management Scheme. A 10 p.m. curfew was enforced by a female police force – a feature of other cordite factories such as ROF Pembrey in Wales. The thinking was that female officers would deal better with female employees and the children they sometimes brought with them. Working independently of the 'proper' male police, they had to buy their own navy blue uniforms out of their £2-a-week salary.

'The girls here are very rough, so are the conditions,' wrote Gabrielle West, who served at ROF Pembrey with the Women's Police Force on 'security duties' between 1916 and the end of the war. 'Their language is sometimes too terrible … The ether in the cordite affects the girls. It gives some headaches, hysteria and sometimes fits. If the worker has the least tendency to epilepsy, even if she has never shown it before, the ether will bring it out.'[22]

Elsewhere, women became acetylene welders and fitters, lens-grinders, plumbers, carpenters, grooms, bus-conductors, couriers, bank clerks … a clean sweep of the professions. But their wages were often kept artificially low by the sharp practice of allowing women to do only part of a job that had previously been done in its entirety by a man. The sight of so many women in trousers, gaiters and overalls was shocking to some. Even female typists at the War Office were required to wear blue overalls – to protect their clothing from ink stains.

'The trained handy woman has arrived!' screamed the *Daily Express*. 'She came yesterday to mend my electric bells, and gave an interesting account of her war-time work. She is an adept at repairs on every sort of contrivance, and gave advice on the management of my sewing machine with the same aptitude as she put up a new roller-blind.'[23] But the shock of the new had little penetrating force, and it took longer for women to permeate the working world than might have appeared to be the case: I. O. Andrews points out that 'as the public came into daily contact with women clerks in banks and business offices … there probably arose an exaggerated idea of the extent to which women did "men's work" during the first year of the war.'[24]

Still, the image of Britain's 'splendid women' making their professional most of these new opportunities was exciting. It gave the impression that full emancipation was imminent; that the struggles of the past fifty years had been magically neutralised. The exotic glamour of it all moved the left-wing Sylvia Pankhurst to high sarcasm: 'Beautiful women in long white coats, flawlessly tailored, already were taking the part of chauffeurs ... How speed-ily they had learnt to drive! It was truly amazing! One scarcely saw women driving before the War ... How important, how joyously important they were ...'[25]

This is slightly mean-spirited. Nevertheless, Sylvia was aware, as many others chose not to be, that women's experience of the war was not the same but shaped distinctly by class and money. With the East London Federation, the splinter suffrage organisation she had founded, she devoted herself to relief work, though she was keen to play down any whiff of upper-middle-class Victorian philanthropy. She helped women whose husbands were fighting to claim the meagre but life-saving 'separation allowance' they had been promised by the government. After appealing in the press for donations of milk and money, Sylvia opened five Mother and Infant Welfare Centres as well as a toy and garment factory. By the end of August 1914, inspired by similar social experiments in the US, she was serving around four hundred customers a day at her small chain of Cost Price Restaurants where a basic meal could be had for two pennies for adults, a penny for children – or nothing if you were 'destitute'.[26] A disused pub, The Gunmakers' Arms, became a clinic-cum-nursery.

Christabel and Emmeline, from whom Sylvia had become estranged, were in a very different place to her politically. While Sylvia was fiercely pacifist, her mother and sister supported the war to what Sylvia thought a 'furious extreme'.[27] Indeed, it became more of a concern to them than suffrage. On 8 September 1914, Christabel emerged from exile to address a crowd at London Opera House on 'the German peril'. The WSPU changed the name of its newspaper from *Suffragette* to *Britannia*. Emmeline made recruitment her focus, her supporters handing out white feathers, a symbol of cowardice, to any men they saw in civilian dress. 'So ends, for the present, the war of women against men,' she wrote. 'As of old the women become the nurturing mothers of men, their sisters and uncomplaining helpmates.' Sylvia wept and called their actions a 'tragic betrayal'.[28]

At London's Imperial War Museum you can see an 8-inch high explosive shell made at the Cunard National Shell Factory in Liverpool – the first ever made by women in Britain. The unusual thing about Cunard was that most of its munitionettes were middle-class and had never worked in a factory before. This meant they could go home after a twelve-hour shift to a warm bed in a quiet, comfortable house. One, Naomi Loughnan, wrote a memoir whose title – *Genteel Women in the Factories* – says it all. 'Inside the gates we are all on a level,' she wrote, and she obviously believed it. But she makes the work sound like a jape, a diversion from which she can escape if she wants:

> The genteel among us wear gloves. We vie with each other in finding the most up-to-date grease-removers, just as we used to vie about hats … As long as we do exactly what we are told … we give entire satisfaction, and are treated as nice, good children. Any swerving from the easy path prepared for us by our males arouses the most scathing contempt in their manly bosoms.[29]

Women were proving themselves to be quick, attentive, reliable workers, so it was hardly a surprise if some of the men felt slightly threatened, refusing to talk to female workers or pass on skills to them.

Outside the factories, organisations such as the Women's Land Army set out to attract single women from the educated middle classes to work on the land, since nearly 60 per cent of male agricultural workers had been called up to serve in the army. One WLA offshoot, the Women's Forestry Corps, specialised in the harvesting of wood. For some reason, however, the 'land girls' of the First World War never enjoyed the cultural cachet of their Second World War counterparts, whose escapades inspired countless books and films.

At least one historian thinks the seeming takeover of the workplace by women was a 'transient phenomenon' more valuable as propaganda than as a blueprint for the future. 'Photographs of women driving trams, buses or ambulances became well known, not because of their typicality but because of their novelty,'[30] says Peter Clarke, pointing out that in 1921, as in 1911, there were only three thousand women employed on the railways, less than 1 per cent of the total. But visibility itself had an important impact: see enough pictures of women in uniforms looking authoritative and that authority becomes real.

The uniform everyone seemed happy for women to wear was a nurse's uniform. However, women who wished to pursue battlefield nursing but were not medically trained had limited options. If they were over twenty-three they could be Voluntary Aid Detachments (VADs) – semi-trained assistant nurses, and there were 38,000 of them by the end of the war. Or they could be FANYs, members of the First Aid Nursing Yeomanry whose duties were more menial and often involved ambulance-driving.

Tensions could run high between professional nurses and the often upper-middle-class, university-educated VADs. Our image of VADs has been formed by *Testament of Youth*, Vera Brittain's enduring account of how in 1915 she interrupted her studies at Somerville College, Oxford to become a military nurse in first England then France and Malta; or as she later put it, 'carried away by the wartime emotion and deceived by the shining figure of patriotism'.[31] At the time, though, her patriotic conviction was absolute. As she wrote to her father when he suggested she return to England:

> *Nothing* – beyond sheer necessity – would induce me to stop doing what I am doing now … I do not agree that my place is at home doing nothing, for I consider that the place now of anyone who is young and capable is where the work that is needed is to be done.[32]

Vera may not have been a natural nurse, but as a writer she was able to convey the horror and pointlessness of war with electrifying clarity, especially in her letters to her Oxford fiancé Roland Leighton, who was serving in France and who would die in December 1915, shot by a sniper as he repaired the barbed wire running in front of his trench. His blood-stained, mud-caked uniform was sent home – a 'heap of horror' mitigated only by the discovery, within it, of a black manuscript book containing his poems.

Despite the horrors, there was no shortage of female volunteers. Almost as soon as war broke out, two female doctors, Louisa Garrett Anderson and Flora Murray, formed the Women's Hospital Corps (WHC). When the War Office rebuffed their approaches they took themselves off to Paris to work in tandem with the French Red Cross. There at Victoria Station to bid them farewell was Louisa's seventy-eight-year-old mother, the great Elizabeth Garrett Anderson, who was heard to say: 'Twenty years younger, I would have taken them myself.' Realising it had gaffed, the War Office later gave the pair permission to run their own female-staffed military hospital in London. Endell Street Hospital opened in May 1915 and served 26,000 patients before it closed in 1919.

Go-getting female medics were often drawn from the ranks of suffrage activists. The Scottish Women's Hospitals, which ran hospitals in France, Russia, Corsica, Salonika, Romania and Serbia, was founded by the Scottish doctor and suffragist Elsie Inglis after she launched an appeal in the NUWSS newspaper *Common Cause*. Inglis had originally wanted to join the WHC. When she had no luck there she approached the Royal Army Medical Corps, only to be advised: 'My good lady, go home and sit still.'

Enraged, Inglis did exactly the opposite. Her first hospital opened at Royaumont, a semi-derelict medieval abbey thirty miles north of Paris, in December 1914. Her crack team of 'seven doctors, ten nurses, seven orderlies, two cooks, a clerk, an administrator, two maids and four chauffeurs' transformed the place from a ruin into a working hospital in a matter of months.[33] It remained open until March 1919, though rather than base herself there Inglis spent most of the war zig-zagging across Europe, establishing her franchise wherever she found a warzone and a suitable disused building. She died of cancer in Newcastle-upon-Tyne on 26 November 1917, the day after she had returned with her unit from Russia. She was just fifty-three.

Some volunteer groups had a rather ramshackle quality. Elsie Knocker was a thirty-year-old nurse and motorbike obsessive who, in 1914, joined the Flying Ambulance Corps (FAC) with her motorbiking friend Mairi Chisholm, an eighteen-year-old tomboy from a well-to-do Scottish family. Knocker left her seven-year-old son with her parents, and – embarrassed that she'd divorced his father – she pretended to be a widow. The FAC was run by Dr Hector Munro, a 'quirky, charismatic bachelor with a natty moustache',[34] who was, as Knocker would later recall, keener on women's rights than most of the women he recruited.

A skilful driver and mechanic, Knocker soon mastered the clunky Napier ambulance and assortment of other vehicles she was made to drive. But she was bad at taking orders and longed to be in charge herself. Increasingly disillusioned by the conditions at the hospital where they were based, she and Chisholm hatched a plan to set up their own Advanced Dressing Station close to the front line, so that wounded soldiers could recuperate before the bumpy drive to the operating table at Furnes Hospital fifteen miles away:

> I had noticed how many of [the soldiers] died of superficial hurts, a broken arm, perhaps, or a gash. They 'died on the way to hospital', or on the pavements or the floors, and I knew why this happened. They were the victims of shock – the greatest killer of them all ... It takes a woman to know these things.[35]

Although Dr Munro disapproved initially, he ended up giving the project his blessing and the pair set up shop in Pervyse in northern Belgium, a small village which had been almost totally obliterated by shell blasts. They found a vacant cellar one hundred yards from the trenches and spent the next three years there, tending the wounded and feeding them home-made soup and hot chocolate. As their local celebrity grew – the media christened them 'the Madonnas of Pervyse' and 'the New Ladies of the Lamp' – so did the steady stream of high-profile visitors, including the pacifist Labour MP Ramsay MacDonald and X-ray pioneer Marie Curie, who arrived one day with her daughter Irene and annoyed the women by not offering to help.

Dr Munro's weirdly dressed women became notorious. 'At first one is inclined to call them masqueraders in their knickerbockers and puttees and caps, but I believe they have done excellent work,' wrote the Scottish novelist, musician and painter Sarah Broom Macnaughtan, who volunteered with the Red Cross Society. 'It is a queer side of war to see young, pretty English girls in khaki and thick boots, coming in from the trenches ...'[36]

For the most part volunteer nurses were neither decorative nor colourful. Most VADs were girls of seventeen or eighteen who had led sheltered, conservative lives before being thrust into the shambles of trench warfare. Their innocence fed into the 'virgin martyr' stereotype – exemplified by the nurse Edith Cavell.

She's memorialised in marble on the north-east corner of London's Trafalgar Square – the first notable female casualty of the First World War. After helping around two hundred Allied soldiers escape from occupied Belgium, Cavell was arrested for treason, court-martialled and sentenced to death: shot by a German firing squad on 12 October 1915. The violent, incredulous response in Britain – on a par with the emotional outpouring following the death of Princess Diana over eighty years later – owed a good deal to the view, promoted in subsequent propaganda, that Cavell was little short of an angel, her virtue grotesquely sullied by the dastardly Germans.

'The frank, open nature of Edith Cavell was ill-fitted for such an atmosphere of fear and deception,' decided William Thomson Hill in his hagiographic *The Martyrdom of Nurse Cavell*, published in the weeks after her death. 'Edith Cavell was suspected, and cunning men sought how they might weave a net of accusation around her.'[37]

Cavell was born in 1865 in the Norfolk village of Swardeston, the daughter of a vicar and the youngest of four. Although pious and obedient on the whole, there were tiny rebellions such as the occasion her father found her smoking a cigarette in his study, a transgression for which she was sent away to boarding school – the sort of low-order education designed to prepare her for life as the wife of a doctor or a clergyman or, if she decided not to marry, a governess: drawing, languages, literature, music.

Initially she worked for several local households as a governess, before moving to Brussels to work for a wealthy lawyer, looking after his four children and their dog. They were friendly and involved her in family life more than she might have expected, but still she felt lonely and adrift in a foreign place, convinced a higher vocation awaited her. 'Someday, somehow, I am going to do something useful,' she wrote to her cousin Eddy.

'I don't know what it will be. I only know that it will be something for people.'[38]

Back at home in Norfolk, both her sisters were training to be nurses, no longer a stigmatised career thanks to the efforts of Florence Nightingale. She returned home in 1895, aged thirty, ostensibly to care for her father, but in December that year applied to the Metropolitan Asylums Board and six days later started work as a trainee nurse at the Fountains Fever Hospital in Tooting in south London. There she learned the value of an industrious, regimented life; how to tell one infectious disease from another; and the harsh truth that most of these diseases were incurable, so the job of a nurse was essentially to be kind, to encourage rest and to keep everything scrupulously clean.

After seven months Cavell moved to London Hospital in Whitechapel to begin her official training – a two-year course. She developed a reputation for being reserved, but also kind beyond the call of duty. When one patient had an operation on his spine without an anaesthetic, Cavell sat with him for three days. But Eva Luckes, the matron, found fault with her 'self-sufficient manner which was very apt to prejudice people against her' – not the last time in Cavell's life that egolessness would be mistaken for arrogance.

In 1907 she returned to Belgium to work as head matron under Dr Antoine Depage, the Belgian royal surgeon, at his new training hospital – the Berkendael Medical Institute. On the day the First World War broke out she was in England visiting her mother. She rushed back to Belgium before its occupation by Germany on 4 August 1914, to help convert the Institute into a Red Cross Hospital that would treat German as well as Allied soldiers. She described her work in a piece she wrote for the magazine *Nursing Mirror*:

> We were preparing 18,000 beds for the wounded; all sorts and
> conditions of people were offering help, giving mattresses and
> blankets, rolling bandages and making shirts ...[39]

The German advance through Belgium had been brutal, characterised by summary executions and other war crimes. Now the
occupation brought with it food shortages, unemployment,
censorship and the deportation of Belgian workers to Germany.
Resistance networks flourished. Cavell's instructions to her nurses
were clear: they were to treat any wounded soldier, friend or foe,
but they should be cautious and watch what they said.

Something in Cavell's nature was changing. She had always
been, says her most recent biographer, 'the most law-abiding of
women', but the Christian duty she felt to help the Allies eclipsed
all other obligations. Where once she had conformed, 'now she
defied. She had been open. Now she was cunning.'[40]

In November 1914, Cavell began sheltering British and French
soldiers and helping them to escape to the neutral Netherlands.
They were given false papers by Prince Reginald de Croy, a former
Secretary at the Belgian Embassy in London, before being taken
to his chateau near Mons which he had turned into a war hospital, then on to other houses, including Cavell's on the rue de la
Culture. They were hidden there until guides were ready to escort
them to suitable holding areas. Some soldiers went to a monastery
at Averbode where they disguised themselves as monks before
crossing the border. Emboldened by her successes, Cavell became
'more entrenched in subterfuge, wily at disguise, coded exchange,
and the art of concealment, and knew – or thought she knew –
who to trust'.[41]

But some of the men she was concealing grew impatient and
indiscreet. They went to cafés, chatted up local girls, drank. A
German command post set up in her road. Her letters to her
mother and others started to contain too much of the wrong sort
of information. Slowly, the net closed around her ...

After her arrest Cavell decided to cooperate completely in the hope that this would spare others. She admitted to helping seventy-five British and French soldiers to escape to Holland and around a hundred French and Belgian civilians. But she knew that the real intention of Lieutenant Bergan, Head of Espionage, and Sergeant Henri Pinkhoff, Chief Officer of Criminal Investigation, was to destroy her, and indeed the deposition they prepared for her was full of errors, her confession contrived and inaccurate.

The problem for Cavell was that, while the Geneva Convention usually guaranteed the protection of medical personnel, a person forfeited this right in a case where espionage was suspected. (The fact that Cavell had been charged with treason rather than espionage seemed not to make a difference.) This meant there was little diplomatically that anyone could do for her. 'Any representation by us will do her more harm than good,' decided Lord Robert Cecil, a committed pacifist who worked for the Red Cross before taking up the post of Under-Secretary of State for Foreign Affairs in the coalition government. 'I am afraid that it is likely to go hard with Miss Cavell; I am afraid we are powerless,' agreed Sir Horace Rowland at the Foreign Office.

It was left to the US mission in Brussels to agitate on Cavell's behalf. American official Hugh Gibson tried to convey to the German police 'the horror of executing a woman no matter what her offence, pointing out that the death sentence had heretofore been imposed only for actual cases of espionage and that Miss Cavell was not even accused by the German authorities of anything so serious'.[42] But no one was listening.

William Thomson Hill describes the moment of Cavell's death:

> At two o'clock in the morning they led her out with bandaged eyes to the place of execution. The firing party stood ready with loaded rifles. At this last moment her physical strength was not

a match for her heroic spirit. She fell in a swoon. The officer in charge of the soldiers stepped forward and shot her as she lay unconscious.[43]

But Diana Souhami, in her brilliant biography from 2010, gives a rather different account, based on evidence rather than sentimental supposition. Here, the nurse's eyes are bandaged, yes – and the soldier who performs the act remarks that they are filled with tears. Then the command is given:

> There was the crack of gunfire. Edith Cavell's face streamed with blood. She jerked forward and three times her body rose up in a reflex action. One shot had gone through her forehead. There was a bullet hole as large as a fist through her heart. She remained upright at the post.[44]

As a nurse she had kept the lowest of profiles. But in death, Edith Cavell became the most famous woman in Britain. When her image was used on recruitment posters, recruitment doubled from 5,000 to 10,000 soldiers a week for eight consecutive weeks. In 1919 her body, hastily buried in Belgium, was exhumed and repatriated before being reinterred in Norwich Cathedral. Even in death, her resemblance to a medieval saint went beyond mere piety: her body, when dug up, was found *not to have decomposed* and her face was still wearing the 'perfectly calm expression' with which Cavell had confronted her killers.[45] Britain used her death to emphasise its own policy of not executing captured female German spies such as Louise Herbert, the wife of a Darlington-based curate, who was imprisoned for six months after admitting she had spied for Germany.

Cavell's death roused the prime minister Herbert Asquith to one of his most tone-deaf Commons speeches: '[Cavell] has taught the bravest man among us a supreme lesson of courage; yes, and in this United Kingdom and throughout the Dominions there are thousands of such women, *but a year ago we did not know it.*[46]

('Pathetic blindness!' remarked Millicent Garrett Fawcett. 'Especially as a great deal of it must have been wilful.')[47]

The question of whether Cavell was, in addition to her resistance work, an agent for MI5 remains only partially answered. The general view seems to be that any spying she did was accidental. After her death, says her most recent biographer, MI5 suppressed any information that might have implicated her as a spy, though the agency's former head, Dame Stella Rimington, conducted additional research in Belgian archives for a radio documentary in 2015 and claimed to have found 'clear evidence that [Cavell's] organisation was involved in sending back secret intelligence to the allies',[48] including information about munitions dumps and the structure of the Germans' trench system. I would love her to have been a spy on top of everything else. But what she achieved – secreting escapees in her house, leading them to safehouses, fixing them up with guides – was remarkable enough. This lily doesn't need gilding.

It took a while for reliable accounts of women's wartime experiences to filter through into public consciousness. Sometimes they encountered a blockage en route. Helen Zenna Smith's *Not So Quiet* purports to be a novel about a group of FANYs doing 'the foulest and most disgusting job it's possible to imagine',[49] ferrying the wounded – sometimes no more than collections of mangled body parts – from the front line to field hospitals. But the novel's history is revealing. Helen Zenna Smith was the pen name of the journalist Evadne Price. Asked by a publisher to write a parody of Erich Remarque's famous 1929 novel *All Quiet on the Western Front*, Price decided she would rather write a serious work which gave an honest account of the role women had played in the First World War. The basis of the novel, however, was the diary of a real-life ambulance driver in France, Winifred Constance Young, who wanted to publish a memoir of her experiences but didn't because she was worried about embarrassing her family. They didn't want to know what she had seen or done during the war. Whatever it was, it was bound to be an affront to respectability, so it was better left unsaid.

As for the women left at home, they 'bore a special burden, dreading the arrival of a telegraph boy on his bicycle'.[50] Grief was one of the few things that transcended class. For all the petty score-settling of Asquith's wife Margot's diaries, her account of the arrival of the news of the death of her stepson at the Battle of the Somme on 15 September 1916 is especially powerful:

> Henry opened the door, and we stood facing each other. He saw my miserable, thin, wet face, and put his arm round me. I said: 'My darling – terrible news.'
>
> He stopped me. 'I know, I've known it – Raymond has been killed.'
>
> I nodded; we walked silently down the little passage into the bridge room.
>
> Henry sat down on the Chinese armchair, put his head on his arms on the table, and sobbed passionately. I flung my arms round him and sat on his knee, silent.[51]

Many women – and indeed men – refused to 'play their part' and flaunted their pacifist credentials from the outset. Others, like Vera Brittain, became pacifists as a reaction to what they had been obliged to see and do; though for her, it seems, a sense that something was amiss gnawed at her early on. Only a few weeks after the war had started she wrote that 'the destruction of men, as though beasts, whether they be English, French, German or anything else, seems a crime to the whole march of civilisation.'[52]

Brittain's childhood was blessed by wealth and stability – her father Thomas made his fortune manufacturing paper; she grew up in the spa town of Buxton in Derbyshire where she was educated first at home by a governess, then at boarding school. None of this protected her, though. The war would rob her of both her brother and her fiancé. Her intellect became her consolation, along with the resolute feminism instilled in her by a sympathetic school teacher, Miss Heath Jones. After the Armistice, Brittain returned to Somerville, switching degrees from English to History, the better to understand 'how the whole calamity had happened, to know why it had been possible for me and my contemporaries, through our own ignorance and others' ingenuity, to be used, hypnotised and slaughtered'.[53]

Some women expressed themselves through their art, apparently sympathetic to the dominant strain of bleak, less-deceived First World War art that takes in works such as Paul Nash's *Void* and Wyndham Lewis' *A Battery Shell*. But their work was rather hidden from view. When the war artists scheme was devised in 1916 only four women artists were commissioned compared to forty-seven men, and of these three had the work they produced rejected.

Some female painters did achieve a recognition of sorts. Anna Airy had been exhibited widely by the time she was commissioned to paint munitions factories.

But much of the female war art that survives from the period is informal and intimate, dealing in real people in real places. Olive Mudie-Cooke had trained as a painter at Goldsmiths but was driving ambulances for the British Red Cross in France when she painted the haunting, phosphorescent *In an Ambulance: a VAD Lighting a Cigarette for a Patient*. Flora Lion's snapshot-like *Women's Canteen at Phoenix Works, Bradford* was commissioned by the Ministry of Information. Her queuing munitions workers look cheerful and buoyed-up, apart from a woman in blue near the front of the queue who gazes blankly ahead, her mug hanging by her side.

For the Bloomsbury Group pacifism was an article of faith. Clive Bell's controversial 1915 pamphlet *Peace at Once* called for a negotiated settlement and alienated pro-war friends. His wife Vanessa Bell remarked to her sister Virginia Woolf: 'I see more and more that we are completely isolated from our kind.'[54] Vanessa moved to Charleston – the Sussex retreat now considered the headquarters of the Bloomsbury Group – partly to support Duncan Grant, who as a conscientious objector was obliged to do farmwork. Her painting/collage *Still Life (Triple Alliance)* refers to the Triple Entente of Britain, France and Russia against Germany but refracts it through images of household items – a soda siphon, a wine bottle and a lamp – created out of paint, a cheque, maps of conflict zones in northern France and newspaper cuttings.

While the Bells might have retreated from the cruel world, some of their contemporaries were rather more active in their pacifism.

One of the leading figures in the pacifist movement was the Liverpool-born teacher and social worker Mary Sheepshanks. Sheepshanks had visited Germany in 1913, finding the country congenial and its people polite and friendly. Why, she wondered, were we suddenly demonising all Germans? Wasn't it better to try to forge bonds of understanding between nations? Asquith dismissed Sheepshanks and her followers as 'sparrows twittering in a tempest'.

At her International Women's Suffrage office on Adelphi Street, Sheepshanks drafted a 'peace manifesto' which began: 'We, the women of the world, view with apprehension and dismay the present situation in Europe, which threatens to involve one continent, if not the whole world, in the disasters and horrors of war …' It appealed to governments to leave untried 'no method of conciliation or arbitration'.[55]

Sheepshanks also turned her attention to the refugee crisis. Holland was struggling with the vast numbers of Belgian refugees arriving there. Together with barrister Chrystal Macmillan, also a leading suffrage activist, Sheepshanks obtained a guarantee of

£200 from the Belgian ambassador to buy food, went to the Lyons' catering headquarters and bought as many loaves of bread, tins of condensed milk and packets of chocolate as she could afford. The cargo was loaded onto lorries and despatched to the docks. Sheepshanks and Macmillan sailed to Vlissingen in Belgium with the convoy across the North Sea – dodging the U-boats – interviewed the refugees and, on her return, Sheepshanks campaigned with Elsie Inglis and Isabella Ford for more of them to be admitted to Britain, giving a rousing speech at Kingsway Hall. She also helped stranded 'enemy aliens' – Germans stuck in Britain at the start of the war – to the anger of the press. 'I have had to open a special file for "anonymous abuse",' she told Bertrand Russell. 'I am rather pleased. I always wanted to be associated with an unpopular cause.'[56] Who said the trolling of high-profile women was a twenty-first-century phenomenon?

When the International Women's Peace Congress was held in The Hague in April 1915, 180 British women were keen to attend. In the face of much government opposition, twenty-four were finally allowed to go, including Sheepshanks. However, Winston Churchill was so opposed to it that he closed the North Sea to British shipping for the duration of the Congress to stop British women attending. Sheepshanks described the frustration of waiting at a hotel on the Thames at Tilbury, the steamer she and her colleagues had been booked on lying at anchor.

Sheepshanks might have had a fractious relationship with the state, but other women were getting jobs at the heart of it. As we've seen, the civil service had employed women as telegraph operators since the 1870s. But the outbreak of war triggered an explosion of paperwork – and women matched the job description. Before long the Foreign Office and new departments like the War Department and the Department of Political Intelligence had significant numbers of female staff. Hilda Johnstone, later Professor of History at Royal Holloway College, worked in the War Trade Intelligence Department. Dorothy Bigby began as a staff officer, then worked in the Librarian's Department, becoming Acting Librarian herself in 1945.

But the glass ceiling was so low it grazed the tops of their heads. As the historian Helen McCarthy points out, women were 'almost wholly absent from the very highest decision-making levels'.[57] She gives the example of Bertha Phillpots, a scholar of Scandinavian literature, history and archaeology who had won a scholarship to Girton College, Cambridge in 1897 but who ended up at the British embassy in Stockholm making files of newspaper cuttings. She'd been hired when she went out there in 1916 to visit her brother Owen, who was already employed as a commercial attaché. He was useless and chaotic – at one point he lost some sensitive papers – so the head of mission asked if she would mind staying on to help him out. She said yes, but was treated as little more than a skivvy and wasn't paid a salary until the following year.[58]

Women did, however, manage to become the backbone of operations at the counter-espionage department MO5 – it became MI5 in 1916. Churchill's old friend from Sandhurst, Vernon Kell, believed it 'increased its value by employing a staff of women' alongside the men. Kell was keen to recruit former pupils from leading girls' schools and women's colleges and actively courted them when the initial system based on informal recommendations failed to yield sufficient candidates. Educated, well-bred women were believed to be more trustworthy – less inclined to blab secrets on the tube – than their social inferiors. Presumably their sense of duty, ingrained in them by their schooling, meant they were also less likely to complain about the bad pay and long hours, including unpaid overtime. I can't help thinking that a system which demanded utter loyalty even as it refused them the vote must have irked them.

Between 1915 and 1919 around six hundred women, most under thirty, worked at MI5's HQ at Waterloo House in Haymarket as clerks, printers, translators and messengers. By November 1918 the postal censorship division known as MI9 had 3,500 women on its payroll – and only 1,300 men. One of them was the future writer and explorer Freya Stark, who hated the way the windows in the cramped offices were always kept open, whatever the weather. She wrote to her mother in February 1917: 'I have just had two days' holiday (they give one weekend every six weeks) and I am so annoyed because I had to spend most of it in bed, stifling a cold …'[59] Women with linguistic or scientific skills were especially valuable. In Room 40 at the Old Admiralty Building, women worked as signallers and cipher decoders under the watchful gaze of Admiral Sir William Reginald 'Blinker' Hall. Their nickname? Blinker's Beauty Chorus.

MI5's H Branch, the so-called Registry of information about known or suspected agents, was almost exclusively female. The controller of the Registry was Edith Lomax – always referred to as 'Miss Lomax' – ably assisted by Elsie Harrison ('Miss Harrison'). Their clerks' work consisted of filing and indexing so that records could be located and accessed almost immediately – tough work in a pre-computer era. One former clerk remembered it as 'so fatiguing that no one was able to keep at it for too long at a stretch'.[60] Hilda Matheson worked for MI5 in Rome as well as London before becoming secretary to the Conservative MP Nancy Astor and joining the BBC as its first Director of Talks in 1927.

'Registry girls' worked an eight-hour shift with half a day off once a week and, when possible, alternate Sundays. The female worker, wrote the male author of one MI5 internal report, 'must have that peculiarly feminine gift of intuition, or the faculty of not only making two and two equal four, but of realising that two and two can equal five'.[61]

This intuition and ability to think laterally, combined with love of detail, made female 'looker-uppers' formidably reliable, though inevitably they were under-appreciated by their male colleagues, one of whom contended that their work 'would have been as well done by men ... of a lower social standing and fewer educational opportunities.'[62]

Some women went on to positions of authority. Charlotte Bosworth rose to deputy assistant censor at MI9 and was posted to Paris where her job was to extract information from German soldiers' paybooks. Meanwhile, thirty-year-old Mary Harris supervised the mostly female staff of the British Mission in Paris.

If women today wrestle with the gender pay gap, in the early twentieth century it was a yawning chasm. Female civil servants were paid no more than £200 a year while their male counterparts earned between £300 and £500. As for job security, most were sacked after the war and replaced with returned-services personnel. This post-war demobilisation of women happened across the board. Liberal prime minister David Lloyd George put them firmly in their place, declaring: 'The workers of today are the mothers of tomorrow.' On the diplomatic side, it wasn't until 1921 that women were hired at the Foreign Office as clerical and executive officers on a permanent basis.[63]

An exception to this was the maverick writer, traveller and archaeologist Gertrude Bell, whose work for the War Office did much to determine the shape of the modern Middle East as laid down at the Cairo Conference of 1921. Not that you'd know from popular history. As her former colleague, T. E. Lawrence, became one of the twentieth century's most fêted figures, his life and military record mythologised in David Lean's film *Lawrence of Arabia*, Bell was reduced to a footnote.

In the film version of *The English Patient*, British soldiers are shown examining a map when one of them asks, 'But can we get through those mountains?' 'The Bell maps show a way,' replies another. To which another responds, 'Let's hope he was right.'[64]

It's classic unconscious bias. Because of course, the maps' author was no 'he', though Bell's more 'masculine' attributes infuriated and confused second-rate men like Sir Mark Sykes, co-author of the Sykes-Picot agreement which after the war carved up the former Ottoman-controlled territories between Britain, France and Russia. Sykes wrote to his wife that Bell was a 'silly chattering windbag of a conceited, gushing, flat-chested, man-woman, globe-trotting, rump-wagging, blethering ass'.[65] Wow!

Born in 1868, the daughter of a progressive, well-connected industrialist, Bell became the first woman to achieve first-class honours (though not, of course, a degree – women weren't allowed to collect those yet) in Modern History at Lady Margaret Hall, Oxford, despite having a tutor who insisted women sit with their backs to him. Too educated to conform to type and marry – though she was briefly engaged in her early twenties – she became instead the archetypal female scholar-traveller: a hardier, more intellectual sub-species of the Victorian ladies who spent their grand tours sketching monuments.

Bell excelled in all fields apparently without breaking into a sweat. T. E. Lawrence thought she was 'born too gifted'. Strong and fit, she could climb mountains as easily as she could master languages and once spent fifty-three hours hanging on a rope in a blizzard while trying to ascend the north-east face of the Finsteraarhorn. But her passion was for what was then known simply as Arabia: the desert lands ruled by the Ottoman Empire.

Bell made her first oriental excursion in 1892, accompanying her Aunt Mary to Tehran where her uncle was ambassador. She returned repeatedly, writing up her observations in books such as *Persian Pictures* (1894) and *The Desert and the Sown* (1907). Armed with detailed knowledge of and respect for tribal protocols, Bell won the trust and even friendship of imams, sheikhs and sundry warring tribes. She rode for up to twelve hours a day in fearsome temperatures, drinking stagnant water from pools, wearing a 'divided skirt' that let her ride like a man. But her caravan included a Wedgwood dinner service and she was careful to dress in the latest fashions so that she looked as regal as her nickname, *khatun* or 'desert queen'. In June 1913 she became one of the first women to be elected a fellow of the Royal Geographical Society.

Forty-six when the First World War began, Bell spent its early stages working as a VAD nurse in the unlikely setting of Clandon Park, the country house near Guildford in Surrey, which had been converted into a hospital. She was then posted to Boulogne where she headed the Red Cross Wounded and Missing Enquiry Department set up to process queries about missing soldiers. It was in chaos when she arrived but she swiftly professionalised it, creating a proper filing system and establishing relationships with local hospitals. In the midst of all this she discovered that the man she loved, Dick Doughty-Wylie, had been killed at Gallipolli.

In November 1915 Bell was asked by the War Office to help set up an intelligence operation in Cairo called the Arab Bureau. 'It's all vaguer than words can say,' she wrote to her stepmother. She and her colleagues, who included T. E. Lawrence, called themselves the Intrusives. Their goal was to persuade the Arab tribes to rise up and overthrow the Ottoman Turks, who were fighting on Germany's side, by promising them self-determination at the end of the war – an empty promise as far as most of them were concerned, though not to Bell. Despite being a colonialist to her fingertips, she believed passionately in Arab self-rule. When the Ottoman Empire crumbled after the war, she produced a detailed report – the first White Paper written by a woman – analysing how this might be achieved. Based in Baghdad, Bell helped to design the constitution and define the borders of Mesopotamia, which was formed out of the Ottoman provinces of Basra, Mosul and Baghdad and renamed Iraq. She organised elections, founded the Iraq National Museum, and worked to establish a constitutional monarchy under the Hashemite King Faisal.

T. E. Lawrence argued that government was a 'doubtful benefit … to give a people who have long done without'.[66] Certainly, Bell's pro-Sunni bias arguably institutionalised sectarian divisions.

This was to have terrible long-term consequences for Iraq after the monarchy was overthrown in 1958. But the task facing her was almost impossible as she acknowledged in her letters home: 'In the light of the events of the last 2 months there's no getting out of the conclusion that we have made an immense failure here,' she wrote to her father in 1920, in the midst of a violent uprising by numerous Arab tribes against the British occupation. 'The system must have been far more at fault than anything that I or anyone else suspected. It will have to be fundamentally changed and what that may mean exactly I don't know. I suppose we have underestimated the fact that this country is really an inchoate mass of tribes which can't as yet be reduced to any system.'[67]

In January 1909 Gertrude Bell found herself sharing a boat with a Mrs Broadbridge, 'an intelligent little woman, wife of an engineer who is now on the W. coast of Africa'. They discussed suffragism and Bell 'enlisted her among the Antis'.[68]

Later that year Bell became Honorary Secretary of the Women's National Anti-Suffrage League. Her ferocious dislike of the women's suffrage movement is hard to understand today. How could a woman who refused to conform to 'normal' Victorian gender roles feel that she either didn't need – or wasn't qualified – to vote? Possibly she thought it an example of women asking for special treatment they shouldn't need. ('[My climbing teacher] says I'm as good as any man … and from what I see of the capacities of the ordinary mountaineer, I think I am,' she wrote to her stepmother Florence on 12 August 1900.)[69]

By the 1920s, Millicent Garrett Fawcett felt that the inevitability of victory for the female suffrage lobby had been obvious from the middle of the war:

Throughout the years 1916 and 1917 conversions of important public men and of leading newspapers kept coming in, not by ones and twos, but by battalions. The Anti-Suffrage Press, which in earlier days had been such an obstacle in the way of our success, was almost wiped out … The wave of appreciation of women's work and place in the world rose higher and higher, and had permanent results; the value of it is felt in many directions; we see evidence of it in the greater courtesy extended to women everywhere; in the greater appreciation of the value of infant life; in the greater willingness of men to share in and help women in their domestic work.[70]

With even Churchill declaring that 'our armies have been saved and victory assured by the women in the munitions factories', the war gave Asquith what Fawcett called 'a ladder down which he could climb in renunciation of his former errors'.[71] Women had proved themselves in the war and now had a special claim to be heard. In private Asquith felt differently, telling an audience in Paisley that the 15,000 women on the register there were a 'dim, impenetrable, for-the-most-part ungettable element … hopelessly ignorant of politics, credulous to the last degree, and flickering with gusts of sentiment like a candle in the wind'. The newspaper proprietor Lord Northcliffe went from opposing suffrage to telling Fawcett, 'The women were wonderful. Their freshness of mind, their organising skill, were magnificent. Men were making too great a mess of the world, and needed helpers without their own prejudices, idleness, and self-indulgence.'[72]

In January 1917, with Lloyd George's coalition government in office, a Speaker's Conference to consider the issue recommended that the vote be given to all adult men *and women* over thirty who owned property and had voted in the local elections, or who were married to men who had.

This wasn't exactly equality – it excluded the factory workers whose efforts politicians had fallen over themselves to praise – but it was a start, and Millicent Garrett Fawcett accepted it in spite of its limitations. Others such as Sylvia Pankhurst and Margaret Llewellyn Davies continued to press for full adult suffrage. They could see that what was proposed was not as radical as it might seem; that politicians were supporting the bill because they knew the older women who had been enfranchised were unlikely to vote for change. Even so, thought Sylvia, 'the breach in the sex barrier had been made.'[73]

On 19 June 1917 the Commons voted by 385 to 55 to accept the Representation of the People's Bill. Lloyd George said the women's vote would 'bring into public life a point of view and spirit which will be of incalculable value to the progress of democracy in these islands'. In the Lords there were dissenters like Lord Curzon. But fears proved unfounded: 143 peers voted for, 71 against, with three abstaining.

The Act enfranchised 8.4 million women – but also 13 million men. In November 1918 women were also able to stand for parliament. The first woman to be elected was Constance Markievicz as Sinn Fein MP for Dublin, though in line with her party's policy she refused to take up her seat – and was in any case imprisoned in Holloway at the time for her involvement in the Easter Uprising.

Sylvia Pankhurst thought that if anything good had come out of the war, it was that it had drawn men and women closer together. They had been bonded by sacrifice and suffering: 'Awed and humbled by the great catastrophe, and by the huge economic problems it had thrown into naked prominence, the women of the suffrage movement had learnt that social regeneration is a long and mighty work.'[74]

On Armistice Day, 11 November 1918, at 8 a.m., the message sent to the armies in the field with the news that hostilities would cease at 11 a.m. was tapped out by a woman, signaller Maude Onions (or to give her her full military title '807', Unit 3, WAAC, L Signals, BEF). She wrote poignantly of her unseen role at this great historic moment: 'In the little Signal Office at Boulogne nothing happened at eleven o'clock, nothing except a silence, and an involuntary glance at the clock. Outside, nothing happened. It was the first great silence of armistice.'

In a daze, Onions wandered down to the military cemetery where British soldiers were buried three deep and struggled through her tears to read the inscribed names of the dead. As she turned to leave, she tripped over a broken piece of wood on the ground which, upon inspection, she realised was the remains of a cross marking the grave of a German soldier. 'Cautiously, afraid of being seen, I stooped and placed some flowers at the foot of the broken cross. Somewhere, a woman was sorrowing.'[75]

4

Between the Wars

1918–39

On a foggy, overcast day in November 1918, Lilian Wyles found herself sitting alongside twenty-four other women in a long corridor at Scotland Yard, the headquarters of the Metropolitan Police on London's Victoria Embankment. All of them had experience of war work. One had driven a tram. Two had been to university. Wyles herself had nurtured an ambition to be a lawyer but abandoned it to work in a hospital once the war started, much to her father's disappointment.

The women had come to Scotland Yard because the Home Secretary, Sir Neville Macready, had agreed to trial a force of one hundred policewomen. He had done this on the condition that a) no, as he put it, 'vinegary spinsters' were given a role, and b) if the experiment failed, the force was immediately disbanded.

Wyles' feeling was that, while the government wanted the experiment to succeed, the Met themselves thought the idea of a female police force laughable, even grotesque. But they were slightly scared of the woman who had lobbied Macready so hard for the opportunity – one Mrs Feo Stanley, who reminded Wyles of a flashing blade, 'exquisite in workmanship but dangerous to engage'.[1] Wyles evidently impressed Mrs Stanley because she passed the interview.

The next step was six weeks of training at Peel House off Vauxhall Bridge Road – the Met's training school before Hendon Police College opened in 1934. Wyles and her peers passed out formally on 16 February 1919, with red ribbons tied round their arms to show they had received their quota of vaccinations. They were taken straight to Harrods to have their uniforms fitted: 'unspeakable apparel' including heavy Land Army-issue boots which left the women's feet covered in blisters and calluses. No make-up was permitted and hair had to be covered by a close-fitting helmet Wyles thought resembled an 'inverted soup plate'.[2]

Mrs Stanley requisitioned 35 Ixworth Place in South Kensington for use as a hostel for policewomen who were unmarried or otherwise lacked a home nearby – a worry being that if the policewomen were housed in ordinary hotels, the other guests might complain. (Ironically, 35 Ixworth Place is now a boutique hotel.) Notwithstanding its 'institution green' walls, Ixworth was comfortable and life there safe and settled, with a cook on hand to prepare meals for the women and fresh flowers in all the rooms.

Wyles was made a sergeant and given responsibility for the whole of central London and the East End. She was allocated five women to work with her – 'well-built, well-covered, a trifle severe of expression and wearing an I'll-stand-no-nonsense air', as she later remembered them.[3] But Wyles' male colleagues, when they weren't openly mocking the women, were obsessing about keeping them safe, not just from the 'criminal element' who might exploit their weaknesses but from members of the public to whom female police were an outrageous provocation. And so the women were made to patrol in pairs with two 'experienced' male policemen following them at a distance of six to ten yards. If they wanted to make an arrest, the women had to enlist the help of their male shadows as they weren't empowered to do it themselves. Understandably, this enraged Wyles:

Why a young man of nineteen or twenty, who had most likely come from a remote Cornish hamlet or from the bogs of Ireland, should have been considered as more suitable to hold the power of arrest than women who for the most part were London-bred and who had a considerable knowledge of the seamy side of life in the Metropolis, I could never understand. There it was! 'Women', quote the wise-acres of Whitehall, 'are so unpredictable, so impulsive.'[4]

Oddly, however, one woman *had* already been given power of arrest way back in August 1915: a former midwife called Edith Smith. Though never formally sworn in she was nevertheless made a police constable and lived in the police station at Grantham in Lincolnshire.

Grantham, with its two army bases, was a den of iniquity during the First World War. Smith's job was to enforce Regulation 40D, an anti-prostitution amendment to the Defence of the Realm Act, controversial among feminists because of its similarities to the woman-blaming Contagious Diseases Act which Josephine Butler had worked so hard to overturn. Smith drew up a blacklist of girls who behaved in an unseemly manner and she even acted as a spy for husbands who wanted their wives' conduct monitored while they were away fighting. The job must have been taxing: Smith lasted two years and, five years after she resigned, she died from an overdose of morphine.

Was Edith Smith the first policewoman? The picture is complicated by the existence of numerous unofficial, voluntary women's police patrols during the war. These were typically based at ports, railway stations and, as we saw in the last chapter, munitions factories, where their role, an extension of the 'rescue work' women had always performed, was to discourage public drunkenness and prostitution.

Lilian Wyles began her career as a member of Mrs Feo Stanley's 'women's patrols', whose success inspired her to lobby the Met. The best known of these patrols is probably the Women Police Volunteers (WPV), co-founded by the former suffragette Nina Boyle and the philanthropist Margaret Damer-Dawson. Edith Smith too had started off as a WPV member.

Boyle and Damer-Dawson parted company after Boyle refused to impose a curfew on women in Grantham, arguing that the curfews recommended under Regulation 40D punished women for their sexual activity under the guise of protecting men from temptation. Damer-Dawson, who had no such qualms, renamed the WPV the Women's Police Service (WPS) and continued to run it with her lover Mary Allen – another woman often called, inaccurately, 'the first policewoman' – long after it was supposed to have been disbanded at the end of the war.

To say tension existed between these rival groups is understating it. In her memoir *A Woman at Scotland Yard* (1952) Lilian Wyles is scathing about 'this organisation of women, calling themselves police' (i.e. the WPS) run by a 'woman of means' (Damer-Dawson):

> Without any authority they appeared on the streets in uniform, patrolling, and pulling up couples or girls who they felt deserved corrective advice … To this day there are many people who are still under the impression that Miss Damer-Dawson and Miss Mary Allen were the original senior officers of the Metropolitan Women Police … Such an impression is entirely erroneous.[5]

We have already met Mary Allen – at the end of my second chapter, staring at the camera with regal hauteur in one of Christina Broom's photographs. Her biographer Nina Boyd describes her, quite correctly, as 'a woman of whom it would be impossible for any liberal-minded reader to approve'.[6] Still, Allen is a fascinating figure because she embodies so many of the tensions that animated British culture between the wars. Her journey from left to right, from suffragette royalty to eccentric outcast, mirrors the journeys of Emmeline and Christabel Pankhurst, who by the end of the 1920s had abandoned the fight for gender equality in favour of, respectively, Conservative politics and evangelical Christianity.

Born in Cardiff in 1878, Mary Allen lived at home with her nine siblings until the age of thirty when she left after arguing about female suffrage with her father, the Chief Superintendent of the Great Western Railway. She joined the WSPU and proved herself a fearless militant. Imprisoned three times for public order offences, including smashing the windows of the Home Office, she was force-fed after going on hunger strike, an ordeal for which she was compensated in the form of a WSPU medal presented by another Emmeline, the activist Emmeline Pethick-Lawrence, in August 1909. Emmeline Pankhurst warned her not to risk imprisonment again, presumably because of the risk to her health. On 14 June 1913 she was chief marshal at the funeral of Emily Davison.

When Emmeline Pankhurst called a halt to militant suffragette activity in 1914, Allen joined Nina Boyle and Margaret Damer-Dawson's WPV. As she explains in the first of her three (!) volumes of autobiography, *The Pioneer Policewoman* (1925), the attraction of the police force to one-time suffragettes accustomed to public scuffles was clear and natural:

> If it did nothing else, this sharp discipline prepared them in
> the grimmest school of endurance for the urgent problems
> the war engendered, inculcating invaluable lessons in
> organisation, obedience, cheerfulness in adversity, fortitude and
> self-control.[7]

For Allen, these 'urgent problems' included so-called 'white slavery': the sex-trafficking of young white girls by non-Europeans – a real and serious issue, to be sure, but also the focus of considerable racist hysteria. Allen's other pressing concern was the morals of working-class women, especially those employed in munitions factories.

To be fair, managing sexual behaviour was a major headache for the police during the war. The combination of changing attitudes, young people leaving home for the first time and new opportunities for liaisons afforded by places like cinemas resulted in a spike in arrests for prostitution and sex-related public order offences. Lilian Wyles' book, published in the early 1950s, is as explicit as the era allowed her to be about the day-to-day reality of dealing with abused child 'prostitutes', who often had tuberculosis and horribly advanced gonorrhea. Much of her work in the early 1920s focused on the grooming of white girls by Lascar sailors in East End 'café' brothels.

Twenty-first century readers, alert to such things, can detect clear evidence of what we'd now call victim-blaming: in cases of sexual assault, Wyles writes, 'adult women are apt to exaggerate'.[8] But she also shows compassion and empathy, refusing to condemn girls from chaotic, broken homes who had come to London in search of off-duty troops who might pay them for sex: 'I would ask myself severely, had I been born and brought up in the same environment as these girls, would I have been any different from them?'[9] Persuaded that these girls were as entitled as anyone else to be treated with dignity, Wyles tried to ensure that any intimate examinations were performed by a female doctor – usually Hannah Billig, an East End-based doctor nicknamed 'the angel of Cable Street' who was formally hired by the Met as a medical officer in 1934.

For these girls Mary Allen seems to have felt hatred rather than compassion. To her, prostitutes fell into the same category as strikers, foreigners and communists. After the war, she and Margaret Damer-Dawson infuriated the official police (to the point where they arrested her for it in 1921) by continuing to wear their own 'uniform' of jackboots and military-style greatcoats and instructing people to call them 'Commandant'. When Damer-Dawson died suddenly in 1920, Allen inherited her fortune and the house they shared. Over the next two decades she travelled the world in uniform as an ambassador for British policewomen (despite not actually being one, as far as the police were concerned), all the while keeping crazy dossiers on people she suspected of running vice rings or being left-wing agitators.

On one such trip to Germany in January 1934, shortly after the Reichstag fire, she met the man who had become her hero: Adolf Hitler. He didn't disappoint her. '[His] hypnotic gestures, his passionate, forceful voice and his visionary eyes held me spell-bound,' she wrote.[10] Like her fellow ex-suffragettes Mary Richardson and Norah Elam, Allen joined Oswald Mosley's British Union of Fascists.

The ever-rightward march of her politics is obvious in her second volume of autobiography, *A Woman at the Cross Roads*, in which she praises dictatorships for keeping youngsters on the straight and narrow, forcing them 'to substitute for all the jargon of "self-expression" a disciplined control in pursuance of any strong presented national ideal'.[11]

While Allen was a tricky, unpleasant character with a mass of toxic hang-ups and prejudices, it's clear that she was also the victim of what we would now call out as homophobia and sexism. It was her sexuality and 'mannish' appearance as much as her authoritarian zeal that led Special Branch, in a report, to conclude that she was a 'crank ... trailing round in a ridiculous uniform'.

Post-war women had a steep, rocky path to tread, both person-ally and professionally. But if you were a lesbian, it was more like the North Face of the Eiger.

Between the wars, there were plenty of women who rejected traditional 'feminine' modes of dress and conduct. You only have to look at photographs to notice the difference between pre- and post-war. Short hair – like the Eton crop for example, or the bobbed 1920s 'flapper' look – and trousers were *de rigueur*, as influences from the American worlds of film and jazz travelled across the Atlantic.

Some of the early twentieth century's highest-achieving women were lesbian. Some, like Mary Allen and the novelist Radclyffe Hall, let their clothes do the talking, donning waistcoats, monocles and ties. Scientists and intellectuals of the time tried to make sense of it all. The sexologist Havelock Ellis characterised lesbians as 'congenital inverts'.

The hysteria around 'masculine' women reached a crescendo with Hall's trial for obscenity after the publication in 1928 of her novel *The Well of Loneliness*. This was the story of upper-class lesbian Stephen Catlin's doomed attempt to find happiness with a woman she meets while driving an ambulance during the First World War. Tame by almost any standard, *The Well of Loneliness* had received polite reviews and offended no one until it suddenly became the target of a vicious campaign by James Douglas, editor of the *Sunday Express*, who called the book 'a seductive and insidious piece of special pleading', concluding: 'I would rather give a healthy boy or a healthy girl a phial of prussic acid than this novel.'

Hall's publisher Jonathan Cape stopped publication at the Home Secretary's request, but secretly leased the rights to Pegasus, an English-language publisher in France. When these French copies started to appear in bookstores, the government acted quickly to suppress them. The resulting show trial got horribly personal, focusing on Hall's own relationship with her partner, the sculptor Una Troubridge.

Although other writers and artists loathed the idea of censorship and supported Hall in principle, the feeling in Bloomsbury circles was that *The Well of Loneliness* was regressive and unsophisticated, both technically and in its self-loathing attitude towards lesbian sexuality. Virginia Woolf, herself in a lesbian relationship with Vita Sackville-West, agreed to defend the novel in court but, to her evident relief, was never called upon to do so. 'Most of our friends are trying to evade the witness box; for reasons you may guess,' she wrote to her nephew Quentin Bell. 'But they generally put it down to the weak heart of a father, or a cousin who is about to have twins.'[12]

New, freer attitudes towards relationships and morality were emerging in tandem with new ways of thinking about human psychology. Sigmund Freud had coined the term 'psychoanalysis' in 1896 to describe his new talking cure for neurosis, hysteria and other mental ailments. By 1913, when Ernest Jones set up the London Psychoanalytical Society, Freud's theories about the workings of the unconscious mind were widely known and discussed in medical circles. But his most devoted British followers were women. Joan Riviere was one of his earliest English translators. Barbara Low enjoyed a big success in 1920 with her book *Psycho-Analysis: A Brief Account of the Freudian Theory* – intended, as she wrote, 'for those who are interested in this subject but cannot yet find time and opportunity to study at first hand the work of Freud and his followers, English and Continental'.[13]

In the interwar period his legacy would be developed by female analysts like Freud's own daughter Anna, who emigrated from Vienna to London with her ailing father in 1938, and Melanie Klein. The British Psychoanalytical Society (as the London Psychoanalytical Society was rechristened) was 40 per cent female by the 1930s.

The final chapter of Barbara Low's book points to a more liberal approach towards female sexuality, debating the dangers of sexual repression and recommending a social system which 'allows some satisfactory measure of freedom to the primitive instincts'.[14]

Of course, if you were a heterosexual man, this system already existed. Even within marriage, men who had affairs were spared the opprobrium that would be heaped on a woman doing the same. Some wives turned a blind eye to these extra-marital dalliances. When Frances Stevenson accompanied the prime minister David Lloyd George to the Paris Peace Conference in 1919, the other delegates assumed she was his secretary, which she was. But she had also been his lover since 1913. Lloyd George was already married, of course, but his wife Margaret remained obligingly in north Wales while Frances lived with him in Surrey. So great was Frances' involvement in Lloyd George's life that, as Martin Pugh puts it, 'in effect Lloyd George had two wives rather than one wife and a mistress'.[15] He eventually married Frances in October 1943, two years after Margaret's death.

H. G. Wells' second wife Jane tolerated the incessant affairs that were part of what he grandly called his 'modus vivendi'. (Jane wasn't even her real name, but one he had given her because he thought it sounded more wifely.) Outside the marriage Wells was attracted to strong, clever New Women like Amber Reeves, Elizabeth Von Arnim and Rebecca West, who were less inclined to do what he told them. West's real name was Cicely Fairfield: she had rechristened herself in honour of the free-thinking hero-ine of Ibsen's play *Rosmersholm*.

West called marriages 'gross, destructive, mutual raids on personality'. But was her part-time relationship with Wells, nursing their child in an isolated cottage by the sea while Wells lived it up in London as a Great Man of Letters, really the best she and other women could hope for? She mused on her status in letters.

> Pale Fabians would say that I was the Free Woman, and
> wanted to be the mother of the Superman, and the older school
> left over from the nineties might say I was his wife in the sight
> of god, and similar clichés.[16]

As Katie Roiphe points out in her fascinating book about married life in early twentieth-century literary circles, *Uncommon Arrangements* (2008), a new, more progressive type of marriage was evolving where there was 'a whole new power dynamic to contend with, as the wife was no longer necessarily subjugated to the husband's will'.[17] One such was Vera Brittain's 'semi-detached' transatlantic marriage to the political scientist George Catlin: he worked in the US as an academic while she maintained her writing career in Britain, neither able nor willing to be what Roiphe calls a 'faculty wife pouring tea'. The arrangement allowed Brittain to remain close to her best friend and former Oxford roommate Winifred Holtby, the feminist writer and author of *South Riding*, who lived with Brittain and her two children, John and Shirley. Contrary to rumour at the time, the relationship seems not to have been a sexual one.

In 1929, three years before Aldous Huxley wrote the sci-fi classic *Brave New World*, Brittain published a curious satirical pamphlet, *Halcyon, or the Future of Monogamy*, imagining how early twentieth-century marriage and sexual relationships would look to a twenty-first-century historian. Brittain's fictional historian, Minerva Huxterwin, looks back on imaginary developments as the introduction in 1971 of ectogenesis (developing embryos outside the uterus), the 1969 Trial Marriages Act and the 1974 State Guardianship of Children Act – giving the state formal guardianship of children alongside parents. These have, Huxterwin tells us, resulted in an 'increasing number of happy monogamous marriages' rather than the 'dark confusion which prevailed little more than a hundred years ago'.[18]

Were interwar marriages darkly confused? If you weren't Vanessa Bell or H. G. Wells conducting a grand bohemian experiment in living, your marriage may have been as blighted by ignorance about sex and fear of unwanted pregnancy as in days gone by. But something was changing, hinted at by the decline in the birth rate and the trend away from large Victorian families: Deirdre Beddoe points out that only 20 per cent of marriages in Britain in 1860 resulted in two children or fewer; whereas by 1925 that figure was 67 per cent.[19]

Not until the advent of the pill in the 1960s would women achieve the full sexual emancipation they sought. But the interwar period saw greater openness about the subject, and a new realisation among women – especially working-class women – that they weren't fated to have large families as their mothers and grandmothers had been. Sex was not just about procreation: it could be had for the sheer fun of it.

Feminist activist Dora Russell, whose marriage to philosopher and mathematician Bertrand was famously open, must have read Barbara Low's potted Freud before she wrote in 1927 that, 'Sex-love is the most intense instinctive pleasure known to men and women, and starvation or thwarting of this instinct causes more acute unhappiness than poverty, disease or ignorance.'[20] That's saying something. What's more, the human bond forged through sex 'would be worth ten million platforms blaring pacifism'.[21]

Naomi Mitchison – the Scottish writer whose taboo-busting novel *We Have Been Warned* (1935) was initially rejected by publishers nervous about its explicit content – had multiple sexual partners on the go, but also a happy, committed marriage. For her, sex was always 'a compromise between what we need and what is allowed us by modern conditions'.[22]

Today, we associate the name Marie Stopes with birth control. But her calling card was the flowery sex manual *Married Love*. When it was published in 1918, it was a *succès de scandale*, which, as Stopes herself put it, 'made Victorian husbands gasp'.

Born in Edinburgh in 1880, Stopes was a botanist by training and continued her important research into the constitution of coal even as she was engulfed by her fame as a writer and activist. In 1907 she had spent eighteen months in Japan at the Imperial University in Tokyo followed by nearly five months in America and Canada between December 1910 and April 1911 working on a geological survey. She had been Lecturer in Paleobotany at both University College London and the University of Manchester – Manchester's first female academic, no less – before the success of *Married Love* steered her onto a different course.

On the face of it Stopes was a well-travelled woman of the world. But in other ways she was naive and closed-off, a victim of Victorian women's ignorance about sex. Incredibly, given its subject matter, she was still a virgin when she wrote *Married Love*. Her first husband Reginald Ruggles Gates, whom she had met in America, was impotent; their marriage was annulled in 1914. She was frank about her inexperience, writing, 'In my first marriage I paid such a terrible price for sex-ignorance that I feel that knowledge gained at such a cost should be placed at the service of humanity.'[23]

So it was that, hiding in libraries or discreet corners of their homes, couples learned from Stopes the 'scientific' Latin names for their private parts; read furtively about the importance of a man and woman – sorry, *husband and wife* – absorbing each other's secretions (one of Stopes' pet theories); wondered at how the vagaries of the 'moon-month' affected a woman's sexual desire; and puzzled over what Stopes called 'the half swooning sense of flux which overtakes the spirit in that eternal moment as the apex of rapture sweeps into its flaming tides the whole essence of the man and woman, and as it were, the heat of the contact vapourises their consciousness so that it fills the whole of cosmic space'.[24] An orgasm, presumably.

Stopes' postbag revealed just how few women were experiencing anything remotely cosmic. One problem, she explained, was that men had grown accustomed to women being passive. Another was the tendency to view women who liked sex as little more than prostitutes, which meant 'most women would rather die than own that they do at times feel a physical yearning indescribable, but as profound as hunger for food'.[25]

Married Love has male ignorance in its sights as well. Too many men barely understood that their wives possessed a sex drive, let alone the mysteries of menstruation (her 'rhythmic sex-tide'). Addressing men who have experience of 'bought "love"', the book urges caution and tenderness when it comes to taking their wives' virginity:

When girls so brought up are married it is a rape for the
husband to insist on his 'marital rights' at once. It will be
difficult or impossible for such a bride ever after to experience
the joys of sex-union, for such a beginning must imprint upon
her consciousness the view that the man's animal nature
dominates him.[26]

Stopes' interest in birth control doesn't show up in her writing
in a major way until her second book, *Wise Parenthood* (1918). By
the 1920s contraception was readily available. Rubber condoms,
made possible by the invention of vulcanisation – a process
which improves rubber's strength and elasticity – had been
introduced as far back as the 1870s, followed in the 1880s by
soluble pessaries and the cervical cap. Generally, though, if
couples practised anything at all it was abstinence or *coitus
interruptus*, with the grim back-up of a dangerous, illegal
abortion if that failed.

But the zeal Stopes brought to championing birth control for
the poor had a less benign motive. Her fascination with the
'science' of eugenics had been simmering since at least 1915 when
she first met Margaret Sanger, the American birth control activist
and sex educator who had fled to Britain after the banning of her
book *Family Limitation* and her subsequent prosecution. Sanger
believed one of the functions of contraception was to 'assist the
race toward the elimination of the unfit'.[27] Stopes found herself
concurring heartily.

In her 1920 book *Radiant Motherhood* Stopes rails against a
society that 'allows the diseased, the racially negligent, the thrift-
less, the careless, the feeble-minded, the very lowest and worst
members of the community, to produce innumerable tens of
thousands of stunted, warped and inferior infants'.[28] This sort of
talk horrifies us now. And if anything, Stopes' views on eugenics
became more extreme as she grew older. When her much-loved
only son married a woman who wore glasses, she cut him out of

her will, outraged that he would consider having children with someone who was, as she saw it, genetically faulty.

Her biographer, Ruth Hall, points out that Stopes' beliefs need to be understood in context. As a scientist Stopes was 'steeped in Darwin, whose theory of natural selection was widely interpreted to mean that if the fittest survived, they deserved to do so'.[29] Eugenic ideas were commonplace between the wars, endorsed by reputable figures like George Bernard Shaw and John Maynard Keynes, before Nazism showed the logical conclusion of such thinking. Vera Brittain's fictional future-dwelling Minerva Huxterwin tells us that 'the general standard of intelligence [in Britain] rose rapidly after the sterilisation of the unfit became law in 1981'.[30] Shameful as it sounds to us now, many among Britain's interwar intelligentsia would have warmly applauded.

On 17 March 1921, in the face of significant opposition from the Catholic church, Stopes and her second husband Humphrey Roe opened the Mothers' Clinic at 61 Marlborough Road in Holloway, north London. Here she dispensed free advice and other kinds of help to all sorts of women, fitting her own brand of cervical cap, a modified version of a French design which she trademarked the 'Prorace'. The clinic was a huge success and over the next few years many others appeared, some run by other birth-control activist groups such as the Malthusian League.

The point of the Holloway clinic, as Stopes herself admitted, was not just the altruistic promotion of sexual happiness and alleviation of distress from unwanted pregnancies, but stopping 'reckless breeding from the C3 [i.e. working-class] end' of society. It was fortunate that other campaigners for contraception, especially those on the feminist left like Naomi Mitchison, Dora Russell and Stella Browne, were around to offer a more enlightened perspective.

Bisexual Stella Browne was a fierce critic of marriage and, like Mitchison and Russell, a champion of free love. She wrote for the radical feminist journal *The Freewoman*, a publication the moderate

Millicent Garrett Fawcett thought so objectionable she is supposed to have torn up its inaugural issue into small pieces. The charismatic Marie Stopes was no shrinking violet. But Browne went where Stopes feared to tread – into the murky moral waters of abortion, to which Stopes was fiercely opposed as she believed the service she provided at her clinics removed the need for it.

Arguing that women should have control over their own bodies, Browne co-founded the Abortion Law Reform Association (ALRA) and spent much of her life campaigning for legalised safe abortion. As she made clear, she had no desire to have children herself:

> I have no experience of maternity, nor of the desire for
> maternity, which is generally attributed to women … As it is,
> many women have no maternal longings at all, and they should
> never become mothers.[31]

This was a daring admission at a time when women were being encouraged to breed for Britain. Rejecting maternity was seen by many as unpatriotic.

Browne's most famous moment came in 1937, when she was giving evidence to the British government's Interdepartmental Committee on Abortion. When asked how she, as an unmarried woman, knew that abortion was not necessarily fatal or injurious to the mother's health, she replied casually that it was because she had had one herself.

In the early days of their marriage Naomi and Dick Mitchison used Stopes' *Married Love* as a manual but still never much enjoyed their sex life. So they took other partners and generally experimented, becoming renowned for the racy parties they threw at their Hammersmith house. One day a friend asked Naomi to tie him up and beat him, which she did, 'making fierce faces and quite enjoying it myself but not, I expect, hurting him as much as he might have preferred'.[32] One of Dick's lovers, Margery Spring

Rice, worked at a birth control clinic in North Kensington and through her Mitchison became involved, 'doing interviews with working-class women, raising funds and even acting as a test subject for birth-control methods'.[33]

Dora Russell was roused to action by the arrest in 1923 of the anarchists Rose Witcop and Guy Aldred for distributing one of Margaret Sanger's pamphlets. 'I could not see why information which a middle-class woman could get from her doctor should be withheld from a poorer woman who might need it far more,' Russell wrote.[34] With Browne and another activist, Janet Chance, she formed the New Generation League to support the pair's legal battle. Russell co-led the Workers' Birth Control Group alongside Browne and the Labour MP Dorothy Jewson, touring the country to spread her message to Labour Party-affiliated women's groups.

She argued that childbearing was, in its own way, as arduous and potentially fatal as coal-mining. So why were women not safeguarded as men were? In 1925 she visited Motherwell in Scotland and wrote that people were '*just ripe* for education about sex … The women blush and are terrified when they hear me say things that they dare not say themselves.'[35]

But her lack of success in attracting Labour's support infuriated her. John Wheatley, Minister for Health in the 1924 Labour government, was a Catholic, and the party was worried about alienating the Catholic Church. 'I hate the Labour Party,' she wrote to Bertrand, 'and men are quite disgusting.'[36]

Eventually, after Labour's modest, heavily qualified victory at the 1929 election – the so-called 'flapper election', as it was the first in which all women over the age of twenty-one could vote – there was a small but significant shift. The Ministry of Health published Memorandum 153/MCW, permitting birth control information to be given to married women by local clinics – but only if there were fears that further pregnancies might damage a woman's health.

Dora Russell is fascinating because of the way she combined radical feminism, in the form of a deep commitment to female sexual liberation, with a love of motherhood. It should, she thought, be possible to sustain multiple sexual relationships within a marriage – as long as both parties were committed to bringing up any children. Both she and Bertrand found this harder in practice than in theory.

For Dora there was no contradiction between loving children and being pro-contraception because 'it is those who love children and care most satisfactorily for their own, who are the strongest and most eloquent advocates of birth control'.[37] Sex and motherhood were intertwined because of the way both made the female body a political space. Her later peace activism – and that of other pacifist feminists such as Helena Swanwick – sprung from the same source: surely women, who gave and nurtured life, were best placed to stop wars?

Dora's political awakening came early, watching her mother have to defend her household spending to her father. But that father was no Victorian villain. He was Sir Frederick Black, a Liberal civil servant committed to female education. Dora was close to him and always remembered standing beside him in Trafalgar Square, aged twelve, listening to the results of the 1906 general election roll in. At Girton College, Cambridge she refined her ideas linking socialism with sexual libertarianism, coming away with a First in Modern Languages.

In 1916, Dora was twenty-two and studying eighteenth-century French literature in London when, one weekend, on a walking trip with friends, she met Bertrand Russell. He asked her what she most desired and was surprised when she replied that it was to marry and have children. Russell was already married, though he and his wife Alys had lived apart since 1911; he had had affairs with numerous women including Ottoline Morrell and the actress and pacifist Constance Malleson. Bertrand and Dora stayed in touch and several years later, at Lulworth in Dorset, became lovers. When they married in September 1921 – Bertrand and Alys had finally divorced earlier in the year – it was his idea; Dora likened it to slavery, though they did not vow to be monogamous. He was forty-nine and she twenty-seven.

Dora keenly felt the pessimism of the years between the wars. Britain was struggling with poverty, unemployment and a sense of what the historian Richard Overy has called 'morbid decline'. Fabian Society lectures and summer schools in the 1920s and 1930s – asking gloomily 'Is Civilisation Decaying?' or 'Capitalism in Dissolution: What Next?'[38] – reflected the prevailing mood, not simply left-wing rhetoric.

Dora absorbed it all, writing in her 1927 personal manifesto *The Right to be Happy*: 'The world as we know it is a hideous nightmare. Human beings have made it, and therefore human beings need to be changed.'[39]

The best way to change them, she decided, was education.

In September 1927 Dora and Bertrand opened their own school, Beacon Hill – partly because they couldn't bring themselves to send their own children to one which already existed. Beacon Hill was one of a number of fee-paying progressive schools founded in the 1920s. Others included Alexander Sutherland Neill's famous Summerhill and Dartington Hall near Totnes in Devon, the experiment of the American philanthropist Dorothy Whitney and her English second husband Leonard Elmhirst. Like the surge in support for communism around this time, especially among intellectuals, these schools were the product of optimistic, utopian thinking and a craving for escape from the gloom of the present.

Beacon Hill's rural location was deliberately Edenic: Petersfield on the South Downs, amid acres of woods and valleys and what the Russells' daughter Kate would remember as 'deer and rabbits and stoats and weasels and huge yew trees we could jump into from higher trees and absolutely magnificent beech trees for climbing'.[40] Its founding principle was, Dora wrote, a sense of each child as a 'unique individual who belongs, not to the State, or even to his parents, but first of all to himself'.[41] According to its prospectus the school aimed to produce 'not listless intellectuals, but young men and women filled with constructive hopefulness'. Dora elaborated on its rules, or rather anti-rules, in a later memoir, *The Tamarisk Tree*:

> There was to be no corporal punishment; the children were free to come into the classroom and work and learn, or not to do so … [There] should be no suggestion that naked bodies, or any part of the body, were obscene or 'dirty'. This meant not scolding for masturbation; it also meant freedom to run around without clothes when the children found it warm enough … [There] was complete freedom of speech, no topic of discussion being ruled out [which] also meant that the grown-ups were not treated with exaggerated respect …[42]

Beacon Hill was popular among the intelligentsia. Sylvia Pankhurst, whose son Richard went there, rented a cottage in the grounds while she was writing her history of the suffragette movement. But as Bertrand admitted, 'The parents who were most inclined to try new methods were those who had difficulties with their children.'[43] The Rousseau-esque experiment came close to failing when Beacon Hill's substantial intake of problem children, combined with the lack of discipline, produced incidents such as the one where two children tried to incinerate another child's pet rabbits on a bonfire.[44] Dora taught French and German, but Bertrand found it impossible to undertake much teaching as he was too busy with his own writing and lecturing, work he was obliged to do to keep the school afloat, as many parents neglected to pay the fees.

In 1930, as Bertrand and Dora's marriage began to collapse under the pressure of their extramarital relationships, Bertrand lost interest in Beacon Hill and withdrew their children from it, sending them to Dartington Hall instead. But Dora kept it going, though it moved several times and struggled financially well before she was forced to close it in 1943.

———————

A commonly held view is that women – correction: *some* women – winning the vote in 1918 transformed everything; that afterwards their lot improved: freedoms previously denied them fell within their grasp, doors formerly closed swung open. Realising how lucky they were, women obligingly gave up their shouty feminism and focused on the important business of repopulating Britain after a war that had wiped out a generation of men.

It's true that the Representation of the People Act was a great victory. And although the full enfranchisement of women on the same terms as men did not come about until 1928, women benefited from masses of other legislation at around this time. The Sex Disqualification (Removal) Act (1919) opened up the professions to women who had been prevented from working as teachers or magistrates once they'd got married. The civil service marriage bar continued until 1946, however. The 1922 Infanticide Act meant women who killed their infant children could no longer be charged with murder – an early recognition of what we now call post-partum psychosis. In 1923 women were granted divorce on the same grounds as men; in 1925 equal guardianship of children. Also in 1925, pensions were paid to widows.

One of the most crucial pieces of legislation was the Eligibility of Women Act (1918) which allowed women to become MPs. Their first opportunity to stand was the December 1918 election, which resulted in a landslide victory for Lloyd George's coalition government. Seven women candidates stood, of whom, as we saw in the last chapter, only Sinn Fein's Constance Markievicz was successful.

The first woman actually to take her seat was Nancy Astor, who became Tory MP for her husband Waldorf's constituency of

Plymouth Sutton when he moved to the House of Lords after his father's death, necessitating a by-election on 28 November 1919. The daughter of an American railway developer, Astor had an unhappy first marriage and moved to England the year after her divorce in 1903, marrying Waldorf in 1906.

Astor loved glitter and publicity. Her campaign was compared to a circus, while her brilliance at putting down hecklers soon became legendary. 'How many toes has a pig?' she was once asked at a meeting. 'Take your shoes off and count them,' she quipped. When asked, on the campaign trail, why she wasn't at home looking after her (five) children, she replied: 'I feel someone ought to be looking after the more unfortunate children. My children are among the fortunate ones.' The kind of abuse hurled at today's female MPs would have come as no surprise to Astor.

Her arrival in Parliament after winning a majority of 5,203 votes was marked by a large delivery of hats from milliners seeking free advertising. But there was nowhere at Westminster to store them: 'Commons Boudoir for Women MP's Hat Problem Still Unsolved' declared the *Daily Express*.[45]

To call Astor's life gilded understates her wealth. She divided her time between her country house Cliveden, a town house in St James' Square and an array of other residences including an estate in the Hebrides. Her head gardener at Cliveden made a fresh buttonhole for her each day which, if she was in London, he would send to her by post. But as the historian Brian Harrison makes clear, she had the gift of empathy and a bunch of good intentions, seeing women as 'the reconciler within both nation and family'.[46] She was what we would nowadays call a social liberal, fighting for causes such as widows' pensions and the raising of the age of consent. She enlisted the help of former suffrage activist Ray Strachey to brief her on debates that were raging on the more radical, intellectual fringes of the movement. A pragmatic feminist who favoured what she called 'real old-fashioned, courageous, sensible, solid, cup-of-tea women', Astor was hugely popular in her constituency, remaining MP for Plymouth until she retired in 1945.

By 1929, the year Margaret Bondfield became the first female cabinet member, there were fourteen women in the Commons. In 1931, there was just one more, despite the fact that the percentage of women in the electorate rose from 39.6 in 1918 to 52.9 in 1931.[47]

The Women's Election Committee, formed in 1920 to promote female candidates, did its best, but the House of Commons remained a male bastion, a gentlemen's club. Within Westminster, men and women inhabited different worlds. Women had their own members' room, and later a dressing room. That's largely where they stayed, away from the drinking, dining and smoking areas where men congregated. But if this meant they missed out on important debate – not to mention gossip – they forged valuable friendships which transcended party divisions. Nancy Astor and the Labour MP Ellen Wilkinson, for example, parried with each other in the debating chamber but they were good friends outside.

As the late Labour MP Jo Cox might have observed, women parliamentarians had more in common than that which divided them. And how they needed that solidarity. The jibes thrown at them – about their health, their constitutions, their children, their husbands – were grossly unfair.

And as Brian Harrison puts it, they were burdened with the duty of 'representing a sex as well as a constituency'.[48] 'As I am the only woman Member of my party in the House, I must say something on this head [topic],' said the Labour MP Ellen Wilkinson during a debate on unemployment on 29 June 1925.

Women MPs tended not to contribute to debates about foreign and defence policy, subjects dominated by men. But they brought to the House a new frankness on social welfare topics. The independent MP Eleanor Rathbone and the Duchess of Atholl (Katherine Stewart-Murray, Scottish Unionist MP for Kinross and West Perthshire) spoke freely in the late 1920s about the horrific practice of female genital mutilation in Kenya which had just started to come to light. Those foresighted MPs might be surprised to learn that nearly a century passed before Kenya got round to banning FGM.

But what of the women the handful of new MPs represented? Sadly, many who had grasped the opportunity for paid employment during the war were either made redundant or intimidated into resigning. In November 1918, six thousand women who had been sacked from Woolwich Arsenal demonstrated at the House of Commons. 'The women formed up in procession with many large and small banners,' reported *The Times*, admitting: 'They did not look in the least like the expensively gowned, highly paid munitions worker of whom so much has been heard, but rather represented the woman worker who is the permanent industrial product.'[49]

In January 1920, seven hundred female clerks at the War Office returned from their Christmas holidays to find that their services were no longer required. When their union complained, Lloyd George replied that 'anybody who places before women the prospect of absolute equality is doing something which is inconsistent with the nature of things'.[50]

Working-class women were 'encouraged' to go back into domestic service – if they didn't, they were told, their benefits would be withheld. Meanwhile, middle-class women's entry into the professions 'proceeded at a snail's pace', says historian Deirdre Beddoe, 'and entry was only the first hurdle: once "in" there were problems of promotion and pay'.[51]

In one profession, the law, women had to be sneaky or downright pushy to get a foot in the door. In 1875, despite having no formal qualifications, Eliza Orme set herself up as a consultant in an office in Chancery Lane. In 1903, Bertha Cave, a butler's daughter, applied to join Gray's Inn – one of the Inns of Court, the professional associations for barristers and judges. When she was rejected she appealed, arguing that other countries had female lawyers, so why not Britain? 'I think we are all of the opinion that the appeal must be dismissed,' declared the Lord Chancellor, Lord Halsbury, arguing there was no precedent: there had never been a female lawyer, therefore there could never be one. The following year, one Christabel Pankhurst appealed to Lincoln's Inn to be let in as a student. Her request too was refused.

The first woman to be called to the bar was Dr Ivy Williams in 1922. But she went into teaching, so the first woman who actually practised as a barrister was Helena Normanton, a feminist who had been a member of the WSPU offshoot the Women's Freedom League. Forty by the time she was called to the bar, also in 1922, Normanton had already enjoyed a successful career as a teacher.

Her decision to switch careers had its roots in family tragedy. When she was four, Helena's piano-maker father had been found dead, lying on a west London railway line with a broken neck. A verdict of accidental death was recorded, but it seems likely that he took his own life: he and Helena's mother had recently separated. Her childhood was chaotic, itinerant, dominated by financial worries and the fear that her mother might lose custody of Helena and her sister. One day, when she was twelve, she accompanied her mother to a solicitor and was horrified by his patronising manner when she failed to understand some legal point. 'I did not like to see my mother nonplussed in that way,' Helena wrote in 1932, 'and I still do not like to see women getting the worst end of any deal for lack of a little elementary legal knowledge which is the most common form among men.'[52]

Her father's death brought home to Helena even as a child that the concept of 'male protection', enshrined in law through the doctrine of coverture, was a nonsense. Likewise, the incident with the patronising solicitor was classic mansplaining – enjoying the sound of his own voice rather than listening and empathising. When women got divorced, Normanton reflected, they had difficulty getting a male lawyer to understand their concerns.

Normanton went on to have a distinguished career, remaining in practice until she was sixty-eight. A lucrative sideline in journalism saw her writing on various legal topics for magazines like the *Pall Mall Gazette* and *Woman*. But she was never as successful as she should have been – she never became a judge, though she did make King's Counsel in 1949 alongside fellow pioneer Rose Heilbron – and on several occasions was accused of 'self-advertising' and subjected to spurious disciplinary inquiries after giving interviews about being a female barrister.[53]

By 1926 there were seventy-seven women barristers.[54] But the difficulty and expense of getting articles remained a constant problem and by 1930 there were still only 2,000 women out of 23,000 Justices of the Peace in England and Wales.[55] Women found it harder to get briefs than men as they weren't part of the same social networks. Lack of cases meant Enid Rosser, one of Helena's contemporaries, had to leave the Bar after her father died and she could no longer count on his financial support.

In teaching, nursing and the civil service, women still had to stop work once they got married, though resistance to the so-called 'marriage bar' was growing. In 1921, St Pancras Borough Council dismissed an assistant medical officer, Dr Gladys Miall-Smith when she got married. The Women's Freedom League organised a demonstration, while the *Woman's Leader* magazine thought marriage only increased Dr Miall-Smith's qualification for the job, because so much of her work involved infant welfare. The *Lancet* protested to the Ministry of Health, saying that 'in view of the special qualification and capability of Dr Miall-Smith, and the present shortage of women medical officers trained in this work, the Borough Council would be well advised to retain her services provisionally if their rules permitted'.[56] But the Council dug its heels in. Undeterred, Dr Miall-Smith moved to Welwyn Garden City where she ran an award-winning baby clinic.

The upshot was that most of the women who achieved professional prominence at this time were either lesbians or proud, self-declared spinsters like teacher Sarah Burton in Winifred Holtby's novel *South Riding*. 'I was born to be a spinster and, by God, I'm going to spin,' she tells herself.[57]

Reading about between-the-wars career women sometimes brings you up short. The intervening years fall away and you feel that you could yourself be in their shoes, being patronised and undermined.

While organising receptions where MPs might meet high-profile women, Nancy Astor's political secretary Hilda Matheson met Sir John Reith, head of the BBC. Reith recognised how well-connected she was, and how accomplished a networker, and hired her as the BBC's first Director of Talks. Matheson came into her own after 1928, when a ban on 'controversy' in broadcasting was lifted, and she was free to persuade the likes of H. G. Wells, Lloyd George and her lover Vita Sackville-West to take part in radio debates and discussions.

Notwithstanding her competence and declared loathing of 'the need for furtiveness and secrecy' about her sexuality,[58] Matheson's relationship with the prudish, autocratic Reith soon deteriorated. A typical Reith tactic was to accuse her of being partisan whenever she covered a topic he disapproved of, for example modern art. Eventually the arguments ground her down. 'They [Reith and his Director of Programmes Roger Eckersley] are always so damned ready to say to any *woman* who disagrees with them that it is unreasonable and shows a lack of balance,' she wrote to Sackville-West. 'I do honestly think that … afterwards when Roger began to say a) that they highly valued my work but b) that I was getting a name for unreasonable truculence I … got a choke in my throat which made me so angry and humiliated I couldn't bear it.'[59] She resigned in December 1931 and went to work for Lord Hailey running the Africa Survey, a blueprint for colonial reform in Sub-Saharan Africa. She died at fifty-two of Graves' disease, an auto-immune disorder, in October 1940.

It must have been tempting for women to conclude that it was easier, if you could afford it, to stay at home than face the hurdles of the workplace. Propaganda to encourage women to do just that arrived in the form of British women's magazines like *Peg's Paper*, launched in 1919, and American imports like *Good Housekeeping*.

The UK version of *Good Housekeeping* appeared in 1922 and was edited by Notting Hill-born Alice Head, a former North London Collegiate girl who had worked as a typist at *Country Life* then as a sub-editor on the venerable Victorian title *Woman At Home*. *Good Housekeeping*'s ultimate owner, the American press baron William Randolph Hearst, was so impressed with Head when he met her on a visit to London that he put her in charge of European operations, on such a large salary that she was reputed to be the best-paid woman in Europe.

Head's job involved sourcing antiques and property for Hearst, including St Donat's Castle in Wales, which he bought after seeing it advertised in *Country Life*. Head would typically spend two months of the year in America, staying at Hearst Castle 'for weeks and weeks' at a time, as she explained to the journalist Sue MacGregor in 1976: 'Marion [Davies, the actress and Hearst's lover] was there and they had lots of film people there ... producers as well as actors and actresses. It was all very entertaining.'[60]

When Margaret Lane launched *Woman* in 1937 she was obliged to defend herself against the charge that its politics were regressive and anti-feminist: 'We are trying to do something which is as difficult, in its way, as the things which they [i.e. old feminists] achieved,' she explained. 'We are trying to blend our old world with the new ... Less aggressive feminists than independently feminine. It is a difficult balance to strike.'[61]

Women who had campaigned together for the vote no longer seemed to be able to agree on anything. The Pankhursts' WSPU withered to nothing. Millicent Fawcett's NUWSS changed its name to the National Union of Societies for Equal Citizenship (NUSEC) in 1918. Eleanor Rathbone replaced Fawcett as president in the following year but alienated old NUWSS hands such as Ray Strachey who had left in 1931 to work for Nancy Astor.

Part of this was a reaction against Edwardian feminism; which seemed, to younger women, to have focused on the vote and equality at the expense of the way most women (certainly working-class women) actually lived – as wives and mothers reliant on a male wage: a 'family wage', as the unions thought of it.

A split emerged between 'old feminists' like Lady Rhondda – whose *Time and Tide* magazine featured stalwarts like Rebecca West and Virginia Woolf – and 'new feminists' such as Dora Russell, Mary Stocks and Eleanor Rathbone. The new breed of equality campaigners championed birth control, 'family allowances' paid to the mother and protective laws to exclude women from jobs involving long hours, heavy lifting or exposure to substances such as lead paint. 'Old feminists' thought such legislation simply gave employers another excuse not to employ women, and that both men *and* women should be protected from dangerous industrial practices.

For such an important figure, Eleanor Rathbone is surprisingly little-known these days, possibly because her forte was lobbying and alliance-building – what her biographer Susan Pedersen calls 'work ... too painstaking and tedious to draw the public eye'.[62] Her legacy is hard to untangle for modern feminists. The historian Martin Pugh calls her work 'a bold and realistic attempt to work with social change and, in effect, to accept that most women aspired to marriage and motherhood'.[63] It's probably fairer to say she was trying to help the women who didn't have the luxury of money or status to 'aspire' to anything beyond marriage and motherhood and who were now struggling horribly – 'the sweated woman worker, the unhappily married wife, and the poor law widow', as Rathbone put it.

Born into a wealthy, liberal, Liverpudlian shipping family, Rathbone was a former suffragette who had also been the first woman on Liverpool's City Council. With her booming voice and old-fashioned manner, she was a strong character with a formidable work ethic. She often had to be reminded to eat and was impatient with what she saw as others' weaknesses – such as a desire to take holidays.

Women's problems were, she thought, too often owned by men – seen through their eyes and discussed in their language. Rathbone thought women should be able to seize control of their own lives. And that didn't mean women having to man-up. 'The more I see of some men, especially politicians, the less I want women to adopt their methods and standards of values.'[64] It's an argument that resonates from the workplace to Westminster today.

Her sense that families could not live on the wages brought home by men alone came from studying labour trends in Liverpool's docks. 'After all,' she wrote, 'the rearing of families is not a sort of masculine hobby, like tobacco smoking or pigeon flying,' so why would you employ the 'clumsy device of paying male wage-earners more than women'?[65]

Her idea was that mothers should be paid a 'family allowance' which would give them both more control over the household budget and, outside the family, a boost in status and confidence. In 1924 she set out her views in a book called *The Disinherited Family*: 'Nothing,' she argued, 'can justify the subordination of one group of producers – the mothers – to the rest, and their deprivation of a share of their own in the wealth of a community which depends on them for its very existence.'[66]

At first the idea was rejected by all three parties. But later, when she became an independent MP in 1929, Rathbone took it to the Fabian economist William Beveridge, chief architect of what became the Welfare State. The Family Allowance Act was finally implemented in 1945, though Rathbone was furious when, initially, plans were made to pay it to the father – a mistake overturned by a Commons vote after intensive lobbying by Rathbone and her supporters.

The Welfare State was still a twinkle in Beveridge's eye, but one moment crystallised contemporary thinking about the lot of the working man (and woman). The Jarrow Crusade, which began on 5 October 1936, caught the imagination in no small part because of the dynamism of the town's diminutive Labour MP, Ellen Wilkinson.

Jarrow on Tyneside had always been a shipbuilding town, but the closure of its shipyard in 1933 – a casualty of the economic slump – had a devastating effect. Visiting it for his book *English Journey* (1933), J. B. Priestley thought Jarrow looked as if it had entered a 'perpetual penniless bleak Sabbath'. It had.

As part of a campaign to win back a steelworks which had been promised to the area then snatched away, two hundred men carried a petition down to London in an oak box, pausing en route to be fêted and fed by local industrialists and politicians. Ordinary members of the public donated boots and clean clothes and food.

There had been other hunger marches, but one of the reasons the Jarrow March lodged in the public consciousness was because of the energy and charisma of 'Red' Ellen Wilkinson, a former communist who had entered Parliament in 1924 at thirty-two and caused a stir with her bright clothes and shingled hair. Like Priestley, Wilkinson was haunted by Jarrow's gloomy stagnancy and the apparent hopelessness of its inhabitants' predicament: 'There was no work,' she wrote in her powerful book about the march, *The Town That was Murdered*. 'No one had a job except a few railwaymen, the workers in the co-operative stores, a few workmen who went out of the town.'

Wilkinson accompanied the marchers most of the way and served as their media spokesperson. When they finally reached Hyde Park, the crowd waiting to greet them was, at around three thousand, smaller than anticipated and it became clear that the marchers' hoped-for meeting with senior government figures wasn't going to happen. But Wilkinson gave a barnstorming performance, weeping in the Commons as she read out the petition and declaring that 'Jarrow as a town has been murdered ... I do not wonder that the cabinet does not want to see us. It does not want anyone to tell the truth about these black areas in the North, in Scotland and in South Wales that have been left to rot.' Wilkinson ended up as Minister of Education in Attlee's government – the second female cabinet minister.

The Jarrow marchers walked almost three hundred miles to London. The very same year, some of the country's young idealists were contemplating an even longer and more perilous journey.

The Spanish Civil War erupted in July 1936 after Spain's elected Republican government was challenged by conservative and Nationalist forces such as the army, landowners and the Catholic Church. The British government preferred not to intervene, but for passionate young Brits, many of whom volunteered to fight with the communist-run International Brigades, it became a rehearsal for conflicts to come. It appeared straightforward, though it was anything but: a clash between fascists and communists with – for some – lashings of radical chic.

Jessica 'Decca' Mitford, sister of fascists Unity and Diana and novelist Nancy, ran off to Spain with her communist lover Esmond Romilly, who had already been out to fight on the Madrid front. She had become obsessed with looking at pictures of 'Spanish guerrilla women fighters in the weekly illustrated papers' and selected as her war outfit 'a brown corduroy ski suit with a military-looking jacket and plenty of pockets'.[67] The novelist Sylvia Townsend Warner and her lover Valentine Ackland worked with a Red Cross unit in Barcelona for three weeks in September 1936. Warner called it 'the nearest thing I shall ever see to the early days of [the] USSR'.[68]

Many ordinary British women volunteered too. The first British volunteer to die was a woman – middle-class artist Felicia Browne, who had studied at the Slade. A communist who was

being monitored by Special Branch, she was in Barcelona sketching athletes at the People's Olympiad when she decided to enlist.
She was shot in August while taking part in a raid on a munitions
train.

Eleanor Rathbone – who, as vice-chair of the National Joint
Committee for Spanish Relief, travelled to Spain on a fact-finding mission – likened the government's response to the escalating
humanitarian crisis in the country as 'that of a fastidious gentleman walking with an averted nose past a butcher's shop'.[69] At first
ministers provided no financial aid; then they contributed £73,000
towards the evacuation of refugees and a further £25,000 towards
the cost of looking after displaced refugees. Eventually, thanks in
part to the efforts of the Labour MP Leah Manning, who had
travelled to Bilbao to assist with evacuation efforts, Britain agreed
to take 4,000 children aged between five and fifteen. They arrived
at Southampton Docks on 23 May 1937. Some were interned in a
purpose-built camp near Southampton; some found their way to
London. Virginia Woolf had been out to Selfridges to buy white-
bait when, returning home, she saw 'a long trail of fugitives – like
a caravan from the desert': 'Spaniards flying from Bilbao which
has fallen, I suppose. Somehow brought tears to my eyes, tho' no
one seemed surprised.'[70]

Soon it wasn't refugees from Spain but from the entire
European continent who urgently needed sanctuary. Another,
bigger war was looming. On 30 September 1938, Chamberlain
returned from the Munich Conference, where he had signed an
agreement over the division of Czechoslovakia in the hope of
preventing war, and addressed the crowds waiting at Heston
Aerodrome. He promised them and the country 'peace for our
time'. But these were empty words. On 9 November, after a
seventeen-year-old Polish Jew shot a German embassy official
in Paris, the Nazis went on a systematic rampage against Jews
in what became known as Kristallnacht – setting fire to
synagogues, smashing up Jewish-owned shops and offices.

Thousands of Jewish men were arrested and sent to concentration camps. The priority for women and children was getting to a place of safety.

Britain refused to relax her tight immigration controls, allowing in only small numbers of refugees it deemed economically viable – women who were willing to work as domestic servants got visas quickest. Three weeks after Kristallnacht, on 2 December 1938, a party of two hundred Jewish children arrived in Harwich – the first of the so-called Kindertransports. Shamefully, some of the families who agreed to foster the children did so with the intention of securing free labour.

'Of course, au-pair jobs were totally against the law,' remembered Hilde Ainger, one Kindertransport child. 'You were only supposed to work if you had a labour permit, which you couldn't get, and so if you had an au-pair job, you would say you came over as a student of the English language and therefore lived with an English family, who didn't tell anybody how they exploited you. They could do what they liked, because you had no rights. I had a few au-pair jobs even without pocket money, you see, and no regular time off or anything. You were incredibly exploited.'[71]

Most, thankfully, had a nobler motive. Stella Rotenberg was billeted with a wealthy old lady who wanted to support and care for Stella rather than see her work, as Stella was expecting to, at a nearby hospital: 'She said to me, this rich old English lady, this ailing old lady: "To you it happened today, it might happen to us tomorrow."'[72]

Quaker volunteers took the lead in processing and welcoming Jewish immigrants. One woman in particular, Birmingham-born former teacher Bertha Bracey, ran the Germany Emergency Committee which dealt with appeals for help from Jews in Germany, Austria and Czechoslovakia.[73] For several years Bracey had organised Quaker relief operations in Germany and the Netherlands, and after Kristallnacht she was one of six Quakers

Octavia Hill had a mission to give inner-city children a taste of England's green and pleasant land. She founded the National Trust to preserve the nation's landscapes and landmarks 'for ever, for everyone'.

In helping organise the London matchgirls strike, Annie Besant enabled female employees at Bryant & May's match factory to fight back against appalling conditions.

Margaret Bondfield exposed shoddy practices at department stores before becoming Britain's first female cabinet minister in Ramsay MacDonald's Labour government.

Elizabeth Garrett Anderson battled against the medical establishment to become the first English woman to qualify as a physician and surgeon.

She's in her finery here, but Dorothy Lawrence dressed up as a soldier, Denis Smith, to get around fusty Fleet Street's refusal to employ her as a war correspondent.

The first notable female casualty of World War I, Edith Cavell helped hundreds of allied soldiers escape from occupied Belgium. She was treated as a saint on her death.

Gertrude Bell won the trust of imams, sheikhs and tribes to help shape the Middle East and win the nickname of 'Desert Queen'.

As one of the first female police officers, Lilian Wyles had to pair up with another woman on patrol, with two experienced policemen following behind.

The first woman to practise as a barrister, Helena Normanton's determination to excel at law stemmed from family tragedy.

Eleanor Rathbone dreamed up the idea of a family allowance after seeing Liverpool dockers struggle to support their families. She just lived to see it become law.

MP 'Red' Ellen Wilkinson took parliament by storm with the Jarrow March, weeping in the Commons as she told how the closure of the shipyard had killed the town.

Motorbike fanatic and engineer Beatrice Shilling was a secret weapon in the Battle of Britain, fixing a fatal flaw in the Spitfires.

Elsie Widdowson was a nutritionist who recommended bolstering the nation's diet during rationing – and whose legacy lives on today in fortified breakfast cereals.

A British Muslim descended from Indian royalty, Noor Inayat Khan spied for Britain in World War II, earning a posthumous George Cross for her bravery.

Textile designer Lucienne Day's colourful, abstract patterns were front and centre at the Festival of Britain, and her 'Calyx' motif became an emblem for postwar society.

Jane Drew was an architect who worked on projects from the rodent house at London Zoo to the new capital of Punjab, Chandigarh.

A gifted X-ray crystallographer, Rosalind Franklin's contribution to the discovery of the double helix structure of DNA was underplayed.

to travel to Berlin on a fact-finding mission. After Chamberlain rejected the Quakers' plan to prioritise child refugees, Bracey successfully lobbied the Home Secretary Sir Samuel Hoare to sanction what became the Kindertransports.

Her committee took over Bloomsbury House, a former hotel in Bloomsbury Street, London. By 1939 Bracey was in charge of 80 staff looking after 14,000 case files.

One staff member, Elizabeth Allen, spent six months there helping to find jobs in British hospitals for qualified and trainee Jewish nurses from Germany and Austria. Interviewed in 1995, she remembered the anger and humiliation she felt at Chamberlain's strategy of appeasement: 'I thought they [the British government] should have stood up to [the Nazis] and if necessary we should have gone to war over the invasion of Czechoslovakia. War was an absolute necessity.'[74]

But many feminists, including Nancy Astor and the peace campaigner Helena Swanwick, supported appeasement in a spirit of optimism and because they felt something – anything – had to be done to avert another war. Swanwick, especially, was a radical pacifist, not a fascist. She did however believe passionately that Germany had been treated unfairly by the Allies after the First World War, humiliated by the Treaty of Versailles – which had stripped it of colonies and assets and imposed a heavy war indemnity – to the point where it could regain its standing in the world only through the use of force.

For this, some historians have accused her of being naive and misguided: Julie Gottlieb has called her 'one of Hitler's most outspoken apologists'.[75] In fact, she simply hated war and believed that women hated war 'more fervently than men ... not because they are better than men, or wiser, but because war hits them much harder and has very little to offer in return.'[76]

What did ordinary women make of the outbreak of war? In August 1939, a twenty-six-year-old payroll clerk Olivia Cockett started to keep a diary of her life in Brockley, south-east London, for the social research project Mass-Observation. The new demands of wartime, like blacked-out curtains, made her feel 'stupid and bewildered', while the sight of evacuee children on their way to train stations and a safer life in the countryside brought her to tears. On the night of 1 September she wrote that she felt 'very depressed at the war atmosphere'. She got herself some milk to drink, went to bed and read a maths book to make herself tired. But she couldn't sleep; she kept imagining 'horror and noises', then had a terrible attack of diarrhoea.

At 11.15 a.m. on 3 September, Chamberlain made his famous broadcast announcing that Britain was at war with Germany. Cockett, who had been summoned to work even though it was a Sunday, to help her office move from central London to Putney, recorded her thoughts. 'Silence and general air of, "That's that." Then the Warning at once … Felt pleased that I was not frightened, but I probably shall be when there are real bangs.'[77]

Listening on the wireless at her house in Hampshire, sitting on a camp bed with her two children, the writer Vera Brittain wept as the extent of her failure as a peace activist sank in.[78] She then went for a walk in the New Forest, though it's unclear whether she found it a blessing or a curse that 'in the sunny quiet and gorse and heather it was impossible to take in the size of the catastrophe'.[79]

The realisation that war was inevitable was too much for Swanwick. In 1938 – aged seventy-six, in poor health and grieving after her husband's death – she had taken in two refugees, orphaned teenage girls from Germany, but they only stayed for a few weeks. Possibly she found herself unable to care for them. It seemed she could barely care for herself. Invited by Nancy Astor to Cliveden in January 1939, she declined by letter: 'I do not now get beyond my garden gate and I have to crawl about in ignominious fashion.' Even writing was beyond her. 'I'm feebly trying to extract another book which is in my head but unwilling to emerge in any presentable order,' she told Astor.[80]

By early November 1939, her frayed nerve endings were exposed and the pain was more than she could bear. She killed herself at her home in Maidenhead with an overdose of the barbiturate Medinal.

5

Daughters of Britain

1939–45

In the late summer of 1940 Virginia Woolf was living at Monk's House, the weatherboarded eighteenth-century cottage near Lewes she and her husband Leonard had bought just after the First World War. Usually it offered respite from the mayhem of wartime London. This time, though, Woolf's sleep was disrupted by planes flying overhead and by the soft crunch of anti-aircraft guns.

'It is a queer experience,' she wrote in her essay, 'Thoughts on Peace in an Air Raid', 'lying in the dark and listening to the zoom of a hornet which may at any moment sting you to death. Yet it is a sound – far more than prayers and anthems – that should compel one to think about peace.'[1] Thinking about peace was, Woolf believed, an urgent necessity. After all, peace was 'the only efficient air-raid shelter'.[2] And yet once again men were fighting; men had been given weapons, while women, at this stage of the Second World War, had not.

Women had to find something else to fight with: ideas. But women's ideas, Woolf believed, were scorned. They had no power because women lacked the political clout to implement them. For now, they had to make do with what Woolf called 'private thinking, tea-table thinking'.[3]

As she wrote, the distant buzzing of the planes changed to a sound like a branch being sawed overhead. Woolf remembered something she read in *The Times* that morning, something Nancy Astor wrote or said in Parliament: 'Women of ability are held down because of a subconscious Hitlerism in the hearts of men.' This sounds pretty harsh. What is 'Hitlerism'? For Woolf it was aggression motivated by an urge to dominate and enslave. And sometimes women seemed complicit in that enslavement, styling themselves as male fantasy figures – clones with crimson nails and painted faces.

Was Woolf right about women's impotence? She may perhaps have felt differently at the end of the war, one that involved women to an unprecedented degree. Tragically, we'll never know. She killed herself in March 1941, fearing another attack of the mental illness that had dogged her throughout her life.

War gave women permission to be someone else. If this was often someone they never imagined they would be, then it was also, occasionally, someone they absolutely *had* to be; someone they'd known they were since they were small. This is probably the best way to describe Beatrice Shilling. When I was in the early stages of thinking about this book and friends asked me about the sort of women it would include, I would always reply 'Women like Beatrice Shilling …' and give a potted history of her life. 'Ah,' they would say. 'Right. We understand now.'

The Battle of Britain, fought in the skies between July and November 1940, was a pivotal moment in the Second World War. The pulverising of Warsaw by the Germans in September 1939 and Rotterdam the following May meant Britain was prepared for aerial bombardment. Until this point, for many at home, nothing much had happened since war was declared, a situation reflected in contemporary nicknames for the conflict's early months – the 'Bore War' or the 'Phoney War'.

During the Battle of Britain the Germans attacked coastal targets and British shipping in the English Channel before moving inland to focus on airfields, ports, communications centres and, of course, London in the series of devastating attacks known as the Blitz. Had Britain failed to defeat the Luftwaffe at this stage, it is likely that Hitler would have gone ahead with Operation Sea Lion, his planned amphibious and airborne invasion of Britain. But although fighting continued into November (and the Blitz didn't stop completely until May 1941), by mid September the Luftwaffe's losses had become unsustainable. Hitler switched his attention to Russia and postponed Operation Sea Lion indefinitely.

You wouldn't necessarily know it from the history books, but one woman was crucial to Britain's victory.

In some ways the Luftwaffe's Messerschmitt 109 fighters and the RAF's Hurricanes and Spitfires were technically much of a muchness. But the Luftwaffe did have one major advantage over the RAF: the 109's fuel-injected Daimler-Benz engines. By contrast, the Rolls-Royce Merlin engines used in the first generation of Spitfires and Hurricanes were carburettor engines with a fatal flaw: if a pilot went into a dive to try to shake off an enemy plane, the 'negative g' momentarily starved the engine of fuel before the 'positive g' created by pulling out of the dive flooded it. The engine would splutter and sometimes cut out entirely.

Pilots were dying unnecessarily. The RAF badly needed a new generation of fuel-injected engines. First, however, it needed to identify the problem with the existing ones and supply a quick fix. Step forward Beatrice Shilling.

The youngest of three daughters, Beatrice was born on 8 March 1909 to Henry and Annie Shilling in Waterlooville, Hampshire, then a small village newly famous for its golf course. She stood out not just because of her talent for what her biographer Matthew Freudenberg calls 'unrepentant brevity'– 'Shan't!' she once said, when asked to apologise for biting her sister – but because she was more interested in Meccano than needlework.[4] Aged twelve, she won a prize in a national competition set by

Meccano Magazine for building a working model of a spinning wheel. By fourteen, she had saved up with her sister Anne to buy a two-stroke Royal Enfield motorbike. When other girls her age were pressing flowers, Beatrice was at the bottom of the garden dismantling and reassembling the Enfield's 225cc engine. At school she excelled at maths and science and decided, aged fifteen, that she wanted to become an engineer.

By 1926, when Shilling left school, the world had opened up significantly for women. They were better educated as a result of the Education Acts of 1902 and 1918 and this led to more job opportunities, mostly in light industries – making electrical goods, for example – or as teachers, nurses and clerks. As we have seen, the Sex Disqualification (Removal) Act of 1919 made it easier for them to go to university and enter certain professions – with strings attached, of course. Even so, as Freudenberg observes, it remained the case that 'for a woman in the 1920s, a career in lion-taming would have been more realistic' than one in engineering.[5]

As we've seen, the First World War created opportunities for women, only to snatch them away in the aftermath as demobilisation returned men to the workplace. It was assumed women would meekly return to their pre-war roles, relieved that the natural order of things had been restored. Men disliked the trespass of women into their professional space and resisted all demands for them to be paid the same. This was a particular problem in engineering. Sir Arthur Percy Morris Fleming, who developed vital radar submarine-detection equipment while working at the British Westinghouse Company during the First World War, stated baldly that 'the average woman does not possess the same engineering instinct as the average man'.

It was to counter such assumptions that two female engineers, propeller-gluer and lathe-turner Verena Holmes and electrical-engineer Margaret Partridge, helped to establish the Women's Engineering Society (WES) in 1919. Partridge had a grand plan:

to install and operate her own power plant in Bungay in Suffolk, having already wired four English villages for electricity. She wanted a female apprentice to train up but had such trouble finding the right person that she resorted to sending a WES circular around girls' schools in the hope that a perceptive teacher might identify a suitable candidate.

When the circular arrived, Shilling's school alerted her mother, who contacted Partridge. Once hired, Shilling thrived at the power plant and with Partridge's help went on to take a degree in engineering at Manchester University, then an MSc in Mechanical Engineering, studying the working temperatures of pistons in different types of diesel engines.

In her spare time she joined the British Motorcycle Racing Club, upgrading her bike to a 500cc Norton with the intention of racing at the 2.75-mile Brooklands circuit near Weybridge in Surrey. Shilling soon became the first woman to lap the circuit at 100mph, winning a Gold Star. When she met and fell in love with another engineer and racing enthusiast, George Naylor, she agreed to marry him only after he had gained a Gold Star himself.

While she may have been able to dictate terms at home, instances of petty sexism dogged Shilling's professional progress. On a trip to an aircraft manufacturer in Bristol to observe engines being assembled, she had to be kept out of sight of the head of the Engine Division because he didn't tolerate women in his factory. Despite this, she managed to forge a long career in aeronautical engineering: on 1 November 1939, two months into the Second World War, she was appointed Technical Officer in charge of carburettor research and development work at the Royal Air Establishment at Farnborough.

The problem of the Merlin engines cutting out had been noted on test flights in 1938 but disregarded. Only in 1940, once the Battle of Britain had begun, did it become clear that aerobatics – swooping, rolling, diving – were an essential element of fighter battles. As long as German pilots were able to perform these feats untroubled by glitches, the bigger the advantage they would enjoy over their RAF counterparts.

The search for a solution took over a year. Shilling and her team worked nineteen-hour shifts, testing and re-testing the engines, trying to recreate the conditions in which cut-outs might occur. Eventually, Shilling solved the mystery of how negative g affected the rate and extent of fuel delivery to the carburettors. The flow of fuel into the float chambers – cavities containing a device which floats on the surface of the fuel and seals off the flow as the level rises – had to be controlled so that there was enough to supply maximum engine power, but not enough to flood the space. Her solution was a brass restrictor – basically, a disc with a hole in it – which could be fitted, without removing the engine from the aircraft, between the end of the fuel intake pipe and the union at the entrance to the carburettor fuel inlet gallery.

To Shilling's apparent amusement, the restrictor was christened 'Miss Shilling's Orifice' by the Rolls-Royce engineer Sir Stanley Hooker and, for better or worse, became known by this name throughout the RAF. Shilling installed it herself, riding from airfield to airfield on her tool-laden Norton, braze-welding the brass collars to the inside of the affected planes' carburettors.

In January 1942, Tilly – as her colleagues called her, strictly behind her back – was promoted to the grade of Senior Technical Officer, becoming head of the Engines and Accessories section. In 1948 she received the OBE for her contribution to the war effort.

Engineering genius she possessed in abundance. Management skills, not so much. As her biographer puts it, 'she could not pretend respect for men she believed did not merit their seniority, and her manner made some of them think of ways of making her disappear, rather than giving her a department to manage.'[6]

Shilling isn't as well known as she should be, but there is a pub named after her in Farnborough in Hampshire, and in 2009 she topped Hampshire County Council's online poll of Hampshire-based historical figures, even beating Jane Austen …

The Second World War has been nicknamed 'the people's war' because of the way it involved Britain's entire civilian population, not just the men who went away to fight. Women had worn uniforms in the First World War – mostly nurses' uniforms – but in the Second they did so with increased status, responsibility and (some of the time) respect; though rarely the same pay as their male colleagues. It seems old habits die hard.

For some men, a sense that female contributions to the war effort were a theatrical indulgence, a sort of rummaging in life's dressing-up box, lingered long after the war had ended. As the historian Sheila Rowbotham has written: 'The exceptional nature of wartime meant that women's extraordinary actions were part of the suspension of normal life; they did not necessarily affect how women were regarded in the long term.'[7] There lingered too a sense that women in uniform weren't quite respectable.

In the early stages of the conflict women were encouraged to volunteer for war work – non-combat of course – so that men were free to fight, and for a while Minister of Labour Ernest Bevin trusted that enough women would do this for enforced mobilisation to be unnecessary. But a report produced by the Manpower Committee under the chairmanship of William Beveridge in December 1940 made it clear that women's involvement wasn't an optional extra, but an essential requirement if Britain was to have any chance of winning the war.

'This war on civilians brings the battlefield into every home,' wrote Anne Stewart Higham in an essay designed to explain the war on the Home Front to Americans, 'and if, as is most often the case the husband, father, or son, sometimes all three, are away in one of the fighting services, the care of the children, the provision of food, the production of armaments, and the defence of the home is the job of the women, young and old.'[8]

Volunteering meant being prepared to do 'every job possible that will release men ... Their responsibility is great for upon them may depend the life of a pilot bailing out, the lives of all on a ship at sea.'[9]

Most female volunteers went into civil defence. The backbone of the war effort on the home front was the Women's Voluntary Service (WVS), founded by Stella Isaacs, Dowager Marchioness of Reading, in 1938 at the request of Sir Samuel Hoare, the Home Secretary. By and large the WVS consisted of well-spoken, middle-class ladies of a certain age who, as Virginia Nicholson puts it, 'played to their perceived strengths as women, making innumerable cups of tea'.[10] 'This organisation is everywhere,' noted Anne Stewart Higham, 'assisting with everything that a woman can do.'[11] Their military-style uniform (a purple blouse with a dark green coat and green hat with a purple band) wasn't compulsory – women could just wear a badge if they wanted – but it gave notice of the tribe's formal fastidiousness.

Nowhere was this attention to detail needed more than in the WVS's earliest and biggest challenge: overseeing the waves of evacuation at the start of the war, what Lady Reading called 'the biggest social experiment since the Exodus' – hordes of mostly working-class inner-city children relocated to the countryside to be puzzled over by rural families who thought they were a different species. At least two WVS escorts accompanied every train out of London. At the peak of the evacuation programme, 51 trains took 41,000 children in one day.

The WVS supported the Air Raid Precautions (ARP) services, running canteens and rest centres for victims of bombing. They made and distributed clothes. They also acted as a kind of customer services interface, assisting people confused not just by the intricacies of ration-book bureaucracy but the broader questions of how and even why the war was being fought. Nicholson thinks many women found it all rather baffling: 'The average housewife, accustomed to leaving difficult decisions about politics and world affairs to her husband, was simply out of her depth.'[12] Others didn't have the time to follow what was going on in newspapers or found the news so depressing that they ignored it completely.

The WVS was not a feminist group: as Helen Jones observes, they 'had no particular interest in furthering the power relations of women in general vis-à-vis government'.[13] You could even argue that the WVS (which was 300,000 strong by September 1939) and similar voluntary societies like the Women's Institute (WI) and the YMCA National Women's Auxiliaries *set back* feminism. By providing the government with an endless supply of untrained women willing to work themselves to the bone for no money – one WVS member in Barnes is supposed to have fed 1,200 bomb victims in one day from her own kitchen – these bodies arguably slowed down women's assimilation into the male professional world.[14] Of the WVS's 3,500 or so administrative staff, only 67 were paid.[15]

But the sense of belonging that came from membership of these groups was clearly beneficial. Stella Schofield, who worked at Mass-Observation, wrote a report in January 1940 concluding that 'inside their organisations women are more consciously critical, more questioningly aware of the war processes. They find themselves once more precipitated into world war by a man-monopolised society. It would be idle to speculate whether or not the present situation could have been avoided had women held executive government positions … but it is very much to the point to realise that, however unorganised the mass of women may be today, they were far less organised in the last war.'[16]

Unevenly implemented in some quarters, the evacuation programme might have been a disaster without the efforts of the WI. There was far more to it than 'jam and Jerusalem', though they did make a lot of jam: 12 million lb of the stuff. A bumper harvest at the start of war led to fears that masses of fruit would rot because there weren't enough workers to pick and store it. So Frances Farrer, general secretary of the WI between 1929 and 1959, secured 430 tons of sugar from the Ministry of Food – her negotiating strategy was to badger ministers on the phone early in the morning, before they had had time to eat breakfast – and invited Britain's nearly 6,000 WIs to order it direct from London.

Having promised that this sugar would be used for preservation only, the WIs set up preservation centres in local schools, town halls, cafés, etc. This jam was sold commercially as well as on market stalls. Cicely McCall, the WI's educational organiser, wrote that jam-making was 'constructive and non-militant ... And for the belligerent, what could be more satisfying than fiercely stirring cauldrons of boiling jam and feeling that every pound took us one step further towards defeating Hitler?'[17]

As Julie Summers explains in her book *Jambusters*, the WI began the war as pacifist and non-sectarian but quickly became if not an instrument of the wartime government then certainly an invaluable asset. With a ratio of one institute per three villages, the WI was in an influential position. Realising this, the government harnessed its power to help find billets for evacuees and implement the 'Dig for Victory!' programme. People were encouraged to grow their own vegetables wherever they could find a bit of spare land, though the WI cautioned against the wholesale digging up of flower beds: 'Many beds, such as narrow front gardens, are not suitable for vegetables, and we shall always need flowers to bring relief from the nervous strain and stress of war-time life,' advised one WI newsletter.

The WI did a huge amount to make disorientated, homesick evacuees feel welcome, from laying on lavish spreads at reception centres – even though the children were often too nervous to eat anything – to knocking on doors demanding that recalcitrant villagers took their fair share of children. They worked tirelessly to facilitate integration, which often took time and occasionally didn't happen at all.

'The woman accustomed to the friendly, quarrelsome crowds of a city street finds little of beauty, but a great empty loneliness in the villages of the fens,' wrote Anne Stewart Higham. 'The darkness and stillness smother her like a wet blanket.'[18] The poverty of some of the urban families shocked countryside-dwellers who had previously considered *themselves* badly off. One diary kept by a WI volunteer spoke of 'a residue [of evacuees] so uncivilised as to completely defeat our efforts at solution'.[19]

The Women's Land Army had existed during the First World War. In June 1939, former suffragette Lady Gertrude Denman fanned its embers and by 1943 there were over eighty thousand Land Girls doing farm work – serious, exhausting farm work at that: ploughing, threshing, lambing, turning hay ... Six thousand women worked in the affiliated Timber Corps, felling trees and running sawmills.

Not everyone who volunteered to be a Land Girl had their offer accepted. Amelia E. King, a young black woman from Stepney, was rejected by the Essex county committee, apparently because farmers and other local residents objected to her being billeted with them. That King's father was in the Merchant Navy and three generations of her family had lived in Britain cut no ice.[20] It's worth noting that some 120 female volunteers from the West Indies were based in Britain during the war. On the whole, says the historian David Olusoga, they experienced little racism, though a 1945 edition of the magazine *John Bull* reported that 'rudeness to colonial service girls in this country is surprisingly common ... a West Indian girl in the ATS [Auxiliary Territorial Service] was refused a new issue of shoes by her officer who added: "at home you don't wear shoes anyway"'. The writer concluded that this was a shameful way to treat troops who 'came to this country to help us win the war'.[21]

From spring 1941, every woman in Britain between 19 and 40 had to register at employment exchanges, submit to an interview and make themselves available for work. In December 1941, the National Service Act (No. 2) formally conscripted women into the armed forces or some other type of war service. At first only single women aged 19 to 30 were called up, but over time this upper age limit rose to 43 and then 50. By mid 1943 almost 90 per cent of single women and 80 per cent of married women were employed in behind-the-scenes work essential to the war effort. The proportion of women employed by the Douglas Aircraft Company rose from 1 per cent in December 1941 to 45 per cent by July 1943.

Women were divided into 'mobile' workers able to work away from home and 'immobile' workers who were not. Mobile workers could be sent anywhere there was a labour shortage – so-called 'scarlet' areas. No mother of children under fourteen living at home had to do war work as her domestic role was considered sacrosanct, though this did not stop many signing up anyway. University students, too, were exempt as long as they could prove that their degrees were going to equip them for work of national importance, such as teaching or medicine.

The Ministry of Labour set up a dedicated Women's Technical Service Register to funnel women with an aptitude for maths and science into the right areas. And to release mothers for factory work, 1,500 subsidised nurseries were opened which in turn employed women as wardens and nannies. During school holidays many schools remained open as play centres. By October 1943, only 24,000 women were registered unemployed.[22]

We worry a lot now about work-life balance. But even in the fraught war years the question of how to balance domestic responsibilities with new roles – particularly for working-class women caring for children – was a pressing one. The Woman Power Committee (WPC), a cross-party pressure group of female MPs and other leading women, debated the issue.

Chaired by the Conservative backbench MP Irene Ward, the WPC met fortnightly at the London home of Nancy Astor from June 1940. Their beef was that, yet again, talented women were being sidelined: out of a sample group of two hundred women with specialist technical qualifications listed on the Ministry of Labour's central register, only twenty-one were employed in appropriate positions in a way that aided the war effort.[23] After a Commons debate on 'woman power' in March 1941 the WPC mutated into the Women's Consultative Committee (WCC), formally advising Minister of Labour Ernest Bevin. This didn't stop one of Labour's staunchest feminists Edith Summerskill from believing that 'the war is being prosecuted by both sexes but directed only by one'.[24]

Ethel Wood agreed. The daughter of Quintin Hogg, founder of what is now the University of Westminster, she was the author of an uncompromising feminist tract, *Mainly For Men* (1943), which argued that the war was actually reinforcing archaic attitudes to women: a glorious opportunity to use women to their full capacity was being passed up.

'What is women power?' she asked.

> To a vast number of people it is the motive force that enables their floors to be scrubbed, their beds nicely made, their meals cooked and cleared away and their clothes mended – and possibly their letters to be typed and filed. But to a large and growing number of thinking citizens, it is the total contribution women have to give the world *if* – oh such a huge, formidable *if* – only they were allowed to pour it into the common stock freely and fully. It is all their qualities of mind and spirit, as well as their purely physical endurance and activity; vision, imagination, initiative, experience as well as muscle and patient drudgery; and it is precisely the more valuable aspects of their equipment that are so frequently wasted and denied expression.[25]

With little in the way of support, female conscription placed a massive strain on families. This wasn't lost on contemporary feminists like Vera Douie, librarian at the Women's Service Library, whose 1949 book *Daughters of Britain* is one of the earliest postwar attempts to assess women's contribution during the Second World War. The idea behind mass mobilisation, she notes, was that 'no skilled person was to do what could be done by an unskilled person, and no man was to do what could be done by a woman'.[26] Simple enough in theory. But to show how onerous this could be in practice, she quotes from a speech given in the House of Commons on 24 September 1943 by Malcolm McCorquodale, then Joint Parliamentary Secretary in the Ministry of Labour and National Service:

> An Hon Member told me a story which, with his permission, I will tell the house, with regard to a man who had permission from his firm to go to work at 8 o'clock instead of 7. A new foreman wished to take away this privilege, and he asked the man why he could not come on at 7 o'clock like the others. His answer was that he had to get the baby up and get it to its granny's. The foreman asked why his wife could not do it, and the man replied that she had to get up at 5.30 to go to another factory at 6 o'clock. Then the foreman enquired whether the grandmother could not get up a little earlier to receive the child, only to be told that the grandmother did not come back from her night shift until 7 o'clock.[27]

You get the sense of a family falling through the cracks. Although the mother should technically have been exempt from *war* work because she had a baby and a husband to support – so-called 'Category R', as determined by her local recruiting officer – it appears that the entire extended family had to work to make ends meet.

What infuriated Ethel Wood was that many of these problems,

especially where childcare was concerned, had been 'obvious to the feminine eye from the first, but were apparently invisible to the male optic till they began to wreck production'.[28] Had women been involved more in the preliminary planning, they might have been avoided.

Meanwhile, war sucked most of the energy out of campaigning for equality. The pressure group Women for Westminster proposed a broad-brush anti-discrimination Equal Citizenship (Blanket) Bill, prepared by Dorothy Evans, former suffragette and member of feminist campaign society the Six Point Group. But debate was dominated by two big issues.

The first was equal pay. Despite working alongside men in factories, wage disparity was marked: by 1943, women comprised nearly 35 per cent of the engineering workforce but earned around 55 per cent of a man's salary.[29] More often than not women soaked up this glaring inequity, not wanting to make a fuss. But sometimes irritation boiled over. At the Rolls-Royce aircraft plant at Hillingdon near Glasgow, union activist Agnes MacLean organised a ten-day strike in November 1944. The government responded with an inquiry which recommended increasing women's wages, though not to the point where they were the same as men's.[30]

The second issue was compensation for war injuries. As things stood, women did not receive the same compensation as men for injuries sustained as a result of enemy action. The Personal Injuries Act of 1939 had based the levels on rates of pay (which were clearly unequal) rather than the cost of living. Mavis Tate and Edith Summerskill – Conservative and Labour politicians respectively – led the Equal Compensation Campaign Committee and on 1 May 1941 tabled a motion to annul the Act. Support for it was substantial, the idea of 'equality of sacrifice' catching the imagination at a time when all the talk was of women fire-watching and operating anti-aircraft guns. In February 1943 a Select Committee report found in favour of the campaign, although, as

Sonya Rose observes, 'this was the only major victory that feminists could claim for gender equity during the war'.[31]

———————————

When the wartime coalition government was formed under Churchill in May 1940 there were only twelve female MPs. In this respect Virginia Woolf's beef about women's influence was justified. Their impact in the Commons was slight, although MPs like Jennie Adamson and Megan Lloyd George sat on advisory committees. Engineer Caroline Haslett, who had been running classes for women in technical institutes across London, advised the Ministry of Labour on the training of women. Beatrice Shilling's old mentor Verena Holmes was appointed technical officer and campaigned against low wages in the munitions industry, complaining that 'women munitions workers had about as much say in agreements on their wages as Czecho-Slovakia had in the Munich agreement'.[32]

So much for Westminster, but what about Whitehall? Some talented women clawed their way into influential positions. Between 1941 and 1944 barrister Sybil Campbell, soon to be the first woman judge, was Assistant Divisional Food Officer (Enforcement) in the Ministry of Food, helping to catch black marketeers. Evelyn Sharp, soon to be the first female Permanent Secretary, was Assistant Secretary in the Ministry of Health. Alix Kilroy, one of the first two women to enter the administrative grade of the civil service by examination, worked at the Board of Trade and in 1943 was put in charge of the Reconstruction Department.

Masika Lancaster worked in a secret, blacked-out room at the War Office building scale models on which the prefab Mulberry Harbours used in the Normandy invasion were based. 'She knew the D Day secrets!' screamed a newspaper profile, quoting Lancaster, whose husband was being held prisoner-of-war in Java, on the discomforts of the job: 'All the work had to be done by electric light ... Often there were hectic rushes. I did not mind staying late and working on Sundays if necessary.'[33] Rousing stuff, but as the historian Helen Jones notes: 'While women were used extensively to implement government policy, and to offer advice on various aspects of the war on the home front ... [they] were not so evident at the policy-making level.'[34]

'On the whole the Civil Service in wartime looks very much like the business and industrial world,' wrote Ethel Wood, reviewing it in 1943 and despairing at the 'departments where there are no women in positions of authority in the Establishment Branches, no signs that any effort has been made to use the permanent women to the best advantage or any policy formulated about temporary ones except to make them the hewers of wood and drawers of water in all classes, just as in business and factories where the management is selfish, prejudiced or uninformed.'[35]

Down the road in the House of Commons it was a similar story, though there were glimmers of light in the darkness. Ellen Wilkinson, the Labour MP for Jarrow, was initially given a minor post at the Ministry of Pensions but in 1940 became one of new Home Secretary Herbert Morrison's Parliamentary Private Secretaries in the wartime coalition government, a position she held until the end of the war. Renowned for her feminism and passionate left-wing oratory, Wilkinson struck many as an unlikely choice for this job. But she had disliked Chamberlain and lobbied behind the scenes to install Churchill. She grew to admire him, and under his influence she moved from the far left to the centre left – a shift 'from principle to pragmatism', as her biographer Matt Perry calls it, that was in keeping with the demands of the wartime administration. What was important, Wilkinson believed, was to place the needs of the nation above sectional interests, even if this involved a degree of apostasy: for example, supporting Morrison's suppression of the communist newspaper the *Daily Worker* and voting for wartime legislation banning strikes in key industries.

Wilkinson fell out with both the Parliamentary Labour Party (PLP) and the unions – one union leader said that she could 'no longer be regarded as a person seeking to assist the emancipation of the workers'[36] – and grew suspicious of the Soviet Union. She abandoned her pacifism, inviting teasing from her friend Nancy Astor who took to calling her 'General Wilkinson', and justified the bombing of German cities with the rather glib, even Trumpish comment: 'They started it and are only getting back what they gave.'[37] This was not mere careerism on her part but an expression of her growing conviction that traditional hard-left ideas were becoming outdated as war altered the landscape. She was however a big fan of the statist wartime economy, believing it to be a trial run for the post-war world.

Wilkinson's patch was civil defence, including fire-fighting and air raid shelter policy – a subject close to her heart as she had witnessed aerial bombardment in Spain while visiting the country with Clement Attlee in December 1936. With terrible irony, on the day her new job was announced her Bloomsbury flat was bombed for the second time. The only possessions she managed to salvage were a few books.

Under its predecessor, Sir John Anderson, her department had been criticised for responding too slowly to the demand for deep shelters, although millions had erected one of the corrugated-iron domestic shelters named after him in their gardens. Wilkinson turned this bad publicity around by making high-profile visits to public shelters with journalists in tow and speaking on the radio. One senior civil servant considered her 'Jarrow-march aura' a 'continuing asset'. In other words, she knew how to connect with ordinary people, how best to dispense what she called 'hygiene and cheer'.[38] She had a habit of producing a notebook from her pocket and taking contemporaneous notes of people's complaints – a bit of theatre that made people feel listened to.

It remained the case, however, that there weren't enough public shelters in the cities that were being most heavily bombed. In

London's East End, 14,000 people were forced to camp out under railway arches, and at the height of the Blitz thousands of Londoners were using tube stations as improvised shelters, often living there for days in cramped, squalid conditions.

Wilkinson recognised this as a major problem. Such people had, she said, become 'divorced from the habits of life' in a way that left them in danger from 'boredom and lack of leadership'.[39] On more than one occasion, her sound judgements were thwarted by government dithering. A report showed that the lower floors of modern steel-framed buildings were practically bomb-proof, so she raised the idea that such buildings, usually offices, could be used as shelters. But this was rejected – likewise the engineer Ove Arup's plan, which she supported, for underground concrete-tunnel shelters. There was an ongoing debate about the virtues of taking cover deep underground versus the official policy of dispersal. In public, Wilkinson defended dispersal while privately agitating on behalf of deep shelters, which were more effective though more expensive and time-consuming to build.[40]

Better – allegedly – than the loathed Anderson shelters, which were cramped and tended to flood whenever it rained, were Morrison shelters, named after the Home Secretary and introduced towards the end of 1941 in a campaign managed by Wilkinson. They were reinforced steel tables with wire mesh sides which lifted up so that you could crawl inside. Earlier in the year, Wilkinson had told the House of her plan to have 'one of the new indoor "table" shelters placed on view in the Tea Room within the next few days'. Conservative MP Sir William Davison grew alarmed, bleating: 'May we ask that a small portion of the room be reserved for teas?'[41]

Much of Wilkinson's shelter work was carried out in tandem with the Ministry of Health, particularly Florence Horsbrugh, parliamentary secretary at the department. She had helped to oversee evacuation and was now responsible for the health and welfare of air raid victims. Wilkinson and Horsbrugh were both valued highly by Churchill, so much so that in 1945 he asked them to attend a conference in San Francisco to help draft the United Nations charter. The pair of assistant delegates were treated as freaks by the media, especially tiny, red-haired Wilkinson, though she insisted sharply that she and Horsbrugh were there not as token women but as 'political figures in our own right'.[42] Afterwards she said: 'We did not create a new world, but we did not expect to. It was really a good piece of cooperative workmanship.'[43]

————

Even in less rarefied spheres than international diplomacy, women's talent for 'cooperative workmanship' was undeniable, Summerskill thought. It just needed teasing out. In her view, conscription would be the making of women: 'The periodic upheaval occasioned by war reveals that women have individualities of their own and are not merely adjuncts of men,' she wrote in *The Fortnightly*. 'They have aspirations and ambitions which become apparent in war time, because only then can they enjoy a real freedom to achieve at least some part of their heart's desire ...'[44]

One argument used to justify not giving women the vote was that they were physically incapable of defending their country. The Second World War had showed this for the nonsense it was. The introduction of conscription meant women suddenly had a choice of auxiliary services to join.

The Women's Royal Naval Service (WRNS), disbanded at the end of the First World War, was re-formed in April 1939. Wrens, as they were known, took up posts as cooks, clerks, telegraphers and drivers, among much else. 'Where will it end?' asked a government booklet. 'That is impossible to say.'[45] Captain Pilkington, Civil Lord of the Admiralty, had a suspicion: 'I have no doubt that if you gave the WRNS half a chance they would be perfectly prepared to sail a battleship,' he told the House of Commons.[46]

Well, yes – but would anyone give them even a quarter of a chance?

The Women's Army Auxiliary Corps (WAAC), another remnant of the Great War, had been re-formed and rebranded as the Auxiliary Territorial Service (ATS) in September 1938. At this point it was strictly voluntary, promoted by adverts which, as Virginia Nicholson observes, made it sound like a slightly racy Girl Guides: 'The Woman's Army is a very human institution – the use of powder is allowed, and even a touch of natural lipstick.'[47] In July 1939 Dame Helen Gwynne-Vaughan, who had been Chief Controller of Queen Mary's Army Auxiliary Corps, took charge and transformed it into a lean, keen, not-quite-fighting-but-almost machine. At first women worked as clerks and cooks and so on; but as the months ticked by they took on new duties such as driving and inspecting ammunition. The ATS's most famous member, Princess (later Queen) Elizabeth, was commissioned as a Second Subaltern and took a Non Commissioned Officer's (NCO) course at No. 1 Motor Transport Training Corps.

The National Service Act (No. 2) stated that no woman should be required to use a lethal weapon without her written consent. So ATS members who wanted to train to use anti-aircraft guns therefore had to declare in writing that this was okay. Women's suitability for 'ack-ack' (anti-aircraft) work was assessed by the WES's Caroline Haslett. In the end mixed batteries, where men and women worked together, were found to be more effective than those operated by men alone. One ageing colonel even told Vera Douie: 'As an old soldier, if I were offered the choice of commanding a mixed battery or a male battery, I can say without hesitation I would take the mixed battery. The girls cannot be beaten in action, and in my opinion they are definitely better than men on the instruments they are manning.'[48]

For poor women, life in the ATS represented freedom and possibility. For middle-class girls, it was often their first encounter with working-class women in a context where they weren't being

served in a shop or having their house cleaned. Churchill's daughter Mary Soames was a junior officer in the ATS and later called
it 'the biggest experience of my life': 'I was catapulted out of my
narrow class background and I was independent.'[49] Shy girls from
sheltered homes learned to mix. They heard crude, unfamiliar
language; got blisters from the endless drilling and training.
Whatever these women had owned before was irrelevant now
that they had little more than a uniform and the knife, fork and
spoon they ate with, which they washed themselves in a trough of
hot water after meals in the Mess. As Mary Soames put it:
'Uniform is a tremendous leveller. We all looked the same, lovely
girls from Liverpool and country bumpkins like me.'[50]

Almost the same, anyway. American author Mary Lee Settle,
who volunteered for auxiliary work in Britain after being rejected
by the American military for her poor eyesight, turned her
unsparing writer's gaze on the mostly working-class women serving alongside her: 'All these very young products of the dole, then
the war, of white bread, "marge" and strong tea, of a hard, city life
already had the shrunken upper body, the heavy-set thighs, white
and doughy, of mature women,' she wrote in her memoir *All The
Brave Promises* (1966). 'My own body, four years older, hard from
sport and protein and sun, was as different … as if I had been of
a different species.'[51]

ATS women could be posted anywhere. Private Yvette Abbott
was sent to Oswestry to be taught how to use ack-ack batteries
– 'plotting' and 'predicting', using the Telescopic Identification
system to pinpoint a plane's location. She was trained to identify
aircraft, to tell friend from foe; then posted to Portsmouth, on the
edge of the naval base, which was enduring horrendous raids. She
slept in Nissen huts with over twenty other women, making cocoa
on a pot-belly stove. Private Angela Cummins volunteered to be
sent abroad and ended up at Caserta near Naples as the battle for
Monte Cassino was raging in 1944. Seconded to the Americans,
she worked as a clerk in Allied Intelligence.[52]

Cooking was considered lowly work. Says librarian Vera Douie: 'There was a regrettable tendency to draft into it women not considered fit for duties requiring high intelligence.'[53] But she tells a great story about a senior ATS commandant who, at the time of the Dunkirk evacuation, was stationed in a village on England's south coast and suddenly found she had eight thousand exhausted, starving men to feed.

> Untrammelled by red tape, she requisitioned (on billeting forms) a flock of sheep grazing nearby and a standing field of cabbages. She got hold of a local butcher, and set the village women to work under her two ATS cooks. A bath, not yet installed, was used as a gigantic stewing pan, a great fire was lit under it – and soon the starving men were enjoying a satisfying meal.[54]

Among the women who really made a mark were those in the Women's Auxiliary Air Force (WAAF), formed in June 1939 to complement the RAF. Run by Jane Trefusis-Forbes, WAAF fed information from radar stations dotted around the coast back to Fighter Command. Other duties included mechanics, signals and telegraphy, parachute-packing and meteorology. WAAFs filled barrage balloons with hydrogen and hoisted them up using cables. By 1943 the WAAF was 180,000 strong, though numbers tailed off towards the end of the war.

The first woman to be awarded the George Cross was a WAAF. Corporal Daphne Pearson had pulled a pilot from a crashed plane loaded with bombs. One of the fifty or so black female servicewomen, Lilian Bader attained the rank of acting corporal in the WAAF, having been asked to leave the Navy, Army and Air Force Institutes (NAAFI) canteen where she worked before because of her colour. And it was a WAAF, Constance Babington Smith – grand-daughter of the 9th Earl of Elgin – who identified the first V1 flying bomb from photos taken over Peenemunde, a German research station on the Baltic, in May 1943.

At the time Babington Smith was working as a photographic interpreter in the Allied Photographic Intelligence Unit. As well as spotting the V1 she identified prototypes of several new German fighter aircraft – the Me 163, He 280 and Me 262. No one was more amazed than Group Captain Frank Whittle, inventor of the jet engine, who paid regular visits to the unit and developed something of a crush on Babington Smith, discreetly asking her colleagues what perfume she wore. (Guerlain's L'Heure Bleue, since you asked.)

The WAAF, the ATS, the WAAC, the WRNS … In among the alphabet soup, one institution no longer needs deciphering: Bletchley.

Women outnumbered men by a ratio of eight to one at the Government Code & Cypher School based at Bletchley Park in Buckinghamshire. An ugly Victorian mansion surrounded by prefab huts, Bletchley was the top-secret centre of codebreaking operations, the place where all the intercepts gathered at listening posts around the coastline were analysed and unravelled.

Bletchley Park's director, Commander Alistair Dennison, liked to employ people he knew, preferably from within his own elevated social circle. He applied this approach to women as well as men. At the start of the war the women at Bletchley tended to divide into aristocratic 'gels', who worked as secretaries and translators, and steely older women who managed the offices. Once the codebreaking 'bombe machines' – designed by maths genius Alan Turing started to arrive at Bletchley in 1940, flocks of Wrens were hired to operate them – 1,676 by 1945. Meanwhile, WAAFs ran the telephone exchange and worked the chuntering teleprinters.

Most of the actual codebreakers were male, but many talented women managed to slip through the net, including Joan Clarke, briefly Turing's fiancée, and Mavis Batey. This was on the say-so of Alfred 'Dilly' Knox, one of the senior cryptographers, who got on better with women than men and so preferred to employ them. Female recruits to 'the Cottage', the set of interlinked houses where he and his team were based, became known as 'Dilly's Fillies'.

Batey, who played a key role in cracking the Italian Enigma codes, always dismissed the rumour that Knox hired only beautiful women, insisting that 'Dilly took us on our qualifications'.[55] Given how much was at stake and how capable women like Batey were, it seems not only churlish but also downright sexist to suggest otherwise. Batey's own account of her initial interview with Knox suggests donnish distractedness more than anything else. His first words to her were, 'Hello, we're breaking machines. Have you got a pencil? Here, have a go.'

'I was then handed a pile of utter gibberish, made worse by Dilly's scrawls all over it. "But I'm afraid it's all Greek to me," I said, at which he burst into delighted laughter and replied, "I wish it were."'[56]

Bletchley historian Sinclair McKay believes Knox had 'somehow found that women had a greater aptitude for the work required. As well as nimbleness of mind and capacity for lateral thought, they possessed a care and attention to detail that many men might not have had.'[57] Rather than treating them as second-class citizens, Knox fought for the women on his team to receive pay rises, writing of one that she was 'actually fourth or fifth best of the whole Enigma staff and quite as useful as some of the "professors"'.[58] And on the whole the female codebreakers were treated with respect in a way that the Wrens frequently were not.

Immortalised – and glamorised – in the film *The Imitation Game*, where she's played by Keira Knightley, Joan Clarke was a clergyman's daughter from West Norwood in south London. She won a scholarship to Newnham College, Cambridge, emerged with a double first in Mathematics though obviously, as a woman, she wasn't awarded a degree. Her Bletchley recruiter was fellow codebreaker Gordon Welchman, a mathematician who had supervised her at Cambridge. 'As with the men,' Welchman remembered in his book *The Hut Six Story: Breaking the Enigma Codes*, 'I believe that the early recruiting [to Bletchley] was largely on a personal-acquaintance basis, but with the whole of Bletchley Park looking for qualified women, we got a great many recruits of high calibre.'[59]

Clarke was one of Bletchley's star codebreakers, exceptionally adept at Turing's cryptanalytic technique – the so-called Banburismus process – and so enthusiastic that she was reluctant to hand over to another person at the end of her shift. But despite Knox's efforts Clarke was still paid less than her male counterparts and denied the official promotion she would have received had she been a man. To their credit, the situation annoyed her supervisors so much that they gave her a bogus promotion to 'linguist grade', even though she didn't speak any foreign languages.

It often feels as if recognition of women's wartime achievements was never as forthcoming as it should have been, even when those achievements were exceptional. Sometimes, though, this is beacuse a veil of secrecy has descended – and with good reason. None of Bletchley's bombe operators would have understood the implications of their work at the time. Not until wartime information was declassified in the mid 1970s did the public hear anything about Bletchley Park, and even then few of the women who worked there felt comfortable talking about it.

Women in the Special Operations Executive (SOE) – the secret volunteer force set up by Churchill after the fall of France to bolster the resistance – didn't have to wait quite so long. SOE agents gathered intelligence, dropped supplies, blew up bridges and trains. Women chosen for SOE roles were trained in sabotage, weaponry-handling and general tradecraft, then placed in the First Aid Nursing Yeomanry (FANY) as a cover. The first female SOE agent to be dropped into France was Yvonne Rudellat. She blew up two trains at Le Mans before being captured by the Gestapo.

The most famous agent, though, remains Violette Szabo née Bushell, a taxi driver's daughter from Brixton whose French husband Etienne, an officer in the Free French forces, was killed in 1942 shortly after the birth of their daughter. Initially thought too temperamental to make a good agent, Szabo turned out to be an amazing shot – the best in the whole SOE, it was said – but was captured at a roadblock near the French village of Salon-la-Tour as she was about to mount a sabotage operation in the run-up to the Normandy landings. She ended up in Ravensbrück concentration camp where she was shot in the back of the head by an SS guard.

Szabo was immortalised only fifteen years after the war in the film *Carve Her Name With Pride* (1958). And hagiographies of female SOE agents – depicting them as heroic martyrs rather than Mata Hari-like 'sexy spies' – began to appear as early as 1952. That was when one of the best known, Jean Overton Fuller's *Madeleine*, was published.

Madeleine tells the remarkable story of Noor Inayat Khan, a British Muslim of Indian descent recruited by SOE's F Section after she had trained as a wireless operator with the WAAF. Given the radio codename 'Madeleine', Khan was dropped into northern France in June 1943 and made her way to occupied Paris where she formed part of a secret radio network codenamed Physician. Even after most other members of the network had been arrested, Khan refused to abandon her post and return to Britain.

She was betrayed to the Germans by a fellow agent and imprisoned at the SS headquarters in Paris. After several dramatic escape attempts, the last of which resulted in her being taken to Germany and placed, shackled, in solitary confinement at Pforzheim, Khan was moved to Dachau. There, on 13 September 1944, in the woods behind the camp's crematorium, she and three other female SOE agents were, like Szabo, shot in the back of the head. This seems to have been the Nazis' standard method of executing SOE agents towards the end of the war.

Both Noor Khan and Violette Szabo were awarded a post-humous George Cross. In the award citation Szabo's escorting officer noted, that 'in a group of heavily armed and equipped men waiting to take off from the same airfield, Violette was slim, debonair. She wore a flowered frock, white sandals, and earrings which she had bought in Paris during her first mission.'[60] Elegant, even in adversity! In 1956, however, the Conservative MP Irene Ward lobbied forcefully for Szabo's George Cross to be converted to a Victoria Cross, awarded for actions 'in the face of the enemy', for fighting rather than a gallant death in captivity.

Ward was the kind of persistent, no-nonsense woman sometimes called a 'battleaxe'. She had been troubled by hints dropped in *Madeleine* and other unofficial SOE histories like Elizabeth Nicholas' *Death Be Not Proud* (1958) that the SOE was so incompetently run that operatives' lives were frequently put at risk.

Was there a conspiracy afoot? Or was this material classified for a good reason? Ward wrote to prime minister Harold Macmillan, demanding SOE files be opened to allow an official history to be written, 'an objective book ... by someone in whom we should have confidence'.[61] Macmillan agreed – though he was more bothered by America and Russia claiming credit for SOE achievements and thought a 'proper history' would set the record straight. The result was military historian Michael Foot's *SOE in France*, finally published in 1966.[62]

Irene Ward's concern was emphatically feminist: that the contributions of women who had risked – and, frequently, sacrificed – their lives should not be underplayed by a male establishment. As she wrote:

There was always the fear – generally expressed by men – that there would be a public outcry against women being employed on dangerous missions. Yet all the time, secure from public comment, women were volunteering for, and serving, in the most dangerous and hazardous of operations, and where physical as well as moral courage was a paramount necessity. To those who understand women their successes come as no surprise, but it is right for future generations to know that women themselves desired no protection when national survival was at stake.[63]

Wartime popular culture did sometimes celebrate daredevil women. Worrals was the fictional female pilot and heroine of a comic-strip created by Captain W. E. Johns of Biggles fame. Though nominally a member of the WAAF – 'Worrals of the WAAF' – she really drew inspiration from the women of the elite flying corps, the Air Transport Auxiliary (ATA). She was a refreshing change from Norman Pett's Jane cartoon for the *Daily Mirror*, about a nubile young thing whose clothes keep accidentally falling off.

The ATA caught the public imagination after the hugely popular magazine *Picture Post* used on its cover a photo of spry, beautiful 1st Officer Maureen Dunlop pushing her hair out of her face as she climbed out of a Fairey Barracuda, a diver bomber. But the editor of *The Aeroplane*, one C. G. Grey, refused to be charmed. While conceding that 'there are millions of women in the country who could do useful jobs in war', he felt strongly that too many of them craved jobs 'which they are quite incapable of doing':

The menace is the woman who thinks that she ought to be flying a high-speed bomber when she really has not the intelligence to scrub the floor of a hospital properly, or want to nose around as an Air Raid Warden and yet can't cook her husband's dinner ... One of the most difficult types of man with whom one has to deal, is that which has a certain amount of ability, too much self-confidence, an overload of conceit, and dislike of taking orders and not enough experience to balance one against the other by his own will. The combination is perhaps even more common amongst women than men.[64]

Using women in the ATA had been suggested by pilot Pauline Gower, a stalwart of the Women's Engineering Society who had written a book on women in aviation, *Women with Wings* (1938). 'I strongly advise the would-be aviatrix to wear breeches or trousers – skirts are uncomfortable and draughty in an open machine,' she wrote.[65]

Gower was such a natural that she made her first solo flight after just seven hours of instruction, gaining her licence in August 1930.

Gower and colleagues like Amy Johnson, who in 1930 became the first aviatrix to fly solo from England to Australia, soon earned the ATA a reputation for formidable efficiency against the odds. As Lord Sempill wrote: 'Miss Gower and her girls have delivered something in the neighbourhood of 3,900 machines to date, and of these only one was a "write-off" and only 14 were slightly "bent". There is no transport organisation of any kind that has such a record as that.'[66] Bear in mind that ATA pilots might have been flying any of 147 different aircraft, had no radios and only basic or broken navigation equipment, and this achievement is all the more impressive.

Lettice Curtis, an Oxford maths graduate, joined the ATA in May 1940 and became the first woman to fly a four-engine bomber. At first women were not allowed to fly operational aircraft like Spitfires, but this changed in the autumn of 1941 when the war situation worsened and the government realised it needed to use every available pilot. Curtis wrote: 'Females landing in either a Hurricane or a Spitfire at an RAF or even an ATA airfield was inevitably a matter for some comment. We felt, therefore, that the less attention we drew to ourselves the better.'[67] Trying not to give people grounds for patronising them was an additional pressure. But they endured it nevertheless.

On one occasion Curtis's friend Joan was flying a Magister from Cowley to Prestwick when she found herself unable to raise its undercarriage: the selector lever was jammed.

'We were very conscious at the time that anything we did tended to be built up into a "good story", and Joan, afraid that if she returned to complain they might attribute it to her small stature and lack of strength, put her foot on the lever and gave it a shove,' Curtis remembered years later.[68] This shove raised the undercarriage, but then the lever refused to return to neutral.

In the event Joan manoeuvred the plane into a belly landing on soft grass and survived. But rather than being relieved, she was worried about the reaction of the Accidents Committee. 'Perhaps it was a little unwise to use her foot, and what would be the effect on women pilots flying Hurricanes as a whole? Would the incident be seized on by those always standing on the side-lines ready to say: "I told you so"?'[69]

There was, however, a temporary breakthrough. From May 1943 female pilots in the ATA were paid the same as male pilots. But wage parity only lasted as long as the war. And the double standard on ability endured throughout. The nickname for male ATA pilots – 'ancient and tattered airmen': many of them were rickety First World War veterans – suggests that despite their superior pay their performance often left a lot to be desired.

Of the eight original members of the ATA's Women's Section, Mona Friedlander was an international ice hockey player; Marion Wilberforce had managed her family's estate from the age of twelve and studied Agriculture at Somerville College, Oxford; and Rosemary Rees was a professional dancer who had toured in Ceylon, China and America. Gower combined her ATA duties with being on the board of the nascent state-owned British Overseas Airways Corporation. She also had to cope with the residual effects of a serious illness she contracted at school.[70]

Sadly, neither Gower nor Johnson enjoyed long lives. Gower died in 1947 while giving birth to twins. Johnson didn't even live to see the end of the war. On 5 January 1941 the Airspeed Oxford she was ferrying crashed into the Thames Estuary en route to RAF Kidlington. She bailed out but her body was never recovered.

Lettice Curtis, however, had a long and happy life. She worked in civil aviation for many years, founded the British Women's Pilots Association, wrote several books and didn't give up flying planes until she was eighty. She died in 2014, aged ninety-nine.

———————

The top film at the British box office in 1942 was *Mrs Miniver*, starring Greer Garson as a plucky middle-class English house-wife. She is portrayed as a well-bred 'flower of England', and just to hammer the point home, the local stationmaster names a rose after her. With her architect husband and troupe of live-in staff, she is living the commuter-belt dream. But in what seems like no time at all, war shatters the idyll.

Her son goes off to fight. Her husband participates in the Dunkirk evacuation. And in the film's most famous scene, Mrs Miniver finds an injured German paratrooper at the bottom of her (massive) garden and slaps him in the face. 'We will come,' the soldier tells her. 'We will bomb your cities.'

Churchill loved the film and is supposed to have said that, in its depiction of British pluck, it did more for the Allies than a flotilla of battleships. Even Nazi propaganda chief Joseph Goebbels praised its 'refined powerful propagandistic tendency'.

By this stage of the war, however, the average British housewife probably feared running out of food and other essential items more than stumbling across a stray Nazi. The pressure to econo-mise dictated a woman's every move. Shopping was a miserable experience characterised by interminable queues for often nonex-istent products. And as for eating ...

'Whether you are shopping, cooking or eating, remember, FOOD IS A MUNITION OF WAR, DON'T WASTE IT,' ran one official edict. And so the nation was guilt-tripped into eating creations like Woolton Pie, an artful melange of root vegetables and grated cheese named after Lord Woolton, head of the Ministry of Food. Women like Marguerite Patten worked hard to persuade people that, actually, you could do a lot with potatoes and egg powder – and whale meat wasn't so bad if you knew how to cook it.

Patten had originally wanted to be an actor but ended up as a cookery demonstrator for the American fridge manufacturer Frigidaire, a job she loved because the company paid for her to travel everywhere first-class. After war broke out she moved to the Ministry of Food, giving cookery demonstrations at local markets and, from 1943 onwards, the Ministry's bureau within Harrods, often to people who had never had to cook their own food before. She combined this with radio appearances on programmes like *Woman's Hour* and *Kitchen Front*.

The question of how to implement rationing in a way that didn't result in the nation becoming malnourished had been a particularly pressing one for the government. Before the Second World War, few people had thought seriously – which is to say, scientifically – about the impact of food on the human body. Luckily for Britain, one of them was Elsie Widdowson.

Born in Surrey in 1906, Elsie was one of only three women in her year at Imperial College, London, where she studied chemistry. After initial work on the distribution of sugars in apples, she switched disciplines to human biochemistry, specifically dietetics – human nutrition and the regulation of diet.

In 1933, as a young postgraduate, she met her lifelong research partner Dr Robert McCance in the unlikely setting of the kitchen at King's College Hospital. McCance kept bringing large joints of meat into the kitchen to be cooked. Why? His current project, he informed Widdowson when he invited her to his laboratory, was an investigation into what the cooking process removed from meat and vegetables.

Among McCance's previous work was a study of carbohydrates in fruits, vegetables and nuts, examining how they were destroyed by acid hydrolysis. When Widdowson read it she realised, based on her own research on apples, that some of his figures were wrong, and told him so. But he was impressed rather than annoyed and asked her to work with him, helping her obtain a grant so that they could do another study together.[71] Their partnership – professional only, as Widdowson never married – lasted for sixty years.

One afternoon in 1934, on a family trip to Box Hill, Widdowson had an idea. What if she and McCance were to compile a set of tables showing the nutritional composition of all foods regularly produced and consumed in Britain? McCance was keen and the result was *The Chemical Composition of Foods*, published in 1940 and for many years the standard text on the subject. Next, the pair became interested in how the body behaved under nutritional duress. How did removing all salt from the diet affect kidney function? How did the body regulate iron absorption? To find out, they injected themselves intravenously with iron.

It was a risky venture. In 1938, after a brief trip to America, Widdowson followed McCance to Cambridge where he had been made a Reader of Medicine. It was there that their fondness for self-experimentation nearly killed them, though with typical understatement they called what happened 'a slight accident'. In a bid to work out how long it took for strontium – a chemical element occurring naturally in various minerals – to be excreted from the body they injected each other with it for a week, measuring its levels daily in their urine and stools.

After twenty-four hours they decided to double the dose, which involved sterilising a second batch of strontium lactate. Unfortunately, this batch became contaminated and less than an hour after injecting it the pair fell seriously ill. Only the chance intervention of a passing colleague who found them slumped in the laboratory saved their lives.

The Chemical Composition of Foods had been bedside reading for government scientists trying to devise a workable rationing programme. Once rationing was up and running, though, Widdowson and McCance wondered about its impact on the population. Could you *really* live on cabbage, bread and potatoes augmented by tiny amounts of protein and be healthy enough to work or fight? Could your children live on such a diet without suffering developmentally?

They and their team followed the restrictive wartime diet to the letter for six months, then took an arduous walking and cycling holiday in the Lake District to test their levels of fitness. Perhaps surprisingly, these turned out to be much the same as they had been on a pre-war diet. The only problem was calcium. Not enough of it was present in the small amount of milk and cheese permitted. And wholemeal bread, which the nation was obliged to eat thanks to shortages of white flour, impaired calcium's absorption by the body.

On Widdowson and McCance's recommendation, 120mg of calcium carbonate (chalk, in other words) was added to every 100g of the 85 per cent wholemeal flour used to make bread at the time. The result was the grey, squidgy, largely unloved National loaf, introduced in 1942. It was a fixture of British life until its abolition in 1956, but Widdowson's influence persisted into a post-war world of water fluoridation and the fortifying of breakfast cereals with vitamins and iron.

After VE Day on 8 May 1945 the decision was made to hold a snap election rather than wait for victory in Japan. Attlee wanted Labour to stay in the coalition, but his Labour colleague Ellen Wilkinson disagreed, preferring to put clear blue water between their own party and the Conservatives. Her threepenny pamphlet *Plan For Peace: How The People Can Win The Peace* argued that the statist hand-holding of the war years should be used as the political launch-pad for a better, fairer society: 'In the modern world full employment, industrial efficiency, social security and well-built houses for all can only be achieved if there is a plan.'[72]

With radio an increasingly important tool, the competing parties put a lot of effort into their campaign broadcasts. Labour fielded nine MPs to participate in BBC talks. Wilkinson was the only woman – a scenario played out on broadcasting networks to this day. Her talk, broadcast on 14 June, focused on post-war economic planning. She dismissed the Conservatives' idea that private enterprise would bring prosperity to the masses as 'the wildest pipe dream of the lot' and called deregulation 'a grim polka to perdition'. The social-research organisation Mass-Observation's survey of responses to the talks found that Wilkinson's had resonated more than the others. 'She says she's going to do it, and somehow, I think she means it,' said a Labour-supporting van driver from East Fulham, while even a Conservative housewife preferred her plain-speaking manner to 'so many of these "Sir Somebody Somebody or other"'.[73]

The nation went to the polls on 5 July. In the event, Labour's victory, especially the magnitude of the swing, took everyone by surprise, even though Churchill's campaign was widely regarded as lacklustre. Labour gained nearly 250 seats.

Women wanted a better, more just world, enacting the social reforms promised in the Beveridge Report, which laid the foundations for the welfare state, and was a bestseller when it was published in November 1942, selling over 600,000 copies. But they also wanted things to return to normal. As Sheila Rowbotham puts it: 'There was a powerful longing for personal life and space to do everything which had been impossible during the war, including going on holiday.'[74] In her book *A Century of Women* (1997) Rowbotham quotes Zelma Katin, a female bus conductor, whose aspirations were heartbreakingly mundane: 'I want to lie in bed until eight o'clock, to eat a meal slowly, to sweep the floors when they are dirty, to sit in front of the fire, to walk on the hills, to go shopping of an afternoon, to gossip at odd minutes.'[75]

Six weeks after VE Day, demobilisation began in earnest. Married women were the first to be released from service. Men were given a 'demob suit', women 56 clothing coupons and an allowance of £12 10s so that they could choose their own Utility outfits. A new world beckoned but, as it had been after the First World War, women's place in it was uncertain. The country was a mess – bomb-ravaged, exhausted, £3 billion in debt to the 'sterling area' of countries that pegged their currencies to the pound or used the pound as currency; no longer able to fall back on the Lend-Lease agreements with the United States that had supplied it with food and oil during the war.[76] The grand project of rebuilding Britain required women to be wives and mothers first. Those who had served needed to put their cherished new freedoms to one side and rejoin civilian society on terms that felt vaguely insulting.

On 6 and 9 August 1945, the United States dropped atomic bombs on Hiroshima and Nagasaki respectively. They were given names – Fat Man and Little Boy. Thousands were killed immediately; thousands more over subsequent months and years from the effects of radiation poisoning. Quite suddenly, the world had changed, as the Scottish novelist Naomi Mitchison recognised. She found she kept 'thinking of this bomb and what it may make the future look like'. The writer Ursula Bloom remembered the exact moment of its announcement: 'My husband looked at me across the lounge of the London flat, and I looked at him. Horror filled us both, and to such a degree that for a moment neither of us could speak.'[77]

But the short-term tactical goal was achieved: within ten days, Japan had surrendered and the Second World War was over. Knowledge of the hideous extent of Nazi barbarism resulted in a new appetite for legislated human rights and freedoms – partly satisfied by the UN Charter, which came into force on 24 October

1945. But it also, as Jill Liddington says in her book *The Road to Greenham Common* (1989), 'put pacifism on the moral defensive'.[78]

Fighting Hitler had been morally necessary. Who, now, was thinking about peace as Virginia Woolf had while planes looped above her? Both she and her fellow feminist Helena Swanwick were dead. Back in 1938, just before the Munich crisis, the writer and pacifist Vera Brittain's husband George Catlin had repeatedly asked her the 'one agitating question. What are you going to do? If war comes, what are you going to do?'[79]

In practical terms Brittain spent the war raising funds for the Peace Pledge Union, her pacifism having acquired a Christian cast. She wrote her fortnightly circular *Letters to Peace Lovers* and protested against the saturation bombing of German cities. Intellectually, however, she was adrift and her obsession with Britain's mistreatment (as she saw it) of the vanquished Germany led her to some bizarre, conspiracist conclusions: in a letter sent to campaigners on 3 May 1945 she made the appalling remark that the British media's coverage of the discovery of the Nazi death camps was 'partly, at least, in order to divert attention from the havoc produced in German cities by allied obliteration bombing'.[80]

After Beacon Hill school closed in 1943, Dora Russell continued her campaigning after a fashion, working for the Ministry of Information as a writer and translator on *The British Ally*, a propaganda English-language newspaper published in Moscow by the British government. The work chimed with Russell's pro-Soviet sympathies. But Britain's great ally was about to become its enemy, one from whom the nuclear secret must be kept at all costs.

As the 1940s shaded into the 1950s, many women would feel betrayed at the casual loss of the progress they had made during the war; infuriated by a burgeoning cult of domesticity that other women — women they had worked alongside, joked with, considered allies — seemed happy to embrace. But none of this was straightforward. Who was to say those homemaker women were wrong? They were only doing what the government was encouraging them to do. The last six years had been hell. Who *wouldn't* opt for peace and stability, if peace and stability were being offered?

'After the war some English women will go on with their new interests; others will return to the demands of family life,' writer Anne Stewart Higham had predicted in 1941, accurately as it turned out:

> There will be diverse economic and social problems. But perhaps there will also be a greater understanding among different types of people, greater understanding of the needs in local administration, housing, health and education. Perhaps the awakening to the real meaning and value of democracy brought on by the impact of war will bear new fruit under the impact of postwar reconstruction. The women of Britain will have their place in this work. The cooperative companionship among all women – in the home, the office, the factory, and on the farm – kindled by the war can do much for peace.[81]

6

Remake, Remodel

1945–61

On 4 May 1951, in a flurry of ceremonial excess – a special service at St Paul's; a forty-one-gun salute and some weird business involving the Lord Mayor of London and a sword – an ailing King George VI declared the Festival of Britain open.

Conceived several years earlier at the height of austerity, the festival was supposed to boost national morale and showcase British talent, much as Prince Albert's Great Exhibition had a hundred years earlier. 'It is a celebration in which the whole of Britain will be able to take part, and in which the whole nation will itself be on show,' promised a brochure published by the Welsh committee of the Festival of Britain Office, adding unconvincingly: 'There has never been anything like it before.'[1]

Unlike the Great Exhibition, which was contained within the Crystal Palace in Hyde Park, the Festival of Britain played itself out in a variety of venues across the country. The focus, however, was a twenty-seven-acre site on London's South Bank where visitors could find, among much else, the Royal Festival Hall (designed by two men); the Dome of Discovery (designed by a man); and Skylon, a slender, cigar-shaped sculpture (designed by three men) which seemed to float above the ground. In the Homes and Gardens Pavilion (designed by four men) you could see two rooms themed around the idea of 'space-saving', which featured smart modern furniture by Robin Day (a man) and colourful abstract-patterned textiles by – hurrah! – a woman: his wife, Lucienne.

As it happened, one of Lucienne's textile designs, Calyx – a quiet riot of Miro-esque cup-shaped petals – soon became a motif for this bright new postwar society. Dark, heavy Victorian furniture had no place in 1950s Britain, nor the mean, spindly Utility furniture of the previous decade. Yet these new designs had to feel immediate and accessible, not like something from a science-fiction novel. As Lucienne Day remembered decades later: 'Robin wanted something that the ordinary man or woman in the street could buy. I took the fabric to Heal's to be made, where I had a contact. They said, "We shan't sell any of this." But they did – it was instantly a great success.'[2]

On the whole there was huge excitement in the run-up to the festival. But not everyone was impressed. 'WHAT a muddle! Hideous buildings in a sea of mud!' wrote Gladys Langford, a middle-aged schoolteacher who kept a diary for Mass-Observation and had made a special trip to the Embankment to check on developments.[3]

Jane Drew, one of Britain's few high-profile female architects (and one of the small number of women involved in the festival's conception), thought the 1940s South Bank 'really looked like a piece of Dickens'.[4] The buildings chosen to fill this wasteland were, with the exception of the Royal Festival Hall, temporary structures thrown up quickly and cheaply using modern materials like concrete, steel and aluminium. They could be demolished quickly too, which would come in handy the following year when the festival was dismantled by a newly re-elected Winston Churchill.

When the invitation came to participate in the festival, Edwin Maxwell Fry – Jane Drew's husband and fellow partner in their architectural practice – was sceptical. He disliked the idea, which he thought the festival promoted, that architecture was a passing distraction rather than central to the way people inhabited and experienced the built world.

Drew disagreed. So while Fry worked abroad, Drew stayed in London and finessed the designs, relishing the opportunity to create forward-looking, abrasive work she wouldn't have been able to get away with in any other context. She later described the festival as 'like lifting the lid off a pressure cooker': 'It was the first time since the war that people were asked to be inventive ... and they responded.'[5]

Indeed, it was almost the first time since the war that Britons had been confronted with design that wasn't boringly utilitarian. The ceramic artist Clarice Cliff, whose hyper-colourful Art Deco 'Bizarre' range of pottery had been such a hit in the 1920s and 1930s, had had to stop her design work as only plain white pottery was permitted by wartime regulations. Dior's New Look, unveiled in Paris in 1947, wasn't allowed in Britain until 1949 because its full skirts required decadent amounts of the wrong sort of fabrics, not to mention corsetry which, under rationing, could only be obtained with a doctor's note. (An exception was made for Princess Margaret, who had a secret Dior fitting at the British Embassy in Paris in 1947.)

Drew and her colleagues were assigned a section at the north end of the festival site. Included in this was the marine-themed Harbour Bar, whose canvas awnings would be much admired, and the Riverside Restaurant, for which Drew fashioned a distinctive undulating cork-and-aluminium roof, prefabricated by a Bristol aircraft manufacturer for hasty on-site assembly. Drew also designed the public entrance from Waterloo Bridge and its adjacent observation tower, commissioning a rotating sculpture from Barbara Hepworth to stand sentry.

Drew is one of those women – we'll meet several of them in this chapter – who defies the docile, obedient, buttoned-up stereotype of the 1950s woman to such a degree that you begin to wonder whether that image bears any relationship at all to reality.

For many women, the 1950s – especially the first half – played out as an extension of the 1940s. But for others opportunity knocked. In 1950 the journalist Katherine Whitehorn arrived in London from Cambridge, where she had been a student, to find 'paralysing fogs that left yellow greasiness over everything'.[6] But as she observes in her memoir *Selective Memory*, it wasn't depressing:

> There's been a tendency to look on the Fifties as simply a damp patch between the battleground of the Forties and the fairground of the Sixties; yet it was anything but. It's true there were still austerities, but we were used to them, and as they gradually ebbed away, we had the heady sense that everything was getting better.[7]

Jane Drew was forty in 1951 but would have struck most observers as part of the younger generation, one whose senses had been sharpened rather than blunted by the experience of war. She was born in the London suburb of Thornton Heath into a wealthy middle-class family: her father made surgical instruments; her mother was a schoolteacher. As a child, Drew liked building things out of bits of wood and bricks – 'a tiny model of the Acropolis, or a sandcastle of sophisticated intricacy'.[8] Her best friends at school were the future Liberal politician and feminist campaigner Nancy Seear and the future actor Peggy Ashcroft. Drew and Ashcroft made a pact that, whatever the pair did in life, if they married they would always use their own names rather than their husbands'. (When once, at a lecture, Drew was introduced as 'Mrs Fry', she tugged the speaker's sleeve hard, prompting the correction: 'I'm sorry Mrs Fry can't be with us tonight, instead Miss Jane Drew has kindly accepted to replace her.'[9])

Studying at the Architectural Association in 1929, Drew was one of only a dozen or so women. She paid her own fees by teaching French in the evenings. After graduating, she had trouble finding work as few architectural practices would appoint women.

Eventually she was taken on by the architect Joseph Hill, working on neo-Georgian pubs as well as more stylish Art Deco theatres and cinemas like the Odeon in Claremont Road, Surbiton. Within a few years, Drew and her first husband James Thomas Alliston had set up their own practice and were designing houses and hospitals; although Drew, her sights set beyond the mundane, was increasingly fascinated by the burgeoning Modern movement and its figurehead, Swiss-French architect Le Corbusier.

In 1937 Drew gave birth to twins, but during the war her marriage to Alliston broke down. She went on to run her own practice in King Street in central London, initially employing only female architects, although she abandoned this policy when the number of candidates proved unworkably small.

Edwin Maxwell Fry was also newly divorced when Drew met him for the first time at the Royal Institute of British Architects (RIBA). They married in 1942, and Drew joined his practice, working on projects like the Rodent House at London Zoo. Much of their work involved designing housing and public build-ings in Britain's colonial territories. Together they evolved a new style of what they called 'tropical architecture' to suit the climate, culture and ecology of countries like India. After partition in 1947, they were commissioned by the Indian prime minister Pandit Nehru to design Chandigarh, the new capital of Punjab, which Nehru envisaged as radical and ultra-modern. Drew persuaded Le Corbusier to become involved. She and Fry spent the best part of three years living and working with him in Chandigarh as part of the Chandigarh Capital Project Team.

On a more humdrum level, Drew was fascinated by new synthetic materials like Formica and enamel and how these might be used in the kitchens of the future. Acting as consultant for the British Commercial Gas Association, she gave her work a femi-nist gloss: 'Every woman agrees that household drudgery must be banished after the war and that's why I'm concentrating on kitch-ens.'[10] Her designs were published as *Kitchen Planning: A Brochure of New Plans and Suggestions for Labour-saving Kitchens* in 1945 and helped promote the idea that kitchens should be integrated with, rather than adjuncts to, the modern household. Admittedly, they deemed the kitchen a female-only zone – one of Drew's design goals was 'to establish the right height for a cooker that would be comfortable for the majority of women'.[11] I think we can excuse this because the prospect of men taking any interest in food storage and preparation was, at this stage, pie in the sky.

To succeed as a female architect you were supposed to be modest and unassuming; bite your tongue rather than make a fuss when, as happened to Drew, the Colonial Office docked your wages by £100 because of your gender.[12] Drew was loudly intolerant of injustice and didn't mind giving offence. As a result, say the architecture critics Iain Jackson and Jessica Holland, her value as a designer 'is often downplayed or dismissed entirely, and Fry seen as the creative talent of the duo' when this is far from the truth.[13]

Maxwell Fry was an ideological modernist who privileged aesthetics over everything else. Drew was always more concerned with how a beautiful idea might work in practice: 'I have to confess that the jobs I've done in my life, I have always been involved in the cause of the job ... It has always mattered to me tremendously that the object should be something very worthwhile.'[14]

Drew was renowned for being difficult, headstrong, opinionated. 'Her personality seemed to either enthral or repel those she encountered,' writes Jackson, 'and even today stories about her misdemeanours abound – nearly all concerned with her supposed amorous appetite and lack of ability as a designer.'[15] In fact, she had designed a village and a school in Kenya before she even met Fry and in 1945 had established the *Architects' Year Book*, a journal featuring writing by key thinkers in the field.

It's surprising – or perhaps not – how many successful creative women from this era acquired reputations for being (to use a recently popularised phrase) 'bloody difficult women'. Lucienne Day didn't suffer fools gladly. The composer Elisabeth Lutyens was the equal of the men who dominated the classical music scene but has been eclipsed by her reputation as a cantankerous, self-destructive alcoholic. The film producer Betty Box, best known for the *Doctor* ... series of hit comedies starring Dirk Bogarde, and her director sister-in-law Muriel Box had to be ruthless in the face of sniping from the likes of Michael Balcon, the head of Ealing Studios, who believed women 'lacked the qualities necessary to control a large film unit'.[16]

Shelagh Delaney's debut play *A Taste of Honey*, about a fiery Salford girl much like Delaney who sleeps with a Nigerian sailor, gets pregnant and is then looked after by a gay art student, was first staged in 1958. The programme notes praised Delaney's 'fierce independence of mind', which is telling. A working-class renegade in an industry dominated by well-spoken upper-middle-class types, Delaney wrote the play aged nineteen after being taken to see Terence Rattigan's *Variation of a Theme* in Manchester and deciding she could do better. She fought attempts to constrain her – she was furious when told she wasn't allowed to spend the money she made from the film rights until she was twenty-one – and ignored the advice of her patron at London's Theatre Royal Stratford East, Joan Littlewood, that she should take time out and learn more about her craft before writing a follow-up.[17] Her theatrical career spluttered out after the relative failure of her second play *The Lion in Love*, although she had a late flowering as a screenwriter, penning the screenplay for Mike Newell's 1985 film *Dance With A Stranger*, about Ruth Ellis, the last woman to be hanged in Britain.

Female novelists seemed to have a better time of it. Finding a publisher was easy and effortless for the young Iris Murdoch, whose first novel *Under the Net* came out in 1954. 'Chatto's taking my novel,' she noted, the only reference to the publishing process in journals that span sixty years. As her biographer Peter Conradi points out, 'her success was instantaneous.'[18]

It was a similar story for Muriel Spark, whose debut *The Comforters* was accepted by Macmillan in 1955 and tells of a woman who hears constant typewriter clicking and comes to realise she is a character in a novel. The book was inspired by hallucinations Spark experienced after becoming addicted, like many women at the time, to the dieting pills Dexedrine – sold over-the-counter in chemists in the 1950s. Macmillan asked her how much money she wanted for the book. She suggested £100.[19] Fine, they said – and that was that.

It's worth pointing out, though, that to get this far, to the point of having written a publishable novel, Spark had had to show a brave disregard for convention, which looked to some like ruthlessness. She abandoned not only her abusive husband but also her son in Southern Rhodesia, where they had all been living, in order to return to Britain. Strong-minded to a tee, she instructed her publishers not to change any punctuation even if it looked wrong and to reinstate passages they had cut on the grounds of mild indecency. When asked to supply a biographical note, she sent them this: 'Born in ice cave of southern Tyrol, year 609 BC of centaur stock, mother descended from Venus. Muriel Spark rose from the waves as is well known. Demands fabulous fees.'[20]

As far as fabulous fees were concerned, the female writer to beat was Agatha Christie. By 1950 the Queen of Crime was more successful than ever, having sold some fifty million books worldwide, even if her creative powers were arguably on the wane.[21] Film and stage adaptations of her murder mysteries proliferated. In 1953 the play *Witness for the Prosecution* became one of her biggest successes, packing out theatres in both London and New York before being filmed to great acclaim by Billy Wilder. The year before, *The Mousetrap* had opened at London's Ambassadors Theatre. 'Too obvious by half' was the verdict of the *Daily Express*. No one could have had any inkling that it would still be running over sixty years and 25,000 performances later.

The Festival of Britain had been a badly needed psychological (if not material) break from a programme of austerity still going strong six years after the end of the war. In some respects things had deteriorated since 1945. A 1948 Gallup poll found that 42 per cent of Britons wanted to emigrate – and in fact 720,000 did between 1946 and 1950, mostly to Australia.[22] Meanwhile, a Mass-Observation report from 1947 observed:

> Shortages in women's clothes are a little less obvious [than men's], though underclothes, gloves, stockings, shoes and handkerchiefs stocks are considerably lower in 1947 than in 1941. To some extent, female clothes stocks have also changed their character: there are more blouses, skirts and jackets hanging in the 1947 wardrobe, and rather fewer dresses and evening dresses. Women mention much more frequently than men that they are 'sick to death' of their present clothes …[23]

In January 1947 the meat ration was cut to lower than its wartime level. Bread hadn't been rationed during the war, but it was for two years from July 1946. The whole business proved too much for Dorothy Crisp, noisy mouthpiece of the right-wing British Housewives' League, who rejected the idea that rationing was the fairest way to distribute goods in a time of scarcity. A Royal Albert Hall rally organised by her League in June 1948 descended into chaos when it was hijacked by left-wing feminists and Crisp was reduced to standing on a platform blowing a police whistle to try to restore order.[24]

A major problem was the acute shortage of housing: many people were still living in temporary accommodation or even bomb shelters. Jane Drew suspected that addressing the postwar housing crisis would involve an even bigger job than architects had had after the last war. Partly that job fell to her: she worked on several post-war social housing projects including the

Downham Estate in Lewisham and the Usk Street Housing Estate in Bethnal Green.

But did Britons want their homes to be the same as they had been before the war? By and large, the answer was no. The desire for privacy was strong after the fraternising that had been forced upon people in wartime. Equally strong was the belief that the home was emphatically a woman's realm. 'The bigger problems – the location of industry, the position of agriculture in our national economy, the gigantic task of finding employment for the people – women leave to their menfolk,' wrote Millicent Pleydell-Bouverie in the *Daily Mail Book of Postwar Homes* (1944). 'But housing is a woman's business. She has to make a home of the houses men build.'[25]

The *Daily Mail* brought in a female architect called Barbara Auld to identify and design the sort of home women wanted. More than 90 per cent of women interviewed by the paper expressed a preference for a house or bungalow. The ideal was a well-built three-bedroom house in a cul-de-sac planted with trees, arranged in a cluster rather than the repetitive strip characteristic of ribbon development. The house needed to be close to amenities such as shops, doctors' surgeries and churches, and within walking distance of public transport. According to the Women's Advisory Housing Council, 52 per cent of women wanted to live in a suburb or small town, 30 per cent in the countryside, and only 17 per cent in a city.[26] Sixty-four per cent of women wanted a separate kitchen that wasn't dark and cramped like the kitchens they'd been used to, but properly designed with fitted units; smooth, easily cleanable work surfaces; and 'tools as up-to-date and as well chosen for their purpose, and as well-placed, as the tools in a modern workshop'.[27] A girl-shed!

'Out of the wholesale destruction caused by war, the revolt against slums and the realisation that God's fresh air and good earth are the natural inheritance of the human race, should arise a new domestic world, a new domestic architecture,' thundered Pleydell-Bouverie. 'The younger generation know and feel it is long overdue.'[28]

By the end of the 1940s austerity would, for some, start to shade into affluence: in 1949 the earnings of a manual worker were 241 per cent of their 1937 level; those of a member of the higher professions 188 per cent.[29] One useful index of affluence is consumer aspiration. Elizabeth David's classic *A Book of Mediterranean Food* was published in 1950, four years before rationing ended. It contained ingredients most people in Britain had never heard of – *aubergines?* – and certainly wouldn't have been able to buy. But it raised the curtain on a more sophisticated Britain unafraid to admit that it might have something to learn from sun-kissed Europe. One cook who swore by David's book in the early 1950s was the scientist Rosalind Franklin. Franklin served her friends such exotic fare as pigeon, rabbit and artichokes and wasn't afraid to use garlic.[30]

In fact, Britain had much to learn from a whole range of countries, particularly the ones it ruled. For by the late 1940s imperial certainties were crumbling. British India was partitioned into the separate states of Pakistan and India, which achieved independence on 15 August 1947. The following year Britain withdrew its authority from Palestine, which it had been awarded as a mandate by the League of Nations in 1922. Over the next few years there would be violence in Kenya – the so-called 'Mau-Mau uprising' of the Kikuyu against colonial settlers, which ran from 1952 until 1960 – and Cyprus, where Greek and Turkish Cypriots fought over whether the island, a British colony since 1878, should become part of Greece. The nail in the Empire's coffin would be Britain's humiliating withdrawal from Egypt after the Suez crisis in 1956.

The nationalisation of the Suez canal by the Egyptian president Gamal Abdel Nasser had given the British prime minister, Anthony Eden, a pretext for invading Egypt in collusion with

France and Israel. Britain's campaign ended after the United States effectively forced a ceasefire by threatening to sell its sterling bonds. Eden's retreat sent a message to former colonial powers that Britain was no longer in a position to defend her assets.

Notoriously, in the aftermath of the crisis, Eden's wife Lady Eden told a group of Conservative women that for its duration she had felt as if the Suez canal was flowing through her drawing room. For other women, it flowed through their offices. Mary Gilbraith was one of seventeen women recruited to the elite administrative grade of the Foreign Service between 1946 and 1951 – 'a tiny fraction of the total intake over that period',[31] as historian Helen McCarthy observes. Unfortunately for Gilbraith, her posting to New York to join the British Mission to the UN coincided with the Suez debacle. She had a 'frightful' time, 'no one knew what was going on', and anti-British feeling within the UN was strong. She was in constant, frenetic contact with London and barely slept, so busy was she drafting speeches and sitting in on Security Council sessions.[32]

Part of the reason for the confusion and anti-British feeling may have been a creeping sense, just starting to be articulated at home, that Britain's status on the world stage was declining. By 1959, when the Labour politician John Strachey published his rumination on Britain's post-imperial future *The End of Empire*, it would be even harder to deny.

Strachey argued that former imperial powers needed to find a new ideal that went beyond 'personal enrichment'. Britain, he noted, had since 1945 developed a 'welfare ideal' in the form of the NHS and other manifestations of the welfare state. But while this was a good start, it wasn't enough: 'Nations, it seems, must aspire as well as simply live, if they are to be healthy.'[33]

It sounds rather haughty, after years of rationing, to talk of people 'simply' living well, as if it were an easy, obvious thing to do. Even in the late 1950s, the NHS would still have seemed miraculous to most Britons – especially women, for whom it had transformed the whole business of child-rearing.

But let's rewind a little. The welfare state arose not only from the emergency planning that had pulled the country through the war, but also from decades of social activism, much of it by women. In fact, the welfare state can be traced back to the work of the pioneering women we met in earlier chapters like Josephine Butler. In the mid 1940s it fell to thinkers like the social scientist Barbara Wootton – one-time president of the Young Suffragist society, committed pacifist and the first woman to lecture at Cambridge University – to put flesh on the concept's bones.

By 1945 the idea that something radical had to be done to improve what we might call 'the condition of Britain' was not in itself radical. Even those on the right conceded that statist central planning had served Britain well since its introduction in 1939. But out in the country at large, there was confusion and uncertainty over what the future might hold. A report by Mass-Observation found that 'five people were pessimistic to every one that was optimistic about reconstruction plans in general after the war, and that proportion increased to nine to one in certain heavily-raided areas'.[34]

The first post-war general election was scheduled to take place on 5 July 1945. The campaign was dirty and bad-tempered as the coalition partners' mask of tolerance and solidarity began to slip. Churchill came out of it worst. The heroic war leader had fought a cheap, unconvincing campaign, telling the country that Clement Attlee's Labour party would only be able to implement its socialist policies – the plans for a welfare state outlined in the Beveridge Report which most Tories also broadly supported – with the help of 'some form of a Gestapo, no doubt very humanely directed in the first instance'.[35]

Still, the scale of Labour's victory was immense and unexpected: suddenly it had 393 MPs, 21 of them women. In fact, the only female MPs who *weren't* Labour were the Conservative Viscountess, Lady Davidson, and the youngest daughter of the former Liberal prime minister David Lloyd George, Megan Lloyd George. The latter, MP for Anglesey since 1929, soon became firm friends with a rookie Labour MP called Barbara Castle. Once, in the Lady Members' Room, the pair pushed two desks together and danced the can-can.[36] Castle, one of 87 female candidates out of almost 1,700, had spent the war as an administrative officer in the Fish Division of the Ministry of Food. Based in the requisitioned Carlton Hotel in London's West End, the Ministry housed its fish stocks in the bathrooms, and as Castle remembered: 'One bathroom was occupied by a bathful of snoek – an evil-looking fish from South Africa.'[37]

A cynic might argue that it is but a short journey from bathfuls of snoek to the House of Commons where, after being elected MP for Blackburn, Castle found herself the youngest woman member, posing shyly for official photos wedged between big beasts like the former Home Secretary Herbert Morrison, now deputy prime minister, and Aneurin 'Nye' Bevan at the Ministry of Health. When her friend Michael Foot, the future Labour leader, tried to take her on a tour of her new home the pair were stopped by a policeman who said, 'I am sorry, Mr Foot, you cannot take visitors there.' Foot replied: 'This isn't a visitor. She is Mrs Barbara Castle, MP.'[38]

In the same cohort was Yorkshire's first female MP, Alice Bacon, elected to represent Leeds North East on a 23 per cent swing from Conservative to Labour. A miner's daughter from Normanton, she had made her first political speech aged sixteen in support of a friend of her father who was standing in a local council election. She understood working-class Labour voters better than anyone, but in the ideological battleground of the 1950s and 1960s would face constant criticism for being insufficiently left-wing. Like most female MPs, she was patronised and belittled by men in Westminster – Hugh Gaitskell called her a 'clever girl';[39] her voice was frequently described as grating, her appearance as plump and dowdy.

But then, this sort of sexism was par for the course. Bacon's fellow Labour MPs Bessie Braddock and Leah Manning were known as 'United Dairies' because they both had large breasts. Taking up her hard-won post, Barbara Castle found she had no desk, let alone an office of her own. The Lady Members' Room was tiny and had just seven desks. Female MPs often had to work with their papers spread out on benches or even the floor.[40]

It would be natural for Castle to feel a bit nervous about making her maiden speech. She seems to have chosen the quietest moment she could: a 4 p.m. Adjournment Debate on a Friday afternoon when hardly anyone was there. But she had no qualms about invading the boys' club that was the Members' Smoking Room, where all the juiciest political gossip was traded. The only thing that stopped her going more often was the expense of buying everyone drinks on her 'derisory' £600-a-year salary.

Castle appears to have made every effort to get along with the boys. In her parliamentary selection meeting she had proclaimed: 'I am no feminist, I want you to judge me only as a socialist.' The MP Rachel Reeves, who many years later would win Bacon's seat for Labour, suggests her predecessor 'took the same line', anxious to be representative of her constituents 'over and above any trail-blazing of the feminist cause'.[41]

There was certainly hard, practical work to be done. Barbara Castle found her weekly surgeries at her constituency of Blackburn in Lancashire revealing: 'Demobilisation, housing, pensions, poverty: the problems came pouring out and I went away awed by the size of the miracles the government was supposed to work overnight.'[42]

Fortunately, legislation designed to enact those miracles was coming thick and fast. There was the Family Allowances Act, the first law to provide child benefit, which Eleanor Rathbone, its champion for decades, just lived to see reach the statute book in June 1945.

In pursuit of its declared goal of full employment, the government nationalised key industries (coal, iron, steel, the railways) and institutions such as the Bank of England. This way, the thinking went, people would be put before profit. The 1944 Education Act introduced free milk and school meals; also the 11-plus exam, after which children would be siphoned off irrespective of social class into one of three different schools: grammars for the brightest, technical schools for the technically minded, and secondary moderns for everyone else. It raised the school leaving age to fifteen, theoretically giving children opportunities their parents had never had.

The 1946 National Insurance Act introduced a comprehensive system of social security, including funeral grants, sickness and maternity benefits and pensions. In 1948 came the National Assistance Act (replacing the Poor Law); the Children Act, revolutionising social work for deprived children; and Aneurin 'Nye' Bevan's National Health Service Act, promising free cradle-to-grave healthcare for all, once a sceptical medical profession had been convinced.

The psychologists Eliot Slater and Moya Woodside were not alone in hoping 'much good will result from the introduction of the NHS'. Researching urban working-class marriages in the late 1940s, they had been shocked by the poor physical condition of the wives, many of whom existed in a state of total ignorance about their bodies. They seemed almost to be rotting away. 'Teeth were on the whole very bad. Eight women, several of them under thirty, had complete sets of dentures; many others had a partial set, or had carious teeth.'[43] In addition, 'menstrual dysfunction was common. Girls are conditioned to expect pain, malaise and partial incapacity at the time of "the curse". The information given to the adolescent is inaccurate or inadequate, and she is left to be influenced by the feelings of fear and embarrassment naturally aroused by the appearance of blood.'[44] An important role for the NHS, they felt, was educational intervention at an early stage: 'Girls should be given some information about menstruation and sexual physiology before puberty, as a knowledge of fact acquired then will determine the later attitude.'[45]

Thanks to the welfare state, Vera Brittain wrote, women had 'moved within thirty years from rivalry with men to a new recognition of their unique value as women'. But the truth was, there was a long way to go.

Take National Insurance, for example. William Beveridge believed that, since wives were supported by their husbands, they didn't need insurance to qualify for benefits like a state pension. Even if they worked, when they lost their jobs their husbands would support them, wouldn't they? There was also a suspicion they were probably only working to earn extra money to spend on fancy clothes and holidays. A 1956 *Picture Post* captured the disapproval several years later, posing the question in an article about day nurseries: 'Is it really necessary in this Welfare State for a woman to go out to work, or do they do it for the ice cream and the TV?' Single women were covered, but lost all their insurance credits as soon as they married. Married women could opt in to the insurance system, but unless they contributed for half their married lives they didn't get a pension when they retired.

By 1951, one in four married women was working. But these women were routinely discriminated against in the workplace: under-deployed, usually the first to be fired, and, if they worked part-time and had opted in to the National Insurance scheme, irritating to employers, who had to pay the same flat-rate contribution for part-time workers as they did for full-time ones. Little wonder some companies like Marks & Spencer actively sought out married women who had 'no interest in their own personal insurability'.[46] Barbara Castle fought for reform of the scheme. From her contact with married women workers in her Lancashire constituency she knew that 'the concept of "dependency" was out

of date ... I instinctively rejected the whole concept of dependency, which visualised most women as satellites of men.'[47]

Then there was education. The tripartite education system
created by the Education Act – whose implementation fell to a
woman, Ellen Wilkinson – produced the women who came to
define second-wave feminism in Britain in the 1960s and 1970s.[48]
But it also made random failures of clever women who faced
discrimination in the 11-plus exam. Girls' 11-plus performances
were weighted differently to boys' so that girls 'achieved fewer
places than their examination results indicated'.[49] The writer and
activist Beatrix Campbell, who ended up at Harraby Secondary
Modern School, has called it 'a disgraceful thing to have happened
to all of us, and didn't mean a damn thing about whether or not
you could do anything, because anybody can do anything'.[50]

Even if they made it to grammar schools, girls were denied the
same opportunities as boys, especially in science and technical
subjects, and all too often left at fifteen before taking any public
exams. This fed into an ongoing debate about the purpose of
educating women.

School was supposed to have a bearing on professional vocation. Some argued that if women abandoned that vocation to have
children, the state was absolved of its responsibility to educate
them. Wasn't it better to stop messing about and simply teach
them how to be mothers? This was the case put by the educationalist John Newsom in his bad-tempered tract *The Education of
Girls* (1948):

> The majority of recent writers on women's education tend,
> somewhat naturally, to be women from an extremely limited
> section of their sex, the intellectually able, university-trained,
> professional educationist. Yet, despite their trained intelligence,
> most of them are inevitably ignorant of what the great
> multitude of ordinary girls and women really think and feel.[51]

Most married women, Newsom argued, *wanted* to stay at home and raise their children. Housework and child-rearing require energy and intellect just as paid work does, so why complain about it? 'Women are not married compulsorily or sold off as wives without being consulted,' he wrote, adding that it is 'a plain fact' that 'the majority of those who fail to reach the altar or the registrar's office would give up overnight their careers and the comforts of a celibate life if ever they got the chance'.[52]

To train girls as doctors, architects and solicitors when 'probably 75 per cent' of them will practise for fifteen years at the most is, thought Newsom, a waste of time and money. If they must work, let women be teachers or nurses as 'in the jargon of psychology, they provide a sublimation of the maternal instinct'.[53] Meanwhile, feminists like the sociologists Alva Myrdal and Viola Klein came down hard on women who gave men like Newsom ammunition, arguing in *Women's Two Roles* (1956) that educated women 'commit a sin against society if they waste the capital of skill invested in them'.[54]

Everywhere you looked there was flux and contradiction. The war had emancipated women but reinforced their status as perpetual volunteers. Women's labour was needed to kickstart the post-war economy, yet many people felt they shouldn't really be working at all. Central to Beveridge's vision was the idea that a woman's role involved domestic work, 'vital though unpaid, without which their husbands could not do their paid work and without which the nation could not continue'.[55] As well as caring for their husbands, this vital unpaid work included looking after any elderly or ill family members. But its main component was childcare: 'The attitude of the housewife to gainful employment outside the home is not and should not be the same as that of the single woman,' wrote Beveridge. 'She has other duties ... In the next thirty years housewives as mothers have vital work to do in ensuring the adequate continuance of the British Race and of British ideals in the world.'[56]

The controversial issue of equal pay was discussed but ultimately kicked into the long grass. The 1946 Equal Pay Report concluded that, while university-educated women with male-style careers as doctors or civil servants might deserve to earn the same as men, women who worked in factories didn't. The reasons given for this were vague and bogus – for example, female manual workers were accused of displaying 'a certain relative lack of flexibility in response to rapidly changing or abnormal situations'[57] – and it was clear the real sticking point was the unions' fear of antagonising the male workforce. There was one small victory, though: women *teachers* were awarded equal pay in 1953.

Towards the end of the war, Geoffrey Thomas conducted a survey for the Office of the Minister of Reconstruction, published as *Women at Work* in June 1944. A shocking 58 per cent of *women* questioned by Thomas 'did not believe in work after marriage, considering that a woman's place was in the home, and only financial necessity justified work for a married woman'.[58]

What of the other 42 per cent? They had an unlikely (given her later pronouncements on the subject) cheerleader in the young Margaret Thatcher.

A grammar-school beneficiary of the 1944 Education Act, Thatcher had read Chemistry at Somerville College, Oxford – she was taught by the future Nobel Prize winner Dorothy Hodgkin, who discovered the structure of vitamin B12 – and worked as a food chemist at Lyon's before switching to tax law after marrying Denis in 1950. (The popular story that she invented Mr Whippy ice cream while at Lyon's seems, sadly, to be a myth.[59]) Hodgkin managed to combine being one of Britain's pre-eminent biochemists with having three children. Perhaps her example played a part in inspiring Thatcher when the future prime minister wrote an article for the *Sunday Graphic* headlined 'Wake up, Women!' arguing for 'more and more women combining marriage AND a career'. It went on:

I should like to see EVERY woman trying to overcome
ignorance of day-to-day affairs; and EVERY woman taking
an active part in local life. And, above all, I should like to see
more and more women in Westminster, and in the highest
places, too.[60]

Reflecting on this period later in her life, Thatcher stated that she
personally needed a stimulating career 'because that was the kind
of person I was' and remembered a maxim she and the MP Irene
Ward often used: 'While the home must always be the centre of
one's life, it should not be the boundary of one's ambitions.'[61]
(This is similar to an epiphany the second-wave feminist academic
Ann Oakley – no Thatcherite – described having in the early
1970s, 'the acknowledgement that you could love your children
very much, find them absolutely wonderful, yet also find the
whole business of looking after them all the time entirely
draining'.)[62]

Thatcher, of course, was both clever and fortunate, not least in
having a wealthy husband whose response, when she told him of
her goals, was, 'Do what you like, love.'[63] Less clever or fortunate
women might have different expectations of home – and indeed
marriage.

As the war sputtered to a close, couples who had been separated
naturally looked forward to what they were sure would be a
glorious reunion. For some, this anticipation bore fruit. Others
weren't so lucky: divorce hit a peak of sixty thousand in 1947,[64] ten
times the prewar figure. In 1951 two psychologists we encountered
earlier, Eliot Slater and Moya Woodside, published their study
Patterns of Marriage, interviewing two hundred families between
October 1943 and January 1946. What they found was all too
predictable: 'The outlook of a wife might seem narrow and
restricted to a husband who had been broadened by life in the
Army ... Men generally did not welcome the increased
independence of women which had been brought by the war, by

responsibilities personally shouldered, by an independent income and out-of-home contacts.'[65] There was paranoia on both sides about wartime infidelities, but a double standard when it came to apportioning blame: husbands away fighting thought it was their right to have affairs or sleep with prostitutes but that their wives had a duty to remain faithful.[66]

In 1943, ATS-girl-turned-singer Odette Leslie had a wartime affair with a drummer she had met in a club. When the relationship petered out she wrote to her husband in Egypt where he was stationed and tried to explain what she had done. By way of reply she received a letter from her husband's commanding officer. 'Well, I've never been torn off quite such a big strip, the whole thing was done on military papers,' Odette remembered. '"You should be totally and thoroughly ashamed of yourself to write such a letter to a serving man fighting for his country ..."'[67] And yet, as Steve Humphries and Pamela Gordon point out in *Forbidden Britain* (1994), rates of venereal disease were around ten times higher among men in the armed forces than among civilians, suggesting they felt no qualms about playing away from home.

Returning soldiers often suffered from what we would now think of as post-traumatic stress disorder, but what Slater and Woodside call neurosis. This obliged their wives to assume a more maternal role, and while most 'felt sympathetic' they were 'often impatient or irritated'.[68] And so once-happy marriages like Cyril and Doreen's (the subjects of one of their case studies) slid into violent dysfunction:

After discharge from the Army, he [Cyril] earned his living as a labourer. On getting home, he might sit and not speak to her for hours, or fly into a rage and say dreadful things. He would go out at weekends or in the evening, and not say where he had been. He would demand intercourse every night, even in the eighth month of yet another pregnancy. In addition, Doreen

Labour minister Barbara Castle was a political giant whose far-reaching legislative reforms ranged from introducing compulsory seat-belts to equal pay.

Claudia Jones was a journalist and activist who founded the Notting Hill carnival and believed that 'a people's art is the genesis of their freedom'.

Dina St Johnston founded Britain's first computer software house and developed the first real-time passenger information systems for airports and train stations.

Businesswoman Margery Hurst overcame entrenched City sexism to found the first secretarial bureau to be floated on the London Stock Exchange.

Astrophysicist Jocelyn Bell Burnell discovered pulsars – rotating stars which have reached the end of their lives – paving the way for groundbreaking work on black holes.

Broadcaster Joan Bakewell endured everyday sexism in the broadcasting industry to host shows such as *Late Night Line-Up*.

Nurse and social worker Cicely Saunders pioneered the modern hospice movement, revolutionising care for the terminally ill.

Jayaben Desai orchestrated one of the defining industrial disputes of the 1970s, the strike at the Grunwick film processing plant, telling managers she and her colleagues were 'lions who can bite your head off'.

A formidable adversary of Margaret Thatcher, Brenda Dean was the first woman elected to lead a big British industrial trade union.

Roma Agrawal is a structural engineer who reached for the stars, helping create the spire of the Shard.

Cressida Dick is the first female Metropolitan Police Commissioner and a powerful LGBT+ role model.

Paris Lees spent time in jail as a teenager but is now an influential journalist and activist for trans rights.

received proof he was associating with another woman whom
he had got into trouble; and still, others were also involved.[69]

The shape of the family was changing as large Victorian families
gave way to nuclear family units with two or three children,
particularly among the middle classes. Women weren't just having
fewer children: they were having them earlier, then going back to
work. A surprise find of the 1944 *Women at Work* survey was that,
while many young women intended to stop working so that they
could have families, 'a considerable number in the higher age
groups [wish] to remain in employment'. The postwar female
workforce, predicted the document, would mainly comprise
women over the age of thirty-five; though equally there were
those who had had their fill of paid work during the war 'and in
later life could only be prompted to [return to work] by boredom
and lack of company at home'.[70]

Some observers agonised over the pressure this 'dual role'
placed on women. Others, like the social researcher Richard
Titmuss (Ann Oakley's father), thought it was ultimately liberating. As he wrote in *Essays on the Welfare State*:

> With an expectation of another 35 to 40 years of life at the age
> of 40, with the responsibilities of child upbringing nearly
> fulfilled, with so many more alternative ways of spending
> money, with new opportunities and outlets in the field of
> leisure, the question of the rights of women to an emotionally
> satisfying and independent life appears in a new guise.[71]

But other factors were keeping women shackled to the nursery.
Natalism – the active promotion of child-bearing and -rearing
– was high on the political agenda and had enthusiastic supporters in the media from figures who included the paediatrician
and psychoanalyst Donald Winnicott. In the late 1940s
Winnicott gave regular radio lectures which were collected in

1957 in a book called *The Child and the Family: First Relationships*. 'Talk about women not wanting to be housewives seems to me just nonsense,' he proclaimed, 'because nowhere else but in her own home is a woman in such command. Only in her own home is she free, if she has the courage, to spread herself, to find her own self.'[72]

Babies starved of motherly affection would, it was widely feared, become 'delinquents' in later life. 'I put it this way,' wrote Winnicott. 'When a child steals sugar he is looking for the good mother, his own, from whom he has a right to take what sweetness is there.'[73]

What, you might well ask, is the role of the 'good father' in this scenario? It wasn't a question anyone seemed very interested in answering.

———————

The plot of Josephine Tey's 1948 novel *The Franchise Affair* turns on the abduction (or not: that is the mystery) of a sixteen-year-old girl, Betty Kane, by two older women desperately seeking a servant to work in their vast, isolated house. Betty accuses them of beating her up and making her perform menial tasks. Her story is so compelling and well-told that even though the women deny the allegations they are unable to refute them satisfactorily when questioned by the police.

Tey based the plot on the real-life tale of an eighteenth-century maidservant called Elizabeth Canning. But its relevance to the so-called 'servant problem' would not have escaped any of Tey's middle-class readers. Once accustomed to having a cook, a nanny and a maid — or at the very least one of the above — they were now finding it harder and harder to fill these positions. 'I know that domestic help is scarce,' says Robert Blair, the solicitor hired by the ladies to defend them, 'but would anyone hope to enlist a servant by forcibly detaining her, to say nothing of beating and starving her?'[74] Probably not. What was becoming clear, however, was that there were certain jobs that native British women were no longer prepared to do. So who would end up doing them?

The welfare state had created a mass of jobs for women as teachers, nurses, social workers, clerical assistants, cleaners and caretakers. Between 1945 and 1951 around one million people migrated to Britain to find work and a better life. Of these around 400,000 were British subjects from her colonies and dominions, 100,000 were Irish, and 31,000 were German.[75] From the late 1940s onwards a steady stream of women willing to do many of these jobs, especially nursing, arrived in Britain.

But by the early 1950s, rather than celebrated as the solution to Britain's acute labour-shortage problem, these immigrants found themselves characterised as feckless parasites, especially if they were black. In July 1952 Osbert Peake, Minister of National Insurance, wrote that 'the public are concerned about the possible abuse of our social services by coloured immigrants from the Colonies. We cannot keep them out – or send them home again – and no doubt our standards of life – even on Assistance – are attractive to them.'[76]

Immigration had been encouraged from the moment the war ended to swell Britain's workforce. Through the European Volunteer Workers scheme, 21,434 Italian women came to Britain to work in the textile districts of Manchester, Lancashire and Yorkshire.[77] Another scheme called Balt Cygnet was designed to attract workers from the Baltic countries; Westward Ho! workers from Eastern Europe.

Niamh, an Irish nurse interviewed by the historian Louise Ryan, remembers being 'aware [of] the way people looked at Irish people here'.[78] Another trainee Irish nurse, Emer, was stung by the widespread British assumption that all Irish women were dirty: 'I can remember, they used to teach us all this stuff about hygiene, cleaning baths and all this, the sister tutor holding up a box of Vim and then she would say, "Of course you Irish girls wouldn't know about this.'"[79] Many Irish women worked in hotels in London's West End. One, the Cumberland, had 2,700 staff of whom over 90 per cent were Irish.

Sixty Polish women were already aboard the Empire Windrush when it docked in Kingston harbour in Jamaica in May 1948. Contrary to popular belief, this captured former Nazi troop ship, renamed and refitted, arrived in the Caribbean on something of a whim, not as part of a grand plan to bring immigrants to London. As Robert Winder puts it in his history of immigration to the UK, *Bloody Foreigners*, 'an enterprising skipper simply took the initiative and advertised for trade to fill his half-empty ship'.[80] There were, however, probably more takers than there would otherwise have been because the British Nationality Act had just been passed, giving British citizenship to inhabitants of Commonwealth countries. Many of them were former service-men whose justified sense of entitlement had been sharpened by the sacrifices they had recently made for the mother country: over fifteen thousand West Indians fought against Hitler in the British armed forces.

Apart from the Poles there were only two women on board: the singer and actress Mona Baptiste, who described herself to immigration on arrival as a clerk; and a stowaway, twenty-five-year-old Trinidadian dressmaker Averill Wauchope, whose passage was paid for by a ship-wide whip-round after she was discovered seven days into the trip.

Windrush has become a potent symbol of multiculturalism in Britain, lending its name to the 'Windrush generation' of West Indian immigrants. But not until the mid 1950s did women arrive in Britain in the same numbers as men: some to join husbands who had already made the journey, others to carve out independent lives. Despite the labour shortage, they still found it hard to get decent jobs; often had to accept positions for which they were overqualified; and even then were paid less than white women doing the same work.

One West Indian woman interviewed by the authors of *The Heart of the Race: Black Women's Lives in Britain* (1985) remembered rising early to get to the Labour Exchange every morning: 'I was actually looking for nursing work, but they wouldn't have me. Someone had told me that they would take me on as an auxiliary nurse and that later on I could train. But when I got to the hospital, the woman there offered me a cleaning job.'[81]

At least this woman had found somewhere to live. Others struggled as 'respectable' landlords turned them away, leaving the field clear for rogues like the notorious slum landlord Peter Rachman. Many black immigrants settled in Brixton in south London, close to the deep-level bomb shelters in Clapham where they had been housed on arrival. Rachman's seedy empire of nightclubs, brothels, mansion blocks and large houses carved up into tiny bedsits was based in Notting Hill in west London. His cheap rents were a magnet for the desperate poor, though what tenants got for their money was appalling.

Notting Hill might be affluent now, but in the early 1950s its core community, especially in the northern area known as Notting Dale, was white, working-class and fiercely tribal. Tension between this old community and what it saw as interlopers had been brewing for a while before it came to a head on 29 August 1958. A domestic argument between a Jamaican painter, Raymond Morrison, and his Swedish wife Majbritt outside Latimer Road tube station triggered an explosion of violence. Hundreds of white would-be supporters of Majbritt marched through Notting Hill armed with knives and other weapons.

The Notting Hill race riots blighted the area for decades. In their wake, though, a handful of mostly female activists like Pearl Prescod and Amy Ashwood Garvey rallied round a charismatic American journalist and activist called Claudia Jones, determined to promote both black resistance and, ultimately, some semblance of cross-cultural harmony.

Jones was born Claudia Cumberbatch in Trinidad in 1915. As a child she had migrated with her family to the US where, in her early twenties, she joined the Young Communist League, inspired by her experience of racial segregation – what she called her 'Jim Crow experiences as a young negro woman, experiences likewise born of working-class poverty'.[82] Imprisoned numerous times for her activism, she was on the verge of being deported to Trinidad and Tobago when its governor refused her entry, fearing she would foment unrest. In 1955, suffering from heart problems aggravated by nine and a half months in prison, Jones was offered sanctuary in Britain on humanitarian grounds. Three years later, a few months before the Notting Hill riots, she founded a newspaper for the black community, the *West Indian Gazette*, which she edited herself from rooms above a barber's shop in Brixton.

Jones was instrumental in initiating what became the Notting Hill Carnival. She did it in the face of opposition from associates who thought a street party a trivial response to racist violence. Since the 1958 riots, Notting Hill had also been the site of the murder of black carpenter Kelso Cochrane by an unidentified white youth. But Jones insisted a carnival would encourage social cohesion and foster a sense of racial identity broader than being a colonial immigrant. The title of the essay she wrote for the souvenir booklet sold at the first carnival in 1959 says it all: 'A People's Art Is the Genesis of Their Freedom.'

'It is as if the vividness of our national life was itself the spark urging translation to new surroundings, to convey, to transplant our folk origins to British soil,' she wrote. 'There is a comfort in this effort not only for the Carnival Committee and the *West Indian Gazette*, for the fine artists participating in our Carnival … but for all West Indians, who strain to feel and hear and reflect their idiom even as they strain to feel the warmth of their sun-drenched islands and its immemorial beauty of landscape and terrain.'[83]

Filmed by the BBC and broadcast in the Caribbean, the 1959 carnival featured steel-band musicians like the Trinidad All Stars and calypsonians like Lord Kitchener. Oddly, it took place not in the streets of Notting Hill but indoors in St Pancras Town Hall – and in winter. Not until after Jones' death in 1964 did the carnival move west and become the outdoor festival it is today, what her biographer calls 'a living testament to the memory of Jones, who was loved, honoured and respected by the entire London Caribbean community'.[84]

Jones wasn't the only woman with an unwavering faith in women's ability to cut across boundaries and create a better society. Across the world, the nuclear threat was growing as tension between the US and the Soviet Union ratcheted up. Britain's incendiary response was to build its own hydrogen bomb.

A mass of competing campaign groups opposed the move. But after 1957, most of them joined forces under the umbrella of the newly founded Campaign for Nuclear Disarmament (CND). Although many of its loudest voices (the likes of Bertrand Russell, J. B. Priestley and Michael Foot) were male, CND was in fact powered by strong women like Priestley's wife, the archaeologist Jacquetta Hawkes; the geneticist Charlotte Auerbach; and especially Peggy Duff and Pat Arrowsmith, who organised the marches to the Atomic Weapons Research Establishment in Aldermaston that first brought CND into the public eye.

The first fully fledged Aldermaston march took place over a wet, miserable Easter weekend in April 1958. Despite it being the coldest Good Friday for 41 years, 4,000 people gathered in Trafalgar Square at the start, while 500 stuck it out for the 50-mile, three-day duration. Among the marchers, travelling in a battered old charabanc from which she handed out sausages and cups of tea,[85] was the pacifist Dora Russell, now in her mid-sixties (and still naively pro-Soviet Russia) but as committed as ever to the cause that had defined her life.

After years of debilitating illness, George VI finally died in February 1952, days after travelling to London Airport to wave off his daughter, Princess Elizabeth, on a tour of the Commonwealth. She had been shouldering some of the burden of her father's duties for some time. In November 1952 Elizabeth opened Parliament for the first time. The society photographer Cecil Beaton, watching her, noted that 'her eyes are not those of a busy harassed person. She regards people with a recognition of compassion – and a slight suggestion of a smile lightens the otherwise cumbrous mouth.'[86] (As the Queen's biographer Ben Pimlott commented: 'Nobody … ever wrote of a male Monarch like this.'[87])

Beneath the pomp, the Coronation was, as Pimlott says: 'a burial service for the Empire'.[88] And, with her youth and innocence, the twenty-seven-year-old Elizabeth stood for the possibilities of a changing Britain. Beyond the gates of Buckingham Palace a storm of progress was brewing. Over the next few years there would be huge shifts in popular culture: the birth of the rebellious, consumerist teenager; a growing lack of class deference; spikiness where there had once been docility. None of these would be reflected in the Queen's behaviour or appearance, though over time they would alter the way the country viewed her and the rest of the Royal Family.

In this frozen moment, however, Britain enjoyed itself to the patriotic full. Shops did a roaring trade in Union Jack flags as well as orbs, sceptres, maces, coaches and crowns. There was a craze for periscopes which enabled bystanders to see over tall people in the crowd. But the big thing – the truly radical thing – was the televising of the Coronation, despite the Queen's initial reluctance. The number of holders of TV licences doubled to 3 million and an estimated 27 million people watched the event live for at least half the day. If they didn't have sets themselves, they went round to the houses of wealthier friends or family who did. The broadcasting experiment was a huge success. But the Queen herself continued to be suspicious of television, and for her first Christmas broadcast instructed the BBC to show only a photograph of her next to a microphone.

The Queen was at the centre not just of a media revolution but of the world's idealising gaze. Cecil Beaton, for one, couldn't get enough of her: 'As she walks she allows her heavy skirt to swing backwards and forwards in a beautiful rhythmic effect. This girlish figure has enormous dignity; she belongs in this scene of almost Byzantine magnificence.'[89] Photographing her at the Palace afterwards, Beaton noted that she looked tired after wearing the heavy crown for three hours. But she had survived the ordeal and made only one mistake, forgetting to curtsey when she got to the North pillar.[90]

As well as stressing the virtues of stability and continuity, the Coronation had all manner of cultural ripple effects, from boosting sales of televisions to introducing the nation to new culinary delights. The gloopy, mildly spiced sandwich-filler favourite Coronation Chicken was created for the Coronation banquet by Rosemary Hume, founder of the Cordon Bleu cookery school. But did the installation of a woman at the centre of British public life do anything for gender equality? It's hard to see it.

As the Queen settled onto the throne, women continued to be sidelined. This might have been the scientific century – the century of penicillin and the nuclear bomb – but by 1951 the Royal Society had admitted only seven women as fellows.[91]

The scientist Rosalind Franklin never called herself a feminist, but we can still be angry with the way her contribution to the discovery of the double helix structure of DNA was underplayed. A gifted X-ray crystallographer whose photographs were renowned for their careful clarity, Franklin was thirty-two in 1953 and, as the Queen was being crowned, preparing to leave King's College London, where she and her research partner Maurice Wilkins had been based, for Birkbeck College.

She couldn't wait to get out. Temperamentally ill-suited, Franklin and Wilkins had had a tense, unhappy working relationship. Franklin had been lured to King's (which she hated) on false pretences by the head of its biophysics unit, and Wilkins had been misled about which project Franklin would be working on. Without Franklin's consent, Wilkins and another scientist, Max Perutz, had shown her research data, including her X-ray photos of DNA, to the Cambridge-based DNA model-builders Francis Crick and James Watson, who needed it so that they could prove DNA's two-strand structure.

Franklin died of cervical cancer in 1958, four years before Crick, Watson and Wilkins jointly received the Nobel Prize. She was so obsessed with getting things right – the X-ray camera could only be aligned with the beam switched on – that she didn't take sufficient care of herself, not bothering to wear a lead apron to protect her from the X-rays.

The scale of her input went unacknowledged for decades. In his bestselling book *The Double Helix*, Watson refers to her as 'Rosy', a name no one called her (at least not to her face) and which she hated, and finds himself wondering 'how she would look if she took off her glasses and did something novel with her hair'.[92] A brilliant scientist, then – but distractingly sexy?

Science in the 1950s was a male domain. By rights, the world of computing should have been a breakaway matriarchy. After all, a British woman – the nineteenth-century mathematician Ada Lovelace, who worked with Charles Babbage on his Analytical Engine – was there at the dawn of it, Eve to Babbage's Adam. Daughter of Lord Byron, Lovelace is credited as coming up with the first algorithm, the world's first computer program.

Tragically, Lovelace died too young to fulfil her potential. And it was more than half a century before another woman built on her legacy. In 1914 a British amateur mathematician called Emma Gifford compiled tables of natural sines (a trigonometric function) for use in the desk calculating machines that were the forerunners of computers. Most other early programmers were American: women like Grace Hopper, who started her computing career in the late 1940s, working on 'compiler' software that converts one programming language into another. Hopper once told a journalist that programming was 'just like planning a dinner. You have to plan ahead and schedule everything so that it's ready when you need it ... Women are "naturals" at computer programming.'[93] Perhaps the Google engineer who almost a century later blamed biological differences for the absence of women in his field of work didn't get the memo.

In the 1950s computers were enormous machines that filled a room and stored data not on discs or memory cards but enormous reel-to-reel tape machines. Many early coders were women because programming was seen (by men) as secretarial drudgery akin to typing. The important bit was deemed to be the creation not of software but of *hardware*, which men oversaw.

In Britain, it took a woman called Aldrina 'Dina' Nia St Johnston (née Vaughan) to question and overturn this orthodoxy. Born on 20 September 1930, Dina was impatient with formal education and left Selhurst Grammar School at seventeen against her father's wishes, taking a job at British Non-Ferrous Metals Research Association and, to please him, studying part-time for a Maths degree. Frustrated when passing this degree failed to bring any increase in salary, she joined the Borehamwood office of a tech company called Elliott Brothers.

In the early 1950s Elliott Brothers produced computer hardware for the military, such as the Elliott 152, which controlled radar-guided guns. It also manufactured a machine called OEDIPUS for GCHQ. After proving herself a skilful programmer, Dina was given the (classified) job of writing software for the Elliott 153 computer, designed for use by the Royal Navy at its Irton Moor intercept station near Scarborough. She went on to write the program used by Elliott Brothers for its payroll and oversaw the first computer purchase by a local council – the Elliott 405 custom-built for Norwich City Council in 1956.

It soon became clear that Dina's gender was not her only distinguishing feature. Colleagues quoted in an appreciation published in *Computer Journal* after her death in 2007 deployed that familiar word 'formidable', hardly ever used to describe a man, and hinted darkly that she was hard to work with. There are echoes here of Beatrice Shilling and, indeed, Rosalind Franklin. One colleague remembered her extreme, almost obsessive accuracy; the way she always wrote using a Parker 51 fountain pen with permanent black ink 'and if there ever was a mistake it had to be corrected with a razor blade'.[94]

Having married the head of Elliott's Computing Division, Andrew St Johnston, Dina left the company in 1959 to found her own, Vaughan Programming Services (VPS). An entrepreneur at heart, she had spotted two big gaps in the market. First: the tech community wasn't reaching out to other industries or preaching the benefits of computer-assisted automation in a loud enough voice. Or as Dina put it: 'There was a shortage of hands-on processor-oriented people who were happy to go round a steel works in a hard hat.'[95]

To understand the second gap she identified, it's important to remember that anyone buying a computer in the early 1950s was, by and large, expected to write all the software themselves: the people who bought them knew how to use them and required minimal support from the manufacturers. The problem, as the novelist and tech journalist Naomi Alderman explains, was that this limited the number of potential customers for computers: 'It was thought no one but a science department or a technical firm employing their own programs would want one.'[96] Dina realised it wasn't practical or cost-effective for hardware companies to produce their own software as well. Instead, independent 'software houses' could design applications to meet companies' specific needs, providing all necessary customer support into the bargain.

At first, VPS was run out of Dina and Andrew's house, a converted pub in Brickendon in Hertfordshire. By the end of

1962, she had a staff of eight, creating bespoke software for blue-chip companies like Unilever, BAA and British Rail. Her company also developed alarm and monitoring systems for the nuclear power plant at Sellafield; an operating system called Master Control Executive (MACE) which ran on eight different types of computer and had a broad range of industrial applications, from warehouse crane control to railway signalling; and, later, its own computer, the 4M, which was mostly used by British Rail to track the position of trains.

VPS's bread and butter, as it prospered in the 1970s and beyond, was the real-time passenger-information systems it developed for airports and train stations. Dina made a point of employing local people and training them up as programming courses were non-existent in the 1950s and 1960s. As Simon Lavington observes, she was 'ahead of her time in believing that computing could be for everyone'.[97] Although VPS was bought out by the US giant GEC, she and Andrew continued working for the company until their retirement in the mid 1990s.

Like Rosalind Franklin, Dina St Johnston symbolised the future – the future of women in STEM; the future of Sheryl Sandberg and Marissa Mayer. But for most women this future was so far away as to be unimaginable. Computers were not yet at the centre of everything. Many in the 1950s would not even have heard of them, and they would have struck most of those who had as both impossibly exotic and excruciatingly dull.

In time, the tech barricade would be stormed, sort of. First, though, there were other battles to fight.

7

It's a Man's World

1961–81

In March 1965, the American magazine *Time* ran an interview with 'one of Britain's richest and most self-esteeming women'. In case that last bit sounded rude, the writer pointed out that Mrs Margery Hurst, fifty-one-year-old founder of the Brook Street Bureau secretarial agency, was self-esteeming 'by her own admission'. 'I never thought for a moment that I could fail,' she declared, and to be fair her confidence seemed justified. Earlier that month Brook Street had been floated on the London Stock Exchange, a first for a 'secretarial bureau'. Within fifteen months its initial share price doubled. Branches in America and Australia followed.

The surprise, given how good Hurst evidently was at running a company, was how long it had taken her to find her vocation. After school, where Hurst was repeatedly told she was good for nothing, she had drifted into acting, experience she would later put to canny use as a charismatic self-publicist. During the Second World War she served in the ATS, the women's branch of the British army. She married a soldier but three weeks after their baby was born her husband walked out of the family home. At the age of thirty-one, broken and humiliated, Hurst accepted her father's offer to cover the rent on their flat. But she was too ashamed to tell him about the overdue rates, so she ended up in court for non-payment.

In her memoir, Hurst describes the moment of epiphany when she realised optimism and resilience were the keys to her recovery. She recognised, as she put it, that 'there is no such thing as the end of your life, only the end of an episode'.[1] Mentally fortified, she rented a room in Brook Street in Mayfair and set herself up as a professional typist. Her first client was a foreign princess (Hurst fails to specify) who lived full time at the Ritz hotel. The princess's fifteen-year-old grandson had written a play and she wanted it typed up for posterity. The only problem, the princess claimed unconvincingly, was that she didn't have much money. Would Hurst consider working for a reduced fee? The standard rate for the job would have been 15 guineas. Aghast at the princess's cheek, Hurst phoned her back and told her the job would normally cost 25 guineas but that she would do it for 23. To her amazement, the princess agreed to the price.

For the first few months Hurst ran Brook Street single-handed 'as one of those many-armed Balinese ladies': 'I was a telephonist, office-girl, receptionist *and* emergency temporary.'[2] She turned up at clients' offices with her baby daughter in a pram. She needed lots more girls on her books, dreamed of having hundreds (and fibbed to people that she did). Within six months she had twenty-five – pretty good going – and contracts to supply clerical staff to several major companies including Shell. Much of her success Hurst attributed to thoroughness, a quality she felt men lacked 'especially in the middle echelon [of a company] where women do so well'. At the top level, she conceded, women were less successful: 'Too often they lack breadth of vision and the boldness for directorships. But this is only lack of experience and training for the top jobs. I believe the time may come when they surprise the world.'[3] Many ambitious women, she knew only too well, saw secretarial work as a route into a company. Being a good secretary was a way of proving to your male boss that you had what it took to climb higher.

Before approving the flotation, the City had demanded that Hurst appoint a male chairman because to have a woman was 'unorthodox'. It was suggested that Hurst's husband, Eric, be chairman and joint managing director with her. No, said Hurst: 'I felt I owed it to women at large to show that it could be done.' The City backed down, but men continued to belittle her: 'Some of the businessmen I met treated me in a half-quizzical, half-patronising way. "Well, well," they would grin, "so the little lady's a tycoon. And how do you shape up with a pan of bacon and eggs?"'[4]

Like so many women of the period, though, Hurst was a mass of contradictions. She disliked the sexist things men did and said, but also disliked the way successful women who needed to make headway in male-dominated industries lost what she thought of as their soft, feminine qualities: 'Nothing is sadder to me than the women who take on a man's job and become so masculine in their attitudes that they turn their back on their own sex.'[5]

In this subtle, stealthy anti-feminism she resembled Mrs Thatcher – who, as prime minister, placed wealth-creating entre-preneurs like Hurst on a pedestal above all others. In 1965, when Hurst was in her expansionist pomp, Thatcher was Shadow Junior Minister of Housing. In the 1950s, as we saw earlier, Thatcher was all for women achieving fulfilment through paid employment. But by the 1970s, after her conversion to monetarism, she seemed to have changed her mind, believing the essentially female (to her) skill of balancing the books was best deployed by women at home. Interviewed in the 1980s by Jenni Murray, Thatcher spoke of her fears of Britain being turned into a 'crèche society' and suggested that mothers who wished to work find a family member who could look after the children for a bit: 'No acknowledgement of a woman's need or ambition to earn her own living at all,' fumed Murray, 'even though she [Thatcher] had always had a job …'[6]

And yet despite Thatcher, the proportion of married women in the total workforce almost doubled between 1951 and 1971, while over the same period the number of men working in Britain dropped from 88 to 81 per cent.[7]

It's easy to see why, for late-1960s feminists like the young Harriet Harman, the funnelling of women into temping and secretarial work felt like part of the problem, condemning women 'forever after to taking direction from their boss and never [having] the opportunity to work their way up the ladder'.[8] Typing and answering the phone was the sort of undemanding 'woman's work' her parents' generation had thought appropriate; the sort of work that could be fitted in around children and family life without too much effort. Harman's parents pitied rather than admired career women. By contrast, she and her friends were 'in rebellion against the lives our mothers ended up leading. My life was certainly not going to be dominated by the wifely duties of cooking and looking after a husband.'[9]

It hardly needs saying that Britain at the beginning of the 1960s was a radically different place from Britain at the end. And by the early 1980s, when this chapter ends, the pace of change had increased so much that the 1960s was already a heritage museum for nostalgists – a parade of resonant images: the Beatles, Christine Keeler naked on a chair, Harold Wilson's pipe …

Outside the big cities, though, the affluent society of the late 1950s had passed many people by. Touring the country for his book *The Other England*, published in 1964, Geoffrey Moorhouse found 'a village not ten miles from Ipswich which, apart from its electricity and its piped water supply, has scarcely budged an inch since the Middle Ages. Some of its cottages are without drains so the housewife has to put a bucket under the plughole every time she wants to empty the sink … Sewerage is unknown in this community.'[10] Not so swinging, then.

In fact, Britain as a whole was adjusting to the post-Suez dip in its fortunes and international standing, notwithstanding prime minister Harold Macmillan's claim in his first television broadcast that Britain 'has been great, is great and will stay great, provided we close our ranks and get on with the job'. What was 'Britain' anyway? In Scotland a new mood of nationalism would lead by 1967 to the election of Glasgow solicitor Winnie Ewing as Scottish National Party MP for Hamilton in Lanarkshire. She won 46 per cent of the vote in what had formerly been a safe Labour seat. Ewing arrived in Westminster with her husband and children in a Scottish-built Hillman Imp, telling the country: 'Stop the world – Scotland wants to get on.' (The Welsh and Scottish Nationalist vote in British general elections rose from 100,000 in 1959 to one million in October 1974.)[11]

Thanks to the baby boom of the mid 1940s there were one million more unmarried 15–21-year-olds in 1960 than there had been in 1950.[12] These young people were strong and plentiful, fewer of them having died in childhood than in previous generations. Keith Waterhouse, in a famous article in the *Daily Mirror*, called them the Beanstalk Generation. As well as health they had money and free time – too much free time, some worried. In 1960 a government paper called the Albemarle Report suggested local councils needed to make more of an effort to provide extracurricular activities for the young. Girls were a particular problem as 'fewer girls than boys are members of youth organisations, and much more thought will need to be given to ways of meeting their specific needs'.[13]

The idea that girls and boys should be treated equally was still thought radical and eccentric – even dangerous. In his Eleanor Rathbone Memorial Lecture of 1960, the influential judge Lord Denning worked himself into a lather on the subject of female equality: 'We ought to remember,' he thundered, 'that there has been one time previously in the history of the world when women achieved a considerable measure of equality. It was in the Roman Empire, and it should serve as a warning of the dangers to which equality may give rise.'[14]

To be fair to Lord Denning, he also campaigned for a common law which would allow a woman to remain in the marital home if she was deserted by her husband. This led to an important piece of feminist legislation, the Matrimonial Homes Act 1967.

But one of his core beliefs was that 'the principal task in life of women is to bear and rear children' – a widely held attitude that explained why, for example, the chemistry sets that were all the rage in the late 1950s and early 1960s were marketed at boys, never mind that a British woman, Dorothy Hodgkin, would win the Nobel Prize for Chemistry in 1964. In September 1963 girls got Sindy, a British version of the buxom US doll Barbie. Fascinatingly, market research had found that British girls disliked Barbie for being too glamorous. Market research also gave Sindy her girl-next-door name. 'Sindy is the free, swinging girl that every little girl longs to be,' explained the doll's manufacturer, Pedigree. 'Sindy has sports clothes, glamour clothes, everyday clothes – a dog, skates, a gramophone – everything …'

The modern woman also now had the pill, a combination of the hormones oestrogen and progestin, which had been developed in the US in the 1950s and approved for release there in 1960. It was introduced in the UK, for married women only, on 4 December 1961. The BBC reported that doctors were in a dilemma over whether it could be prescribed for 'social as well as medical reasons'. There was concern too about its long-term effects on the body. The BBC quoted Sir Charles Dodds, 'Britain's leading expert on the drugs contained in the pill', who compared the female body to a clock: 'Even if you thoroughly understand the mechanism of a clock, provided it is going well it is very much better to leave it alone. To interfere with it if you do not understand it can be disastrous.'[15]

By the summer of 1962, 150,000 women were taking the pill, rising to 480,000 by 1964. The historian Dominic Sandbrook is surely right when he says that this figure is 'nowhere near large enough to bear out the common claim that the pill was a major cause of the sexual revolution'.[16] Not until 1970 did it become widely available through the Family Planning Association and it wasn't prescribed regularly by doctors until 1975. But early-adopters included the writer Lynn Barber, who started taking it in 1963 during her second year at Oxford. 'It made a huge difference,' she says. 'In my first year I don't think you could get it at all unless you were married. By my second year you had to say – not prove – that you were engaged and they gave you a bit of a lecture about being careful and serious. But basically you could get it and that was good because up till then we'd all been borrowing a Dutch cap!'[17]

In 1967 the Abortion Act, proposed by the Liberal MP David Steel, legalised abortion in England, Scotland and Wales – though emphatically not Northern Ireland – in the first twenty-eight weeks of pregnancy as long as two doctors were satisfied that it was necessary on medical or psychological grounds. Massive progress, then – even if, in all likelihood, the doctors performing that assessment would have been male. The Family Planning Act 1967 further removed restrictions on women's access to local-authority contraception services in England and Wales.

Meanwhile, some of the most advanced work on women's reproductive systems was being conducted in London and Edinburgh by a woman, Anne McLaren – a developmental biol-ogist specialising in mammalian genetics. Only a few years earlier, working with John Biggers, McLaren had produced the first litter of mice grown from embryos developed outside the uterus, then transferred to a surrogate mother. Within three decades this tech-nique, known as in-vitro fertilisation or IVF, would have trans-formed (and created) thousands of human lives.

Given how much women had contributed in the fields of science and engineering during the Second World War, STEM (Science, Technology, Engineering and Maths) roles were oddly thin on the ground in the 1960s. Maybe there was less for them to do? Or maybe, now that there was no longer a war to act as a catalyst and route women into those careers, it was the inevitable result of too few women studying science subjects at university?[18]

Since the launch of Sputnik, Britain had watched from afar as America and Russia competed to send satellites, animals and finally men into space. In America, as we know from the Hollywood film *Hidden Figures*, women – and in particular black women, who had additional hurdles to overcome – played a key role as computational analysts and programmers at NASA.

In Britain, the 'brainy woman' seemed to crop up in science-fiction with more reliability than she did in the country's fledgling space programme. Think of Dr Venus, the 'doctor of space medicine' in the early Gerry Anderson puppet series *Fireball XL5*. Like the more famous Lady Penelope from *Thunderbirds*, Dr Venus was created and voiced by Anderson's wife and business partner Sylvia who, it's worth observing, had a degree from the LSE in sociology and political science.

Britain's modest space programme amounted to the Ariel series of satellite launches, masterminded by the Science and Engineering Research Council. Ariel 1 blasted off in 1962 from Cape Canaveral in America. The available evidence suggests Ariel was pretty much a male-only endeavour, notwithstanding the contributions of a Mrs Quirk – wife of a Mr R. Quirk at the Ministry of Science – who gave the project its Shakespearean name,[19] and an astrophysicist called Miss D. M. C. Gilmore, who in 1957 co-authored an important paper, 'The Effect of the Earth's Oblateness on the Orbit of a Near Satellite'.[20]

All five Aerial probes – the last launched in October 1974 – were powered by American rockets. Britain's post-war rocket programme had sputtered out in the mid 1960s after the government withdrew funding. As it happens, this programme had been kick-started by a woman, Joan Bernard, who worked for the army's Special Projectile Operations Group after the war. Bernard was the brains behind what became known as Operation Backfire, the plan to seek out and fire unused German V2 rockets so that the technology behind them could be studied.[21]

Even when women made amazing discoveries, it seems they didn't promote themselves the way men might have done. In 1967 a doctoral student called Jocelyn Bell Burnell, one of the few women studying Astronomy at Cambridge at PhD level in the 1960s, noticed an anomaly on a chart tracking radio signals from across the cosmos. It turned out to be a pulsar, a rotating star that has reached the end of its life and run out of fuel.

The implications were huge. If pulsars existed then so too, possibly, did black holes, regions of deformed space-time created by stars which have undergone gravitational collapse. But some combination of Burnell's Quaker upbringing and natural humility stopped her from selling herself as the new Crick and Watson (and Franklin). Although her subsequent hugely successful career has taken in working on the Ariel programme; heading up the Physics department at the Open University, where she doubled the number of chairs held by female professors; and (her current role) being Visiting Professor of Astrophysics at Oxford, her personal philosophy focuses on humility and acceptance. In 1974, Burnell's supervisor was awarded a Nobel Prize for their discovery, but she was not singled out. Burnell has always been sanguine about this, saying: 'You can actually do extremely well out of not getting a Nobel prize, and I have had so many prizes, and so many honours, and so many awards, that actually, I think I've had far more fun than if I'd got a Nobel Prize.'[22]

In 1996 she told the editors of the book *Beyond the Glass Ceiling* that she thought 'the element of bravado is stronger in men than in women. In physics and astronomy there's a culture that's confident and assertive. There is a distortion of the kind of values that I would like to work with.'[23]

If only some of that confidence and assertiveness had been on display in government. Harold Macmillan had been prime minister since 1957 when Anthony Eden was forced to resign after the Suez crisis. His first term notched up some successes. There was a rise in prosperity, the cue for Macmillan's famous observation at a Tory rally on 20 July 1957 that 'most of our people have never had it so good'. At the 1959 election, seeking a third term in government, the Conservatives increased their overall majority to 101 seats over Hugh Gaitskell's Labour party and Jo Grimond's Liberals.

By 1962, however, the fairy dust had come off. Britain's first attempt to join the EEC was blocked by the French president Charles de Gaulle. On 13 July 1962, bruised by some poor by-election results, Macmillan abruptly sacked seven members of his Cabinet, a reshuffle that was christened the 'night of the long knives' in a slightly tasteless nod to the extra-judicial executions carried out by the Nazis in Germany in 1934.

Macmillan looked fusty and inept; ripe for indignant mockery, which duly arrived in the form of the early-1960s satire boom. This took in the Cambridge revue *Beyond the Fringe*, first performed on 22 August 1960; the magazine *Private Eye*, originally a pamphlet distributed in cafés; Peter Cook's Establishment comedy club in Soho; and the groundbreaking and irreverent TV show *That Was The Week That Was* (or *TW3*, as it became known).

TW3's short life – it was cancelled less than a year later, by which time Macmillan had been replaced by Sir Alec Douglas-Home – belies the size of its impact. Never before had television's power been used to mock politicians and public figures. But while *TW3*'s loose format and bold content pointed somewhere new, the gender make-up of its cast told a boy's own story.

TW3 shared much of its cast and writing team with Cook's Establishment club. As far as women's involvement was concerned, the warning signs were visible early on. Reviewing a show at the club, the critic Kenneth Tynan noticed that 'some essential is lacking', identifying as the problem the fact that while 'the girls are clever and personable' they were 'not encouraged to be funny; in a curious way they are frozen out'.[24]

It sounds very much like the age-old Funny Women Problem – one that persists to this day in the form of token women being included on comedy panel shows, only for their contributions to be reduced so much in the edit, it's as if they were never there.

The 'girls' in question at the Establishment were Hazel Wright and Carole Simpson. When Wright left the cast she was replaced by Cook's Cambridge contemporary, the brilliant Eleanor Bron.

Sadly for lovers of funny women in Britain, Bron was touring America with the Establishment during filming so she only appeared in the pilot of *TW3*. After that she joined the cast of its successor *Not So Much A Programme, More A Way of Life*, then mostly left comedy behind for straight acting. *Beyond The Fringe* rightly made stars of Alan Bennett, Jonathan Miller, Peter Cook and Dudley Moore. But in some ways the man who benefited most from *TW3* was David Frost. This is rather odd, because if you watch an episode of *TW3* today it isn't the stiff, uncomfortable-looking Frost you notice but Millicent Martin.

Although she went on to be hugely successful as a singer and actor in America, discussion of Martin's role on *TW3* now tends to focus not on how funny she was, but on the fact that she sang the theme song. She also gets blamed for the show's weakest moments, for example the sentimental ballad about John F. Kennedy which she sang in the deliberately not funny edition of *TW3* broadcast twenty-four hours after his assassination.

Born in 1935, Martin had trained at the Italia Conti stage school and appeared in numerous West End musicals. The most experienced performer in the *TW3* cast, she was chosen as a singer because of how quick she was at learning songs. This was an important skill because the *TW3* title song had new lyrics written for it each week which Martin had to learn off by heart because the primitive autocue couldn't keep up with the music. Martin never expected *TW3* to take off and, when offered a contract for the first series, considered turning the show down in order to honour a prior commitment to appear in panto in Bromley.

In his account of the satire boom *That Was Satire That Was*, Humphrey Carpenter comments on Martin's 'ultra-professional polish' in the first show, transmitted on 24 November 1962, noting that other performers 'frequently fluff words and look at the wrong cameras'.[25]

By this time television was firmly established at the centre of British cultural life. As Joan Bakewell observes: 'It wasn't something people did if there was nothing better to do: it was seen as the thing to do.'[26] Yet other women were suspicious of it. The novelist Doris Lessing felt it disrupted family life, especially in working-class communities, killing conversation and replacing it with blank passivity: 'Soon the big kitchen table had been pushed along the wall, chairs were installed in a semi-circle and, on their chair arms, the swivelling supper trays. It was the end of an exuberant verbal culture.'[27]

But television undoubtedly gave women new opportunities and new visibility, both as presenters and behind the scenes as producers and writers. It also brought ordinary women's stories to a mass audience. The playwright Nell Dunn's adaptation of her 1963 novel about backstreet abortion *Up the Junction* was one of a number of breakthrough dramas that included Ken Loach's film *Cathy Come Home*. Surprisingly, given the bold, honest way she wrote about working-class lives, Dunn herself was upper-class, the daughter of Sir Philip Dunn, a gentleman farmer. But she had rejected her privileged background and moved across the river from Chelsea to Battersea to work in a sweet factory.

Mary Whitehouse, self-appointed guardian of the nation's morals as the founder of the deeply conservative National Viewers' and Listeners' Association, reserved special scorn for the work of Dunn and her ilk. 'We are told that the dramatists are portraying real life,' she complained to an audience in Birmingham, 'but why concentrate on the kitchen sink when there are so many pleasant sitting rooms?'[28]

Joan Bakewell anchored the pioneering discussion programme *Late Night Line Up* on BBC2, launched in 1964. One of the first presenters to be shown on TV in colour, she laboured under the dismissive nickname 'the thinking man's crumpet' bestowed on her by the comedian Frank Muir.

Bakewell's television career began in the mid 1950s as a studio manager at the BBC. She was bad at it, she says, and made to do the training course twice. Her then husband, Michael, was a drama producer. This was her ambition too, but husbands and wives were not allowed to work in the same department as it was considered 'bad for morale'.[29] Once, she asked Derek Amoore, the BBC's head of news, why there were no female newsreaders. He replied that, one, their voices were too shrill; two, their clothes would distract viewers; and three, if there was a serious catastrophe, they wouldn't be able to keep their emotions hidden.[30]

Should women read the news? *Could* they? Mary Marquis was already the main newsreader for BBC Scotland in 1975 when Angela Rippon became the first woman permanently employed to read the national TV news. Rippon has said that when she started in broadcasting there was no sexism 'because nobody had thought of it then': 'You didn't have token women. If you could do the job, that was it.'[31] Bakewell remembers it differently. She says that sexual harassment, especially, was 'a matter of routine' in the TV industry in the 1960s: 'I took it for granted. A quick squeeze, a salacious leer.'[32] (Of course, sexism comes in different shapes and sizes. When I first moved into TV, I was shocked by how often I heard unflattering stories about my childhood journalistic heroine Kate Adie — like the famous one that Adie had allegedly been filmed scrabbling in the sand for her lost pearl earrings while reporting on Operation Desert Storm. Adie later called this out as a 'ridiculous fiction'.)

Behind the scenes the BBC was by no means exclusively male. In 1965 the veteran news producer Grace Wyndham Goldie retired after a long and illustrious career. Her protegé, future Director-General of the BBC, Alasdair Milne, would remember her as 'a small, birdlike woman with a striking, finely chiselled face'. For David Attenborough, it was her personality that left the strongest impression – she was a 'ferocious battleaxe'.

A few years earlier Goldie had watched the filming of the pilot of *TW3* and been unimpressed. The satirical broadcaster and director Ned Sherrin observed that she was 'not without humour, but only in the sense that the equator is not without ice if you ship in a refrigerator'.[33] As a former journalist on the BBC's magazine *The Listener*, Goldie had been one of the first people to realise how huge and important television – 'this miracle, this phenomenon' – was going to be. It had, she wrote, 'a vividness which we cannot get from sightless broadcasting and a combination of reality and intimacy which we cannot get from the films'.[34]

She joined the BBC proper in 1944 and was requisitioned by its fledgling television wing four years later, by which time she was already in her forties. She would revolutionise current affairs broadcasting, turning *Panorama* into what she called 'the voice of authority' and launching the magazine show *Tonight*, which ran five times a week from 1957 to 1965. Fiercely loyal both to the BBC and to the Reithian idea that broadcasting served an important civic function, she spent her last two years there as Head of Talks and Current Affairs, though her departure was marred by a dispute over her pension.

Talking to the writer Charlotte Higgins for her history of the BBC *This New Noise*, Melvyn Bragg remembered her holding court, perching on a bar stool while 'toughies' like Milne and Attenborough waited their turn to talk to her. Higgins concludes that she was 'an object of fascination as a powerful woman, an exotic creature within the BBC'. If Goldie was sometimes brusque and unpleasant, then that was because she had to be. Higgins notes the way colleagues describe her 'in terms subtly different from those employed to assess her male peers'.[35]

On the drama-production side women were in seriously short supply. Verity Lambert began her TV career in the PR department at Granada, one of the companies that made up ITV, the commercial network which had launched in 1955. She had grown up in Hendon in north London during the Second World War, but at the age of eleven was sent to the boarding school Roedean, where she found it hard to fit in. Lambert left school at sixteen after the headmistress told her she wasn't university material, and took herself off to the Sorbonne to study French. On returning to London, she wandered into the Granada job by accident after someone misread 'Roedean' as 'RADA' on her CV. A stint in New York working in stage management followed; then, back in England, a job on the popular ITV show *Armchair Theatre* where she won plaudits for the way she handled a crisis – the actor Gareth Jones dying in the middle of a live broadcast. Lambert had to keep the show going, micro-managing the camera opera-tors from the control room while the director and the other actors rapidly reworked the plot and dialogue. The episode sparked a broader ambition to direct, but back in England she found she 'couldn't make any headway because I was a woman'.[36]

One day in 1963 she was phoned by Sydney Newman who had been the producer of *Armchair Theatre* and was now working in the BBC's drama department. Did she know anything about chil-dren? Absolutely nothing, she replied. Evidently it didn't matter: Lambert got the job, producing a curious science-fiction confec-tion about a man who could travel through time. It was called *Doctor Who*.

Doctor Who was supposed to run for a year, but the initial response to it was disappointing. The BBC was about to junk the programme when suddenly the Daleks were introduced, at which point viewing figures soared. 'As a woman I did have to work twice as hard,' Lambert remembered.

You really had to be good. When I went to the BBC I was the only woman producer and considerably younger than most of the other producers in the department. Meeting me was a shock to a lot of people. I would be introduced to someone and

I could see horror flit across his face before he rearranged it
into a sort of a smile. People were amazed and I think that they
thought that I was sleeping with the head of the department. I
am sure they thought that, and people did ask me.[37]

Sadly, Lambert was neither the first nor the last woman in the
media to be the object of such a misapprehension. And despite
winning a BAFTA award for an adaptation of some Somerset
Maugham short stories, she was 'let go' by the BBC, a blow she
later rationalised as the best thing that could have happened as
it made her independent and self-reliant. She went to London
Weekend Television for a bit, then returned to the BBC to make
a series of plays about the suffragettes. In the 1970s and 1980s
she ran both the independent Euston Films and EMI's film
division before founding her own company, Cinema Verity,
which employed mostly women, not out of any feminist
compulsion but because 'when women came along they seemed
to be better'.

———————

Philip Larkin's second most famous poem dates the first phase of
the 1960s sexual revolution to the period between the lifting of
the ban on buying D. H. Lawrence's *Lady Chatterley's Lover* on 2
November 1960 and the release of the Beatles' first album *Please
Please Me* on 22 March 1963.

Lawrence conceived sex as quasi-religious but at the same time
earthbound and animalistic. 'Tha's got the nicest arse of anybody,'
gamekeeper Mellors tells aristocratic Connie. 'An' if tha shits an'
tha pisses, I'm glad.' Addressing the jury as they went off to
ponder their verdict at the end of the Chatterley trial, chief pros-
ecutor Mervyn Griffith-Jones asked them to consider if the novel
was the kind of book 'you would wish your wife or servants to
read'. In acquitting Penguin Books, the jurors answered in the
affirmative.

Indeed, as the historian Brian Harrison observes, 'The 1960s merely rendered public much of what had long been going on privately among ever-widening circles.'[38]

Newspaper reporting of the divorce of Margaret Campbell, Duchess of Argyll from her second husband in 1963 baffled many Britons with its euphemistic discussion of Polaroid photos stolen from her room which showed a 'headless man' – in reality the Duchess's lover, shown from the neck down while she fellated him. In July 1961 John Profumo, Secretary of State for War in Harold Macmillan's government, had had a fleeting affair with a nineteen-year-old dancer and would-be model called Christine Keeler. Profumo had met Keeler – half-naked, trying to cover herself with a towel after climbing out of his swimming pool – through his osteopath friend Stephen Ward who rented a cottage in the grounds of Cliveden, Profumo's country estate. The scandal turned ostensibly on the security implications of the fact that Keeler was also sleeping with a naval attaché at the Soviet embassy, Yevgeny Ivanov. But it ended up providing an excuse to discuss sex in and beyond public life.

Profumo lied to Parliament about his involvement with Keeler and resigned after the truth emerged. Doomed to walk the earth as a symbol of establishment hypocrisy, he had the consolation of his wealth and status and redeemed himself over time through his charitable works. No such absolution was available to Keeler, brought up by her mother and stepfather – her father had walked out – in a house made from two railway carriages bolted together. After a brief period of celebrity, she sank back into poverty.

The moral judgements passed on Keeler and the 'promiscuous' Duchess of Argyll over the years reek of misogyny. Giving his 160-page verdict on the 'headless man' divorce trial, Lord Justice Wheatley called the Duchess 'a highly sexed woman who has ceased to be satisfied with normal sexual activities and has started to indulge in disgusting sexual activities to gratify a debased sexual appetite'.[39]

Keeler, meanwhile, always seems to be written off as a 'slut', a 'good time girl' or a 'prostitute'.

Increasing openness about sex wasn't the same as increasing openness about how it was used by the powerful to oppress the weak. The big British cinematic success story of the early 1960s was the James Bond films, laden with rape gags and jokey threats of violence against women; almost as nasty as the Ian Fleming novels on which they were based. For Bond, sex is a service women provide. 'I think my mouth is too big,' Tatiana Romanova tells Sean Connery's Bond in *From Russia with Love*. 'It's just the right size,' he quips back. 'For me, that is.'

Sex as described by women was, of course, rather different. Frequently the tables were turned. Writer and journalist Virginia Ironside was twenty in 1964 when she published her first novel *Chelsea Bird*. 'It had the first ever bed scene, apart from *Lady Chatterley*,' she says. 'It was a very bleak one which started off: "He fumbled with my bra. I hoped he wasn't going to be a two-hour man."'[40] In Nell Dunn's work, too, sexuality is celebrated as something women own and control. Dunn thinks 'the most subversive thing in [her 1967 novel] *Poor Cow* [is] when Joy says, "I began to enjoy different men's bodies."'[41]

A fascinating document of the time is Dunn's 1965 book *Talking to Women* – edited transcripts of frank conversations with her female friends about life, the universe and everything. Some of these friends, such as the actress and pop artist Pauline Boty and the writer Edna O'Brien, were either famous or on the cusp of fame. But there were regular people too like twenty-six-year-old Kathy Collier, who worked in a butter factory, was married at sixteen and had a ten-year-old son.

Collier spoke of her bouts of depression during which she imagined gassing herself; of how she went off sex after having her son, leading to the breakdown of her marriage. 'If these girls have anything in common,' Dunn wrote in the preface, 'it is a belief in personal fulfilment – that a woman's life should not solely be the struggle to make men happy but more than that a progress towards the development of one's own body and soul.'[42]

Until her recent rediscovery, not least her part in Ali Smith's 2017 novel *Autumn*, Dunn's friend Pauline Boty was one of the great lost figures of the 1960s. Although she died in 1966 (from cancer: she was twenty-eight) when the decade was just over halfway through, she was everywhere while she had the chance. She knew Bob Dylan, who wrote a song about her, and she interviewed the Beatles. She worked as a stage designer; as an actor in film and TV – blink and you'll miss her in the hit Michael Caine comedy *Alfie*; as a music journalist; as a dancer on pop show *Ready Steady Go!*; and, most successfully, as an artist.

In the TV programme that introduced Pop art to the masses, Ken Russell's BBC Monitor documentary from 1962 *Pop Goes the Easel*, Boty is the only woman featured. Russell's film makes for fascinating viewing, the paternalistic smoothness of Huw Wheldon, who introduces it, at surreal odds with the director's jumpy, kaleidoscopic approach. Russell certainly makes the most of Boty's acting skills. In one nightmarish sequence she is chased along a never-ending corridor (actually BBC TV Centre) by an evil-looking old woman in a wheelchair. Boty explains later that her vivid dreams influence her collages. We see her backcombing her hair and making coffee in her bedsit, its walls covered in photos, postcards and magazine cut-outs – the contemporary images from which she would make art that, as Ali Smith says, 'is so full of energy and life and bravura and intelligence that something about it refutes tragedy'.[43]

Boty was twenty-five when she and Dunn had their conversation. It's loose and rambling, slightly studenty in its idealism but always delightful. Boty talks about the difficulties of dating married men and how rare it is for men genuinely to like women as people – a theme Germaine Greer would toy with at the end of the decade. She talks about her depression and her boredom with the way women are depicted in sex scenes in popular novels;

about how frustrated she is by the way men find it so hard to accept that some women are cleverer than they are.

Shockingly – well, it would have been shocking to readers in 1965 – Boty confides that as a child she 'felt guilty about having an ugly cunt'. This guilt has 'a very good basis', she explains, 'because when I was very little and surrounded by my brothers and everything, who kept yelling, "Shut up, you're only a girl," I wanted to be a boy. I used to pull – you know that sort of skin you have – I used to pull it you see and I slightly deformed it to make it sort of longer and so I used to spend all my time when I went to bed with someone thinking, "They'll find out."'[44]

Did this new frankness about sex mean women were having more of it, and outside wedlock? On the basis of research conducted in the late 1960s, sociologist Geoffrey Gorer felt confident enough to declare in 1971 that promiscuity was 'not a prominent feature of teenage sexual behaviour' and that England 'still appear[ed] to be a very chaste society'.[45] Lynn Barber, who says she slept with over fifty men in two terms at Oxford, admits her promiscuity was unusual by the standards of the time, but thinks increasing use of the pill inevitably encouraged experimentation:

> Lots of girls had been worried about having sex before because of the fear of getting pregnant, which was huge. I could generalise and say they were then happy to sleep with their boyfriends. My promiscuity was a bit odd and very short-lived, just a couple of terms. And I did get a reputation for sleeping around. So I wouldn't say everyone [was having sex]. But at a pop concert or something people would say to you, "Do you want to fuck?" whereas a few years earlier they would never have dreamed of saying that. Before the pill, you only slept with a man if you were seriously aiming to marry him. Lots of girls aimed to get pregnant in order to force a shotgun marriage. Then suddenly you could sleep with people just because you liked it! That was a terrific change of mindset.[46]

In 1967 the Sexual Offences Act would partially decriminalise (though not legalise – a big difference) male homosexuality. Notoriously, the law didn't allow for the possibility that lesbians existed, but this didn't stop them from suffering discrimination and abuse. Gina Ware, manager of the Gateways club in London's Chelsea from the mid 1950s until its closure in 1985, made the club 'female-only' in 1967 to create a safe, friendly space for lesbians.

The novelist Maureen Duffy was one of the first women in British public life to declare herself a lesbian. On a celebrated edition of *Late Night Line Up* in 1967, shortly before the Act was passed, she argued for gay women and men to be seen not as afflicted abstractions but as 'real live people'. When her fellow panellist, the Conservative MP Ray Mawby, complained that homosexuality risked damaging the social fabric, she replied brilliantly: 'What is so special about our social fabric that it can't do with a radical overhaul?'

Yet lesbian visibility was surprisingly low, especially outside London. Barber, who hardly lived a sheltered life, says: 'If you'd asked me in my twenties whether I knew any lesbians I'd have said, "Oh, I think one of my teachers at school might have been." but I didn't know any my own age, or at least I didn't realise I did.'[47]

Meanwhile, ignorance and suspicion continued to surround transgenderism, which as Brian Harrison notes was 'hardly yet understood' as a category in the 1960s. In 1951 former fighter pilot Robert Cowell had become Roberta, the first transgender woman to undergo gender reassignment surgery – a vaginoplasty carried out by the plastic surgery pioneer Sir Harold Gillies. Although her story was covered rather salaciously in the British media in the mid 1950s, by the 1960s and into the 1970s transgender people were still not clearly distinguished in the public imagination from transvestites or homosexuals.[48] In 1972 the Welsh writer and historian Jan Morris transitioned from male to female but had to travel to Morocco for surgery because no British surgeon would perform it unless Morris and her wife Elizabeth Tuckniss divorced.

In her 1974 memoir of her transition, *Conundrum*, Morris noted that middle-aged people were surprised and excited by her gender change much more than the young and wondered about the broader shift in attitudes this represented. Perhaps sex was 'past its heyday' and had 'lost the sanctity it commanded in our grandmothers' day':

> Degraded by publicity, made casual by tolerance, defused by post-Freudian psychiatry, made unnecessary by artificial insemination, it is already becoming a matter not of the spirit but of the mechanism.[49]

It's odd, considering what a force it would become just five years later, how unsure of itself the women's movement seemed in the mid 1960s. Nell Dunn's work feels uncompromisingly feminist, as do Pauline Boty paintings like *It's a Man's World II*, which uses pornographic images only to subvert them. But while the sociologist Hannah Gavron's 1966 study of the anxieties of housebound wives *The Captive Wife* is now regarded as a groundbreaking piece of feminist sociological writing, at the time it was hard for Gavron to persuade her academic supervisors – the book was based on her doctoral thesis – of the study's value.[50] Depressed over a failed relationship, she killed herself before the book was published.

For many clever young women, feminism felt joyless and retrograde. The historian Sheila Rowbotham, later a stalwart of the movement, admits that in her teens she associated the word with 'shadowy figures in long old-fashioned clothes who were somehow connected to the headmistresses who said you shouldn't wear high heels and make-up. It was all very prim and stiff and mainly concerned with keeping you away from boys.'[51]

In his Beatles biography *Shout!*, Philip Norman sketches a fashion-conscious girl of the early 1960s – a Mod-ette for whom feminism would probably not have been a pressing concern:

> Her hair, teased up into a huge, hollow 'bouffant', represented hours at the salon and in arduous, private backcombing and curling. Her face was a deathly white, with Woolworths' 'Minors' make-up, save for her two, huge, coal-black 'Dusty Springfield' eyes. Her dress, tight-bodiced, ballooned with stiff petticoats given every stiffness by soaking in sugar and water. Her shoes, matching her handbag, were white, with Italian 'winkle-picker' points and stiletto heels, banned as a destructive agent from so many ballroom floors.[52]

When, in 1963, the Beatles learned that their second single 'Please Please Me' had gone to Number One they were on tour support-ing Helen Shapiro, a sixteen-year-old girl from Hackney who had attended the same stage school as another singing sensation, Alma Cogan. A couple of years earlier Shapiro had had two Number Ones herself, 'You Don't Know' and 'Walkin' Back To Happiness'. Next to the Beatles, though, she looked prim and old-school and by the end of the year her run of big hits was over. It was a similar story for Cogan – dropped by EMI in 1965, her final album a collection of Beatles covers. She died of ovarian cancer the following year aged just thirty-four.

The Beatles were a classic male gang; tightly bonded, musically as well as socially, after their apprenticeship playing in seedy clubs in Hamburg's red-light district. They also wrote their own mate-rial. By contrast, female British pop stars like Cogan, Shapiro, Sandie Shaw and Dusty Springfield stood alone and sang other people's songs.

Songwriting was a male-dominated industry. The job of women was to consume, not create. In Soho's songwriting centre of Denmark Street there was no female equivalent of the American

Carole King, who in partnership with her husband Bobby Goffin wrote a mass of hit songs such as 'Will You Love Me Tomorrow' and 'The Locomotion' (a gift to their babysitter, Little Eva). As the sociologist Candy Leonard notes in her book *Beatleness*: 'Girls loved the music ... but, for the most part, were not socialised to see themselves as people who create it ... Girls' love for the music was expressed through close listening, singing along with it, dancing to it, connecting with their friends through it, and focusing on the lyrics – that's what the culture permitted.'[53]

This state of affairs persisted for over a decade. Growing up in the early 1970s, Viv Albertine, guitarist in all-female punk band the Slits, thought playing the electric guitar was 'something you had to have a willy to do'.[54] Not until 1973 did a woman win an Ivor Novello Award for songwriting: Lynsey de Paul for 'Won't Somebody Dance With Me'. And as Albertine points out, it would take the advent of punk in 1976 to persuade women that they could participate in pop music on something approaching the same terms as men:

> I've always thought that my particular set of circumstances –
> poor, North London, comprehensive school, council flat, *girl* –
> haven't equipped me for success. As I watch the Sex Pistols I
> realise that this is the first time I've seen a band and felt there
> are no barriers between me and them.[55]

Women did, however, see themselves as people who *wrote* about pop music – and luckily newspaper editors concurred. Maureen Cleave obtained unique access to the Beatles because John Lennon, a fan like Cleave of Richmal Crompton's *Just William* books, thought Cleave wrote in a similar style. It was to her in 1966 that Lennon made his notorious remark that the Beatles were 'more popular than Jesus now'. The interview passed unnoticed in Britain, where it ran in London's *Evening Standard*, but the outcry it provoked in America after it was picked up for syndication there contributed to the Beatles' decision to give up live performance and focus on studio recording. So in a roundabout way we have Maureen Cleave to thank for their masterpiece, *Sergeant Pepper's Lonely Hearts Club Band*.

The journalist Virginia Ironside started her career at the *Sunday Telegraph*, then went to the *Daily Mail* when she heard they needed a rock correspondent. 'It was so easy in those days,' she says. 'I just applied and got the job because I knew what Tamla Motown was and they had no idea. There was no mixing of the classes in those days. These mostly working-class bands were terrified of me because I seemed posh and I was scared of them because they were famous. Terror was the name of the game.'[56]

Women like Cleave and Ironside blasted a path for writers like Caroline Coon (also an important artist and activist) and Julie Burchill who dominated music journalism in Britain in the 1970s. Coon would go on to manage punk band the Clash.

The Merseybeat scene which produced the Beatles did throw up an all-female band, the Liverbirds, who took over the Beatles' slot at the Star-Club in Hamburg. But although they had some success in Germany, they made little impression back home and weren't, if we're being honest, terribly good.

Apart from the screaming fans and the WAGs (Lennon's wife Cynthia, Ringo's wife Maureen, Paul's fiancée Jane Asher), women weren't a big feature of the Beatles' story until its end in 1969, at which point Linda McCartney and Yoko Ono became hate figures, blamed for breaking up the group. They were both tough, uncompromising women: Yoko an avant-garde artist connected to the Fluxus movement whose work, at that stage, inspired mockery rather than respect from critics; Linda casual and insouciant, refusing to be demure or agree with journalists that she was 'lucky' to have 'snared' a Beatle.

A woman mentioned infrequently in accounts of the Beatles' career but who was vitally important in keeping the show on the road was Wendy Hanson, Brian Epstein's smart, well-spoken,

Yorkshire-born assistant. Hanson had moved to the US in the early 1960s to work as an au pair before drifting into the music industry, working first as a PA to the conductor Leopold Stokowski and then at Capitol Records, the Beatles' US label.

Concerned that the practical pressures of coping with the band's popularity were overwhelming Epstein and his team, Capitol sent Hanson to help out during the Beatles' 1965 US tour. Scenes of chaos greeted her upon her arrival at Epstein's New York hotel. 'He was in a terrible state when I walked in there,' Hanson later recalled. 'There was a queue of people in the hall, many of whom had been waiting for hours and all of whom he seemed to be trying to avoid.'[57] At one point she was bitten by an over-enthusiastic fan who trampled on the roof of her car.[58]

Undeterred, Hanson returned to London with Epstein afterwards and worked in his Albemarle Street office of his company NEMS. There, says Philip Norman, her job was 'to provide anything a Beatle wanted, from new Asprey luggage for Ringo to a Coutts bank account for Paul'.[59] This makes her sound like a mere factotum. In fact, Hanson kept the overstretched office functioning, covering for the frequently absent Epstein as his mental health deteriorated. By the time Epstein killed himself in 1967, Hanson had left and been replaced by another secretary, Joanne Newfield. It was Newfield who went to Epstein's flat and found his body.

Hanson fielded the fuss over John Lennon's 'bigger than Jesus' remarks – 'You'd better get on top of this,' she told Epstein as Beatles records were burned on bonfires across middle America. But the job she remembered most fondly was tracking down all the still-alive celebrities whose cut-outs appeared on the cover of *Sergeant Pepper* and arranging to pay them royalties for the use of their image: 'I spent many hours and pounds on calls to the States. Some people agreed to it, but others wouldn't. Fred Astaire was very sweet and Shirley Temple wanted to hear the record first. I got on famously with Marlon Brando, but Mae West wanted to know what she would be doing in a lonely-hearts club.'[60]

What was the connection between this new world and those who sought to govern it? Having united the squabbling Labour movement behind him, Harold Wilson scraped to victory in 1964 promising a 'dynamic, expanding, above all purposive Britain' that would be forged in the 'white heat of the technological revolution'. Despite the liberal social reforms it pushed through, the Wilson government would prove a disappointment: pragmatic rather than inspired, especially in its handling of the economy – Wilson was pushed into devaluing sterling in 1967 – and Rhodesia, where Ian Smith's white supremacist government declared unilateral independence (UDI) in November 1965. But whatever his flaws, Wilson was, as the Labour-turned-Liberal Democrat politician Shirley Williams has said, 'quite exceptional regarding women'.[61] Just as female entrepreneurs like the clothes designers Mary Quant and Barbara Hulanicki did well out of Swinging London, so female politicians did well out of Wilson.

Williams entered Parliament in the 1964 election as Labour MP for Hitchin. By 1971 she was shadow Home Secretary. Judith Hart had several ministerial posts under Wilson before he promoted her to Paymaster-General in 1968. She would go on to be Minister of Overseas Development in every Labour government between 1969 and 1979. The previous incumbent in this job – it had been a new post when she took it on in 1964 – was one Barbara Castle, probably the most charismatic, high-profile female politician of the 1960s and 1970s apart from Margaret Thatcher.

Hart was made Minister of Overseas Development after Castle was promoted to the Transport department. A self-confessed non-driver, Castle became a male-hate figure in 1967 for introducing the 70mph speed limit, breathalyser tests for drivers suspected of drinking, and compulsory seat-belts in new cars. Reading about the abuse she received for this makes you wonder how much worse the reaction would have been in the age of Twitter. One letter wished her an 'evil Christmas and a whole bunch of unhappy days'. Another, from a darts team resentful that their right (as they saw it) to drive back from matches drunk had been curbed, called her a 'bitchy old cow'. But in the year after the test was introduced, road deaths in the UK dropped by 1,200. Castle knew she'd won when an ambulance driver told her that the difference was so stark, he and his team now spent the hours after closing time playing cards rather than attending traffic accidents.

Castle's mettle was to be tested further, when, in May 1968, 187 sewing machinists at Ford's Dagenham plant went on strike, believing they deserved to be on a higher pay grade.

The Dagenham strike, which has passed into legend and inspired both a film and a musical, was not originally about 'equal pay' as such – but as the strikers acknowledged, it rapidly became that way. 'We're just cheap labour, like most other women,' one (unnamed) woman told the *Guardian*. 'If Ford's would pay the right rate for the job, they'd get plenty of men machinists, they want us because it costs less. The strike is officially about upgrading our rate, but really it's about sex discrimination.'

Not all women were sympathetic to the cause, though. One striker observed that the biggest opposition they faced was from other women: 'The wives of other Ford workers who have been laid off are all against us. They say we do it just for pin money and why should their men's money be cut off because of us?'[62]

After three weeks the strikers returned to work when Castle promised them an extra 7d – 7 pence – an hour. Although the Ford machinists had to wait until 1984, when they went on strike for a second time, to win full skill and pay parity, in the short term the strike catalysed the Equal Pay Act 1970, of which more in a moment.

More catastrophic for Castle, potentially, was her effort to introduce trade-union reform against the overwhelming opposition of union-backed MPs led by the future prime minister Jim Callaghan. Both she and Wilson believed reform was overdue and that the conclusions of Lord Donovan's 1968 Royal Commission – that the problems would be solved by setting up an Industrial Relations Commission to settle grievances – were hopelessly optimistic. Her draft White Paper, called *In Place of Strife*, suggested a twenty-eight-day conciliation period followed by a compulsory ballot – anathema to many left-wing Labour MPs – and the threat of legal sanctions if unions did not ultimately fall into line. The legislation was rejected by Labour's ruling National Executive Committee and the Trades Union Congress and on 18 June 1969, Wilson and Castle were forced to concede defeat.

But Castle fought back. On the opening day of the 1970 Labour Party conference she announced that the government would introduce equal pay for women. Companies were given five years to prepare themselves, but by the end of 1975 it would be illegal to discriminate against women by paying them less than men.

The last piece of legislation to reach the statute book before Labour's defeat at the 1970 election, the Equal Pay Act was a step in the right direction. But the veteran human rights lawyer Lord Anthony Lester calls it 'a mouse of a law, the product of a deal done with employers and trade unions – both sides male-dominated. It dealt only with crude forms of sexual discrimination. It covered equal pay for the same work, but not for different work of equal value.'[63]

In the late 1970s Lester acted for the Equal Opportunities Commission, set up after the Sex Discrimination Act became law in December 1975. One case which illustrates the Equal Pay Act's shortcomings involved a factory manager called Wendy Smith who took her employer, Macarthys Ltd, to court when it paid her less than the man she had replaced, even though she was doing the same job. As Lester explains: 'Read literally, the Equal Pay Act allowed her to compare her work and pay only with a man working at the same time, not with a predecessor. In the Court of Appeal, only Lord Denning was willing to read the legislation sensibly, in light of the European principle of equal pay for equal work.'[64]

The case ended up going to the European Court of Justice which ruled in Wendy Smith's favour.

It's astonishing to think that, nearly half a century after the Equal Pay Act was introduced, women from Asda check-out staff to BBC presenters are still battling for the wages their male colleagues take for granted.

Another important Harold Wilson appointment was Jennie Lee, who served as Minister of the Arts between 1964 and 1970 and was so much loved by the public that, when she attended a play, the audience would applaud her as she took her seat. The arts establishment was more sceptical, but needn't have been. Although Lee never claimed to be highbrow, she was passionate about making the arts more accessible to ordinary people. As she put it: 'I am determined that all our children should be given the kind of education which was the monopoly of the privileged minority in the past.'[65]

Lee was a miner's daughter, born in 1904 in Lochgelly, Fife, into a passionately political family. Her grandfather had established the Fifeshire Federation of the Independent Labour Party (ILP); her father went on to chair it, and as a child Lee attended Socialist Sunday School. Aided by bursaries, she trained to be a teacher at Edinburgh University but dreamed of making politics her profession. She didn't have long to wait: in 1929, only two years after graduating, Lee became the ILP MP for North Lanark and, at twenty-four, the youngest member of the House of Commons.

By 1964, though, four years after the death of her husband, Aneurin 'Nye' Bevan, the founder of the NHS, Lee was lost and adrift. She had spent years in Nye's shadow, furthering his career at the expense of her own. Harold Wilson tried to find a post for her and initially offered her to Richard Crossman at the Department of Housing. Crossman rejected the sixty-year-old on the grounds that she was only 'good for opening bazaars'.[66] His loss was Britain's gain. Wilson created the role of Minister of the Arts for Lee, and to say she made it her own is an understatement.

In the mid 1960s the importance of the arts was held to be inarguable and by today's standards they were lavishly endowed. Lee beefed up the Arts Council and made sure the regions received as much money as London. She saved the National Youth Orchestra, which had been struggling since its founder Ruth Railton withdrew her subsidy in 1962, and she was a great supporter of the National Film School, which opened in 1971. At the same time, she oversaw the redevelopment of the old Festival of Britain site on the South Bank and fought for the long-mooted new National Theatre to be located there.

Her biggest, most ambitious achievement, though, was over-seeing the creation of the Open University. This 'university of the air', using TV and radio to give large numbers of people a univer-sity education they would not otherwise have had, was Harold Wilson's pet project. But it was very much a rough sketch on a beermat at the point when Wilson asked Lee to produce a White Paper on it.

The Open University was a perfect match for Lee, who knew all about what she called 'the struggle for self-education' and whose favourite novel was Thomas Hardy's *Jude The Obscure*, about a stonemason who dreams of becoming a scholar at 'Christminster' – Hardy's stand-in for Oxford. She herself liked to trace the Open University's roots 'back to when Nye Bevan and myself were together. We knew, we both of us, from our backgrounds, that there were people in the mining villages who left school at four-teen or fifteen who had first-class intellects. The problem was how could you devise a scheme that would get through to them without excluding other people?'[67]

The educationalist and historian Norman MacKenzie, who worked with Lee on the project, felt that she 'always had a mental picture of her father in a break in the day's mining with his headlight on, sitting reading Karl Marx in a mine'.[68]

With the help of the chair of the Arts Council, Lord Goodman, and in the face of massive, snarky opposition from civil servants, the press, the Cabinet and the opposition (with the exception, to give her credit, of Margaret Thatcher), the Open University opened for business in January 1971. By 1975 it had fifty thousand students, many of whom, like the heroine of *Educating Rita*, Willy Russell's hit play about a young hairdresser who embarks on an Open University course, had no formal qualifications.

Forceful and belligerent, Jennie Lee made enemies as easily as she did friends. Among the former was Roy Strong, then Director of the National Portrait Gallery, which, he told Patricia Hollis, was 'not her thing at all'. He remembered 'shipping in a mass of Council children to keep her happy': 'These she lectured on the terrible times the working classes and children had in the last century, which made one groan.'[69]

Over at the National Gallery, the joke was that the not-exactly-svelte Lee cared more about the coffee shop than the paintings. But as the Gallery's director Sir Michael Levey later admitted, the coffee shop was awful and Lee had been right to care about it. Once again, it was all about access. Young families needed somewhere to feed children, older people somewhere to sit down. Lee approached museums and galleries from the viewpoint of ordinary punters who might have their lives transformed by what they saw. Hollis tells a revealing story about a time Lee overheard a mother hushing her child in one of the National Gallery's rooms. She rushed up to the woman and told her crossly: 'Don't do that or she will associate the National Gallery with restrictions!'[70]

Meanwhile, in the control centre of Wilson's Number 10, a woman ruled the roost; a woman well enough known by the late 1960s for an obscene cartoon of her to appear on the cover of a hit single – the Move's 'Flowers in the Rain', the first song to be played on BBC Radio 1. She sued, and to this day all royalties from the song go to charity. Her fame persisted well into the 1970s. When President Nixon visited Downing Street in April 1974 he is supposed to have asked of a female press officer: 'Say, is that the one we've been reading about?'

The woman wasn't Wilson's wife Mary, who liked to remain as detached as possible from politics, but Marcia Williams, his political secretary and the empress of his so-called 'kitchen cabinet'.

Ben Pimlott, Wilson's biographer, calls the pair's close, almost symbiotic relationship – which was never proved to be sexual, despite the rumours – 'one of the most famous, and mysterious, partnerships of modern political history'.[71] The daughter of a builder from Northamptonshire, Williams had read history at Queen Mary College, London – chosen over Oxbridge so that she could be near Westminster, where she wanted to work. After graduating in 1955 she got a job at Transport House as Wilson's secretary. Widely expected to go into politics herself, she ended up channelling her energy and ambition into helping Wilson climb the ladder: she had 'diagnosed his possibilities', as Pimlott elegantly puts it.[72]

In some ways Williams behaved as if she *were* Wilson's wife. In public she berated him like a child – 'You silly little boy', she was overheard calling him after one City function – and her memoir of life at Number 10 includes such bizarre trivia as what Wilson liked to drink at lunchtime: 'Harold likes coffee, but his first cook, a very nice Irish girl, Mary Wright, produced tea after lunch and that somehow became the custom.'[73]

Williams certainly made enemies. When in 1976 Harold Wilson sent the queen his resignation honours list – one that rewarded what Roy Jenkins tactfully called 'some adventurous business gentlemen, several of whom were close neither to him nor to the Labour Party' – a rumour quickly spread that Williams was its author. The list became known as the 'lavender list' after the colour of the notepaper she was supposed to have used.

But Williams has always denied involvement and certainly no evidence exists to suggest she had any. When, in 2006, the journalist Francis Wheen wrote *The Lavender List*, a docudrama repeating the allegations, Williams sued successfully, winning £75,000 in damages and a promise from the BBC that the programme would never be repeated.

It often feels as if the freewheeling, hedonistic 1960s and 1970s belong to youth. But attitudes to the elderly were undergoing something of a revolution too. Writing in 1961, the pioneer in geriatric care Margaret Hill noted the paradox that 'everyone wishes to live as long as possible, but no one wants to be old'.[74]

As women of her class had done in previous decades, Hill threw herself into voluntary work while her brothers, the economist John Maynard Keynes and the surgeon Sir Geoffrey Langdon Keynes, went on to successful traditionally 'male' careers. In 1940 Hill had fashioned Hill Homes out of specially requisitioned properties in Highgate in north London. What we now call sheltered accommodation, Hill Homes were designed to house elderly people who had been displaced or otherwise affected by the war. Over the next twenty years Hill established several new Hill Homes, some intended for people who were mentally as well as physically frail. She only gave up chairing committee meetings in 1964 when she was seventy-nine.

The very cold winter of 1962–63 saw a sharp rise in cases of hypothermia in old people. This led in turn to a rise in general concern about their welfare. In January 1965 the psychotherapist Barbara Robb paid a visit to the now-closed Friern Hospital in north London where an elderly former patient of hers, Amy Gibbs, had been transferred to a long-stay 'back ward'. Appalled by the dehumanising conditions in which Gibbs was being kept, Robb founded the pressure group Aid for Elderly in Government Institutions (AEGIS) and in 1967 published the book *Sans Everything*, a horrifying litany of abuses perpetrated against old people in hospitals.

It took a long time to convince the likes of Kenneth Robinson, then Minister of Health, that Robb hadn't simply made this stuff up. But the message got through, and thanks to her, malpractice in hospitals received closer scrutiny and geriatric medicine evolved from rather unfocused general care to a distinct field of expertise.

Death, too, was a taboo that was about to be shattered. Hospices have always existed, even if they weren't described as such, but despite – or perhaps because – many were run by religious orders, there was little direct discussion about what went on in them.

The founder of the modern hospice movement, Cicely Saunders, changed all of this irrevocably. Spurred on by a strong Christian faith tempered by scientific pragmatism, she revolutionised care for the dying, encouraging doctors to see death, as Brian Harrison puts it, 'not as a professional failure but as a prize opportunity for a multi-disciplinary sharing of expertise'.[75]

Saunders was born in Barnet, north London on 22 June 1918 into a prosperous middle-class family. Her father was a successful estate agent and the young Cicely boarded at Roedean before going up to St Anne's College, Oxford in 1938 to read PPE. She interrupted her studies to train as a nurse during the war, but after hurting her back was invalided out, returning to Oxford in 1944 to finish her degree.

Saunders' interest in improving the way the terminally ill were cared for developed in the late 1940s when, while working at London's Archway Hospital, she formed a close friendship with David Tasma, a forty-year-old Polish-Jewish emigré who was dying of cancer. At a time when death and cancer were not much discussed, and certainly not with patients, Tasma and Saunders had frank conversations about what Tasma required as a dying person and how much of this Saunders could provide. Tasma told her he wanted 'what is in your mind and in your heart' – in other words, medical expertise delivered with the utmost understanding and compassion. To achieve this, Saunders reasoned, friends, family, social and religious workers should ideally be involved as well as medical professionals in the final stages of life.

Inspired by Tasma, Saunders took the unusual step of training as a doctor relatively late in life: she didn't earn her medical qualification, the MBBS, until 1957, by which time she was thirty-nine. In 1959 she published a series of six articles in *Nursing Times* which developed her 360-degree approach to what we now call palliative care. Central to this was her emerging concept of 'total pain'. Pain in the terminally ill was, she realised, complex and multi-faceted. It was emotional and social as well as physical, to the point where it sometimes became hard for patients to tell one kind from another. As one anxious patient with financial worries told Saunders when asked where she was hurting, 'The pain began in my back, but now it seems that all of me is wrong.' This pain was different from, say, an acute stabbing pain pointing to a particular ailment. Rather, Saunders wrote, it was 'a situation in which the patient is, as it were, held captive'.

In the summer of 1967, after years of planning and fundraising, Saunders finally opened her own institution devoted to end-of-life care – St Christopher's Hospice in the south London suburb of Sydenham. Here she was able to put into practice her belief that the dying most needed love, security, a listening ear and relief from physical pain. To achieve the latter she tore up existing rules dictating the frequency with which patients could be given painkillers. Her mantra was: 'Constant pain needs constant control.' If you were dying anyway, did it really matter if you became addicted to diamorphine?

St Christopher's continues to lead the field in palliative care. Although she retired from full-time work there in 2005, Saunders continued to write, lecture and assist with the running of her foundation at King's College, London into her eighties. But in 2002 she developed breast cancer. She died three years later in the Nuffield Ward of the hospice she had worked so hard to bring into being.

Had she lived, Saunders would have been impressed by the determination shown by Tessa Jowell in the last months of her life, especially her moving speech to her fellow peers in the House of Lords in January 2018 which led, after her death, to a doubling in funding for brain cancer research and better diagnostic tests in NHS hospitals. The speech's most beautiful line – 'In the end, what gives a life meaning is not only how it is lived, but how it draws to a close' – could have come from Saunders' own mouth.

On the evening of 20 November 1970, some twenty-five million British TV viewers settled down to watch the annual Miss World competition, broadcast live from London's Royal Albert Hall and compèred by the American comedian Bob Hope. Miss World was, by this time, the bête noire of a feminist movement which had become increasingly radical since the apathetic days of the mid 1960s.

Hope told a series of unfunny, misogynistic jokes and mocked the protesters outside, many of whose banners compared the event to a cattle market. 'I've been backstage, checking out the calves,' he said, smirking. But then, hearing a curious rattling sound, he looked up. From somewhere in the stalls women were waving football rattles and shouting, 'We're not beautiful, we're not ugly, we're angry.'

Suddenly, a flour bomb landed on the stage behind him. Hope looked disorientated, even a little scared. 'What the hell was that?' he asked.

All this you can see from surviving footage of the show that's been posted on YouTube. What you can't see is Hope subsequently trying to leave the stage but being prevented from doing so by Julia Morley, the wife of the event's organiser, Eric Morley. Persuaded to carry on, he tried to make light of the demonstration: 'Anybody that would try to break up an affair as wonderful as this with these kind of proceedings ... have [sic] got to be on some kind of dope, ladies and gentlemen, believe me.'

The protesters, about a hundred in all, had rushed down the aisles when the rattle sounded – that was the designated signal for action – throwing stink bombs and distributing leaflets and, in some cases, plastic mice. 'There was a sense of exhilaration that we were making our mark,' remembered Sally Alexander, one of the organisers. 'We dressed up. We wanted to fit into the audience so we went in with our handbags, looking good. Inside our handbags we had little scrunchy-scrunchy bits of paper, flour bombs to flick around ... You felt: Oh my God, I've got to do this. You felt terrified.'[76]

If the suffrage movement was first-wave feminism, this was the breaking of the second-wave. Earlier in 1970, between 27 February and 1 March, six hundred women had gathered at Ruskin College, Oxford for the first National Women's Liberation Conference. It speaks volumes about the state of gender relations at the time that Alexander, who helped to arrange it, was amazed when a woman from the shopworkers' union USDAW revealed that when her household ran out of toilet paper 'either my husband or I go out and buy some more'. Whoever heard of a man doing the shopping? Hardly anyone: the historian Jane Lewis says that in the mid 1970s 'husbands performed less than one-quarter of all domestic work and less than 10 per cent of routine domestic work'.[77] In 1974 Ann Oakley attacked the idea, starting to be floated by male sociologists, that men did more around the house than they used to. She expressed frustration at the way 'no one suggested that the domestic incompetence of men might be a result of insufficient experience'.[78]

Shortly after the conference on 8 March – International Women's Day – thousands of women marched through London's West End singing 'Stay young and beautiful if you want to be loved'.

The book that kicked off second-wave feminism, the American social scientist Betty Friedan's *The Feminine Mystique*, had been published back in 1963. Friedan's interest, like Hannah Gavron's a few years later, was in the suburban wife's sense of bleakness and alienation, what she called 'the problem without a name'. In the book's most famous passage Friedan describes a wife – ostensibly content, with all the material things she could want – lying beside her husband at night and being 'afraid to ask even of herself the silent question: "Is this all?"'[79]

Joan Bakewell remembers reading it at the time of publication: 'It changed my life … From now on I was alert to the snares and delusions of male values: I was eager to see change and improvement for women.'[80] But by 1968 the decade had taken an angrier, more political turn. Friedan's question was no longer silent and the answer was deafening: *No*.

Out of this new radicalised scene emerged writers and thinkers like Juliet Mitchell, Sheila Rowbotham and Germaine Greer, whose *The Female Eunuch* (1970) smuggled radical feminism into ordinary homes across Britain, its uncompromising language goading women into examining the way they had lost touch with their sexuality. Women, argued Greer, are afraid of freedom and too often blind to their social conditioning. They also 'have very little idea of how much men hate them'.[81]

An Australian studying for her doctorate at Newnham College, Cambridge, Greer was one of the few women to make a proper mark in the journalism of the late-1960s counterculture – magazines like *Time Out*, *International Times* and *OZ*. *OZ*, which regularly printed objectifying photos of naked women, was edited by another expat Australian, Richard Neville.

Possibly what feels exploitative to us now, in an age of omnipresent internet porn, made a kind of sense at the time, when debate raged over the political significance of nudity and indeed the meaning of the word 'obscene': 'Obscene is not the picture of a naked woman who exposes her pubic hair,' wrote the philosopher Herbert Marcuse in his *An Essay on Liberation*, 'but that of a fully clad general who exposes his medals rewarded in a war of aggression.'[82]

In July 1970, Germaine Greer co-edited a 'female energy' issue of *OZ* which she wanted to call the 'cunt power' issue. But for all its determination to subvert society and attack the hypocrisy of the older generation, the counterculture was embarrassingly male-dominated. As Beatrix Campbell and Anna Coote observe in their history of post-war 'women's lib' *Sweet Freedom*: 'Men led the marches and made the speeches and expected their female comrades to lick envelopes and listen.'[83]

Neville's girlfriend, Louise Ferrier, was the movement's poster girl and appeared nude on *OZ*'s cover. Beautiful and glamorous, she was generally assumed to be a major player on the scene. But the truth is more predictable, reinforcing a point made by the historian of the British counterculture Elizabeth Nelson, that women were 'never considered as suitable candidates in the search for allies'.[84] 'I was a very silent person, a very naive person,' Ferrier told an Australian newspaper in 2013. 'I was around and I was doing all the stuff, the secretarial stuff I guess.'[85]

Actually, she did more than this. Along with another *OZ* veteran, Marsha Rowe, Ferrier had the idea for a feminist women's magazine to be called *Spare Rib*, though she had bailed out by the time it launched in July 1972 under the editorship of Rosie Boycott. Through 21 years and 239 editions, *Spare Rib* was a cerebral, politicised alternative to traditional fluffy women's mags, running features on compulsive eating, the importance of learning self-defence, what to do with body hair and the plight of lesbian mothers threatened with losing their children.

And out of *Spare Rib* grew another now-venerable institution – the publisher Virago, whose green-spined 'modern classics' series brought unjustly forgotten writers like Elizabeth Taylor,

Antonia White and Rosamond Lehmann back into circulation. Virago was founded in 1973 by Rowe, Boycott and another Australian, Carmen Callil, who had been doing PR for *Spare Rib* when she had the idea for a publishing house that would 'break a silence … make women's voices heard … tell women's stories, my story and theirs': 'How often I remember sitting at dinner tables in the 1960s, the men talking to each other about serious matters, the women sitting quietly like decorated lumps of sugar. I remember one such occasion when I raised my fist, banged the table and shouted: "I have views on Bangladesh too!"'[86]

A bigger problem wasn't so much what men said, but what some of them did.

Recognition of the dangers of male violence had been growing. In 1971 in the west London suburb of Chiswick, Erin Pizzey set up Britain's first refuge for abused women. 'There were women and children everywhere,' remembered Jenny Smith, who sought sanctuary there from her violent, unstable husband. 'There were lengths of brown hessian hanging at the windows as curtains; mattresses snaked out of the bedrooms and up the hallways in any space that we could get them. It was a bit like a refugee camp, but it was wonderful … I cannot get away from the fact that Chiswick saved my life. You felt safe, you knew your children were safe; there was safety in numbers.'[87]

Pizzey's book *Scream Quietly or the Neighbours Will Hear* shocked with its frank testimonies from survivors of domestic abuse. Her subsequent falling out with women's lib gives some insight into the diverse range of views it accommodated – or failed to. Pizzey accused the movement of promoting the idea that men were intrinsically violent. 'All men are rapists' was a radical feminist meme long before the American author Marilyn French popularised it in her 1977 novel *The Women's Room*. Was it possible for a man to be a feminist? Most women's libbers of the 1970s would have said no. The ground has shifted since, as we shall see, but versions of this argument continue to be played out.

Second-wave feminists were also under fire over what they had to offer beyond the white, middle-class coterie who bought the T-shirt. There was growing awareness of what fans of jargon now call 'intersectionality'. It's a big word for a simple idea. Feminism has historically done more for middle-class white women than any other kind. For women of colour, who face the additional hurdle of racial discrimination, the idea of 'consciousness-raising' – discussing the private, subjective experience of being a woman – so central to mainstream white feminism felt like a luxury. This kind of feminism was opposed by the Brixton Black Women's Group, founded in 1973 by the activist Olive Morris. Meanwhile, Amrit Wilson, the writer and current chair of the black feminist refuge group Imkaan, was active in the Organisation of Women of Asian and African Descent. In books like *Finding a Voice* (1978) Wilson stressed the complex ways gender is shaped by race – not news some white feminists, who would 'cry and say our words were hurtful', necessarily wanted to hear. 'Terms like "privilege" are not nuanced and why should they be?'[88]

In retrospect these seem like healthy expressions of difference. But the result at the time was a fracturing of the feminist project into a mass of divergent groups.

With Britain's social kaleidoscope in flux, the business of government went on – or didn't. The economic problems which beset Edward Heath's government culminated in the 'three-day week' of January 1974 to conserve fuel. In February he called an election, asking 'Who governs Britain?' – in other words, was it the government or the unions? The public couldn't make up its mind, returning a hung parliament. A weary, slightly disengaged Harold Wilson trudged back into Number 10, subsequently calling another election in October. Labour won, but with a majority of only three seats. Economic disasters piled up, the worst being a collapse in the pound's value which led to Britain being bailed out humiliatingly by the International Monetary Fund.

Wilson resigned in March 1976, pleading exhaustion, but in the year before he went a raft of progressive legislation was passed. The toothless but well-meaning Equal Pay Act became law in 1975; ditto the Social Security Pensions Act, which gave unemployed women full pension rights, and the Employment Protection Act. This last enshrined maternity leave as a statutory right, forbade dismissal on the grounds of pregnancy and forced employers to give women their jobs back within twenty-nine weeks of giving birth.

This *annus mirabilis* for women also saw the Sex Discrimination Act 1975, after which it was illegal to advertise for jobs specifying applicants' desired gender, as in this example from *The Times* on 10 March 1971: 'Attractive girl required to be receptionist on show at Paris Air Show.'[89] Slowly the language began to change: 'Ms' was used instead of 'Miss' or 'Mrs' so that a woman's married status wasn't made explicit, for example.

The Sex Discrimination Act did significant work opening up professions to women, and the Equal Opportunities Commission, founded in the Act's wake, made sure the press knew its success stories. In 1977 Camden Council made Claudine Eccleston their first woman plumber. Linette Simms, a mother of six who had come to Britain from Jamaica in 1953, became the first woman to drive a school bus for the Inner London Education Authority and Margaret Gardner the first female guard on the Underground. Jacqueline Abberley trained to be a train driver. At the age of forty-five, Yvonne Pope became a commercial airline pilot for Dan-Air, a step up from the air traffic controller she had been before. Ellen Winser became one of the first women members of the Stock Exchange and Judith Bell a Marine Broker at Lloyds.[90]

But despite the success stories, the 1970s were a bitter struggle for many women. One such was a railway station cleaning lady, May Hobbs, who was so frustrated by the way three women were expected to 'clear up in one night an area the size of at least five football pitches'[91] that in 1972 she set up the Cleaners Action Group. By getting organised, she and her cleaning comrades won a series of victories by targeting high-profile government buildings, securing widespread media coverage.

Few walk-outs were as high-profile, though, as the strike at the Grunwick film processing plant in Willesden in north-west London. Owned by an Anglo-Indian family, Grunwick employed mostly Indian and Pakistani immigrants who had settled in East Africa before subsequently heading to Britain when countries like Kenya and Uganda gained independence.

Although Grunwick's workforce was mostly female, the dispute focused not so much on gender as issues like poor overtime rates and working conditions; petty regulations such as a 'no talking' rule in the mail-order room; and Grunwick's steadfast opposition to its employees joining the union Apex.[92] When in 1975 some staff were sacked, ostensibly because work was short, a rumour circulated that it was because they had been trying to start a branch of the Transport & General Workers' Union at Grunwick. The dispute rumbled on for months at a low level, then flared up in the hot summer of 1976, triggered by an argument over the sorting of some crates of mail for posting.

The orchestrator of the mass walkout on 23 August was a diminutive (at 4 feet 10 inches) mother-of-two, Jayaben Desai, whose dignity and charisma were complemented by a wonderful turn of phrase. 'What you are running is not a factory, it is a zoo,' she told her manager. 'But in a zoo there are many types of animals. Some are monkeys who dance on your fingertips. Others are lions who can bite your head off. We are those lions, Mr Manager.'

Desai made a rota for the picket, ensuring that nobody stood on it for longer than two hours. This gave women time to go home and do the cleaning, washing and child-rearing. She needed this too – her husband was working at night so he'd be asleep during the day. She'd make sure she and her sons had food to heat up. In addition, Desai and other committed strikers visited waverers at their homes to try to persuade them to strike too.

In this way she became a symbol of what Jack Dromey, then secretary of the Brent Trades Council, called 'a world of super-exploitation in 1970s Britain – exploited migrant labour'.[93] But by her refusal to play meek or helpless, Desai bucked the 'strikers in saris' stereotype, wrong-footing both politicians and her managerial-class opponents. As Andy Beckett observes: 'Often doubly discriminated against, used to balancing domestic and workplace burdens, and more awkward to confront aggressively than their male counterparts, Asian women could seem infuriatingly dogged, disconcerting strikers to unthinking British employers.'[94]

The strike fizzled out in July 1978 after the House of Lords supported the Grunwick boss George Ward's right not to recognise Apex.

Dominated by violence on the picket lines (there were over five hundred arrests) and a high-level legal challenge, the Grunwick strike was one of the defining industrial-relations disputes of the 1970s and contributed to a perception that the unions were out of control. At heart it was a struggle for supremacy between left- and right-wing forces – the unions, backed by the government whose Scarman Inquiry had recommended the workers' union recognition and reinstatement, and on the right the Conservatives and the pressure group the National Association for Freedom (NAF). This libertarian outfit stepped in to help Grunwick's managers after local post-office workers showed solidarity with the strikers by refusing to handle the company's mail.

The NAF's efforts were applauded by the then opposition leader Margaret Thatcher, who called George Ward a champion of freedom. Once in office, she was quick to crack down on the secondary picketing – that is, picketing anywhere besides an employee's own place of work – that had made the Grunwick strike so hard to manage.

Although the October 1974 election was the second election he'd lost in the same year, Edward Heath refused to resign. But behind the scenes other Conservatives were starting to tire of him. Only four days after the election the 1922 Committee voted for a leadership contest. But who would replace Heath? Some favoured Keith Joseph, others Willie Whitelaw. No one thought forty-nine-year-old Margaret Thatcher had a chance. As Education Secretary between 1970 and 1974, she had made little impression, apart from achieving a dubious notoriety by cutting free school milk for children over seven to help Heath meet his election pledges on tax. This had earned her the nickname 'Milk Snatcher'.

More pertinently, she was from the wrong side of the tracks – a lower-middle-class grocer's daughter from Grantham, of all places. The *Sunday Times* acknowledged that her 'sheer ability' made her a contender 'despite the apparent handicap that she is a woman'. Bernard Levin thought the country wasn't yet ready for a female leader; also that Thatcher was too chilly to be likeable, a failing that might be corrected were she to 'burst into tears occasionally'. (Remember that Britain's second female prime minister Theresa May faced similar criticism, only to be berated for admitting to shedding a few tears when she failed to land the stonking majority she'd been predicted. If you're a woman in power, you're damned if you do and damned if you don't.)

Enoch Powell thought Thatcher's selection unlikely because 'they would never put up with those hats or that accent'. All of which proves Andy Beckett's point that there was 'often a crude misogyny behind how [Mrs Thatcher] was regarded, but in Britain in the seventies – and afterwards – for all the impetus of women's lib, misogyny remained a potent political and electoral force'.[95]

At first Thatcher threw in her lot with Keith Joseph to the point where, she wrote in her memoirs, she 'virtually [became] Keith's informal campaign manager'.[96] But then Joseph gave a bizarre speech in Edgbaston in which he praised Mary

Whitehouse and appeared to argue for the enforced sterilisation of working-class women because 'our human stock' was threatened by the sort of children they produced. The subsequent uproar prompted him to withdraw from the contest.

Thatcher stood instead. Having seen off Heath at the first ballot, she beat her closest rival Willie Whitelaw by 77 votes at the second on 11 February 1975. The first female leader of a major British political party would become, in due course, Britain's first female prime minister.

On 4 May 1979 Thatcher stood in front of Number 10 and, at the behest of her speechwriter Ronald Millar, quoted St Francis of Assisi: 'Where there is discord, may we bring harmony ... Where there is despair, may we bring hope.' In doing this she seemed to be placing herself in a grand tradition of female peace-makers. And as her biographer Hugo Young observes, when asked by the BBC on the campaign trail whether she had doubts about her ability to do the job she had 'replied with thoughts few men would have spoken': 'Of course you have doubts, and you're tremendously aware of the responsibility. I just hope that people will take me as I am for what I can do.'[97]

The cover for her insecurity was a *modus operandi* which totally belied it. 'Her style was built on domination,' writes Young. 'None of her colleagues had ever experienced a more assertive, even overbearing leader ... Certitude was her stock in trade, the commodity with which she planned to exorcise the vapid compromises of post-war politics.'[98]

Thatcher's imperturbable self-belief was to transform Britain for ever.

8

What You Really, Really Want

1981–2017

People often ask me what Margaret Thatcher was like, assuming I must have met her. But by the time I started writing about politics for the *Financial Times* in the late 1990s, Britain's first female prime minister had exited stage right – notwithstanding her occasional interventions on, say, Europe – and she was regarded by many as irrelevant, or worse. The Conservative MP Edwina Currie noted in her diary that when Thatcher appeared in the Commons during the premiership of her successor, John Major, only the hardcore faithful spoke to her: 'Everyone else slides past, as if she's a turd on the pavement.'[1]

Thatcher is not a hidden or overlooked figure. But her attitude to gender, especially where it touched on her own femininity, affected the careers and livelihoods of countless women in Britain throughout the 1980s and beyond. Thatcher was strong and purposeful, a *bona fide* conviction politician, and it's only fair to acknowledge her successes as well as her failures. The Britain she inherited from James Callaghan's Labour government was a mess, crippled by rampant inflation and toxic industrial-relations disputes. By fair means and foul, she reversed what felt at the time like unstoppable national decline. She cut an imposing figure on the world stage. She encouraged aspiration and entrepreneurialism. She took enormous risks and picked enormous fights.

Crucially for a politician, she genuinely didn't care if people liked her or not.

But she did almost nothing for women. She left even her own mother out of her entry in *Who's Who*. It was her father, alderman and shopkeeper Alfred Roberts, who commanded her love, for instilling in her solid Methodist values like thrift and self-reliance when she was growing up in Grantham.

One consequence of what Thatcher's biographer Hugo Young calls the 'competing and contradictory aspects of her gender'[2] was her blind faith in meritocracy. Anyone who suggested this was a crazy conviction in the face of so much that impeded women's progress was found guilty of that cardinal left-wing sin, whining. 'The battle for women's rights has been largely won,' she declared in 1982. 'The days when they were demanded and discussed in strident tones should be gone forever. I hated those strident tones that you still hear from some Women's Libbers.'[3]

Of course, Thatcher's awareness of the stridency (or in gendered parlance 'shrillness') of her *own* tone led her to employ voice coaches so that hers would have a more masculine pitch. And although she insisted 'I don't notice that I'm a woman',[4] you can't help wondering if she suspected something was up when, despite being Prime Minister and First Lord of the Admiralty, she was refused membership of that Tory establishment bastion the Carlton Club for just this reason.

Interestingly, given how publicly dismissive Thatcher was of affirmative action, her government did take steps to improve gender diversity in the civil service. Equality officers were appointed and in 1984 Anne Mueller became the most senior woman in the civil service when she was made Second Permanent Secretary in the Management and Personnel Office, although a 1994 assessment of the initiative commended only 'modest progress ... from a very low starting point'.[5]

One or two other female-friendly policies followed. In 1988 her Chancellor of the Exchequer Nigel Lawson reformed the personal taxation system so that a man was no longer responsible for his wife's taxation: 'The present system ... takes the income of a married woman as if it belonged to her husband,' he said in his Budget speech. 'Quite simply, that is no longer acceptable.' Finally, in 1990, a White Paper was published proposing the creation of the Child Support Agency (CSA). This body, launched in 1993, benefited women insofar as it ensured that absent parents (usually the fathers) paid appropriate child maintenance, although it had been designed with the more Thatcherite aim of curbing the rising cost to the public purse of lone parenthood.

A body like the Equal Opportunities Commission (EOC), however, was never going to appeal to someone like Mrs Thatcher. She loathed it – and Elspeth Howe, wife of her longest-serving Cabinet minister, Geoffrey Howe, who was its deputy chair-woman between 1975 and 1979. (Elspeth Howe loathed her back, accusing her of suffering from 'Queen Bee Syndrome': "I made it. Others can jolly well do the same."[6]) In the 1980 budget, Thatcher cut the EOC's funding so that its staff numbers had to be reduced from 400 to 148. This made it less effective and so easier to criticise and mock.

Thatcher only ever included one woman in her cabinet – Baroness Young, who did a brief stint as Leader of the House of Lords and once tied herself in knots trying to analyse Thatcher the woman: 'Women have to make instant decisions, admittedly of a minor kind, like what shoes to buy for the children and what to have for supper,' she explained. 'This gives them a natural deci-siveness which applies itself to larger fields. But there is also great caution, again very feminine. An anxiety in human terms about the effects of an action. It could be seen in Mrs Thatcher during the Falklands. The men were discussing the casualties in cold figures, but you could see that wasn't the way she was thinking about them.'[7]

Or could you? Thatcher was capable of great private kindness but notoriously bad at empathising with grand-scale human suffering. Is empathy a largely female attribute? So much of the debate around Thatcher seems to involve grading her personality on a gender spectrum. Even Hugo Young, still her shrewdest analyst, weighs her 'hard' masculine qualities against 'soft' female ones, like crying frequently, which Young alleges she did.

Meanwhile, other talented Tory women went unpromoted, among them Lynda Chalker, who put her time as Minister for Overseas Development & Africa to good use after she left Parliament when she founded the Africa Matters consultancy; Angela Rumbold, who did her biggest job, as Deputy Chairman, under John Major; and Sally Oppenheim-Barnes, who never rose higher than Minister for Consumer Affairs in the Department of Trade. 'Mrs Thatcher offers her own life and career as proof of the folly of feminism,' wrote Wendy Webster in her book *Not A Man To Match Her*. 'Since she has achieved power and success, she sees no reason why other women could not do so if they wanted. But curiously, she usually does not think they ought to want to.'[8]

As we saw earlier, this was not always Thatcher's view. In the 1950s she championed the right of women to work, especially herself – remember her comment about needing a career 'because that was the kind of person I was'? Once she became prime minister, though, she preferred women to conform to the traditional Conservative model of the housewife and mother.[9] Part-time work was fine if you had no other choice or wanted some pin money, but the demands of a career had to be weighed against the responsibility of bringing up children – which was, it went without saying, a woman's work. In the February 1989 edition of *She* magazine, Thatcher was asked whether her government would introduce tax allowances for working mothers. Her reply is both revealing and ridiculous:

> No, there would be the most terrible abuses. Women make
> their own arrangements now and they can carry on doing so.
> Where women are going out and earning money while their

children are still young, they have some basic fundamental decisions to make. Can they, in fact, go out at all at that stage in their children's development, *or should several women get together and arrange that one looks after the children while the rest go out part time?* [my incredulous italics]

Once or twice this attitude led to unintentional comedy as she praised women whose achievements were emphatically professional or political for other things entirely. In July 1982, in a speech commemorating the suffragist Liberal politician Margery Ashby, Thatcher noted bizarrely that the suffragettes had had 'the inestimable privilege of being wives and mothers and they pursued their public work against the background of full and happy domestic lives. They neglected no detail of those lives – so that they were warm as well as immensely capable women.'[10] This would have come as a surprise to the many lesbian suffrage campaigners such as Cicely Hamilton and Edith Craig, who managed somehow to be warm and capable without male assistance.

Despite not really being one, Thatcher promoted herself as a housewife. She claimed to buy her underwear from Marks & Spencer, just like ordinary women. Her most trusted prop was her handbag, from which she would produce notes, quotes and other documents. Altercations with her became known as 'handbaggings'. The housewife stood for thrift, so possessed an intuitive understanding of Tory economic policy: they 'know I know from experience the sort of thing which they encounter daily', as she told the BBC in 1979. Whether this was true or not, it resonated. In 1983, 46 per cent of women voted Conservative compared to 42 per cent of men. MORI data from the period shows that women were more likely to support Thatcher personally than men; more likely to share her economic vision; and more likely to support her policies on education. Throughout her term as prime minister, middle-aged and older women especially stuck with her, though over time younger women swerved to the left.[11] As Laura Beers concludes in her study of female-voting patterns in the 1980s: 'While feminists viewed Thatcher as an enemy of women's liberation, on average women voters were less likely to view Thatcher as anti-feminist.'[12]

In her speech to the Conservative Party Conference in 1969, Thatcher quoted Socrates' aphorism, 'Once a woman is made equal to a man, she becomes his superior.' But how was that equality to be attained? For all Thatcher's love of meritocracy, the playing field had been levelled for her by the wealth of her husband Denis. It enabled her first to stop working as a chemist and train as a lawyer, then to hire a nanny to look after her twins. (Presumably she was unwilling to take her own advice and patch together ad hoc childcare with the help of random female acquaintances.) Many women would have been encouraged to stay at home by their husbands – and come under enormous social pressure to do so. It's remarkable, and very much to his credit, that Denis was so happy for his wife's success to transcend his own.

We don't think of Thatcher in her prime as being belittled by men, especially those within her circle. But it did happen. One of her former advisers, Alfred Sherman, once observed: 'Lady Thatcher is great theatre as long as someone else is writing her lines; she hasn't got a clue.'[13] According to this view, she was just an opportunist whose belief in free markets, privatisation, monetary control, spending cuts and low taxation happened to coincide with those of the clever boys at the Centre for Policy Studies (CPS), the right-wing think tank which Sherman co-founded (with Thatcher and Keith Joseph), and from which Thatcherism emerged in the late 1970s.

Thatcher liked to tell a story about how influenced she had been at university by *The Road to Serfdom*, the Nobel Prize-winning economist Friedrich Hayek's 1944 broadside against central planning, which argues that empowering the state disempowers the individual. It's one of Thatcherism's key texts. But in 2006, shortly before he died, Sherman told the journalist Andy Beckett: '[Thatcher] came from Grantham with her mind made up. She brought Grantham with her. I doubt whether she ever read Hayek.' As for her rise to power: 'It was chance.'[14]

In Mrs Thatcher's wake came other no-nonsense Tory women who, like her, attracted equal-parts desire and loathing. Ann Widdecombe, known for her socially conservative views on abortion and gay rights, entered Parliament in 1987 as MP for Maidstone; Edwina Currie, junior health minister between 1986 and 1988, as MP for South Derbyshire in 1983. Both were frequently caricatured in misogynistic and, in Currie's case, anti-semitic terms – Widdecombe nicknamed 'Doris Karloff', Currie called a 'pushy Jewess'.[15]

And then there was Virginia Bottomley. Married to the MP Peter Bottomley, she became an MP herself, for South West Surrey, in 1984 after a by-election, but only really entered the public consciousness in 1992 when she joined John Major's Cabinet as Secretary of State for Health. Tasked with major structural reforms to the NHS, including the closure of the London hospital St Barts, founded in 1123, she developed a reputation for insincerity and for giving statistic-heavy, Teflon-coated answers to journalists' questions.

This was hardly unusual behaviour for an MP. Why, then, was she so disliked? Because she was felt to have performed a gender-betraying ideological U-turn. Although her mother, a teacher, had been a Conservative councillor, Virginia was educated in something of a progressive-left bubble – a Sociology degree at Essex University, then an MSc in Social Administration at the London School of Economics. Initially her career proceeded along these lines. She worked for the Child Poverty Action Group, where she lobbied to ensure Child Benefit was paid to mothers rather than fathers through the tax system, then for the NHS for ten years as a psychiatric social worker. People felt entitled to ask how on earth she had ended up a senior figure in a government that seemed to want to privatise healthcare.

The apparent mismatch between Bottomley's 'feminine' looks and 'masculine' views was remarked upon by journalists. 'And of course she is a woman, with all the caring connotations that implies, and much beauty besides,' wrote the *Independent*'s Geraldine Bedell in a 1994 profile: 'The wide, lipsticked mouth engulfs people in smiles, the eyes are wide and concerned-looking, the skin is clear, the shoes sensible; she is an ideal of a certain kind of modest, intelligent womanhood.' She is, Bedell continues, 'the type whose composure men frequently long to disturb'.[16] The MP Hywel Williams echoed this assessment, calling Bottomley 'the kind of assured, attractive, bossy woman whom a certain type of English professional male wants to harm physically'.[17]

Back in those halcyon pre-Weinstein days it seemed okay to suggest that Tory women were inherently rapeable, especially if they had a distractingly sexy air of competence.

Even left-wing women found themselves compared to Thatcher, for no other reason than that they knew their minds. One of Thatcher's most tenacious 1980s adversaries was Brenda Dean, head of the Society of Graphical and Allied Trades (SOGAT) union which represented Fleet Street's printers. In January 1986, News International, publisher of *The Times*, *The Sunday Times*, the *Sun* and the *News of the World*, decided to move its operations from Fleet Street to Wapping in east London, frustrated by the intransigence and strike-prone nature of the print unions, and wanting to replace the old 'hot metal' method of newspaper typesetting with computer technology. When four thousand SOGAT members went on strike in protest, they were sacked. Dean went into bat on their behalf and became a frequent sight at rallies and on television. To those on the right, she was a union firebrand. But those on the left saw her as an appeaser who had dared to break bread – well, eaten barbecued lamb-chops –

with News International's owner Rupert Murdoch at his house in Beverly Hills.

Born in Eccles, Lancashire in 1943 in the middle of an air-raid, Dean was the first woman ever elected to lead a major British industrial trade union, despite having been taught at school that 'as girls we were destined only to be reliable, conscientious assistants to men'.[18] With her bouffant blonde hair she did bear some resemblance to Thatcher, though Edwina Currie is overstating it when she says that Dean 'could have passed for the Prime Minister's younger sister'.[19]

Elsewhere, force of circumstance brought Thatcherish (as opposed to Thatcherite) zeal and conviction to quarters where it had never existed before. During the 1984 miners strike, strong women who had once left the room when the news came on the TV became fiercely political. Women like Betty Cook from Woolley, a pit village near Barnsley in Yorkshire, ran communal kitchens, addressed rallies and found themselves at the sharp end of the police's attempts to restore order on picket lines: Cook had her knee broken in three places by a truncheon.[20]

Cook's life had been untouched by the predominantly urban, middle-class phenomenon of feminism: 'During the strike, my eyes were opened and after it I divorced my husband ... I had always been told I was thick and I was stupid by my husband but I learned I wasn't. During the strike my mother told me I wasn't fit to be a mother or a wife. Underneath, she was proud of me for going on the picket line but she didn't like me going out of the women's traditional role.'[21]

In truth, few people *did* like this. In the early 1980s, outside Greenham Common air base near Newbury in Berkshire, women protesting against the storage of ninety-six American cruise missiles there – part of a planned European-wide NATO deployment – were rewarded for *their* convictions by being bullied and abused. Camped out along the nine-mile perimeter fence in makeshift 'benders' of plastic sheeting, the women were more interested in staying warm than looking beautiful. And while it wasn't inaccurate to describe the camps as dirty, the women's blackened cooking utensils and supposedly infrequent washing provoked a grotesquely misogynistic response. Auberon Waugh wrote that the women smelt of 'fish paste and bad oysters'.[22] Local youths smeared the camp with excrement and poured pig's blood over the women while they slept. Soldiers leaving the camp in coaches would bare their buttocks at the women as they drove past.

The protest was symbolic, mostly peaceful, even spiritual. But it was also about physically stopping the missiles from entering the base. In March 1982 the women formed their first major blockade, only to be dragged along roads and thrown into ditches.[23] Later, they occupied the base itself and climbed on to the missile silos. In one sense the women failed in their goal – the missiles arrived in November 1983 – but they had provoked a national conversation about the safety and value of nuclear weapons, embarrassing the government and the military into the bargain.

Ann Pettitt, who co-led the original march from Cardiff to Greenham Common that resulted in the camp being founded, wrote that 'women were far more concerned about nuclear weapons than were most men ... In fact, women in general seemed to just be less easily blinded than men by visions of technological advance ...'[24]

Is this true? For all that the Greenham protest was an inspiring example of feminist pacifism, it exposed the dangerously thin ice beneath the concept of 'women in general'. Not all women opposed war, after all – they also served, increasingly successfully, in the armed forces. In August 1982 the Army Board ruled that members of the Women's Royal Army Corps (WRAC) could bear arms (though women could not be employed in a position that would place them in direct combat and could not serve in any post that, in a time of war, would be filled by a man). Relatively late in the day – March 1984, by which time the women had been at the camp for three years – the novelist Caroline Blackwood spent time at Greenham, recounting her experience in a book, *On the Perimeter*. She found it was local women in Newbury who were among the most hostile to the activists. 'I really loathe them,' one housewife told Blackwood. Others spread myths, for example that Newbury's swimming baths had had to increase their levels of chlorine because the women used them.[25]

In 1987 the Soviet Union and the United States signed the INF treaty, after which all the missiles were removed and destroyed. In February 1993 Greenham Common air base was closed and sold off – it is now common land once more, replete with dog-walkers and grazing cattle – although a hardy band of campaigners remained there until September 2000.

Can the women claim credit for the base's closure? To some degree I think, even if they didn't directly influence government policy. As Suzanne Moore has written, the protest had a different kind of power: 'It taught my generation about collective action, about protest as spectacle, a way of life, incredibly hard but some-times joyous. Still the image of resistance for me … is the picture of Greenham women dancing in 1982: witchy, unarmed women dancing on a missile silo. This magical, powerful image shows how the peace camp both played on traditional images of the feminine and then subverted them. Greenham created an alternative world of unstoppable women. It changed lives.'[26]

With its long debates running late into the night and macho boozing culture, Westminster was rigged to make female MPs' lives difficult. But few of the female politicians of the 1980s and 1990s who wanted change (and of course, some didn't) believed they had the power to enact any. The author and psychotherapist Susie Orbach once described Edwina Currie as part of 'that generation of women politicians who did not join forces to chal-lenge the system; rather they saw their predicament as an individual burden that could only be resolved on their own'.[27] (Memorably, Currie once helped to resolve *her* burden by pouring a glass of orange juice over the Labour MP Peter Snape after the filming of a TV show on which she felt he had behaved abusively towards her.)

This might be true of Tory female politicians. But over on the Labour benches, MPs like Harriet Harman, Joan Ruddock and Barbara Follett put women's rights and the battle for equality at the centre of their agendas, appalled by the fact that there were more MPs called John than there were women in Parliament. When Harman became an MP in 1982, 97 per cent of MPs were male. She set up the Parliamentary Labour Party Women's Committee to push for change by expanding the ambit of debate. As she put it: 'It's sometimes hard to remember now, but in the eighties, while politics included discussion of the mines, motorways and money supply, issues such as maternity leave, childcare and domestic violence were just not on the political agenda.'[28]

When, the following year, Harman returned to work after having her first child, she was told off by the Sergeant at Arms for taking her baby into the Division Lobby during a vote, hidden under her coat. Someone – a man – had seen her and complained. But Harman knew she hadn't done any such thing. What the man had thought was a baby was just post-pregnancy 'baby fat'.[29] For the sterling work she was doing, decades before it became fashionable to declare yourself a feminist, Harman earned the nicknames 'Harriet Harperson' and 'Harridan Harman'.

Harman was promoted under Tony Blair, serving as both Secretary of State for Social Security and the first ever Minister for Women. But she was made a scapegoat for one of New Labour's most ill-advised policies, the removal of a benefit premium paid to single parents. Actually, this had been a Tory idea, but in their 1997 manifesto Labour had pledged to honour their predecessors' welfare cuts. Loyally but without enthusiasm, Harman defended the policy in the Commons in Blair's absence.

Partly as a result of the fiasco – forty-seven Labour MPs rebelled – Harman lost her job in a reshuffle in July 1998. Why, she later wondered, was she blamed for the cuts rather than her colleagues Gordon Brown and Alistair Darling? The answer was depressingly obvious: 'You tend to be more exposed in this kind of crisis if you are a woman.'[30]

Tessa Jowell seemed to sidestep the mistreatment endured by other New Labour women, possibly because of her conciliatory nature – she had that rare gift for making people like her and want to do things for her. A Blair loyalist with a pragmatic approach, she was praised by him as 'sensible'. But this was code for 'canny' and 'clever'. Jowell knew how to put the pressure on when she had a firm goal in mind. Were it not for her polite but persistent lobbying, the UK might not have bothered to mount its winning bid to host the 2012 Olympics.

In 1987 Diane Abbott made history by becoming the first black woman to hold a seat in the House of Commons. Born in London in 1953, the daughter of a welder and a nurse who had migrated from Jamaica, she went to grammar school (where she was the only black girl in her class) then read History at Newnham College, Cambridge (where she was the only black woman in the university not from a private school), despite having been told by her history teacher that she 'wasn't up to it' and accused of copying someone else's work when she got an A-grade in an English assignment.[31] 'The biggest challenge I faced was racism,' she has said. 'People simply didn't think I could do it – that I could be elected as a black woman. But I learned a long time ago that you just have to get on with it; you can't let racism hold you back from what you want to achieve.'[32] (It would take until 2003 for a black woman to sit in the Cabinet: after Clare Short's resignation, Valerie Amos became Secretary of State for International Development in Tony Blair's government. Not until January 2018 did a woman Muslim minister speak from the Commons dispatch box – Nus Ghani, recently promoted to Transport Minister.)

Motherhood always came into the equation for female politicians in a way that fatherhood rarely did for men. Harman remembers being wary of giving the impression that family commitments compromised her ability to be a good MP, meaning she was 'too busy with my own family to help others'.[33] Worst of all was the fear of being exposed as an insufficiently 'good' mother. When in 1993 it was revealed that Clare Short had put the son she had had aged seventeen up for adoption, she worried it would be the end for her: 'My expectation was that I would be criticised and drummed out of politics as a wicked woman.'[34]

Shirley Williams remembered as an MP in the mid 1960s dashing home to give her small daughter supper and a bedtime story before returning to the Commons for a 10 p.m. vote 'and perhaps an hour or two's work after that'.[35] But her artful combining of public and private roles rankled with her first husband, the philosopher Bernard Williams. As she explained: 'People in the 1970s could be cruel to the husbands of well-known women, and they would refer to him as Mr Shirley Williams, or as my consort. He was a generous, brilliant man and a great philosopher, but being treated like that grated with him.'[36]

Williams was, of course, one of the 'Gang of Four' Labour moderates who left Labour in 1981 in protest at its commitment, under leader Michael Foot, to far-left policies such as unilateral nuclear disarmament, founding the Social Democratic Party (SDP). After some initial success – including a personal triumph for Williams when she won the 1981 Crosby by-election with 49 per cent of the vote, becoming the first SDP MP – the SDP fizzled out, merging with the Liberal Party later in the 1980s. In 1988, her daughter grown up, Williams moved to the United States and taught at Harvard, returning to Britain in 1993 when she was created a life peer. As Baroness Williams of Crosby she served as Leader of the Liberal Democrats in the House of Lords between 2001 and 2004.

In 1992 the number of women standing for Parliament hit a new high – 144 Liberal Democrats, 138 Labour and 59 Conservative. Not until 1997, however, did things really change. The 1993 Labour conference had voted for all-women shortlists as part of then-leader John Smith's programme of modernising the party in readiness for government. The result was 'Blair's Babes' – the name given by the *Daily Mail* to the 101 Labour women who won seats in the 1997 election. Notoriously, the newly elected prime minister Tony Blair insisted on posing with 96 of them on the steps of Church House for an iconic but unhelpful photograph. (When Harriet Harman warned Number 10 that it would send the message that Blair was a ram surrounded by sheep, she was told to stop being a prima donna.[37])

Initial media coverage was friendly. But Blair's Babes rapidly became symbolic of everything people loved to hate about New Labour, especially unthinking adherence to the party line. Singled out for ridicule in a manner that felt slightly bullying was the newly elected Peterborough MP Helen Brinton (now Clark), who professed her loyalty to Blair in a *Newsnight* interview. She became emblematic of what former *Daily Mirror* political editor Kevin Maguire called 'this new breed of robotic Labour MP'.[38] Brian Sedgemore MP compared the Babes to 'Stepford Wives … who have a chip inserted into their brain to keep them on message'.[39]

The 1997 intake boasted a number of talented women, among them Yvette Cooper; Maria Eagle, whose sister Angela was already an MP; and Anne Begg, who became the first MP who uses a wheelchair. But the expectation that they would, as Blair had boasted, transform the political culture weighed heavily on some of them, especially those who bore the double burden of being mothers as well. As the journalist Rachel Cooke observed in a piece for the *Observer* published to mark ten years having elapsed since the Blair's Babes photo, 'at least some of these women were grinning in the face of deep logistical anxiety'.[40]

Claire Curtis-Thomas, MP for Crosby, confessed to Cooke: 'I was never meant to come here [i.e. Parliament]. I'd been told my seat was unwinnable. I kept telling the north-west office that I thought I'd do it and with a good majority. I subsequently found out that they'd labelled me clinically insane. They insisted that voters were telling me lies and I believed them, to the extent that my husband and I decided to go ahead and have another baby. When the results came out, I burst into tears.

'We lived in Crewe, but had committed to moving to Crosby during the campaign. I had two children, one with severe learning difficulties, and I was pregnant. When I arrived in Westminster, everybody else was going to champagne receptions, but I had appalling morning sickness. All I was interested in was finding the nearest toilet.'[41]

Cooke uncovered a lot of unsisterly bad feeling too. From the start, Helen Clark felt excluded and patronised by

> a little band who were really snotty and snooty. I discovered later, thanks to the papers, that these were the women tipped to be the first Labour woman Prime Minister, the first Chancellor. They were well-connected. They were the poster girls and they got jobs because they were always going to get them. We all know who they are: Ruth [Kelly], Yvette [Cooper], Oona [King], Claire Ward and Lorna [Fitzsimons]. They were pushed. I thought it was a meritocracy, but it wasn't. I could have done the most wonderful speech. It would never have made any difference; I was always going to moulder on the backbenches.[42]

Fiona Jones, elected as MP for Newark, had the position of Labour whip withdrawn from her after she was accused of failing to declare her full election expenses. Convicted of election fraud in March 1999, she became reliant on alcohol to cope with the stress. Even though her conviction was overturned and she returned to the Commons, the damage had been done. She died of alcoholic liver disease in 2007. 'If she had not become an MP, she would be here today,' her husband Christopher Jones observed. 'It was Fiona's greatest achievement and dream. But ultimately it killed her.' Jones too had been a victim of nasty gossip. 'People bitched that she'd muscled her way next to Blair in that photo,' remembered Jones, 'but she laughed about it because *he'd* stood next to *her.*'[43]

During the 1997 election campaign, Blair's team invented 'Worcester Woman' as a symbol of the type of female voter they needed to attract. Worcester Woman was a struggling mother with two children and little if any interest in politics. In the past she had voted Tory out of habit, but would happily switch if she could be persuaded that a Labour government would improve her family's quality of life. She was not a feminist and had no interest in gender equality per se. But she ended up being well catered for, theoretically at least, by New Labour policies such as the minimum wage, introduced in April 1999; working families' tax credit (WFTC), introduced in October 1999; the National Childcare Strategy, launched in May 1998; and the Employment Act of 2002 which gave employees with children under the age of six or with disabled children under the age of eighteen the right to apply for flexible working.

Despite these successes, New Labour's attitude to women was confusing. Harriet Harman might have been the first ever Minister for Women, but the fact that she was also Secretary of State for Social Security gave the impression that the 'women's' job wasn't a 'proper' one. When Joan Ruddock became Harman's deputy, it was only on the basis that she wasn't paid. This put her in the position, as Harman notes, of having to fight for equal pay for women while her own role was deemed unworthy of remuneration.[44] And when Baroness Jay took over Harman's role after Harman and Ruddock's sacking, she declared herself not to be a feminist: 'In politics, feminism is seen as negative, complaining about things, it's perceived to be about separateness, putting up a brick wall between men and women. I don't think you have to be negative like that ...'[45]

Around this time, Helen Wilkinson from the Blair-friendly think tank Demos identified a 'new laddish' tendency within Blair's 'internal coterie'. She argued that 'men remain in charge, with old Labour's macho, labourist culture replaced by a subtler, covert and insidious laddishness — all the more alienating for being steeped in predominantly middle-class values.'[46]

Implicit in this laddishness were assumptions about how women should behave. This may partly explain Mo Mowlam's sidelining after she contributed so much to teeing up the Good Friday Agreement as Secretary of State for Northern Ireland. The public loved Mowlam — in 1998, the year she received a standing ovation in the middle of Blair's conference speech, her popularity rating among the public stood at 86 per cent — but this seemed to infuriate certain figures at the top of New Labour.

Mowlam's unconventional behaviour — removing at 'inappropriate' moments the wig she wore to hide the baldness caused by her cancer treatment; conducting meetings while sitting on the toilet with the door open; talking about tampons and how much her new bra was hurting her — disarmed some men but freaked others out. *They* swore all the time, but when a woman did the same it was regarded as coarse, undignified, 'disinhibited' behaviour. Gossips were quick to link it to the brain tumour which, perhaps wrongly given the sensitive nature of her job, she had tried to keep a secret. Those who knew her well insisted she had always behaved that way.

Labour's laddishness simply reflected changes in the culture at large. The 1980s had found some men taking stock, recognising that their behaviour and attitudes towards women weren't all they could be and modifying them. There had even been talk of New Men who pushed prams, changed nappies and held babies hunkily like the men in the posters sold by the high street store Athena.

But the New Man turned out to be an elusive creature. As the historian Peter Clarke points out, in 1984 nine out of ten married women still coped alone with the washing and ironing; seven out of ten with cleaning; and five out of ten with shopping.[47] By 1988 the number of children born to unmarried mothers reached 25 per cent, compared to around 10 per cent in the 1970s. While many of these would have been raised in stable two-parent relationships, those that weren't were usually brought up by the mother on her own.[48]

By the 1990s men were said to be exhausted by feminism and what they judged to be its extreme, humourless demands; and by the effort of suppressing their 'true nature' as feckless, immature idiots. A new phrase floated about, 'post-feminist', though it was never clear what it meant. Sometimes it was used as a prefix, as in 'post-feminist irony', to justify the sexist soft porn of *Loaded* magazine, launched in 1994 to entertain men who, its editor James Brown explained, 'have accepted what we are and have given up trying to improve ourselves'.[49]

To some late-1990s commentators, high-profile 'new lass' women such as the TV presenters Zoe Ball and Sara Cox were complicit in their own exploitation – competing with the lads to see who could drink the most or be the most crude. Was this way of behaving, popularised in the media as 'girl power', the same as feminism? It depends. If feminism for you meant opposing the male objectification of women, then no. But it's hard not to hear echoes of feminist sexual libertarians like Dora Russell in Cox's celebration of women's new sexual freedoms: 'Women are choosing to have one-night stands, to have sex with whoever they want. Women can now talk about shagging and not feel obliged to bring in the romance or the commitment or what he actually thinks or whether there's any love there.'[50]

And while it's easy to mock the Spice Girls, they were important role models for many. No mere Barbies, they were rough around the edges, dressed in the sort of clothes their fans could afford. Ordinary girls forced into an extraordinary situation. As Ciara Green, who grew up on a council estate in Belfast struggling with her sexuality, told the journalist Caroline Sullivan: '[Geri] was loud and obnoxious, and there weren't many women like that on TV. I knew to an extent that I was a lesbian but I wasn't sure – I had an affiliation with loudmouthed, tomboy women, and Geri [Halliwell] was quite loud and had the qualities associated with men. Women weren't allowed to be like that in public and to see them on *Live & Kicking* and getting completely arseholed seemed funny and brilliant. That ladette culture they were part of helped me to accept the way I was.'[51]

To some degree, ladette culture and its associated moral panics have always been with us. Whether flappers or ordnance workers, young women have always liked to drink and get drunk.[52] But as the 1990s shaded into the 2000s, there were worries that what had seemed like a passing fad was becoming entrenched behaviour with disastrous health implications. According to the Office for National Statistics, women drinking to excess increased from one in 10 in 1988–89 to one in six in 2002–3. 'The number of young women drinking excessively on a regular basis has more than doubled in the past decade,' worried the *Telegraph* in 2004. 'Statistics show the national rise in drinking above safe limits is almost entirely down to female binge drinkers or so-called "lager loutettes".'[53] The then home secretary David Blunkett warned that pub culture was changing. Where women might once have exerted a civilising influence on their male co-drinkers, this was happening less and less.[54]

More worrying than whether women were saving men from themselves was the connection between this sort of self-destructive behaviour and an emerging 'raunch culture' that legitimised, supposedly playfully, porn emblems like the *Playboy* bunny and sex-industry practices like pole dancing. Often this meant women abasing themselves for the entertainment of men, but in a context that gave them the illusion of being empowered – or at the very least in on the joke.

One old-school feminist who tried to square this circle was Germaine Greer, who in 2001 wrote in praise of the fun-loving, hard-drinking 'Essex girl', putting her in her historical context:

> Historic precedents for the twenty-first-century phenomenon of the Essex girl can be found in ballad literature, workhouse records and crime pamphlets, which abound with foul-mouthed molls and bludgets. Essex was always noted for its ducking stools and scolds' bridles, and for 'witches', which is just another name for uncontrollable women.[55]

But historical memory is short, which is why hard-won battles are taken for granted. How many binge-drinking ladettes in 1997 knew that only fifteen years earlier two women had had to take a wine bar to court to obtain the right to be served alongside men? It sounds ridiculous. And yet it happened.

The bar in question was El Vino on Fleet Street, in what was then the beating heart of London's newspaper industry. El Vino had a rule that women had to sit in a back room away from the bar while they waited for table service. In its defence El Vino cited 'old fashioned ideas of chivalry', though the ban was thought to date back only as far as the Second World War when it had been introduced to deter prostitutes. Sick of this nonsense, in November 1982 solicitor Tess Gill and journalist Anna Coote finally achieved victory at the Court of Appeal, having lost their two previous legal challenges.

From then on, women were allowed to stand alongside men at the bar. But the dispute wasn't just about the right to buy booze. As one of the Appeal Court judges, Lord Justice Griffiths, pointed out, El Vino's status as Fleet Street's pre-eminent 'gossip shop' meant female journalists had, for years, been professionally disad-vantaged by being shunted into the back. For him the principle at stake was crystal clear: 'There is no doubt whatever that she is refused facilities that are accorded to men, and the only question that remains is: is she being treated less favourably than men? I think that permits only one answer: of course she is. She is not being allowed to drink where she wants to drink ...'[56]

They never won the approval of Margaret Thatcher, who preferred to see them hoovering the sitting room rather than holding forth in a boardroom, but many female entrepreneurs prospered during the 1980s and into the 1990s.

Sophie Mirman, whose mother had been milliner to the Queen, co-founded Sock Shop with her husband Richard Ross in 1983 using a £45,000 bank loan. Mirman had begun her career in the typing pool at Marks & Spencer's head office, rising to the post of PA to the company's then-chairman, Lord Sieff. With his encouragement, she studied the nuts and bolts of store management, then in 1981, at the age of just twenty-four, became managing director of Tie Rack where her husband-to-be was finance director.

Mirman's shops selling tights, socks and stockings were mostly found in railway and underground stations – the first branch opened in Knightsbridge station – and for a while the company could do no wrong: when it floated on the Unlisted Securities Market in 1987 the offer was more than fifty times oversubscribed and Mirman won Veuve Clicquot Business Woman of the Year. But unwise expansion into America caused problems which ultimately forced the firm into administration. Undaunted, Mirman and Ross subsequently opened the successful childrens-wear store Trotters.

Margaret Seymour found huge success as managing director of the Scottish swimming pool engineering firm Seymour, which she founded in 1980. Frustrated by the low numbers of women in business, she also co-founded the Scottish Women's Enterprise

Group. In her experience women lacked both confidence and the desire to push themselves forward and 'get up off their butts': 'It is not enough that [women] are as good or better at their business than their male counterparts – they must get out to events and meet people,' she told the *Sunday Herald* in 1993. 'They should get away from their desks and take their enthusiasm out into the networking situation and spend £100 on that lunch. It is money well spent.'[57]

In 1993, at the age of just thirty-three, Penny Smith became president of Coca-Cola in the UK and Ireland, having success-fully overseen the company's merger with Schweppes a few years before. Two years later, pregnant with her first child, she left the post to a chorus of cheers and jeers. 'Coca-Cola boss says moth-erhood is the real thing,' ran the *Daily Mail's* headline, the paper seemingly relieved that Smith had, as Aminatta Forna puts it, 'bowed to the inevitable, given way to nature and fulfilled her true destiny'.[58] In fact, Smith soon returned to the fray, taking on an assortment of well-paid non-executive director (NED) roles at companies like Vodafone, the Mirror Group and The Body Shop which gave her the flexibility she had not possessed at Coca-Cola. This approach, known as 'going plural' – dividing time and energy between several companies rather than devoting it to one – appealed particularly to women. Mair Barnes, former managing director of Woolworths, and Ann Burdus, the former clinical psychologist who became chairman and chief executive of adver-tising agency McCann, followed similar paths.

Perhaps the highest profile businesswoman of the 1980s and 1990s was Anita Roddick. The daughter of Italian immigrants, Roddick founded the ethical skincare chain The Body Shop in Brighton in 1976 and, with the help of her husband Gordon, turned 'capitalism with a conscience' into a feminist mission. Taking her cue from masters of self-promotion like Virgin's Richard Branson, Roddick put herself at the centre of the brand, campaigning for human rights and the environment – she invested in a wind farm in Wales to show support for renewable energy – and against domestic violence and the testing of cosmetics on animals.

The company's most memorable gimmick, refillable bottles, Roddick later revealed to have been inspired by necessity as much as concern for the environment: 'We didn't have enough bottles.' Though she also said it was inspired by her mother's wartime habits. The brilliance of the idea was that it 'translated across cultures, across geographical barriers and social structures. It wasn't a sophisticated plan, it just happened like that.'[59] At its peak, as Roddick pointed out, The Body Shop's 2,045 stores served more than 77 million customers in 51 different markets in 25 different languages and across 12 time zones.[60]

A formidable achievement. Put her in a room with a male CEO, though, and Roddick was still mansplained to death. In a 1996 *Guardian* debate between Roddick and Stanley Kalms, CEO of the electrical chain Dixons, about the moral duties of business, Kalms cast his own approach as 'focused', 'rational', 'ordered' and 'studied'; Roddick's, on the other hand, he considered 'scattered', 'frenetic' and 'self-righteous', and told her so. Roddick saw immediately what he was trying to achieve by using these gendered words: 'Now I know where you're coming from. I'm the irrational female imposing my world view on employees, ignorant of how markets work.'[61]

The London Stock Exchange had admitted its first female stockbrokers – Anthea Gaukroger, Audrey Geddes, Susan Shaw and Muriel Wood – in 1973, although they had all been working in the sector for some years before that. Actually, female stockbrokers have worked in London since the eighteenth century but had to trade on an unregulated, informal market along with others excluded for whatever reason from formal Stock Exchange membership. These female 'jobbers' based themselves in and around the Rotunda of the Bank of England. Their work involved a certain amount of standing around. So inevitably some male historians have raised doubts 'as to how far they were dealing in stock and how far plying an even older trade',[62] ho ho.

By 1985, partly because of attitudes like this, only 52 out of 4,000 stockbrokers at the London Stock Exchange were women.[63] In a documentary filmed that year, broker Elizabeth Sullivan spoke frankly about the hostile, predatory atmosphere on the trading floor. 'We used to walk onto the floor and go and ask a jobber a price. And [men] would sort of congregate behind you as though you were from Mars. And they'd stand there watching you … waiting for you to make a mistake. And they'd jeer and laugh and shout.'[64]

In the male citadels of corporate finance, something was stirring … But it never roused itself fully awake. In 1986, aged just thirty-two, Lesley Knox became the merchant bank Kleinwort Benson's first ever female group director. Looking back on her career in a 2006 interview, Knox conceded: 'The City is certainly a very tough environment. I've had lots of experiences that these days you could sue for if you chose to write them down.' But to succeed, it seems, Knox had to tread carefully: 'It's fair to say I've never positioned myself as a professional female. Being a woman brings both positives and negatives. As many times as someone has said, "I'm not dealing with a fucking woman," someone else remembers you, and when you do a good job is more likely to say so.'[65]

What does it mean, though – 'never positioning yourself as a professional female'? Does it mean, when a man says to you, 'I'm not dealing with a fucking woman,' replying, 'Don't worry, I'll find a man for you to deal with'? Or, as I hope most women would nowadays, 'You fucking are, mate'?

We're back in Thatcher's delusional gender utopia where good women rise on merit and those who fail do so not because they have been held back by sexism and circumstance but because they are deficient. Is biological deficiency really a convincing explanation for why it took until 1997 – 1997! – for a woman (Marjorie

Scardino) to become chief executive of a FTSE 100 company (Pearson)? Or for why it took female membership of the Institute of Directors nearly twenty years to rise from 2 per cent in 1975 to a measly 6 per cent in September 1994?[66]

Sometimes women are their own worst enemies. In August 1994, a twenty-eight-year-old aviation insurance broker called Samantha Phillips sued her former employer, Willis Corroon, for unfair dismissal. She claimed that, having refused her boss's sexual advances on a work trip to Denmark – he had tried to touch her breasts on the dance floor – she had been sacked in a 'steamroller' fashion after she complained. (Willis Corroon claimed Phillips had been fired for gross misconduct after misleading an under-writer.) The tribunal chairman exonerated her boss but conceded that Phillips would not have been 'catapulted out of the door' without the right to appeal had she been a man. She was awarded 75 per cent of damages for unfair dismissal and sexual discrimina-tion (£13,500) plus a further £4,500 for 'injury to feelings'.[67]

The astonishing thing about the case, which generated quite a lot of coverage at the time, is the way Phillips was not supported by the women in her office, thirteen of whom wrote to the *Guardian* to praise the company's 'non-sexist attitude' and accuse Phillips of being unable to survive 'the normal rough and tumble, cut and thrust of office life'.[68] Phillips, for her part, described a 'swaggering atmosphere' at the firm.

I can't help wondering how many of these thirteen women would have described themselves as feminists. Even clever, high-achieving women seemed to flinch at the word in the way that historian Sheila Rowbotham had in the mid 1960s. It felt fusty, joyless, antique. When, in 1981, Sue Brown became the first woman to compete in the Oxford v. Cambridge Boat Race – she coxed the winning Oxford VIII – she told the *Glasgow Herald* she had been happy to accept a bouquet from the crew because she was 'not a feminist'.[69] After giving up rowing in 1986, Brown went into the City. By the mid 1990s she was working in the research department of a multinational securities dealer in Tokyo[70] – the kind of environment where not being a feminist was presumably an advantage, and still is. As recently as 2010, two former employees at the Japanese bank Nomura, Maureen Murphy and Anna Francis, exposed a culture where it was considered acceptable for a man to say to a female colleague, 'Oh, you don't have your honkers [breasts] out today, I see,' and, apropos a discussion about hiring a cleaner, 'That's where women belong – at home, cleaning floors.'

The pair lost their £3 million claim for unfair dismissal after a tribunal panel ruled that the remarks were 'trivial, not intended to be offensive … The comment made by a trader that women should be at home cleaning floors does not in isolation amount to an act of sex discrimination.'[71] Which is a bit like saying that a single struck match does not, in isolation, start a fire.

What about women further down the ladder? As Sue Innes points out: 'The dominant female image of the "post-feminist" 1980s, the besuited sleekly sexy high-flyer, never came near most women's lives.'[72] Their wages had largely stuck, having risen from roughly half those of men in 1970 to 60 per cent by 1980.[73] Why were other women not making progress? Overt gender discrimination was of course illegal. But covert discrimination was just as invidious; ditto women's sense of themselves as unworthy of success. Ginny Nevill's 1990 report *Women in the Workforce* concluded: 'Lack of confidence, self-blame and the feeling that female self-interest is in some way wrong seem to act as a ball and chain on women climbing towards higher levels of work or entering male bastions.'[74] Some companies, said Nevill, were even sending women on assertiveness training courses to 'release them from some of the learned behaviour of their upbringing'.[75]

The 1990s saw the appointments of some high-profile women to prestigious jobs. In one year alone, 1992, former Labour MP Betty Boothroyd became Speaker of the House of Commons, Barbara Mills Director of Public Prosecutions and Stella

Rimington Director General of MI5. But the overall picture for women at this time was stasis. A report by the Women's National Commission advisory committee published in 1994 found that while some women were living better lives than previous generations, many were still trapped in poverty, incomes of the poorest households having fallen by 17 per cent since 1984, and were 'trapped by violence and intimidation in their own homes'.[76] Women able to find work, said the report, 'often have to take jobs that are well below their capabilities in order to combine work and family responsibilities'.[77] Perhaps inevitably, it was older women who suffered the most: 69 per cent of women aged seventy-five and over were living on their own in 1991 compared to 35 per cent of men of the same age. Thanks to disrupted careers and a failure to pay into a pension (often because they had always relied on men for financial security), these women were more likely to be living on restricted incomes.[78]

In 1992, in the introduction to the British edition of her bestselling book *Backlash: The Undeclared War Against Women*, the American journalist Susan Faludi mocked the assumption, then prevalent, that to be a woman at the close of the twentieth century was the essence of good fortune. How much freedom women had now! *Far* too much ... As a result of this freedom, they were burning out in the workplace, leaving it too late to have children, struggling to snare the men on whom their happiness depended. For those who subscribed to this view, feminism had failed, washed most women out to sea, leaving on the shore a spluttering hardcore residue of harpies, spinsters and (whisper it) lesbians.

Of course, as Faludi pointed out, this was nonsense. The freedoms women supposedly enjoyed were, in reality, barely worthy of the name. And crises like 'female burn-out' and 'the infertility epidemic' that so exercised newspapers and magazines had their origins 'not in the actual conditions of women's lives but in a closed system that starts and ends in the media, popular culture and advertising – an endless feedback loop that perpetuates and exaggerates its own false images of womanhood'.[79]

At that stage, before mass media, and in particular social media, had started to proliferate like poisonous mushrooms in a forest, Faludi had no way of knowing how much worse things would get. But one woman, someone we have met several times, had had an inkling nearly a decade before. Towards the end of her life, in a book she published in 1983 called *The Religion of the Machine Age*, Dora Russell set down her worries about the impact of industrialisation on humankind and the environment. The difference between 1983 and the 1910s and 1920s, when she and writers such as E. M. Forster first latched on to the term 'the machine' to describe the coming age of automation, is that the computer has worked its way into the heart of this vast apparatus.

Russell worries that we will be unable to keep the machine under control. Rather than emancipating us, the 'persecuting religion' of technology will 'threaten liberty, and make an end of democracy as we then understood it', because it will invariably end up being 'run by an elite of oligarchs or a dictator at the top, holding the key to the clockwork'. She continues: 'I had a vision of the machine invading ever more territory of individual labour, running the full twenty-four hours, setting times and hours of shifts, impinging on every detail of our personal lives.'[80] Most presciently, Russell cautions against 'our habit of living through externalised aids and gadgets, rather than from inherent personal initiatives'.[81]

Although it feels like a century ago, I first surfed the internet and sent an email in 1996. A year out of university, I was a rookie journalist covering what we used to call 'new media' for the trade magazine *Media Week*. If there was excitement about the internet – where it might lead; how it might transform our lives – there was also scepticism about the potential reach of what was then clunky, user-unfriendly technology. With dial-up modems the norm, people joked about the 'world wide wait' while their computers tried to access graphics-heavy websites. E-commerce was in its infancy. Amazon existed, but nobody had worked out yet how to make serious money from the web. Google was two years off. As for Facebook, well – Mark Zuckerberg was just twelve years old.

What became the internet had its roots in the US military's desire for a decentralised communications system that could withstand a nuclear conflict. By the late 1980s it comprised around eight hundred networks but was fiendishly difficult to find your way around; the preserve, more or less, of computer scientists and academics. That all changed in 1991 when Tim Berners-Lee, a British software engineer at the Geneva-based particle physics laboratory CERN, invented a filing system for the internet which enabled users to jump between files using hypertext: the World Wide Web (WWW).

Histories of the internet have one thing in common: women are almost entirely absent from their early chapters. One who sometimes makes the cut is Nicola Pellow, one of Berners-Lee's assistants and arguably the first British woman to be involved in the internet at an architectural level. A maths student at Leicestershire Polytechnic (now De Montfort University), Pellow had secured a one-year internship at CERN's computer division. As she later admitted, when she arrived there in September 1990 she had 'no knowledge of any computing languages really, apart from using a bit of Pascal and FORTRAN as part of my degree course'.[82] Concerned that she didn't have enough to do, Berners-Lee asked her to create a 'line mode' web browser – a simple prototype of what would, many years down the line, become Internet Explorer and Google Chrome. The browser was simple because it had to run on any platform, not just the NeXT computer on which Berners-Lee had created the WWW. But as James Gillies and Robert Cailliau put it in their book *How the Web Was Born*, it was 'the vehicle that allowed the Web to take its first tentative step on to the world stage'.[83]

In 1992, after finishing her degree, Pellow returned to CERN and worked on what was intended to be the first web browser for the Apple Macintosh, Samba. In the event, Samba was beaten to the market by the more sophisticated Mac browser Mosaic. But Mosaic wouldn't have existed without Pellow's earlier coding efforts.

This was a vibrant, romantic time, full of utopian possibility. That the internet would, by transforming the way we communicated, usher in an era of unsurpassed peace and stability was regarded as a given. Why should technology not be harmonising as well as revolutionary? No reason at all, despite Dora Russell's fears. But where there is revolution there is ferment, followed in this case by a gold rush.

So it was that in the late 1990s and early 2000s a mass of young entrepreneurs, many in their twenties or younger, rushed to establish internet start-ups, then issue stock. The fact that many of these companies were totally unproven – how could they be otherwise? – and run by people with little relevant experience seemed not to bother investors, who succumbed to the madness of crowds and kept pouring the money in. A speculative bubble ensued, fuelled by excitable journalists.

The most talked-about British internet company was lastminute.com, briefly valued at nearly £800 million when it floated on the LSE in March 2000. In many respects it was a British version of the American priceline.com, a means for people to pick up cheap flights, rooms and other services like theatre tickets and restaurant tables which suppliers were struggling to offload. (Priceline stock was valued at nearly $10 billion when the company was initially floated on Nasdaq. Two years later, after the dotcom crash, it was trading at $7 a share.) The difference between Britain and America, as John Cassidy points out in his history of the dot.com boom *Dot.con*, was that here the start-up phenomenon was 'largely restricted to a small group of young, highly educated professionals, who lived and worked in London, or so it appeared from afar'.[84]

Within this grouping, the educated professional who attracted the most publicity – indeed, became the poster girl for the whole dot.com boom in the UK – was Martha Lane Fox, co-founder of lastminute.com with Brent Hoberman, her former colleague at the media strategy consultancy Spectrum. Lane Fox's job there, her first after leaving Oxford where she had read ancient and modern history, focused on the growing impact of the internet on media and telecoms, putting her in an ideal position to exploit this collision.

Lane Fox credits Hoberman with the idea for lastminute.com, but the pair worked together on hiring staff, building the technology and generally selling the concept to potential investors, funding themselves by hiring out rooms in their flats. (I'm sure Lane Fox would be the first to admit she was lucky to be in a position to own property so early in her career.) Although they managed to secure investment relatively easily, Lane Fox was surprised by how few women she came across in the process of finding it. Talking to Danielle Newnham for her book *Female Innovators at Work*, Lane Fox admitted to having encountered sexism – but also, in that classic female double-bind, to having benefited from male interest. 'You know, [being a woman] attracted attention – not the sort of attention I wanted. It was incredibly sexist on one level but it meant that if I went to the opening of an envelope, it was in the papers. Unbelievable!'[85]

Lane Fox has also been outspoken about sexism within the venture-capital community, arguing that female entrepreneurs are often given short shrift. 'I mean, why are so many bloody gadgets funded by venture capitalists? Because they want to fly them around their garden. And why are there so few actual real innovations around some of the things women would like?'[86]

At its height, lastminute.com had a workforce of two thousand and outposts across Europe. Lane Fox served as group managing director until 2004, the year before it was acquired by Sabre Holdings for £577 million. Her first move subsequently was to found the chain of karaoke bars Lucky Voice – a fun passion project. More recently she has joined the board of Twitter and founded the independent think tank Doteveryone to try to resolve the ethical challenges that bedevil tech companies.

Other female tech entrepreneurs also did well out of the boom years and, like Lane Fox, used their fortunes to try to do good. When Dame Stephanie 'Steve' Shirley's software consultancy FI Group was floated in 1996 it was worth £121m. (FI Group had its roots in Freelance Programmers, the revolutionary software company Shirley founded in 1959 to create job opportunities for women with dependents.) Immediately, seventy employees became millionaires. Shirley sold a controlling interest in 1991 and made £150 million from the sale and flotation. But the company continued to grow and prosper – an attractive proposition because it was solidly profitable as well as innovative. By 2000 it was worth nearly four times the offer price and Shirley was able to anticipate a future in which her wealth would increase exponentially every year without her having to do anything. This troubled her as much as it pleased her. 'Having spent half my life working 70- or 80-hour weeks trying to keep alive a young company that was paying me only a minimal salary, I found this prospect odd, and faintly obscene. Wealth as a reward for hard work, I could understand; wealth simply as a reward for wealth seemed wrong.'[87]

The philanthropy to which Shirley subsequently devoted her life had a personal as well as an ethical motivation. Her son Giles, who died in 1988, was severely autistic and required specialist care. Shirley spent much of her fortune on autism projects, including the specialist residential school Prior's Court in Berkshire. In 2001 she donated £10 million towards the founding of the Oxford Internet Institute, a research body devoted to studying the way the internet, especially social media, impacts on society. 'My life's legacy is not going to be my company, which I thought for many years it would be,' she has admitted. 'When I give, I try to think in terms of investing in society. I give only to things that I know, understand and care about – and that is information technology and autism.'[88] Shirley has spoken often of her need to justify the fact that, as a Kindertransport refugee child, she was saved when so many other Jewish children died in the Holocaust: 'It makes me driven to ensure that each day was worth saving, so I try not to fritter my life away.'[89]

Part of the internet's utopian appeal in the early days – before it became the portal for porn, abuse and fake news it can sometimes feel like – was that it might end up having a different social and gender dynamic from offline 'reality'. As we know, that hasn't happened. On the contrary, many of the most popular and influential websites remain male-dominated. A 2008 survey found that fewer than 13 per cent of Wikipedia's contributors worldwide were women. A follow-up survey in 2011 found things were going backwards: globally, 9 per cent of contributors were women, though that figure rose to a still-pathetic 15 per cent in the US. In 2015 Jimmy Wales, founder of the Wikimedia Foundation which runs Wikipedia, admitted the organisation had failed to meet its goal of increasing women's participation in the site to 25 per cent by 2015.[90] One study by the Illinois Institute of Technology, of reviews posted on IMDB, found that 'even when they resemble men's reviews linguistically, women's reviews still enjoy less prestige and smaller audiences'.[91] Linguistic analysis by the report's authors suggested that, to get round this, female contributors were adjusting their writing styles to sound more male – using fewer pronouns and worrying less about being polite and conciliatory.[92]

Faced with this reality, women have sought to carve out space for themselves. The tagline of Mumsnet, the hugely successful parenting support website co-founded by sports journalist Justine Roberts and TV producer Carrie Longton in 2000, is 'by parents, for parents'. Its name clearly tells a more gender-specific story, while even a cursory visit shows how angled towards the female parenting experience it is.

According to a Mumsnet census conducted in the autumn of 2013, men make up only 16 per cent of all users. No great surprise there, although interestingly the behaviour of Mumsnet's female users has struck academics who have studied it as 'male': one paper found posters on its forums to have 'a robust posting style', a 'tolerance of behaviour such as flaming and swearing' and 'an appreciation of witty entertainment' – qualities usually associated with male-dominated internet spaces, i.e. most of the internet, as far as I can work out.[93]

So successful has Mumsnet been that Roberts and Longton are regular fixtures on 'female power' lists. They were even credited with the power to sway the result of a general election: the 2010 election was nicknamed the 'Mumsnet election' as it was believed the site's 1.3 million members, many of them floating voters, would play a key role in determining the outcome. This, says Roberts, was when they first noticed misogyny creeping into the conversation around Mumsnet: 'There was a backlash, which almost said to me, women know your place, this isn't your territory, who do you think you are?'[94]

———————

Who do you think you are? Usually asked covertly rather than directly, this strikes me as the question most commonly directed at women in the twenty-first century. *Who do you think you are, working alongside men and expecting to be paid the same as them? Who do you think you are, complaining when your bottoms are pinched?*

In the two years since I began work on this book the world has changed considerably. Brexit, Trump, Weinstein – these phenomena weren't inconceivable, nor did they come out of nowhere; but they were unexpected and it will take a while to recover from the aftershock. As I write this, in April 2018, I can hardly believe it is only six months since *The New York Times* published its original story detailing decades of alleged sexual harassment by Hollywood producer Harvey Weinstein. The impact continues to reverberate in the form of the #MeToo and other associated movements and there is widespread hope that we might be on the verge of real change. At this year's Golden Globe awards almost all female attendees wore black, a symbolic protest against the everyday degradations endured by women in the film industry.

Yet on the day this development was being reported, another story broke in the UK. The BBC's experienced, hugely respected China editor Carrie Gracie had resigned in protest at the way her colleagues, male international editors Jeremy Bowen and Jon Sopel, were paid 'at least 50 per cent more' than she was. Accusing the BBC of possessing a 'secretive and illegal' pay structure, she stressed that she didn't want more money – she turned down a £45,000 pay rise – but to be paid the same as the men. Instead, she would be leaving China and returning to her former position in the TV newsroom where, she said, she hoped to be paid equally. 'It's the job of my generation to help fix [this problem],' she told me. 'If we don't fix it now then our daughters will be having to fix it twenty years from now.' What about the justification put forward by some that Sopel, the BBC's North America editor, was on screen more? Or *Newsnight* presenter Evan Davies' comment that what Gracie did was 'showbiz', a realm in which evaluating talent pay is hard? This was how Gracie responded to that question when I asked her directly on *Channel 4 News*: 'I speak Chinese. I've been reporting China for thirty years. The BBC repeatedly says I'm very hard to replace. It's a very difficult job with lots of surveillance, police harassment, pollution … Getting everybody from yak-herders to communist party officials in front of the camera in a one-party state. That is not easy … I'm not in showbiz! I challenge anyone to come to China, trek around in a minibus, work all the hours of the night, get jostled and thrown in a detention cell (briefly) by the Chinese police. That is not showbiz!'[95]

As I was putting the finishing touches to this book, a clause of the 2010 Equality Act came into force requiring every company with 250 or more employees to publish its gender pay gap. The results confirmed my worst fears. Nearly eight out of ten firms, 78 per cent of the 10,000-plus that reported their data, paid their male employees on average more than their female ones. One of the worst offenders was Ryanair, with a 71.8 per cent pay gap – the result of almost all their pilots being men. This lack of women in senior roles, the main reason for the gap,[96] is a problem across the board, including at ITN where I work and where the gender pay gap is a frankly shocking 19.6 per cent – worse than the BBC.

Since 7 May 2015 Britain has had its second female prime minister, Theresa May. Compared to Mrs Thatcher, May is a radical feminist. As Home Secretary, May lobbied her predecessor David Cameron for compulsory sex education and pushed colleagues to do more to tackle domestic violence – introducing laws criminalising coercive control, domestic-violence protection orders and a disclosure scheme through which women could find out whether their partner had a history of abuse offences.

It's too early to predict how May's premiership will be regarded by future historians. So far, it's not looking good. But nor are headlines like 'Theresa May's incompetence has set women back decades'[97] – a recent example from the *Independent* – very helpful. Just because a woman makes an error of judgement – for example, calling an election with the aim of boosting her majority only to end up with a hung parliament – does not mean she is a benchmark against which all other women should be judged. We shouldn't be made to own the failure of every other woman.

Of course, we shouldn't need reminding that, compared to women in some other countries, most British women have it easy. Or that attempts to advance the female cause too often end up advancing white middle-class women rather than BAME, working-class or disabled women. The writer and Black Feminist activist Lola Okolosie is absolutely right that too many white middle-class feminists – and I must put my hand up here – have been slow to see beyond their own preoccupations.[98]

In a thoughtful lecture to the think tank Demos, Alison Wolf noted that the cheap labour on which modern elites depend to clean and look after their children is by and large female: 'Workers in these sectors are low-paid. They are also overwhelmingly female. Without them, today's two-career, two-salary elite families simply could not exist.'[99] Wolf's excellent point is that poor women get an exceptionally raw deal and usually end up poorer than the poorest men. But too many critiques of modern feminism seek to divide and rule, either by dismissing issues like board-room representation as relevant only to a privileged few – another strand of Wolf's lecture – or setting up emotive but unhelpful oppositions between, say, access to abortion and warzone rape; Hollywood actresses and trafficked women; a BBC correspondent on £135,000 a year (Carrie Gracie's salary at the time of her resignation) and a professional carer on £7.36 an hour.

The conclusion that sexism and misogyny can only be conquered if men are prepared to buy into feminism underpinned the UN's ambitious 2014 campaign HeForShe, launched by the actress and UN Women Goodwill Ambassador Emma Watson. Watson began her speech by checking her Western privilege, acknowledging that 'my parents didn't love me less because I was born a daughter. My school did not limit me because I was a girl. My mentors didn't assume that I would go less far because I might give birth to a child one day.'[100] She went on to make the point that men too are imprisoned by gender stereotypes, particularly the compulsion to show strength through aggression: 'If men don't have to be aggressive in order to be accepted women won't feel compelled to be submissive. If men don't have to control, women won't have to be controlled.'[101]

Watson is the public face of HeForShe. But the project was conceived by the political scientist Elizabeth Nyamayaro, Senior Adviser for UN Women. As a child, Nyamayaro survived on

UNICEF food parcels when the small village in Zimbabwe where she and her family lived was hit by a drought. Aged ten, she went to live with an aunt in Harare and attended a private school alongside British children. As she told *Elle*: 'At school I was way behind everyone else; I couldn't read or write English. But during the holidays I would go back to my village and I no longer fitted in there. I felt guilty because I realised how privileged I was. I wanted to do something about it.'[102]

Nyamayaro left Zimbabwe when she was twenty-one and moved to London, studying first at a small college in Notting Hill, then at the London School of Economics where she took an MSc in Politics. After further studies at Harvard she worked at the pharmaceutical company Merck as Director External Affairs & Policy, Africa, and in their corporate strategy office.

HeForShe is a great example of a successful, feminist, social media-driven awareness-raising movement and Nyamayaro's ambition to 'make it an advocacy platform to change public policy and the law' is commendable.[103]

Another fantastic example of an awareness-raising platform is Everyday Sexism. Founded as a website in 2012, Everyday Sexism is a collection of stories uploaded by women detailing their experiences of sexist abuse and harassment. Former actress Laura Bates was inspired to found it after enduring what she calls 'another week of little pinpricks': a man who seized her hand outside a café and refused to let go; another who followed her off the bus and 'propositioned me all the way to my front door' ... She started for the first time to consider 'how many of these little incidents I was putting up with from day to day'.[104] Just how many other women were experiencing them too is astonishing. By December 2013, the site had 50,000 entries; by April 2015, 100,000.

But for her efforts Bates found herself abused and vilified on social media, the recipient of thousands of rape and death threats from men, some bizarrely detailed: 'People talk about specific serial killers they admire and who they would like to emulate and about the different weapons that they fantasise about using on you and in what order. It is quite twisted stuff.'[105]

It was a similar story for Caroline Criado-Perez, the Brazilian-born British feminist activist who succeeded in getting an image of Jane Austen onto the £10 bank note. The Bank of England had announced that Winston Churchill would replace the prison reformer Elizabeth Fry on the £5 note from 2016, meaning the only woman on notes issued by the Bank was the Queen. This enraged Criado-Perez, who had already launched her online directory of female experts, The Women's Room, to tackle the problem of women's media invisibility after listening to discussions on Radio 4's flagship *Today* programme about teenage pregnancies and breast cancer which featured no contributions from women experts.[106] Thanks to Criado-Perez's efforts, which included an online petition, a letter to the Bank accusing it of breaching the Public Sector Equality Duty and frenzied social (and other) media activity, the Bank caved in. But like Laura Bates before her, Criado-Perez's reward was staggering levels of online abuse. Two of her most persistent trolls, John Nimmo and Isabella Sorley, were jailed in 2014. Nimmo had also trolled the feminist Labour MP Stella Creasy. On being released, he continued to offend, emailing the Jewish Labour MP Luciana Berger a picture of a large knife and the message 'watch your back Jewish scum'. He was jailed again in February 2017.

I know from personal experience that this kind of abuse is frightening, depressing and exhausting – yet another layer of crap to deal with. Time and again, and not because of anything they have or haven't done, women are forced into the role of 'victim'. An American movement called Women Against Feminism blames feminism for encouraging this self-identification. But this is ridiculous. Women are victimised; therefore they are victims – of violence, abuse, oppression and inequality. And as someone once (nearly) sang, sisters are not doing it to themselves.

Sometimes the stories make me want to scream with frustration. In February 2018 the head of the London Fire Brigade, Dany Cotton, got the full 'you stupid cow, why don't you die?' treatment after launching a campaign to encourage people to talk about 'firefighters' rather than 'firemen'. When it was put to her that this would mean the cartoon character Fireman Sam being rechristened Firefighter Sam, she was obliged to point out that it wouldn't because 'he is not real. He is not a person, he is a cartoon – I just want him to join us and call himself a firefighter'.[107]

This is all about male fear. And we have been here before. The feminist literary critic Elaine Showalter identified a similar phenomenon at the end of the nineteenth century as New Women and the promise of suffrage chipped away at male supremacy: 'In periods of cultural insecurity,' she writes, 'when there are fears of regression and degeneration, the longing for strict border controls around the definition of gender, as well as race, class and nationality, becomes especially intense.'[108]

It's important to appreciate how freaked out some men have been by #MeToo. In a matter of months, everything seems to have changed. Office conduct which once struck men as innocuous – a wink here, a bottom pat there – has been reappraised as harassment. Add to this the growing sense that gender is less fixed than people once thought and where does that leave some men who feel they have nothing to be proud of except the accident of having been born male?

But this isn't a book about them. It is about a hundred – and more – years of bloody brilliant women. So I want to end by thinking about this generation of BBWs – as I've taken to calling them.

Pleasingly, there's no shortage. These are just examples from off the top of my head – some well known, some not – and I invite you to add your own …

Clever, talented female politicians exist across the spectrum, from Nicola Sturgeon and Mhairi Black (SNP) to Leanne Wood

(Plaid Cymru), Jess Phillips and Angela Rayner (Labour), Eleanor Smith – the West Midlands' first MP from an African Caribbean background, in Enoch Powell's old seat – Margot James and down-but-not-out Amber Rudd (Conservative). Let's not forget Sophie Walker of the Women's Equality Party, founded by Sandi Toksvig and Catherine Mayer in 2015.

Cressida Dick's appointment as Commissioner of the Metropolitan Police in February 2017 – the first woman to serve in the role – was very exciting. The high-achieving daughter of academics, Oxford-born and -educated Dick joined the police in 1983 as a constable. She had a low profile until 2005 when, while she was Gold Commander of Operation Kratos, designed to combat suicide bombers, the Brazilian electrician Jean Charles de Menezes was shot at Stockwell tube station in a tragic case of mistaken identity. (At the inquest, Dick was exonerated of blame.) At a difficult time for the Met, with knife-crime soaring and terrorism a constant threat, Dick will doubtless be braced for battles over funding, and attacks on her gender, and, as a lesbian, on her sexuality.

There are so many powerful female writers around at the moment that it feels invidious to single any out, but I would be surprised if future generations didn't look approvingly upon Hilary Mantel, queen of the historical novel; Carol Ann Duffy, probably my favourite living poet; Naomi Alderman, British heir to Margaret Atwood; Ali Smith, gleeful enthusiast and inspired experimentalist; Sarah Waters, peerless storyteller; Caitlin Moran, who did so much to extend the reach of feminism with her salty, empowering 2011 bestseller *How to Be a Woman*; and of course J. K. Rowling. No one's going to forget J. K. Rowling in a hurry, are they?

The current crop of determined, resilient female campaigners bear comparison with their early twentieth-century counterparts – a point that surely won't be lost on future historians. Collectively they target a broad spectrum of injustices. Leyla Hussein and

Nimco Ali have worked to combat gender-based violence against women, especially female genital mutilation; while the likes of Avon & Somerset Constabulary's brilliant DCI Leanne Pook try valiantly to prosecute its practitioners within Britain. Arminka Helić, now Baroness Helić, first came to Britain as a Bosnian Muslim refugee in the early 1990s. While working as Special Adviser to William Hague when he was Foreign Secretary, Helić and her Foreign Office colleague Chloe Dalton spearheaded a campaign to end sexual violence in warzones. She is currently doing inspirational work with Angelina Jolie at the not-for-profit foundation she co-founded with Jolie and Dalton.

Shaista Gohir at the Muslim Women's Network deserves a special mention. She founded the charity, which offers specialised help and support to Muslim women, after tiring of constantly seeing only men from the Muslim Council of Britain representing her community on TV. As she told the *Guardian*: 'They were the only [Muslim] voices on TV, the only ones talking to the government. It didn't seem right that they were all men.'[109] As director of Liberty for thirteen years, Shami Chakrabarti did incomparable work promoting human rights before accepting the role of Shadow Attorney General in Jeremy Corbyn's Labour party. Paris Lees has moved the often fraught conversation around gender and identity into the mainstream with grace and charm, using positive dialogue to advance the transgender cause.

On the arts side, Jude Kelly has done amazing work as Artistic Director of the Southbank Centre. In 2010 she founded the Women of the World (WOW) festival: music, film, comedy, talks and celebrating girls and women. It's now a global phenomenon – there have been more than 40 WOWs in 23 countries across six continents – and I feel privileged to have taken part in its speed-mentoring sessions for school-age girls on the London Eye … As I write this, Kelly has just announced that she is stepping down from the Southbank Centre after twelve years to concentrate on WOW.

There are City women like Helena Morrissey, who combined being CEO of Newton Investment Management with being a mother of nine – and found time to set up the 30% Club to encourage better female representation in boardrooms. (In a great example of HeForShe role reversal, her husband Richard gave up his job as a financial journalist to look after their ever-increasing brood. He has subsequently trained as a Buddhist priest. 'He used to hate it when people asked him what he did, hated the term "house husband" and felt the social pressure on men to conform,' Morrissey admitted to the *Daily Telegraph*.[110])

She's provided a timely update to Sheryl Sandberg's advice, questioning the value of 'leaning in' to a patriarchal system. Rather than aping men by bossing their way to the top, Morrissey argues that women need to remake the system so that it works for them.

The self-confessed 'only senior black woman in the advertising industry', Karen Blackett is chief executive of the UK's largest media agency, Mediacom, where she has done sterling work improving access to the industry and encouraging diversity. As she has put it: 'There is a clear business case for diversity. In the UK, 83 per cent of all purchase decisions are made by women and we need to do more in terms of marketing ourselves to a diverse range of talent to reflect this.'[111]

One woman who has defied the under-representation of black women in science is Maggie Aderin-Pocock. An Honorary Research Associate at University College London's Department of Physics and Astronomy, she overcame both dyslexia and being warned off science at school to devote admirable amounts of energy to conveying the magic of it, both on TV shows like *The Sky at Night* and through her company, Science Innovation.

Then there are the women who have had power thrust upon them by tragedy. For Jo Cox it happened posthumously, not that the dedicated Labour MP hadn't already achieved a great deal by the time she was shot and stabbed multiple times by right-wing recluse Thomas Mair on 16 June 2016. Similarly, the horrific racist murder of her son Stephen in 1993 drove Doreen Lawrence to become a fierce, forensic campaigner for police reform.

It's easy, when reflecting on the progress made by women over the last hundred years, to be outraged and think, 'Well of course, that wouldn't happen now ... We would recognise and champion the brilliance of (for example) Rosalind Franklin.'

But when you read that women accounted for only 11.5 per cent of applicants for engineering jobs in 2014, your heart sinks all over again. We need more women like the structural engineers Roma Agrawal, who spent six years developing the foundations and spire of the tallest building in Western Europe, London's Shard, and Alex Mitchell, who worked on Crossrail's Connaught Tunnel project.

As new channels for communication have proliferated, so new mechanisms for silencing women have evolved. Women may not be ignored and overlooked as they once were. But they are shouted down, humiliated, not taken seriously – and so locked out of the centres of power. As Mary Beard has written in her excellent book *Women & Power*: 'For a female MP to be Minister of Women (or of Education or Health) is a very different thing from being Chancellor of the Exchequer, a post which no woman in the United Kingdom has yet filled.'[112]

And most shameful of all, women still bear the brunt of male violence, with two killed every week in England and Wales by a current or former partner. If #MeToo is to mean anything, it has to be rewriting that tragic narrative.

———————

So as we look to the future, it seems fair to ask if posterity works differently for women. Does it *mean* different things for women?

Early nineteenth-century Romantic culture favoured a genius-will-out theory of posterity. But with the exception of *Frankenstein* author Mary Shelley, all those geniuses – Wordsworth, Shelley, Coleridge – turned out to be men. (For most of the Victorian era women's writing was judged secondary and ephemeral. The sight of a woman's name on a book cover sent an instant signal that it was a frivolous, light-hearted romance, hence the use of male pseudonyms by George Eliot and the Brontës, and Elizabeth Gaskell's decision to publish her first novel *Mary Barton* anonymously. Though modesty was also a factor with Mrs Gaskell.) Wordsworth dedicated two poems to his young writer friend Maria Jewsbury, but Jewsbury herself was under no illusion that anything *she* wrote would stand a similar chance of lasting. Did it even deserve to last? 'A man may erect himself from such a state of despondency; throwing all his energies into some great work, something that shall beget for him "perpetual benediction"; he may live for, and with, posterity,' she wrote. 'But a woman's mind – what is it? – a woman – what can she do? – her head is, after all, only another heart; she reveals her feelings through the medium of her imagination; she tells her dreams and dies.'[113] (Again, Mary Shelley confounds this diagnosis. Her dream, or rather nightmare, will outlive us all.)

Posterity found Jane Austen. She never sought it. We don't even have a clear, reliable sense of what she looked like. After Jane's death, her sister Cassandra destroyed the vast bulk of her letters, saving from the fire a small number not for posterity but to give away as mementoes. Our knowledge of Austen's life is full of gaps which even the best biographies hedge and stutter trying to plug.

There is a theory that Austen owed her place in the canon to the fact that her novels chimed strongly with men, who then wore their devotion like a Victoria Cross. Virginia Woolf, who was agnostic about Austen – she found her 'difficult to catch in the act of greatness' – noted this tendency and mocked in *A Room of One's Own* what she called the 'twenty-five elderly gentlemen living in the neighbourhood of London who resent any slight upon [Austen's] genius as if it were an insult to the chastity of their aunts'.

At the risk of earning Virginia's disapproval, I am *not* agnostic about Jane Austen. I believe in her absolutely.

Last autumn, on our way back from a camping trip to the South Downs, my husband, daughters and I stopped off in Chawton to visit the house where Austen spent the last seven years of her life. My daughters were fascinated by Chawton Cottage, though puzzled about why Jane, Cassandra and their mother lived as charity cases in such a small house while her brother Edward Austen Knight, the favoured heir of their father's cousin, got to live in Chawton House, the Elizabethan manor up the road ... 'It's complicated,' I said. 'But basically it's to do with something called patriarchy.' Oh, I am such a barrel of laughs.

Jane was close to her brother and a frequent visitor to his house. 'I went up to the Great House between 3 & 4, & dawdled away an hour very comfortably,' she wrote in 1814. Beautifully restored by the American philanthropist Sandy Lerner, Chawton House is now a library devoted to neglected and forgotten women writers from 1600 to 1830 such as Mary Astell, Aphra Behn, Maria Edgeworth, Ann Radcliffe and Charlotte Smith.

Sadly, last year Lerner stepped down from its Board of Trustees and Chawton House's long-term future is uncertain. Hopefully a new funding stream will be found soon. Because it really is an extraordinary, inspiring place. Walking in its exquisite walled garden, with its herb garden inspired by Elizabeth Blackwell's *A Curious Herbal* (1737–39), I was struck afresh by the importance of instilling in women a sense of continuity so that present-day oppressions (and triumphs – it's not all bad news) can be connected to those of the immediate and distant past.

In Austen's time an elegant, well-stocked garden was seen as an agent of moral growth; a link, for women, between the domestic life of the house and the outside world with all its dangers and temptations. To be a 'disciple of flora' was a noble thing. Flowers are pretty, after all. But the sharp warning with which Mary Wollstonecraft opens *A Vindication of the Rights of Women* (published in 1792, when Austen was sixteen) comes wrapped in a gardening metaphor: the current conduct and manners of women, she writes, 'show clearly that their minds are not in a healthy state; as with flowers planted in soil that is too rich, strength and usefulness are sacrificed to beauty; and the flamboyant leaves, after giving pleasure to viewers, fade on the stalk, disregarded, long before it was the time for them to reach maturity.'

I'm optimistic that today's women are built for the long haul; that they have what it takes to smash through glass ceilings, be heard over the massed ranks of haters and follow in the footsteps of the women you have just been reading about.

So let's raise a glass to strength, usefulness and not fading on the stalk – and the coming generations of bloody brilliant women.

Acknowledgements

This book was inspired by conversations with many people. Some of those suggested women to include, books and/or authors I should check out or avenues I might explore. Others offered other kinds of support and advice, answered queries or kindly let me interview them. Many books went into the making of this one, as the notes and bibliography show. I especially enjoyed (and found useful) David Kynaston's panoramic Tales of a New Jerusalem sequence; Dominic Sandbrook's similarly thorough accounts of the same twentieth-century period; Andy Beckett's histories of the 1970s and 1980s; Martin Pugh's *The Pankhursts*; Brian Harrison's *Seeking a Role: The United Kingdom 1951–1970* and *Finding a Role?: The United Kingdom 1970–1990* and books by feminist historians and sociologists such as Sheila Rowbotham, Deirdre Beddoe and Elizabeth Wilson.

I owe a more personal debt and enormous thanks to: Nimco Ali, Matt Baker, Lynn Barber, Harriet Bell, Liz Bell, Rosie Bennett, Monroe Bergdorf, Ian Blandford, Simon Blendis, Iwona Boesche, Sarah Boyd, Amelia Brauer, Eleanor Bron, Martin Brookes, Louise Casey, Shami Chakrabarti, Sarah Champion, Lisa Connell, Chloe Dalton, Dana Denis-Smith, Julie Etchingham, Ali Goldsworthy, Julia Goring, Kate Halpin, Harriet Harman, Mary-Anne Harrington, Professor Brian Harrison,

Stephen Heath, Arminka Helic, Charlotte Higgins, Margaret Hodge, Jo Hodges, Lucia Hodgson, Mathew Horsman, Matthew Hotopf, Virginia Ironside, Margot James, Theresa Johansen, Tessa Jowell, Nicole Kleeman, Emma Clark Lam, Andrea Leadsom, Paris Lees, Anthony Lester, Toby Litt, Anne Longfield, Jo McGrath, Nicky Morgan, Gavin Morrison, Shaminder Nahal, Martina Olusi, Lucy Parham, Katie Perrior, Jo Potts, Alice Rawsthorn, Rachel Reeves, Emma Staples, Tom Stone, Michiko Takahashi, Jane Taylor, Ruth Taylor and Leigh Wilson.

My heartfelt thanks go to my ITN colleagues for putting up with me while I was writing this, especially my editor Ben De Pear; his deputy Nevine Mabro; the *Channel 4 News* director Martin Collett; my co-presenters Jon Snow, Krishnan Guru-Murthy, Matt Frei, Jackie Long and Fatima Manji; our director of communications Hayley Barlow; and Dorothy Byrne, Ian Katz and Alex Mahon at Channel 4.

A big thanks to my broadcast agents Helen Purvis and Sue Ayton at Knight Ayton Management, my literary agent Antony Topping at Greene & Heaton, my fantastic editor Arabella Pike and everyone at HarperCollins.

But above all, I'd like to thank my parents Julia and David, my sister Sarah and her partner Paul, my two girls Scarlett and Molly and their father, my husband John O'Connell. He not only helped me with mountains of research but, just as importantly, gave me endless love and moral support as the deadline loomed. Without him this book would never have made it into print.

Selected Bibliography

Viv Albertine, *Clothes Clothes Clothes Music Music Music Boys Boys Boys* (Faber, 2014)

Bonnie S. Anderson and Judith P. Zinsser, *A History of Their Own: Women in Europe from Prehistory to the Present, Vol. II* (Penguin, 1990)

Joan Bakewell, *The Centre of the Bed* (Hodder, 2003)

Andy Beckett, *When the Lights Went Out* (Faber, 2009)

Andy Beckett, *Promised You A Miracle: Why 1980–82 Made Modern Britain* (Faber, 2015)

Deirdre Beddoe, *Back to Home and Duty: Women Between the Wars 1918–1939* (Pandora, 1989)

Nina Boyd, *From Suffragette to Fascist: The Many Lives of Mary Sophia Allen* (History Press, 2013)

Beatrix Campbell, *The Iron Ladies: Why Do Women Vote Tory?* (Virago, 1987)

Humphrey Carpenter, *That Was Satire That Was* (Gollancz, 2000)

Barbara Castle, *Fighting All the Way* (Macmillan, 1993)

Shami Chakrabarti, *Of Women* (Allen Lane, 2017)

Peter Clarke, *Hope and Glory: Britain 1900–1990* (Allen Lane, 1996)

Rachel Cooke, *Her Brilliant Career: Ten Extraordinary Women of the Fifties* (Virago, 2013)

Nell Dunn, *Talking to Women* (Pan, 1966)

Carol Dyhouse, *Girl Trouble: Panic and Progress in the History of Young Women* (Zed, 2014)

Millicent Garrett Fawcett, *What I Remember* (Unwin, 1924)

Kate Figes, *Because of Her Sex: The Myth of Equality for Women in Britain* (Macmillan, 1994)

Matthew Freudenberg, *Negative Gravity: A Life of Beatrice Shilling* (Charlton, 2003)

Jeffrey Green, *Black Edwardians: Black People in Britain 1901–1914* (Routledge, 1998)

Ruth Hall, *Marie Stopes: A Biography* (Virago, 1978)

Emily Hamer, *Britannia's Glory: A History of Twentieth-Century Lesbians* (Cassell, 1996)

Harriet Harman, *A Woman's Work* (Allen Lane, 2017)

Brian Harrison, *Prudent Revolutionaries* (Clarendon Press, 1987)

Brian Harrison, *Seeking a Role: The United Kingdom 1951–1970* (Clarendon Press, 2009)

Charlotte Higgins, *This New Noise: The Extraordinary Birth and Troubled Life of the BBC* (Faber/Guardian, 2015)

Patricia Hollis, *Jennie Lee: A Life* (OUP, 1997)

Georgina Howell, *Queen of the Desert: The Extraordinary Life of Gertrude Bell* (Pan, 2007)

Margery Hurst, *No Glass Slipper* (Arlington, 1967)

Helen Jones, *Women in British Public Life 1914–50: Gender, Power and Social Policy* (Routledge, 2000)

David Kynaston, *Austerity Britain 1945–51* (Bloomsbury, 2007)

David Kynaston, *Family Britain 1951–57* (Bloomsbury, 2009)

Henrietta Leyser, *Medieval Women: A Social History of Women in England 450–1500* (Weidenfeld & Nicolson, 1995)

Sue Lloyd-Roberts, *The War on Women* (Simon & Schuster, 2016)

Helen McCarthy, *Women of the World: The Rise of the Female Diplomat* (Bloomsbury, 2014)

Sinclair McKay, *The Secret Life of Bletchley Park* (Aurum, 2010)

Brenda Maddox, *Rosalind Franklin: The Dark Lady of DNA* (HarperCollins, 2002)

Joe Moran, *Armchair Nation: An Intimate History of Britain in Front of the TV* (Profile, 2013)

Virginia Nicholson, *Among the Bohemians: Experiments in Living 1900–1939* (Viking, 2002)

Virginia Nicholson, *Singled Out: How Two Million Women Survived Without Men after the First World War* (Penguin, 2008)

Virginia Nicholson, *Millions Like Us: Women's Lives in War and Peace 1939–1949* (Viking, 2011)

Sybil Oldfield, *Spinsters of this Parish* (Virago, 1984)

David Olusoga, *Black and British: A Forgotten History* (Pan Books, 2017)

Richard Overy, *The Morbid Age: Britain Between the Wars* (Allen Lane, 2009)

Sylvia Pankhurst, *The Suffragette Movement* (1931; Virago, 1984)

Susan Pedersen, *Eleanor Rathbone and the Politics of Conscience* (Yale University Press, 2004)

Matt Perry, *'Red Ellen' Wilkinson: Her Ideas, Movements and World* (Manchester University Press, 2014)

Melanie Phillips, *The Ascent of Woman* (Little, Brown, 2003)

Martin Pugh, *The Pankhursts* (Allen Lane, 2001)

Martin Pugh, *We Danced All Night: Britain Between the Wars* (Bodley Head, 2008)

Rachel Reeves, *Alice in Westminster* (IB Tauris, 2017)

Jane Robinson, *Bluestockings: The Remarkable Story of the First Women to Fight for an Education* (Viking, 2009)

Katie Roiphe, *Uncommon Arrangements: Seven Portraits of Married Life in London Literary Circles 1910–1939* (Virago, 2008)

Sheila Rowbotham, *A Century of Women* (Viking, 1997)

Sheila Rowbotham, *Dreamers of a New Day: Women Who Invented the Twentieth Century* (Verso, 2010)

Dora Russell, *The Right to Be Happy* (Routledge, 1927)

Dominic Sandbrook, *Never Had It So Good 1956–63* (Little, Brown, 2005)

Dominic Sandbrook, *White Heat: A History of Britain in the Swinging Sixties* (Little, Brown, 2006)

Simon Schama, *A History of Britain: The Fate of Empire 1776–2000* (BBC, 2002)

Diana Souhami, *Edith Cavell* (Quercus, 2010)

Graham Stewart, *Bang! A History of Britain in the 1980s* (Atlantic, 2014)

Alwyn W. Turner, *A Classless Society: Britain in the 1990s* (Aurum, 2014)

Julie Wheelwright, *Amazons and Military Maids* (Pandora, 1989)

Elizabeth Wilson, *Only Halfway to Paradise: Women in Postwar Britain 1945–1968* (Tavistock, 1980)

Lilian Wyles, *A Woman at Scotland Yard* (Faber, 1952)

Hugo Young, *One of Us* (Macmillan, 1989)

Notes

1 Introduction: Education, Education, Education

1. Helen Castor, *She-Wolves* (Faber, 2010), p. 31
2. Doris Stenton, *The English Woman in History* (Allen & Unwin, 1957), p. 28
3. See Pauline Stafford, 'Women and the Norman Conquest', Transactions of the Royal Historical Society (Vol. 4, 1994), pp. 221–49
4. Henrietta Leyser, *Medieval Women* (Weidenfeld & Nicolson, 1995), p. 20
5. Quoted in Richard W. Unger, *Beer in the Middle Ages and the Renaissance* (University of Pennsylvania Press, 2013), p. 106
6. Elizabeth Norton, *The Lives of Tudor Women* (Head of Zeus, 2016), p. 103
7. Quoted in Elaine V. Beilin, *Redeeming Eve: Women Writers of the English Renaissance* (Princeton University Press, 2014), p. 22
8. Katie Whitaker, *Mad Madge: Margaret Cavendish, Duchess of Newcastle* (Vintage, 2004), p. 168
9. Bonnie S. Anderson and Judith P. Zinsser, *A History of Their Own: Women in Europe from Prehistory to the Present, Vol. II* (Penguin, 1990), p. 113
10. Janet Todd, *Sensibility: An Introduction* (Methuen, 1986), p. 17
11. Anderson and Zinsser, *A History of Their Own*, p. xviii
12. Stephanie J. Snow, *Blessed Days of Anaesthesia* (Oxford University Press, 2008), pp. 76–7
13. Quoted in Jack Dewhurst, *Royal Confinements* (Weidenfeld & Nicolson, 1980), p. 181

14. Simon Schama, *A History of Britain: The Fate of Empire 1776–2000* (BBC, 2002), p. 154
15. Virginia Nicholson, *Singled Out* (Penguin, 2008), p. xi

2 Old Battles, New Women: 1880–1914

1. Stephen Inwood, *A History of London* (Macmillan, 1998), p. 411
2. Robert Winder, *Bloody Foreigners* (Little, Brown, 2004), p. 99
3. Peter Ackroyd, *London: The Biograpahy* (Chatto & Windus, 2000), p. 714
4. See Jeffrey Green's study *Black Victorians* (Frank Cass, 1998)
5. For more on Ira Aldridge and his legacy see Alex Ross, 'Othello's Daughter', *New Yorker* (29 July 2013)
6. Green, *Black Victorians*, pp. 211–12
7. Jeffrey Green, *Black Edwardians: Black People in Britain 1901–1914* (Frank Cass, 1998), p. 71
8. Frederick E. Forbes, *Dahomey and the Dahomans: Being the Journals of Two Missions to the King of Dahomey, Vol. II* (Longmans, 1851), p. 208
9. Letter to Charles Darwin, 22 December 1866, www.darwinproject.ac.uk/letter/DCP-LETT-5316.xml
10. Beatrice Webb, *My Apprenticeship, Vol. 1* (Longmans, Green & Co, 1926), p. 206
11. John Ruskin, 'Sesame and Lilies' in *The Works of John Ruskin, Vol. 18* (G. Allen, 1905), p. 122
12. Emily Davies, *The Higher Education of Women* (1866; A & C Black, 1988), p. 14
13. Ibid., p. 12
14. See Kate Summerscale's brilliant *Mrs Robinson's Disgrace* (Bloomsbury, 2012) for a full account of this case.
15. Mary Wollstonecraft, *The Wrongs of Woman: or, Maria, A Fragment* (1797; Broadview Press, 2012), p. 248
16. Quoted in George Robb and Nancy Erber, *Disorder in the Court: Trials and Sexual Conflict at the Turn of the Century* (Springer, 1999), p. 102
17. Ibid., p. 103
18. Lois S. Bibbings, *Binding Men: Stories About Violence and Law in Late Victorian England* (Routledge, 2014), p. 173
19. Anderson and Zinsser, *A History of Their Own*, p. 253
20. Flora Thompson, *Lark Rise to Candleford* (1939; David R. Godine, 2009), p. 158
21. Anderson and Zinsser, *A History of Their Own*, p. 134
22. Letter to *Crewe Chronicle*, 5 May 1894

23. Quoted in Alison Twells, *British Women's History: A Documentary History from the Enlightenment to World War One* (I.B. Tauris, 2007), p. 111

24. Annie Besant, 'To the Shareholders of the Bryant & May Company, Limited', *The Link*, 14 July 1888

25. Quoted in Sheila Blackburn, *A Fair Day's Wage For a Fair Day's Work?: Sweated Labour and the Origins of Minimum Wage Legislation in Britain* (Routledge, 2016), p. 6

26. Lucy Deane, 'Report on the Health of Workers in Asbestos and Other Dusty Trades' in *HM Chief Inspector of Factories and Workshops 1899, Annual Report for 1898* (HMSO, 1899), pp. 171–2

27. George Eliot, *Middlemarch* (1871–2; Penguin, 1985), p. 302 – a wonderful line, cited in Deborah Cohen's excellent *Household Gods* where I came across it.

28. Deborah Cohen, *Household Gods: The British and their Possessions* (Yale University Press, 2006), p. 118

29. Katharine Chorley, *Manchester Made Them* (1950; Silk Press, 2001), p. 17

30. Ibid., p. 156

31. Ibid., p. 108

32. Ibid., p. 157

33. Gwen Raverat, *Period Piece* (Faber, 1953), p. 119

34. Ibid., p. 119

35. Mary P. Ryan, *Women in Public: Between Banners and Ballots 1825–1880* (Johns Hopkins University Press, 1990), p. 86

36. Martha Vicinus, *Independent Women: Work and Community for Single Women 1850–1920* (University of Chicago Press, 1988), p. 297

37. Virginia Woolf, *The Pargiters: The Novel-Essay Portion of* The Years (Harcourt Brace Jovanovich, 1978), p. 37

38. Mary Higgs, *Glimpses into the Abyss* (P. S. King, 1906), p. v

39. Ibid., p. x

40. Ibid., p. 99

41. Ibid., p. 109

42. Ibid., p. 106

43. Letter to Lady Elizabeth Eastlake (1868), quoted in Lynn McDonald (ed.), *Florence Nightingale on Women, Medicine, Midwifery and Prostitution* (Wilfrid Laurier University Press, 2005), p. 91

44. Quoted in Diana Postlethwaite, 'Mothering and Mesmerism in the Life of Harriet Martineu', *Signs* (University of Chicago Press, 1989), pp. 583–609

45. Quoted in F. Elizabeth Gray (ed.), *Women in Journalism at the Fin de Siècle: Making a Name for Herself* (Palgrave Macmillan, 2012), p. 131

46. Quoted in Peter Cole and Tony Harcup, *Newspaper Journalism* (Sage, 2012), p. 68

47. Quoted in Maurice Edelman, *The Mirror: A Political History* (Hamish Hamilton, 1966), p. 6

48. Quoted in Brian Winston, *Messages: Free Expression, Media and the West from Gutenberg to Google* (Routledge, 2006), p. 139

49. Quoted in Eilat Negev and Yehuda Koren, *First Lady of Fleet Street: The Life, Fortune and Tragedy of Rachel Beer* (JR Books, 2011), p. 256

50. Josephine Butler, *Woman's Work and Woman's Culture* (Macmillan, 1869), p. xxxvii

51. Josephine Butler, letter to Stanley Butler, quoted in Jane Jordan, *Josephine Butler* (John Murray, 2001), p. 55

52. Ibid., p. 58

53. Ibid., p. 67

54. Josephine Butler, *Personal Reminiscences of a Great Crusade* (1896; Cambridge University Press, 2010), p. 20

55. Quoted in Helen Blackburn, *Women's Suffrage* (Williams & Norgate, 1902), pp. 110–11

56. Steven King, *Women, Welfare and Local Politics 1880–1920: 'We Might Be Trusted'* (Sussex Academic Press, 2010), p. 206

57. Hannah Mitchell, *The Hard Way Up* (Faber, 1968), p. 208

58. Beatrice Webb, *The Diary of Beatrice Webb: Glitter Around and Darkness Within, 1873–1892* (Harvard University Press, 1982), p. 168

59. Roy Porter, *London: A Social History* (Penguin, 2000), p. 271

60. Sheila Rowbotham, *Dreamers of a New Day* (Verso, 2010), p. 28

61. Octavia Hill, 'Organised Work Among the Poor; Suggestions Founded on Four Years' Management of a London Court', *Macmillan's Magazine* (July, 1869)

62. Octavia Hill, *Letters to Fellow Workers 1872–1911* (Kyrle, 2005), p. 257

63. Quoted in Inwood, *A History of London*, p. 532

64. Tristram Hunt, 'Octavia Hill Revisited', *Guardian*, 6 May 2008

65. Maud Pember Reeves, *Round About a Pound a Week* (1912; Persephone Books, 2008), p. 6

66. Helena Swanwick, *I Have Been Young* (Gollancz, 1935), p. 58

67. Ibid., p. 118

68. Quoted in Louisa Garrett Anderson, *Elizabeth Garrett Anderson* (1939; Cambridge University Press, 2016), p. 108

69. Quoted in William Knox, *Lives of Scottish Women: Women and Scottish Society 1800–1980* (Edinburgh University Press, 2006), p. 80

70. Edith Pechey, letter to the *Scotsman*, 13 July 1871

71. Quoted in Margaret Jackson, *The Real Facts of Life: Feminism and the Politics of Sexuality c.1850–1940*, (Taylor & Francis, 1994), p. 28

72. Quoted in Anne Jordan, *Love Well the Hour: The Life of Lady Colin Campbell 1857–1911* (Matador, 2010), p. 124
73. Victoria Cross, *Anna Lombard* (1901; University of Birmingham Press, 2003), p. 6
74. W. T. Stead, 'A Novel of the Ethics of Sex', *Review of Reviews* – quoted in Gail Cunningham's introduction to Victoria Cross, *Anna Lombard* (1901, University of Birmingham Press, 2003), p. xvi
75. Quoted in Margaret Drabble, 'A Room of Her Own', *Guardian*, 2 April 2005
76. Quoted in Brian Harrison, *Separate Spheres: The Opposition to Women's Suffrage in Britain* (1978; Routledge, 2012), p. 116
77. Quoted in Joyce Marlow (ed.), *Suffragettes: The Fight for Votes for Women* (Virago, 2015)
78. Martin Pugh, *The Pankhursts* (2001; Vintage, 2008), p. 17
79. Ibid., p. 32
80. Quoted in Rowbotham, *Dreamers of a New Day*, p. 43
81. Sylvia Pankhurst, *The Suffragette Movement* (1931; Virago, 1977), p. 186

3 Of Soldiers and Suffrage: 1914–18

1. Dorothy Lawrence, *Sapper Dorothy Lawrence: The Only English Woman Soldier* (Lance, 1919), p. 40
2. Ibid., p. 93
3. Ibid., p. 128
4. Ibid., p. 133
5. Ibid., p. 175
6. Ibid., p. 189
7. Flora Sandes, *The Autobiography of a Woman Soldier: A Brief Record of Adventure with the Serbian Army 1916–1919* (Witherby, 1927), p. 9
8. Julie Wheelwright, *Amazons and Military Maids* (Pandora, 1990), p. 41
9. Quoted in ibid., p. 104
10. Millicent Garrett Fawcett, *Women's Suffrage* (TC & EC Jack, 1912), p. 14
11. Mabel Potter Daggett, *Women Wanted: The Story Written in Blood Red Letters on the Horizon of the Great War* (Hodder & Stoughton, 1918), p. 67
12. A. J. P. Taylor, *The First World War: An Illustrated History* (Penguin, 1966), p. 21
13. Ibid., p. 16
14. James Bryce, *Committee on Alleged German Outrages – Report* (Crown, 1915), p. 38

15. Quoted in Ray Strachey, *Millicent Garrett Fawcett* (John Murray, 1931), p. 280

16. Olive Schreiner, *Woman and Labour* (Stokes, 1911), p. 178

17. Gerry Holloway, *Women and Work in Britain Since 1840* (Routledge, 2007), p. 132

18. Peter Clarke, *Hope and Glory: Britain 1900–1990* (Allen Lane, 1996), p. 94

19. Nigel Fountain (ed), *Women at War 1914–91: Voices of the Twentieth Century* (Michael O'Mara, 2002), p. 50

20. See Juliet Bernard's blog at www.huffingtonpost.co.uk/juliet-bernard/knitting-for-soldiers-in-the-first-world-war_b_5591340.html

21. *Barrow News*, 14 October 1916

22. Avalon Weston (ed.), *Menus, Munitions and Keeping the Peace: The Home Front Diaries of Gabrielle West* (Pen & Sword, 2016), pp. 137–8

23. *Daily Express*, 22 November 1916

24. I. O. Andrews, *The Economic Effects of the World War upon Women and Children in Great Britain* (Oxford University Press, 1921), p. 33

25. Sylvia Pankhurst, *The Home Front* (Hutchinson, 1932), p. 38

26. Sheila Rowbotham, *A Century of Women* (Penguin, 1999), p. 80

27. Sylvia Pankhurst, *The Suffragette Movement* (1931; Virago, 1984), p. 593

28. Ibid., p. 595

29. Naomi Loughnan, *Genteel Women in the Factories*, quoted in Marvin Perry, Matthew Berg, James Krukones, *Sources of European History: Since 1900* (Cengage Learning, 2010), p. 59

30. Clarke, *Hope and Glory*, p. 95

31. Quoted in Mark Bostridge and Paul Berry, *Vera Brittain: A Life* (Chatto & Windus, 1995), p. 61

32. Vera Brittain, *Testament of Youth* (1933; Fontana, 1979), p. 213

33. Anne Powell, *Women in the War Zone: Hospital Service in the First World War* (History Press, 2009), p. 16

34. Diane Atkinson, *Elsie & Mairi Go to War* (Preface, 2010), p. 42

35. Quoted in Angela K. Smith (ed.), *Women's Writing of the First World War* (Manchester University Press, 2000), p. 213

36. Quoted in Anne Powell, *Women in the War Zone* (History Press, 2001), p. 48

37. William Thomson Hill, *The Martyrdom of Nurse Cavell* (Hutchinson, 1915), p. 23

38. Quoted in Diana Souhami, *Edith Cavell* (Quercus, 2010), p. 38

39. 'Nursing in War Time', *Nursing Mirror*, 22 August 1914, quoted in Souhami, *Edith Cavell*, p. 153

40. Souhami, *Edith Cavell*, p. 184

41. Ibid., p. 233
42. Herbert Leeds, *Edith Cavell, her Life Story, a Norfolk Tribute* (Jarrold & Sons, 1915), p. 58
43. Thomson Hill, *The Martyrdom of Nurse Cavell*, p. 46
44. Souhami, *Edith Cavell*, p. 327
45. Ibid., p. 415
46. Quoted in Millicent Garrett Fawcett, *What I Remember* (Unwin, 1924), p. 229
47. Ibid.
48. 'Edith Cavell, Shot by Germans during WW1, Celebrated 100 Years On', *Guardian*, 12 October 2015
49. Helen Zenna Smith, *Not So Quiet* (1930; Feminist Press, 1989), p. 59
50. Clarke, *Hope and Glory*, p. 81
51. Quoted in Roy Jenkins, *Asquith* (1964; A & C Black, 2013), p. 466
52. Brittain, *Testament of Youth*, p. 97
53. Ibid., p. 471
54. Quoted in Frances Spalding, *Vanessa Bell: Portrait of the Bloomsbury Artist* (I.B. Tauris, 2015), p. 147
55. Quoted in Sybil Oldfield, *Spinsters of this Parish* (Virago, 1984), p. 178
56. Ibid., p. 184
57. Helen McCarthy, *Women of the World: The Rise of the Female Diplomat* (Bloomsbury, 2014), p. 56
58. Ibid., p. 53
59. Quoted in Tammy M. Proctor, *Female Intelligence: Women and Espionage in the First World War* (NYU Press, 2006), p. 63
60. Ibid., p. 64
61. Quoted in Thomas Hennessey and Claire Thomas, *Spooks: The Unofficial History of MI5* (Amberley, 2010)
62. Ibid.
63. 'Women in Diplomacy 1782–1999', *History Notes* (Foreign & Commonwealth Office, 1999), p. 6
64. All credit to Georgina Howell for noticing this!
65. Quoted in Georgina Howell, *Queen of the Desert: The Extraordinary Life of Gertrude Bell* (Pan, 2007), p. 259
66. Letter to Sir Hugh Bell, quoted in Howell, *Queen of the Desert*, p. 449
67. Letter to Sir Hugh Bell, 23 August 1920 (Newcastle University/ Gertrude Bell Archive)
68. Diary entry, 21 January 1909 (Newcastle University/Gertrude Bell Archive)
69. Letter to Dame Florence Bell, 12 August 1900 (Newcastle University/Gertrude Bell Archive)

70. Fawcett, *What I Remember*, p. 229
71. Ibid., p. 236
72. Ibid., p. 240
73. Pankhurst, *The Suffragette Movement*, p. 607
74. Ibid., p. 608
75. Maude Onions, *A Woman at War: Being Experiences of an Army Signaller in France in 1917–1919* (Daily Post Printers, 1929), p. 58

4 Between the Wars: 1918–39

1. Lilian Wyles, *A Woman at Scotland Yard* (Faber, 1952), p. 15
2. Ibid., p. 24
3. Ibid., p. 27
4. Ibid.
5. Ibid., p. 102
6. Nina Boyd, *From Suffragette to Fascist: The Many Lives of Mary Sophia Allen* (History Press, 2013), p. 10
7. Mary Allen, *The Pioneer Policewoman* (Chatto & Windus, 1925), p. 13
8. Wyles, *A Woman at Scotland Yard*, p. 163
9. Ibid., p. 67
10. Mary Allen, *The Lady in Blue* (Stanley Paul, 1936), p. 148
11. Mary Allen, *A Woman at the Cross Roads* (Unicorn Press, 1934), p. 143
12. *The Letters of Virginia Woolf, Volume 2* (Harcourt Brace Jovanovich, 1975), p. 555
13. Barbara Low, *Psycho-Analysis: A Brief Account of the Freudian Theory* (Allen & Unwin, 1920), p. 9
14. Ibid., p. 158
15. Martin Pugh, *We Danced All Night* (Bodley Head, 2008), p. 134
16. Letter to Violet Hunt, quoted in Victoria Glendinning, *Rebecca West: A Life* (Knopf, 1987), p. 58
17. Katie Roiphe, *Uncommon Arrangements* (Virago, 2008), p. 16
18. Vera Brittain, *Halcyon, or the Future of Monogamy* (K. Paul, Trench, Trubner & Co, 1929), pp. 87–8
19. Deirdre Beddoe, *Back to Home and Duty* (Pandora, 1989), p. 104
20. Dora Russell, *The Right to be Happy* (G. Routledge, 1927), p. 128
21. Ibid., p. 132
22. Naomi Mitchison, *Comments on Birth Control* (Faber/Criterion Miscellany, 1930), No. 12, p. 5
23. Marie Stopes, *Married Love* (1918; OUP, 2004), p. 11
24. Ibid., p. 78
25. Ibid., p. 37

26. Ibid., p. 33
27. Margaret Sanger, 'Birth Control and Racial Betterment', *Birth Control Review* (February 1919)
28. Marie Stopes, *Radiant Motherhood* (1920; Putnam, 1921), p. 236
29. Ruth Hall, *Passionate Crusader: The Life of Marie Stopes* (Harcourt Brace Jovanovich, 1977), p. 112
30. Brittain, *Halcyon, or the Future of Monogamy*, p. 87
31. Quoted in Ann Taylor Allen, *Feminism and Motherhood in Western Europe 1890–1970* (Springer, 2005), p. 184
32. Quoted in Virginia Nicholson, *Among the Bohemians: Experiments in Living 1900–1939* (Penguin, 2003), p. 51
33. Stephen Brooke, *Sexual Politics: Sexuality, Family Planning and the British Left from the 1880s to the Present Day* (OUP, 2011), p. 76
34. Dora Russell, *The Tamarisk Tree, Vol. 1: My Quest for Liberty and Love* (Elek/Pemberton, 1975), p. 169
35. Letter to Bertrand Russell, February 1925, quoted in Brooke, *Sexual Politics*, pp. 54–5
36. Letter to Bertrand Russell, March 1925, quoted in Brooke, *Sexual Politics*, p. 63
37. Quoted in Brooke, *Sexual Politics*, p. 54
38. Richard Overy, *The Morbid Age* (Allen Lane, 2009), p. 55
39. Russell, *The Right to be Happy*, p. viii
40. Katharine Tait, quoted in Deborah Gorham, 'Dora and Bertrand Russell and Beacon Hill School', *Russell: The Journal of Bertrand Russell Studies* (Summer 2005), pp. 39–76
41. Dora Russell, *The Tamarisk Tree, Vol. 2: My School and the Years of War* (Virago, 1980), p. 211
42. Ibid., p. 16
43. Bertrand Russell, *Autobiography, Vol. 2: 1914–44* (Allen & Unwin, 1968), p. 154
44. Nicholson, *Among the Bohemians*, p. 87
45. Quoted in Brian Harrison, *Prudent Revolutionaries* (Clarendon Press, 1987), p. 78
46. Harrison, *Prudent Revolutionaries*, p. 82
47. Brian Harrison, 'Women in a Men's House: The Women MPs 1919–1945', *The Historical Journal*, 29, 3 (1986), pp. 623–54
48. Ibid.
49. *The Times*, 20 November 1918, quoted in Fiona Montgomery, *Women, Politics and Society in Great Britain 1770–1970: A Documentary History* (Manchester University Press, 2006), p. 140
50. *The Woman Clerk* (January 1920), p. 15, quoted in Cheryl Law, *Suffrage and Power* (I.B. Tauris, 2000), p. 81
51. Beddoe, *Back to Home and Duty*, p. 77

52. Helena Normanton, *Everyday Law for Women* (Clay & Sons, 1932), p. 6
53. Judith Bourne, *Helena Normanton and the Opening of the Bar to Women* (Waterside Press, 2016), p. 175
54. Beddoe, *Back to Home and Duty*, p. 78
55. Harrison, *Prudent Revolutionaries*, p. 303
56. *The Lancet, Vol. 2* (Onwhyn, 1921), p. 725
57. Winifred Holtby, *South Riding* (1936; Random House, 2011), p. 44
58. Quoted in Charlotte Higgins, *This New Noise* (Guardian/Faber, 2015), p. 31
59. Ibid., p. 32
60. Radio interview with Sue MacGregor, *BBC Woman's Hour*, 3 May 1976
61. *Woman*, 5 June 1937, quoted in Pugh, *We Danced All Night*, p. 176
62. Susan Pedersen, *Eleanor Rathbone and the Politics of Conscience* (Yale University Press, 2004), p. 3
63. Pugh, *We Danced All Night*, p. 188
64. Quoted in Beddoe, *Back to Home and Duty*, p. 139
65. Quoted in Pedersen, *Eleanor Rathbone and the Politics of Conscience*, p. 152
66. Eleanor Rathbone, *The Disinherited Family* (Arnold, 1924), p. 274
67. Quoted in Angela Jackson, *British Women and the Spanish Civil War* (Routledge, 2003), p. 131
68. Quoted in James Hopkins, *Into the Heart of the Fire: The British in the Spanish Civil War* (Stanford University Press, 1998), p. 200
69. Eleanor Rathbone, *War Can Be Averted* (Gollancz, 1938), p. 66
70. Virginia Woolf, *A Writer's Diary* (HMH, 2003), pp. 273–4
71. Quoted in 'Arrival in Great Britain', document produced by the Association of Jewish Refugees (ajr.org.uk)
72. Ibid.
73. See Dr Jennifer Taylor, 'The Missing Chapter: How the British Quakers Helped to Save the Jews of Germany and Austria from Nazi Persecution', October 2009, remember.org
74. Interview with Elizabeth Allen, Imperial War Museum sound archive (www.iwm.org.uk/collections/item/object/80015834)
75. Julie V. Gottlieb, 'Guilty Women', *Foreign Policy and Appeasement in Inter-War Britain* (Springer, 2016), p. 97
76. Quoted in Cambridge Women's Peace Collective, *My Country is the Whole World: An Anthology of Women's Work on Peace and War* (Pandora, 1984), p. 123
77. Olivia Cockett, *Love and War in London* (History Press, 2016), p. 13
78. Overy, *The Morbid Age*, p. 359

79. Quoted in Richard Overy, *1939: Countdown to War* (Penguin, 2009), p. 95

80. Letter to Nancy Astor, 9 January 1939 (Reading University, Lady Astor MSS 1416/1/2/203)

5 Daughters of Britain: 1939–45

1. Virginia Woolf, 'Thoughts on Peace in an Air Raid', *Selected Essays* (OUP, 2008), p. 216

2. Ibid.

3. Ibid., p. 217

4. Matthew Freudenberg, *Negative Gravity: A Life of Beatrice Shilling* (Charlton, 2003), p. 7

5. Ibid., p. 8

6. Ibid., p. 116

7. Sheila Rowbotham, *A Century of Women* (Penguin, 1999), p. 229

8. Anne Stewart Higham, 'Women in Defense of Britain: An Informal Report', *Journal of Educational Sociology*, Vol. 15, No. 5, Women in National Defense (Jan 1942), pp. 293–300

9. Ibid.

10. Virginia Nicholson, *Millions Like Us: Women's Lives in War and Peace 1939–1949* (Viking, 2011), p. 24

11. Higham, 'Women in Defense of Britain: An Informal Report', pp. 293–300

12. Nicholson, *Millions Like Us*, p. 50

13. Helen Jones, *Women in British Public Life 1914–50* (Routledge, 2000)

14. Ibid.

15. Higham, 'Women in Defense of Britain: An Informal Report', pp. 293–300

16. Dorothy Sheridan, *Wartime Women: A Mass-Observation Anthology 1937–45* (Weidenfeld & Nicolson, 2009), pp. 73–4

17. Cicely McCall, *Women's Institutes: Britain in Pictures* (Collins, 1943), p. 31

18. Higham, 'Women in Defense of Britain: An Informal Report', pp. 293–300

19. Julie Summers, *Jambusters* (Simon & Schuster, 2013), p. 76

20. Peter Fryer, *Staying Power: The History of Black People in Britain* (University of Alberta, 1984), p. 364

21. David Olusoga, *Black and British: A Forgotten History* (Pan, 2017), p. 486

22. Gail Braybon and Penny Summerfield, *Out of the Cage: Women's Experiences in Two World Wars* (Routledge, 1987), p. 158

23. S. Grayzel and P. Levine (eds), *Gender, Labour, War and Empire: Essays on Modern Britain* (Springer, 2008), p. 94

24. Quoted in Jones, *Women in British Public Life 1914–50*, p. 195

25. Ethel Wood, *Mainly for Men* (Committee on Woman Power, 1943), p. 9

26. Vera Douie, *Daughters of Britain* (1949; George Ronald, 1950), p. 10

27. Ibid., p. 18

28. Wood, *Mainly for Men*, p. 18

29. Mary Evans and David Morgan, *The Battle For Britain: Citizenship and Ideology in the Second World War* (Routledge, 2002), p. 97

30. Ibid.

31. Sonya O. Rose, *Which People's War? National Identity and Citizenship in Wartime Britain 1939–45* (Oxford University Press, 2004), p. 115

32. Quoted in Jones, *Women in British Public Life 1914–50*, p. 190

33. I haven't been able to identify the newspaper, but the cutting – along with others relating to the construction of the Mulberry Harbours – can be found at www.mulberryharbour.com/wp-content/uploads/2014/05/Mulberry-Harbour-Press-Cuttings-Jun-16-1944.pdf

34. Jones, *Women in British Public Life 1914–50*, p. 193

35. Wood, *Mainly for Men*, pp. 46–7

36. Quoted in Matt Perry, *'Red Ellen' Wilkinson: Her Ideas, Movements and World* (Manchester University Press, 2014), p. 360

37. Ibid., p. 353

38. Quoted in Betty Vernon, *Ellen Wilkinson 1891–1947* (Croon Helm, 1982), p. 188

39. Quoted in Perry, *'Red Ellen' Wilkinson*, p. 357

40. Perry, *'Red Ellen' Wilkinson*, p. 358

41. *Parliamentary Debates: Official Report, Volume 369* (HMSO, 1941), p. clxxxvi

42. Quoted in Helen McCarthy, *Women of the World: The Rise of the Female Diplomat* (Bloomsbury, 2014), p. 155

43. Quoted in Perry, *'Red Ellen' Wilkinson*, p. 364

44. Edith Summerskill, 'Conscription and Women', *The Fortnightly*, Vol. 157 (Chapman & Hall, 1942), p. 210

45. Quoted in D. Collett Wadge (ed.), *Women in Uniform* (1946; Imperial War Museum, 2003), p. 61

46. Ibid.

47. Nicholson, *Millions Like Us*, p. 12

48. Douie, *Daughters of Britain*, p. 41

49. 'Father Always Came First, Second and Third', *Daily Telegraph*, 16 August 2002

50. Ibid.

51. Extracted in Sayre P. Sheldon (ed.), *Her War Story: Twentieth Century Women Write About War* (SIU Press, 1999), p. 171
52. These examples are taken from Collette Drifte, *Women in the Second World War* (Pen & Sword, 2011)
53. Douie, *Daughters of Britain*, p. 35
54. Ibid., pp. 35–6
55. Sinclair McKay, *The Secret Life of Bletchley Park* (Aurum, 2010), p. 14
56. Mavis Batey obituary, *Guardian*, 20 November 2013
57. McKay, *The Secret Life of Bletchley Park*, p. 58
58. Ibid., p. 87
59. Gordon Welchman, *The Hut Six Story: Breaking the Enigma Codes* (McGraw-Hill, 1982), p. 86
60. Quoted in Kate Adie, *Corsets to Camouflage: Women and War* (Hodder/Imperial War Museum, 2003), p. 201
61. Quoted in Christopher J. Murphy, 'The Origins of SOE in France', *The Historical Journal*, 46, 4 (Cambridge University Press, 2003), pp. 935–52
62. See ibid.
63. Irene Ward, *FANY Invicta* (Hutchinson, 1955), p. 209
64. Quoted in Adie, *Corsets to Camouflage*, p. 140
65. Pauline Gower, *Women with Wings* (J. Long, 1938), p. 218
66. Quoted in Douie, *Daughters of Britain*, p. 85
67. Lettice Curtis, *Lettice Curtis: Her Autobiography* (Red Kite, 2004), p. 67
68. Ibid., p. 68
69. Ibid.
70. Lois K. Merry, *Women Military Pilots of World War Two* (McFarland, 2010), p. 150
71. My source for much of the information about Elsie in this section is a short but wonderful biography written by the nutritionist Margaret Ashwell – part of the Biographical Memoirs of Fellows of the Royal Society series (1 December 2002)
72. Ellen Wilkinson, *Plan For Peace: How the People Can Win the Peace* (Labour Party, 1945)
73. Quoted in Perry, *'Red Ellen' Wilkinson*, p. 366
74. Rowbotham, *A Century of Women*, p. 243
75. Quoted in ibid., p. 243
76. Arthur Marwick, *British Society Since 1945* (1982; Penguin, 1996), p. 19
77. Ursula Bloom, *Trilogy* (Hutchinson, 1954), p. 159
78. Jill Liddington, *The Road to Greenham Common* (Syracuse University Press, 1989), p. 176
79. Vera Brittain, *Testament of Experience* (1957; Fontana, 1979), p. 134

80. Quoted in Oliver Kamm, 'Pacifists Failed Vera's Britain', *Jewish Chronicle*, 22 January 2015
81. Higham, 'Women in Defense of Britain: An Informal Report', pp. 293–300

6 Remake, Remodel: 1945–61

1. *The Festival of Britain 1951* (Festival of Britain Office, 1951), p. 7
2. Interview with Charlotte Higgins, 'Adventures in Polypropylene', *Guardian*, 7 February 2001
3. Quoted in David Kynaston, *Austerity Britain 1945–51* (Bloomsbury, 2007), p. 623
4. Quoted in Iain Jackson and Jessica Holland, *The Architecture of Edwin Maxwell Fry and Jane Drew* (Ashgate, 2014), p. 132
5. Ibid., p. 133
6. Katherine Whitehorn, *Selective Memory* (Virago, 2007), p. 44
7. Ibid.
8. Shusha Guppy, 'Jane Drew: Obituary', *Independent*, 1 August 1996
9. Ibid.
10. Quoted in Jackson and Holland, *The Architecture of Edwin Maxwell Fry and Jane Drew*, p. 117
11. Guppy, 'Jane Drew: Obituary'
12. Iain Jackson, 'Jane Drew (1911–1996)', *The Architectural Review*, 4 July 2014
13. Quoted in Iain Jackson and Jessica Holland, *The Architecture of Edwin Maxwell Fry and Jane Drew* (Ashgate, 2014), p. 101
14. Quoted in Iain Jackson and Jessica Holland, *The Architecture of Edwin Maxwell Fry and Jane Drew* (Ashgate, 2014), p. 4
15. Jackson, 'Jane Drew (1911–1996)'
16. Rachel Cooke, *Her Brilliant Career* (Virago, 2013), p. 175
17. See Michael Billington, 'Shelagh Delaney Gave Working-Class Women a Taste of What Was Possible', *Guardian*, 21 November 2011
18. Peter J. Conradi, *Iris Murdoch: A Life* (HarperCollins, 2001), p. 368
19. Martin Stannard, *Muriel Spark: The Biography* (Hachette, 2009), p. 164
20. Ibid., p. 177
21. This is the view of her biographer Laura Thompson, who considers the novels she wrote immediately after the war as 'highly competent, Agatha Christie on majestic auto-pilot'. See Laura Thompson, *Agatha Christie: An English Mystery* (Headline Review, 2007), p. 359
22. Paul Addison, *No Turning Back: The Peacetime Revolutions of Postwar Britain* (OUP, 2010), p. 54

23. M-O file report no. 3073, 'Middle-class: Why' (1947), pp. 54–5
24. Beatrix Campbell, *The Iron Ladies: Why Do Women Vote Tory?* (Virago, 1987), p. 80
25. Millicent Pleydell-Bouverie, *Daily Mail Book of Postwar Homes* (Daily Mail, 1944), p. 12
26. Ibid., p. 25
27. 'Post-War Homes: Design and Equipment', Standing Joint Committee of Working Women's Associations (1943)
28. Pleydell-Bouverie, *Daily Mail Book of Postwar Homes*, p. 33
29. Ross McKibbin, *Classes and Cultures: England 1918–51* (OUP, 1998), p. 118
30. Brenda Maddox, *Rosalind Franklin: The Dark Lady of DNA* (HarperCollins, 2002), p. 139
31. Helen McCarthy, *Women of the World: The Rise of the Female Diplomat* (Bloomsbury, 2014), p. 257
32. Ibid., p. 256
33. John Strachey, *The End of Empire* (Gollancz, 1959), p. 231
34. Quoted in Kynaston, *Austerity Britain*, p. 43
35. Barbara Wootton, 'Freedom Under Planning', *Can Freedom Be Democratic?* (Fabian Society/Routledge, 1944), p. 49
36. Barbara Castle, *Fighting All the Way* (Macmillan, 1993), p. 126
37. Ibid., p. 110
38. Ibid., p. 127
39. See Rachel Reeves' revealing biography of Bacon, *Alice in Westminster* (I.B. Tauris, 2017)
40. Reeves, *Alice in Westminster*, p. 40
41. Ibid., p. 40
42. Castle, *Fighting All the Way*, p. 131
43. Eliot Slater and Moya Woodside, *Patterns of Marriage* (Cassell, 1951), p. 244
44. Ibid., p. 245
45. Ibid., p. 248
46. Virginia A. Noble, *Inside the Welfare State: Foundations of Policy and Practice in Post-war Britain* (Routledge, 2008), p. 25
47. Castle, *Fighting All the Way*, p. 135
48. See Phillida Bunkle, 'The 1944 Education Act and Second Wave Feminism', *Women's History Review* (Vol. 25, March 2016)
49. Rosemary Deem, 'State Policy and Ideology in the Education of Women 1944–1980', *British Journal of Sociology of Education* (Vol. 2, No. 2, 1981), pp. 131–43
50. Quoted in www.bl.uk/sisterhood/articles/girls-in-formal-education
51. John Newsom, *The Education of Girls* (Faber, 1948), p. 15
52. Ibid., pp. 25–6

53. Ibid., p. 33
54. Alva Myrdal and Viola Klein, *Women's Two Roles* (Routledge, 1956), p. 159
55. William Beveridge, *Social Insurance and Allied Services* (HMSO, 1942), p. 49
56. Ibid., p. 53
57. Royal Commission on Equal Pay 1944–46 (HMSO, 1946)
58. Geoffrey Thomas, *Women at Work* (Central Office of Information, 1944)
59. www.newyorker.com/news/news-desk/ the-margaret-thatcher-soft-serve-myth
60. Margaret Thatcher, 'Wake Up, Women', *Sunday Graphic*, quoted in George Gardiner, *Margaret Thatcher: From Childhood to Leadership* (Kimber, 1975), p. 50
61. Margaret Thatcher, *The Path to Power* (HarperCollins, 1995), p. 80
62. Kira Cochrane, 'Ann Oakley: "Barbara Wootton Was Too Visionary"', *Guardian*, 7 July 2011
63. Carol Thatcher, *Below the Parapet: The Biography of Denis Thatcher* (HarperCollins, 1997), p. 68
64. Steve Humphries and Pamela Gordon, *Forbidden Britain: Our Secret Past 1900–1960* (BBC, 1994), p. 58
65. Slater and Woodside, *Patterns of Marriage*, p. 223
66. Humphries and Gordon, *Forbidden Britain*, p. 58
67. Quoted in ibid., p. 69–70
68. Slater and Woodside, *Patterns of Marriage*, p. 230
69. Ibid., p. 235
70. Thomas, *Women at Work*, p. 2
71. Richard Titmuss, *Essays on the Welfare State* (1958; Beacon Press, 1969), p. 102
72. D. W. Winnicott, *The Child and the Family: First Relationships* (Tavistock Press, 1957), p. 88
73. D. W. Winnicott, *The Child and the Outside World* (1957; Routledge, 2013), p. 184
74. Josephine Tey, *The Franchise Affair* (1948; Folio Society, 2001), p. 20
75. Inge Weber-Newth and Johannes-Dieter Steinart, *German Migrants in Post-War Britain: An Enemy Embrace* (Routledge, 2006), p. 15
76. Note to Secretary of the NAB from Osbert Peake (Chairman NAB), 8 July 1952 (National Archives: Public Record Office, AST 7/1210)
77. Louise Ryan and Wendy Webster (ed.), *Gendering Migration: Masculinity, Femininity and Ethnicity in Post-War Britain* (Ashgate, 2008), p. 36

78. Ibid., p. 126
79. Ibid.
80. Robert Winder, *Bloody Foreigners* (Little, Brown, 2005), pp. 257–8
81. Beverley Bryan, Stella Dadzie and Suzanne Scafe, *The Heart of the Race: Black Women's Lives in Britain* (Virago, 1985), p. 23
82. Quoted in Jennifer Tyson, *Claudia Jones 1915–1964: A Woman of Our Times* (Camden Black Sisters, 1988), p. 6
83. Claudia Jones, 'A People's Art is the Genesis of Their Freedom' (Carnival Committee, 1959)
84. Carole Boyce Davies, *Left of Karl Marx: The Political Life of Black Communist Claudia Jones* (Duke University Press, 2007), p. 182
85. My account of this comes from Virginia Nicholson, *Perfect Wives in Ideal Homes* (Viking, 2015), p. 390
86. Cecil Beaton, *The Strenuous Years* (Weidenfeld & Nicolson, 1973), p. 120
87. Ben Pimlott, *The Queen: A Biography of Elizabeth II* (HarperCollins, 1996), p. 190
88. Ibid., p. 204
89. Beaton, *The Strenuous Years*, p. 143
90. Pimlott, *The Queen*, p. 215
91. Maddox, *Rosalind Franklin*, p. 134
92. James Watson, *The Double Helix* (Weidenfeld & Nicolson, 1968), p. 61
93. Rose Eveleth, 'Computing Used To Be Women's Work', Smithsonian.com, 7 October 2013
94. Simon Lavington, 'An Appreciation of Dina St Johnston (1930–2007) Founder of the UK's First Software House', *Computer Journal*, 26 March 2008
95. Quoted in ibid.
96. Naomi Alderman, 'Women in Computing: The 60s Pioneers Who Lit Up the World of Coding', *Guardian*, 13 October 2014
97. Lavington, 'An Appreciation of Dina St Johnston (1930–2007). Founder of the UK's First Software House'

7 It's a Man's World: 1961–81

1. Margery Hurst, *No Glass Slipper* (Arlington, 1967), p. 67
2. Ibid., p. 74
3. Ibid.
4. Ibid., p. 177
5. Ibid., p. 182
6. 'What Did Margaret Thatcher Do for Women?', *Guardian*, 9 April 2013

7. Brian Harrison, *Seeking a Role* (Clarendon, 2009), p. 251
8. Harriet Harman, *A Woman's Work* (Allen Lane, 2017), p. 5
9. Ibid., p. 3
10. Geoffrey Moorhouse, *The Other England* (Penguin, 1964), p. 72
11. Harrison, *Seeking a Role*, p. 426
12. Francesca Carnivali, Julie Marie Strange (eds), *20th Century Britain: Economic, Cultural and Social Change* (Routledge, 2014), p. 298
13. *The Albemarle Report* (HMSO, 1960), paragraph 57
14. Quoted in Elizabeth Wilson, *Only Halfway to Paradise* (Pandora, 1989), p. 162
15. http://news.bbc.co.uk/onthisday/hi/dates/stories/december/4/newsid_3228000/3228207.stm
16. Dominic Sandbrook, *White Heat* (Abacus, 2006), p. 489
17. Interview with author, 11 October 2007
18. Harrison, *Seeking a Role*, p. 236
19. Harrie Massey and M. O. Robins, *History of British Space Science* (Cambridge University Press, 2009), p. 86
20. Ibid.
21. Brian Harvey. *Europe's Space Programme: To Ariane and Beyond* (Springer, 2003), p. 19
22. http://www.quakersintheworld.org/quakers-in-action/366/Jocelyn-Bell-Burnell
23. Sian Griffiths (ed.), *Beyond the Glass Ceiling* (Manchester University Press, 1996), p. 21
24. Quoted in Humphrey Carpenter, *That Was Satire That Was* (Gollancz, 2000), p. 149
25. Carpenter, *That Was Satire That Was*, p. 149
26. Joan Bakewell, *The Centre of the Bed* (Hodder, 2003), p. 168
27. Doris Lessing, *Walking in the Shade* (HarperCollins, 1997), p. 16
28. Quoted in Joe Moran, *Armchair Nation: An Intimate History of Britain in Front of the TV* (Profile, 2013), p. 158
29. Interview with Joan Bakewell by Hunter Davies, *Independent*, 19 April 1993
30. Ibid.
31. 'Sexism? No One Had Thought Of It When I Started?', *Guardian*, 14 August 2000
32. Bakewell, *The Centre of the Bed*, p. 176
33. Carpenter, *That Was Satire That Was*, p. 212
34. Quoted in Charlotte Higgins, *This New Noise* (Guardian/Faber, 2015), p. 75
35. Higgins, *This New Noise*, p. 89
36. Susan Vinnicombe and John Bank, *Women with Attitude: Lessons for Career Management* (Routledge, 2003), p. 192

37. Interviewed in ibid.
38. Harrison, *Seeking a Role*, p. 481
39. 'The Scarlet Duchess of Argyll: Much More Than Just a Highland Fling', *Independent*, 17 February 2013
40. Interview with author, 3 October 2017
41. www.thefword.org.uk/2016/06/it-was-such-a-laugh-writer-nell-dunn-in-conversation/
42. Nell Dunn, *Talking to Women* (1965; Pan, 1966), p. 9
43. 'What Makes a Man Booker Novel?', *Guardian*, 14 October 2017
44. Dunn, *Talking to Women*, p. 24
45. Geoffrey Gorer, *Sex and Marriage in England Today* (Nelson, 1971), p. 30
46. Interview with author, 10 October 2017
47. Ibid.
48. Harrison, *Seeking a Role*, p. 243
49. Jan Morris, *Conundrum* (1974; Faber, 2011), p. 186
50. Jeremy Gavron, *A Woman on the Edge of Time* (Scribe, 2015), p. 129
51. Quoted in Dominic Sandbrook, *State of Emergency: Britain: The Way We Were 1970–74* (Penguin, 2011)
52. Philip Norman, *Shout!: The True Story of the Beatles* (Corgi, 1981), p. 201
53. Candy Leonard, *Beatleness* (Arcade, 2014), p. 44
54. Viv Albertine, *Clothes Clothes Clothes Music Music Music Boys Boys Boys* (Faber, 2014), p. 48
55. Ibid., p. 86
56. Interview with author, 3 October 2017
57. Quoted in Bob Spitz, *The Beatles: The Biography* (Aurum, 2005), p. 465
58. Spitz, *The Beatles*, p. 583
59. Norman, *Shout!*, p. 201
60. Quoted in Keith Badman, *The Beatles: Off the Record* (Omnibus, 2009)
61. Quoted in Andy Beckett, *When the Lights Went Out* (Faber, 2009), p. 163
62. 'Women Strikers at Ford Dagenham Sense Victory', *Guardian*, 20 June 1968
63. Anthony Lester, *Five Ideas to Fight For* (Oneworld, 2016), p. 72
64. Ibid., p. 76
65. *Socialist Commentary* (January 1967), p. 279
66. Patricia Hollis, *Jennie Lee: A Life* (OUP, 1997), p. 254
67. Quoted in Daniel Weinbren, *The Open University: A History* (Manchester University Press, 2014), p. 43
68. Ibid.

69. Quoted in Hollis, *Jennie Lee*, p. 273
70. Hollis, *Jennie Lee*, p. 278
71. Ben Pimlott, *Harold Wilson* (HarperCollins, 1993), p. 199
72. Ibid., p. 201
73. Marcia Williams, *Inside Number 10* (1972; NEL, 1975), p. 70
74. Margaret Hill, *An Approach to Old Age and its Problems* (Oliver & Boyd, 1961) p. 55
75. Harrison, *Seeking a Role*, p. 288
76. Interview with BBC Witness programme: www.bbc.co.uk/programmes/p01tdrl6
77. Jane Lewis, *Women in Britain Since 1945* (Blackwell, 1992), p. 88
78. Ann Oakley, *The Sociology of Housework* (Robertson, 1974), p. 157
79. Betty Friedan, *The Feminine Mystique* (1963; Norton, 2013), p. 15
80. Bakewell, *The Centre of the Bed*, pp. 161–2
81. Germaine Greer, *The Female Eunuch* (MacGibbon & Kee, 1970), p. 249
82. Herbert Marcuse, *An Essay on Liberation* (1969; Harmondsworth, 1972), p. 18
83. Anna Coote and Beatrix Campbell, *Sweet Freedom* (Blackwell, 1982), p. 5
84. Elizabeth Nelson, *British Counter-Culture 1966–73* (Springer, 1989), p. 140
85. 'OZ Era's Feminist Offspring', *The Australian*, 26 March 2013
86. 'The Stories of Our Lives: Carmen Callil', *Guardian*, 26 April 2008
87. 'Domestic Violence: How the World's First Women's Refuge Saved My Life', *Guardian*, 28 April 2014
88. 'In Defence of Feminist Dissent', *Guardian*, 7 March 2014
89. Quoted in Pamela Harper, *Life in Britain in the 1970s* (Batsford, 1988), p. 20
90. James Heartfield, *Equal Opportunities Revolution* (Duncan Baird, 2017), p. 88
91. May Hobbs, *Born to Struggle* (Quartet, 1974), p. 76
92. See Beckett, *When the Lights Went Out* for a brilliantly detailed account of the strike
93. Quoted in Beckett, *When the Lights Went Out*, p. 367
94. Beckett, *When the Lights Went Out*, p. 370
95. Ibid., p. 262
96. Margaret Thatcher, *The Path to Power* (HarperPerennial, 1995), p. 261
97. Quoted in Hugo Young, *One of Us* (1989; Pan, 1993), p. 137
98. Young, *One of Us*, p. 137

8 What You Really, Really Want: 1981–2017

1. Edwina Currie, *Diaries 1992–1997* (Biteback, 2012), p. 231
2. Hugo Young, *One of Us* (1989; Pan, 1993), p. 303
3. Speech on 'Women in a Changing World' (26 July 1982) https://www.margaretthatcher.org/document/105007
4. Deborah L. Rhode, *Women and Leadership* (Oxford University Press, 2016), p. 50
5. Dr Joe Devanny and Dr Catherine Haddon, *Women and Whitehall: Gender and the Civil Service since 1979* (Institute for Government, 2015), p. 33
6. Charles Moore, *Margaret Thatcher, The Authorised Biography, Volume 1: Not For Turning* (Allen Lane, 2013), p. 353
7. Quoted in Young, *One of Us*, p. 311
8. Wendy Webster, *Not A Man To Match Her* (Women's Press, 1990), p. 4
9. Young, *One of Us*, p. 305
10. Speech on 'Women in a Changing World'
11. Laura Beers, 'Thatcher and the Women's Vote' in Ben Jackson and Robert Saunders (eds), *Making Thatcher's Britain* (Cambridge University Press, 2012), p. 113
12. Ibid., p. 114
13. 'Sir Alfred Sherman: Obituary', *Daily Telegraph*, 28 August 2006
14. Andy Beckett, *When the Lights Went Out* (Faber, 2009), p. 280
15. Robert Philpot, *Margaret Thatcher: The Honorary Jew* (Biteback, 2017)
16. 'Ginny Knows Best', *Independent on Sunday*, 27 February 1994
17. Hywel Williams, *Guilty Men: Conservative Decline and Fall 1992–1997* (Aurum, 1998), p. 56
18. Brenda Dean, *Hot Mettle: SOGAT, Murdoch and Me* (Politico, 2007), p. 4
19. Edwina Currie, review of Brenda Dean's book *Hot Mettle*, *The Times*, 31 March 2007
20. 'I Was Always Told I Was Thick. The Strike Taught Me I Wasn't', *Guardian*, 10 May 2004
21. Ibid.
22. David Morley, *Home Territories: Media, Mobility and Identity* (Routledge, 2002), p. 70
23. 'The Greenham Common Peace Camp and Its Legacy', *Guardian*, 5 September 2006
24. Ann Pettitt, *Walking to Greenham* (Honno, 2006), p. 41
25. Caroline Blackwood, *On the Perimeter* (Flamingo, 1984), p. 69

26. 'How the Greenham Common Protest Changed Lives', *Guardian*, 20 March 2017

27. Quoted in Cristina Odone, 'In Defence of Edwina Currie, the Woman Who Dared', *New Statesman*, 7 October 2002

28. Harriet Harman, *A Woman's Work* (Allen Lane, 2017), pp. 73–4

29. Ibid., p. 89

30. Quoted in Anna Coote (ed.), *New Gender Agenda: Why Women Still Want More* (IPPR, 2000), p. 27

31. Diane Abbott, 'Having the Last Laugh', *New Statesman*, 17 January 2017

32. Diane Abbott, 'You Can't Let Racism Hold You Back', *Guardian*, 20 September 2012

33. Harman, *A Woman's Work*, p. 102

34. Clare Short, *An Honourable Deception? New Labour, Iraq and the Misuse of Power* (Free Press, 2004), p. 53

35. Shirley Williams, *Climbing the Bookshelves* (Virago, 2009), p. 146

36. 'Shirley Williams: My Family Values', *Guardian*, 15 May 2015

37. Coote (ed.), *New Gender Agenda*, p. 23

38. Ibid., p. 26

39. Ibid.

40. 'Oh Babe, Just Look At Us Now', *Observer*, 22 April 2007

41. Ibid.

42. Ibid.

43. 'Drink, Deception and the Death of an MP', *Guardian*, 6 February 2007

44. Harman, *A Woman's Work*, p. 198

45. 'The Betrayal of Feminism', *Independent*, 13 November 1998

46. Quoted in Alwyn W. Turner, *A Classless Society: Britain in the 1990s* (Aurum, 2013), p. 444

47. Peter Clarke, *Hope and Glory: Britain 1900–1990* (Allen Lane, 1996), p. 365

48. Ibid., p. 366

49. Quoted in Christopher E. Forth, *Masculinity in the Modern West* (Palgrave, 2008), p. 227

50. Quoted in Tom Hickman, *The Sexual Century* (Carlton, 1999), p. 237

51. 'The Spice Girls at 20: "Women Weren't Allowed to Be Like That in Public"', *Guardian*, 7 July 2016

52. See Carol Dyhouse, *Girl Trouble: Panic and Progress in the History of Young Women* (Zed, 2014)

53. 'The "Lager Loutette Culture Doubles in Ten Years"', *Telegraph*, 30 July 2004

54. Ibid.

55. Germaine Greer, 'Long Live the Essex Girl', *Guardian*, 5 March 2001
56. Quoted in Michael Boella and Alan Pannett, *Principles of Hospitality Law* (Cengage, 1999), p. 159
57. 'A Successful Woman Is One in the Swim', *Sunday Herald*, 29 July 1993
58. Aminatta Forna, *Mother of All Myths: How Society Moulds and Constrains Mothers* (HarperCollins, 1998), p. 18
59. 'Anita Roddick, Capitalist With a Conscience, Dies at 64', *Independent*, 10 September 2007
60. Ibid.
61. Quoted in Lia Litosseliti, *Gender Identity and Discourse Analysis* (Routledge, 2014), p. 259
62. E. V. Morgan and W. A. Thomas, *The Stock Exchange: Its History and Functions* (St Martin's Press, 1971), p. 53
63. 'Sexism in the City: Why is Banking Stuck in 1985?', *Telegraph*, 7 August 2015
64. Interviewed in Bob Bentley's film for the Central Office of Information, *A Woman's Place: The City* (1985)
65. 'Opportunity Knox', *Daily Telegraph*, 29 January 2006
66. Sue Innes, *Making It Work: Women, Change and Challenge in the 1990s* (Chatto & Windus, 1995), p. 32
67. 'Sacked Broker Wins £18,000', *Independent*, 10 August 1994
68. Innes, *Making It Work*, p. 18
69. *Glasgow Herald*, 18 February 1981
70. 'Where Are They Now?: Sue Brown', *Independent*, 22 March 1994
71. 'City Workers Shouldn't Take Offence at Sexist Comments, Tribunal Rules', *Telegraph*, 15 April 2010
72. Innes, *Making It Work*, p. 17
73. Clarke, *Hope and Glory*, p. 363
74. Ginny Nevill, *Women in the Workforce* (Industrial Society Press, 1990), p. 40
75. Ibid.
76. Women's National Commission, *Women in the '90s* (Women's National Commission, 1994), p. 6
77. Ibid., p. 7
78. Ibid.
79. Susan Faludi, *Backlash: The Undeclared War Against Women* (Chatto & Windus, 1992), p. 9
80. Dora Russell, *The Religion of the Machine Age* (Routledge & Kegan Paul, 1983), p. 199
81. Ibid., p. 245

82. James Gillies and Robert Cailliau, *How the Web Was Born: The Story of the World Wide Web* (Oxford University Press, 2000), p. 203

83. Ibid.

84. John Cassidy, *Dot.con* (2002; Penguin, 2003), p. x

85. Danielle Newnham, *Female Innovators at Work* (Apress, 2016)

86. Ibid.

87. Stephanie Shirley, *Let IT Go* (AUK, 2012)

88. 'First-Generation Immigrants Are Wealth Creators', *Director*, 21 October 2016

89. Ibid.

90. 'Why Do So Few Women Edit Wikipedia?', *Harvard Business Review*, 2 June 2016

91. Libby Hemphill and Jahna Otterbacher, 'Learning the Lingo? Gender, Prestige and Linguistic Adaptation in Review Communities' (Illinois Institute of Technology, 2012)

92. Ibid.

93. Sarah Pederson, '"It Took a Lot to Admit I Am Male on Here". Going Where Few Men Dare to Tread: Men on Mumsnet' published in Einar Thorsen, Heather Savigny, Jenny Alexander, Daniel Jackson (eds), *Media, Margins and Popular Culture* (Palgrave Macmillan, 2015), p. 249

94. 'Mumsnet Founder Justine Roberts', *Director*, 4 April 2011

95. Interview on *Channel 4 News*, 8 January 2018

96. 'Gender Pay Gap: How Women Are Short-Changed in the UK', *Financial Times*, 5 April 2018

97. Headline from the *Independent*, 9 June 2017

98. 'Emma Watson's Willingness to Face the Truth About Race is Refreshing', *Guardian*, 10 January 2018

99. Alison Wolf, 'Changing Families and Feminist Blind Spots' (Demos, 14 January 2015)

100. 'Emma Watson: Gender Equality Is Your Issue Too', unwomen.org, 20 September 2014

101. Ibid.

102. 'My Story: Elizabeth Nyamayaro', *Elle*, 23 September 2016

103. 'Meet the Woman Behind Emma Watson's Viral Feminism Campaign', *Fortune.com*, 18 December 2014

104. '"Enough Is Enough": The Fight Against Everyday Sexism', *Guardian*, 29 March 2014

105. 'Lucy Kellaway Interviews Everyday Sexism Founder Laura Bates', *Financial Times*, 1 August 2014

106. 'Who Expects Death Threats for Asking For a Woman on a Bank Note?', *Financial Times*, 10 November 2017

107. 'London Fire Chief Tells of Sexist Abuse Over "Firefighters" Campaign', *Guardian*, 1 February 2018
108. Elaine Showalter, *Sexual Anarchy: Gender and Culture at the Fin de Siècle* (Virago, 1992), p. 4
109. Shaista Gohir 'I Wish the Words Shame and Honour Could Be Deleted', *Guardian*, 19 January 2015
110. 'Helena Morrissey "I'm Not Superhuman ..."', *Daily Telegraph*, 2 September 2016
111. 'Mediacom's Karen Blackett is a New Breed of Leader', *Campaign*, 20 March 2017
112. Mary Beard, *Women & Power* (Profile, 2017), p. 31
113. Maria Jewsbury, *The Three Histories* (Frederick Westley and A. H. Davis, 1830), p. 134

Image Credits

Page 7: © Robin & Lucienne Day Foundation/photo: Studio Briggs

Page 8, top: Charles Hewitt/Stringer/Getty Images

Page 8, bottom: Universal History Archive/Contributor/Getty Images

Plate section 2

Page 1: PA/PA Archive/PA Images

Page 2: Tophams/Topham Picturepoint/Press Association Images

Page 3, top: https://artsandculture.google.com/asset/dina-st-johnston/cQEk345REeKfhQ

Page 3, bottom: Keystone Pictures USA/Alamy Stock Photo

Page 4: Daily Herald Archive/Contributor/Getty Images

Page 5: David Cairns/Stringer/Getty Images

Page 6, top left: Frank Barratt/Stringer/Getty Images

Page 6, top right: Graham Wood/Stringer/Getty Images

Page 6, bottom: United News/Popperfoto/Contributor/Getty Images

Page 7, top: Image courtesy of Nicola Lyn Evans

Page 7, bottom: WPA Pool/Pool/Getty Images

Page 8: Ryan Harding/REX/Shutterstock

Index